Scott Foresman
Science

See learning in a whole new light

PEARSON
Scott Foresman

Editorial Offices: Glenview, Illinois • Parsippany, New Jersey • New York, New York
Sales Ofices: Needham, Massachusetts • Duluth, Georgia • Glenview, Illinois
Coppell, Texas • Ontario, California • Mesa, Arizona
www.sfscience.com

Series Authors

Dr. Timothy Cooney
Professor of Earth Science and Science Education
University of Northern Iowa (UNI)
Cedar Falls, Iowa

Barbara Foots
Science Education Consultant
Houston, Texas

Dr. James Flood
Distinguished Professor of Literacy and Language
School of Teacher Education San Diego State University. San Diego State University
San Diego, California

Dr. M. Jenice Goldston
Associate Professor of Science Education
Department of Elementary Education Programs
University of Alabama
Tuscaloosa, Alabama

Dr. Shirley Gholston Key
Associate Professor of Science Education
Instruction and Curriculum Leadership
Department College of Education
University of Memphis
Memphis, Tennessee

Dr. Diane Lapp
Distinguished Professor of Reading and Language Arts in Teacher Education
San Diego State University
San Diego, California

Sheryl Alicia Mercier, Ma.Ed.
Classroom Teacher
Dunlap Elementary School
Dunlap, California

Dr. Karen Ostlund
Director
UTeach | Dell Center for New Teacher Success
The University of Texas at Austin
Austin, Texas

Dr. Nancy Romance
Professor of Science Education & Principal Investigator
NSF/IERI Science IDEAS Project
Charles E. Schmidt College of Science
Florida Atlantic University
Boca Raton, Florida

Dr. William Tate
Chair and Professor of Education and Applied Statistics
Department of Education
Washington University
St Louis, Missouri

ISBN: 0-328-14962-4

Dr. Kathryn C. Thornton
Professor
School of Engineering and
Applied Science
University of Virginia
Charlottesville, Virginia

Dr. Leon Ukens
Professor of Science Education
Department of Physics, Astronomy,
and Geosciences
Towson University
Towson, Maryland

Steve Weinberg
Consultant
Connecticut Center for
Advanced Technology
East Hartford, Connecticut

Dr. Jim Cummins
Professor
Modern Language Center
& Curriculum Department
Ontario Institute for Studies
in Education
Toronto, Canada

Consulting Author

Dr. Michael P. Klentschy
Superintendent
El Centro Elementary School District
El Centro, California

Science Content Consultants

Dr. Frederick W. Taylor
Senior Research Scientist
Institute for Geophysics
Jackson School of Geosciences
The University of Texas at Austin
Austin, Texas

Dr. Ruth E. Buskirk
Senior Lecturer
School of Biological Sciences
The University of Texas at Austin
Austin, Texas

Dr. Cliff Frohlich
Senior Research Scientist
Institute for Geophysics
Jackson School of Geosciences
The University of Texas at Austin
Austin, Texas

Brad Armosky
McDonald Observatory
The University of Texas at Austin
Austin, Texas

NASA Content Consultants

Adena Williams Loston, Ph.D.
Chief Education Officer
Office of the Chief
Education Officer

Clifford W. Houston, Ph.D.
*Deputy Chief Education Officer
for Education Programs*
Office of the Chief
Education Officer

Frank C. Owens
Senior Policy Advisor
Office of the Chief
Education Officer

Deborah Brown Biggs
Manager, Education Flight Projects Office
Space Operations Mission Directorate,
Education Lead

Erika G. Vick
NASA Liaison to Pearson Scott Foresman
Education Flight
Projects Office

William E. Anderson
*Partnership Manager
for Education*
Aeronautics Research
Mission Directorate

Anita Krishnamurthi
Program Planning Specialist
Space Science Education and
Outreach Program

Bonnie J. McClain
Chief of Education
Exploration Systems
Mission Directorate

Diane Schweizer
Program Scientist
Earth Science Education

Deborah Rivera
Strategic Alliances Manager
Office of Public Affairs,
NASA Headquarters

Douglas D. Peterson
*Public Affairs Officer,
Astronaut Office*
Office of Public Affairs,
NASA Johnson Space Center

Nicole Cloutier
*Public Affairs Officer,
Astronaut Office*
Office of Public Affairs,
NASA Johnson Space Center

Reviewers

Dr. Maria Aida Alanis
Administrator
Austin ISD
Austin Texas

Melissa Barba
Teacher
Wesley Mathews Elementary
Miami, Florida

Dr. Marcelline Barron
Supervisor/K-12 Math
and Science
Fairfield Public Schools
Fairfield, Connecticut

Jane Bates
Teacher
Hickory Flat Elementary
Canton, Georgia

Denise Bizjack
Teacher Dr. N. H. Jones
Elementary
Ocala, Florida

Latanya D. Bragg
Teacher
Davis Magnet School
Jackson, Mississippi

Richard Burton
Teacher
George Buck Elementary
School 94
Indianapolis, Indiana

Dawn Cabrera
Teacher E.W.F. Stirrup School
Miami, Florida

Barbara Calabro
Teacher
Compass Rose Foundation
Ft. Myers, Florida

Lucille Calvin
Teacher
Weddington Math &
Science School
Greenville, Mississippi

Patricia Carmichael
Teacher
Teasley Middle School
Canton, Georgia

Martha Cohn
Teacher
An Wang Middle School
Lowell, Massachusetts

Stu Danzinger
Supervisor
Community Consolidated
School District 59
Arlington Heights, Illinois

Esther Draper
Supervisor/Science Specialist
Belair Math Science
Magnet School
Pine Bluff, Arkansas

Sue Esser
Teacher
Loretto Elementary
Jacksonville, Florida

Dr. Richard Fairman
Teacher
Antioch University
Yellow Springs, Ohio

Cecelia Ferguson
Teacher
School District of Lee County
North Fort Myers, Florida

Joan Goldfarb
Teacher
Indialantic Elementary
Indialantic, Florida

Deborah Gomes
Teacher A J Gomes Elementary
New Bedford, Massachusetts

Sandy Hobart
Teacher
Mims Elementary
Mims, Florida

Tom Hocker
Teacher/Science Coach
Boston Latin Academy
Dorchester, Massachusetts

Shelley Jaques
Teacher
Moore Public Schools
Moore, Oklahoma

Marguerite W. Jones
Teacher Spearman Elementary
Piedmont, South Carolina

Kelly Kenney
Teacher
Kansas City Missouri
School District
Kansas City, Missouri

Carol Kilbane
Teacher
Riverside Elementary School
Wichita, Kansas

Robert Kolenda
Teacher
Neshaminy School District
Langhorne, Pennsylvania

Karen Lynn Kruse
Teacher
St. Paul the Apostle
Yonkers, New York

Elizabeth Loures
Teacher
Point Fermin
Elementary School
San Pedro, California

Susan MacDougall
Teacher
Brick Community Primary
Learning Center
Brick, New Jersey

Jack Marine
Teacher
Raising Horizons Quest
Charter School
Philadelphia, Pennsylvania

Nicola Micozzi Jr.
Science Coordinator
Plymouth Public Schools
Plymouth, Massachusetts

Paula Monteiro
Teacher
A J Gomes Elementary
New Bedford, Massachusetts

Tracy Newallis
Teacher
Taper Avenue Elementary
San Pedro, California

Dr. Eugene Nicolo
Supervisor, Science K-12
Moorestown School District
Moorestown, New Jersey

Helen Pedigo
Teacher
Mt. Carmel Elementary
Huntsville Alabama

Becky Peltonen
Teacher
Patterson Elementary School
Panama City, Florida

Sherri Pensler
Teacher/ESOL
Claude Pepper Elementary
Miami, Florida

Virginia Rogliano
Teacher
Bridgeview Elementary
South Charleston, West
Virginia

Debbie Sanders
Teacher
Thunderbolt Elementary
Orange Park, Florida

Grethel Santamarina
Teacher
E.W.F. Stirrup School
Miami, Florida

Migdalia Schneide
Teacher/Bilingual
Lindell School
Long Beach, New York

Susan Shelly
Teacher
Bonita Springs Elementary
Bonita Springs, Florida

Peggy Terry
Teacher
Madison District 151
South Holland, Illinois

Jane M. Thompson
Teacher
Emma Ward Elementary
Lawrenceburg, Kentucky

Martha Todd
Teacher
W. H. Rhodes Elementary
Milton, Florida

Renee Williams
Teacher
Central Elementary
Bloomfield, New Mexico

Myra Wood
Teacher
Madison Street Academy
Ocala, Florida

Marion Zampa
Teacher
Shawnee Mission
School District
Overland Park, Kansas

Unit A Life Science

What are some ways to classify living things?

Life Science in Indiana

Chapter 1 • Classifying Plants and Animals

Chapter 2 • Energy from Plants

What features help plants to make their own food and reproduce?

Unit A Life Science

How do organisms interact with each other and with their environment?

How do changes in ecosystems affect our world?

Chapter 3 • Ecosystems

Chapter 4 • Changes in Ecosystems

Chapter 5 • Systems of the Human Body

How do the systems in your body keep you alive?

Unit B Earth Science

How does Earth's water affect weather?

Earth Science in Indiana

Chapter 6 • Water Cycle and Weather

Chapter 7 • Hurricanes and Tornadoes

How do storms affect Earth's air, water, land, and living things?

Unit B · Earth Science

How can rocks tell us about Earth's past, present and future formation?

How is Earth's surface shaped and reshaped?

Chapter 8 • Minerals and Rocks

Chapter 9 • Changes to Earth's Surface

Chapter 10 • Using Natural Resources

How can living things always have the natural resources they need?

Unit C Physical Science

Physical Science in Indiana

How can matter be compared, measured, and combined?

How does heat energy move from one object to another?

Chapter 13 • Electricity and Magnetism

What are some ways that forms of energy can change?

Unit C Physical Science

How do sound and light travel?

Chapter 14 • Sound and Light

What causes motion and how does it affect us?

Chapter 15 • Objects in Motion

Chapter 16 • Simple Machines

How do simple machines make work easier?

Unit D · Space and Technology

Space and Technology in Indiana

What can daily and seasonal cycles tell us about the Earth, Moon, and Sun?

How is Earth different from other planets in our solar system?

Chapter 19 • Effects of Technology

How do the devices and products of technology affect the way we live?

How to Read Science

A page like this one is toward the beginning of each chapter. It shows you how to use a reading skill that will help you understand what you read.

Before reading

Before you read the chapter, read the Build Background page and think about how to answer the question. Recall what you already know as you answer the question. Work with a partner to make a list of what you already know. Then read the How To Read Science page.

Target Reading Skill

Each page has one target reading skill. The reading skill corresponds with a process skill in the Directed Inquiry activity on the facing page. The reading skill will be useful as you read science.

Real-World Connection

Each page has an example of something you might read. It also connects with the Directed Inquiry activity.

How to Read Science

Reading Skills

Cause and Effect

A **cause** is why something happens. An **effect** is what happens. Sometimes clue words such as *because* and *since* signal a cause and effect. Sometimes there are no clue words or the author does not tell why something happened. The student who wrote the lab report observed the effects of having too many plants growing close together.

Lab Report

Procedure

Day	Procedure	Observations
1	We planted radish seeds in two small milk cartons. We filled each milk carton with garden soil. We planted 3 radish seeds in carton A, and 20 radish seeds in carton B.	The cartons are the same size and contain the same amount of soil. The only difference is the number of seeds.
7	We watered the seeds in each carton every few days.	The seeds are beginning to grow. We can see a few plants in carton A. We see more plants in carton B.
14	The plants have been growing for two weeks.	The plants in carton A are very tall and full. The plants in carton B are much smaller and look crowded.

Apply It!
Make a graphic organizer like the one at the right. Use it to show what happened to the carton with more seeds and why it happened.

Cause		Effect
A cause is why something happens.	→	An effect is what happens.

109

Graphic Organizer

A useful strategy for understanding anything you read is to create a graphic organizer. A graphic organizer can help you think about the information and relate parts of it to each other. Each reading skill has a certain graphic organizer.

Species Then and Now

Fossils show us that life on Earth has not always been the same as it is now. Over long periods of time, changes in the environment have caused species to change or adapt as well. Scientists can compare fossils of organisms that lived long ago to organisms that are alive today.

Woolly mammoths lived long ago. They have since become extinct, but many are preserved as fossils. Some mammoths have been frozen solid. Scientists compare these frozen mammoths with modern elephants. They both have large tusks and long noses. Their skeletons are also very much alike. Both the woolly mammoth and modern elephants are classified in the same family.

Fossils can also tell us about the environment long ago. Sometimes fossils of marine creatures are found in dry climates. This tells scientists that long ago shallow seas must have covered the area where the fossils were found.

In ancient times, many kinds of sea lilies filled the oceans. Many sea lilies have been preserved as fossils.

1. ✓**Checkpoint** When are species considered threatened?
2. ◐ **Cause and Effect** Why do organisms become extinct?

Today only a few species of sea lilies remain. These flower-like animals attach themselves to the ocean floor.

121

◉ During reading

As you read the lesson, use the checkpoint to check your understanding. Some checkpoints ask you to use the reading target skill.

◉ After reading

After you have read the chapter, think about what you found out. Exchange ideas with your partner. Compare the list you made before you read the chapter with what you learned by reading it. Answer the questions in the Chapter Review. One question uses the reading target skill.

These are some target reading skills that appear in this book.

☐→☐   Cause and Effect

◯◯   Compare and Contrast

Sequence of Events

☐→☐   Predict

Draw Conclusions

☐·☐·☐·☐   Summarize

Main Idea and Supporting Details

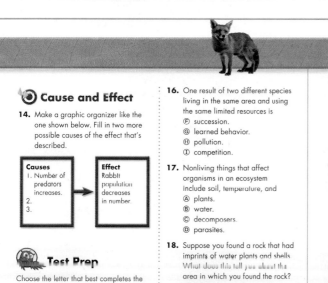

◐ Cause and Effect

14. Make a graphic organizer like the one shown below. Fill in two more possible causes of the effect that's described.

Causes	Effect
1. Number of predators increases. 2. 3.	Rabbit population decreases in number.

🦗 Test Prep

Choose the letter that best completes the statement or answers the question.

15. A pet-store gerbil has lived alone in a cage. Suppose you were to put it in a cage with two other gerbils. How can the pet-store gerbil survive in its new environment?
  Ⓐ It must wait to eat until the other gerbils have finished.
  Ⓑ It must build a new home.
  Ⓒ It must compete with the other gerbils for resources.
  Ⓓ It must hide in the cage.

16. One result of two different species living in the same area and using the same limited resources is
  Ⓕ succession.
  Ⓖ learned behavior.
  Ⓗ pollution.
  Ⓘ competition.

17. Nonliving things that affect organisms in an ecosystem include soil, temperature, and
  Ⓐ plants.
  Ⓑ water.
  Ⓒ decomposers.
  Ⓓ parasites.

18. Suppose you found a rock that had imprints of water plants and shells. What does this tell you about the area in which you found the rock?
  Ⓕ It was once under water.
  Ⓖ It was once a forest.
  Ⓗ Dinosaurs once lived there.
  Ⓘ Many predators lived there.

19. Explain why the answer you chose for Question #15 is best. For each of the answers you did not choose, give a reason why it is not the best choice.

20. Writing in Science **Expository** Explain how predators and parasites are different and alike.

135

How Scientists Use Scientific Methods

Ask a Question

Tropical rain forests. Grasslands. Deserts. What do these very different ecosystems have in common? All are biomes, plant and animal communities spread over a large area. Each has a specific climate, filled with plant and animal life. And each has a unique type of soil. What are the effects on soil if the climate warms? Dr. Elissa Levine, a soil scientist at NASA's Goddard Space Flight Center, used scientific methods to dig into this question.

The tropical rain forest is one of the biomes of the world.

Make a Hypothesis

Scientific methods are organized steps in solving problems. Scientists use them, but each does so in his or her own way. So one scientist's method might be different from another's. The order of the steps might change. It all depends on the problem. As you read, you'll learn how Dr. Elissa Levine used these steps to answer her question about soil changes.

A **hypothesis** is a likely explanation of the problem. A hypothesis might not be *the* answer. It might only be one *possible* answer. It must be tested. When Dr. Levine makes a hypothesis, she considers whether it specifically answers the question she is dealing with. She focuses on a hypothesis that deals with global warming. She makes sure that it will answer her question and help pose the next set of questions. Her hypothesis was that when the temperature rises, the amount of water in the soil decreases.

What factors does Dr. Levine consider in making a hypothesis? She considers whether her question will represent the study of global warming. She thinks of how it will affect an entire area and not just one tiny piece of it.

*When Dr. Levine studies biomes she has never visited, she **communicates** with local soil scientists like this one to help her learn about the biome.*

As global warming continues, changes take place in ecosystems. This dried up piece of land was once a river, home to plant and animal life.

Collect Data

Experiments are used to test a hypothesis. They help scientists collect **data.** Dr. Levine and her team use **observations** of an ecosystem to understand how it functions. They **collect data** about soil, climate, and land cover. Depending on what they are studying, they might collect data every 15 minutes, once a day, or just one time in the entire experiment.

Anything that could be changed in their experiment, such as a temperature increase, is called a **variable.** Setups of an experiment have only one variable changed at a time. That way, scientists can be sure that results occurred because of that variable. A **control** is a setup that does not have the variable being tested. Dr. Levine and her team controlled other factors that might influence their data. For example, storms could cause the data to have variability. "It's important to have confidence in the data," says Dr. Levine.

Dr. Levine and her team also **used simulation models** to see what kind of run-off and drainage would occur in soil as temperatures were increased. They first ran the model with current temperatures. Then, they increased the temperatures by 2 degrees, up to 10 degrees.

This scientist is using a computer to help him study soils.

Students take measurements of their soil study sites for GLOBE. This data is valuable for scientists like Dr. Levine and for others around the world.

How would you feel if scientists in the field used **data** that you had collected? It would be exciting, wouldn't it? Well, students participating in the GLOBE program have this opportunity! GLOBE is a worldwide science and education partnership between scientists, teachers, and students. Through GLOBE, students take **measurements** of soil and other parts of the ecosystem. They report their **collected data** by using the Internet. Scientists and students around the world have access to the **data.** Dr. Levine, a principal investigator for GLOBE, used student data in her experiment.

Analyze Data

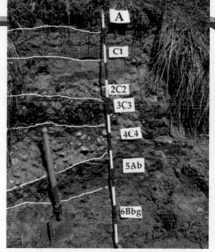

The purpose of an experiment is to **collect more data** about the problem to be solved. Data are pieces of information from the experiment. Data can take the form of written descriptions or drawings. Data can also be lists of numbers or other recorded information. Dr. Levine and her team had a good deal of data to **analyze,** or study. They put it into computer models as input and integrated information in a spreadsheet.

Through the models she creates, Dr. Levine can make **predictions** over a long period of time. "With a computer model, we don't have to wait for years for things to happen!" she says.

Dr. Levine also placed data into visual form, using graphs, plots, and statistics—information presented in number form. The visual forms allowed her to **interpret,** or understand, the data and **draw conclusions** about what was meant. Dr. Levine also checked the quality of the data, to be sure that nothing was missing and that she was confident in it.

Dr. Levine believes that **communication** is an ongoing part of the scientific process. She talks to scientists in other areas of her field. She also speaks with those in different fields. She always seeks their input and interpretations.

Dr. Levine conducted a data experiment, rather than a field one. That means that she did not go out into the field. Instead, students like you collected samples and shared their data. They send photos like this to the GLOBE program.

A spreadsheet is a computer program that places numerical data into individual cells. The format allows quick and easy access to information.

Make Conclusions

When scientists make conclusions, they see if their data supports their hypothesis. Dr. Levine concluded that when the temperature rises, the amount of water in the soil decreases. Dr. Levine also learned that evaporation and transpiration increase. That's because more energy comes into the system. **Data** supported her hypothesis.

Using Scientific Methods

Scientists such as Dr. Elissa Levine use scientific methods as they try to solve problems. Scientific methods are organized ways of finding answers and solving problems. Scientific methods include certain parts. The order of how each scientist uses the parts can change. Here are some parts of a scientific method that you can use.

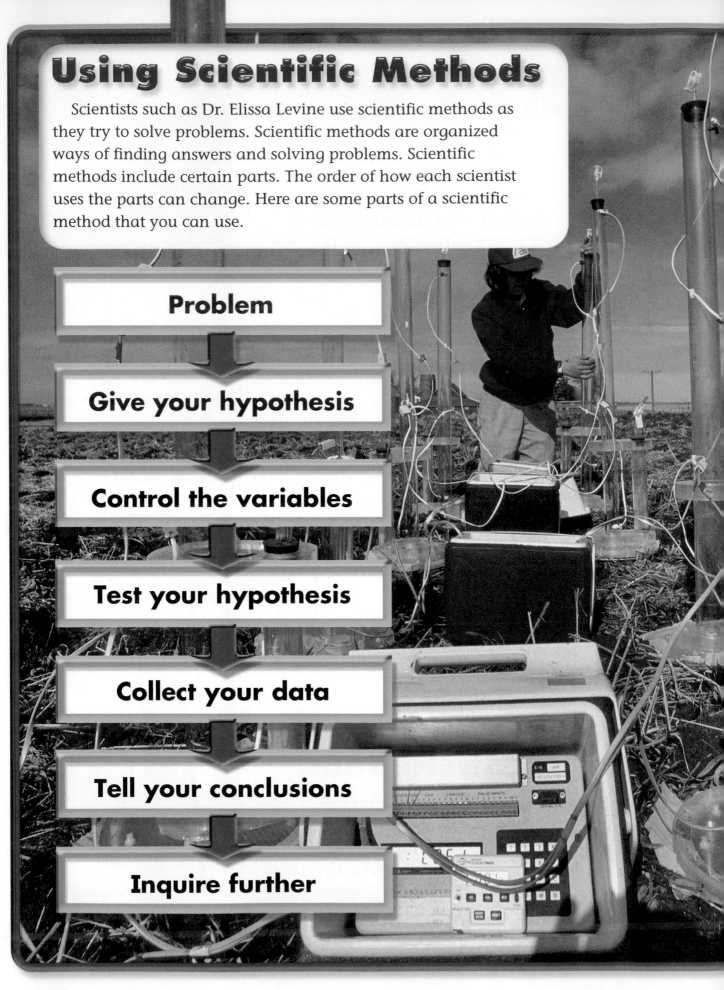

Problem

Give your hypothesis

Control the variables

Test your hypothesis

Collect your data

Tell your conclusions

Inquire further

Using Science Process Skills

Scientists use process skills as they do their research. As you do science activities, you will use these same skills.

Observing Use your senses to find out about objects, events, or living things.

Communicating You can use words, pictures, charts, graphs, and diagrams to share information.

Classifying Arrange or sort objects, events, or living things according to their properties.

Estimating and Measuring Tell what you think an object's measurements are. Then measure it in units.

Inferring Draw a conclusion or make a reasonable guess based on what you have learned or what you know.

Predicting Tell what you think will happen.

Making and Using Models Models can be made of materials. Sketches or diagrams are models too.

Making Operational Definitions Define or describe an object or event based on your own experience with it.

Forming Questions and Hypotheses Think of how you can solve a problem or answer a question.

Collecting Data Gather observations and measurements into graphs, tables, or charts.

Interpreting Data Use the information you collected to solve problems or answer questions.

Identifying and Controlling Variables Change one thing, but keep all the other factors the same.

Investigating and Experimenting Plan and do an investigation to test a hypothesis or solve a problem.

Science Tools

Scientists use many different kinds of tools. Tools can make objects appear larger. They can help you measure volume, temperature, length distance, and mass. Tools can help you figure out amounts and analyze your data. Tools can also help you find the latest scientific information.

You can use a **telescope** to help you see the stars. Some telescopes have special mirrors that magnify things that are very far away, such as stars and planets.

You can use a **magnifying lens** or **hand lens** to make objects appear larger and to show more detail than you could see with just your eyes.

A **hand lens** doesn't enlarge things as much as microscopes do, but they are easier to on a field trip.

Pictures taken with a **camera** record what something looks like. You can compare pictures of the same object to show how the object might have changed.

Microscopes use several lenses to make objects appear much larger, so you can see more detail.

Funnels are used when pouring a liquid such as water or a solid such as salt into a container.

You can use **filter paper** to separate solids from liquids.

Timers are used to measure the amount of time that has passed.

You can use **graph paper** to make charts and graphs to display data.

You can talk into a **sound recorder** to record information you want to remember. You can also record different sounds made by organisms or objects.

A measuring tape can be used like a meter stick or ruler to measure length, but it is flexible to measure around objects.

You use a **thermometer** to measure temperature. Many thermometers have both Fahrenheit and Celsius scales. Scientists usually use only the Celsius scale when measuring temperature. Thermometers also can be used to measure the gain or loss of energy.

Scientists use **barometers** to measure the air pressure, which can be a good indicator of weather patterns.

A **weather vane** is used to determine the wind direction.

You can look at a **wind sock** to see which way the wind is blowing.

A **rain gauge** is used to measure the amount of rain that has fallen.

Terminals are used in electrical circuits to allow or prevent the flow of electricity.

The **multimeter** can measure several characteristics of electricity.

Calculators make analyzing data easier and faster.

You can use **computers** in many ways, such as collecting, recording, and analyzing data.

Science Safety

Scientists know they must work safely when doing experiments. You need to be careful when doing science activities too. Follow these safety rules.

- Read the activity carefully before you start to do it.
- Listen to the teacher's instructions. Ask questions about things you do not understand.
- Wear safety goggles w hen needed.
- Keep your work place neat and clean. Clean up spills right away.
- Never taste or smell substances unless directed to do so by your teacher.
- Handle sharp items and other equipment carefully.
- Use chemicals carefully.
- Help keep plants and animals you use safe.
- Tell your teacher if you have an accident or you see something that looks unsafe.
- Put materials away when you finish an inquiry.
- Dispose of chemicals properly.
- Wash your hands well when you are finished.

Unit A
Life Science
in Indiana

Did you know that some bald eagles make their winter homes in Indiana? A population of bald eagles spends the winter months in Indiana. Conservationists are trying to make Indiana more attractive to bald eagles.

Life Science in Indiana

How are a river, a flower, forests, and basketball alike? They all provide opportunities for learning about life science in Indiana. You will learn more about the science behind them in Unit A.

Grand Calumet River

All living things are made of up cells. Cells are the smallest unit of living things. Scientists at Purdue University in West Lafayette measure the level of pollution to prevent it from entering the cells of plants and animals along Grand Calumet River. You will learn more about cells in Chapter 1.

Butterfly Milkweed

Butterfly milkweed, a common wildflower in Indiana, has colorful flowers that attract butterflies. Butterflies assist plants in the process of pollination. You will learn more about the reproduction of plants in Chapter 2.

Forests

Forests cover about one-fifth of Indiana. Indiana's forests are ecosystems. An ecosystem is a group of living and nonliving things in an environment and the ways they interact. You will learn more about ecosystems in Chapters 3 and 4.

Basketball

Roberts Stadium in Evansville hosts a basketball tournament every year. Indiana has a long history of high school, college, and professional basketball. Athletes depend on their skeletal, muscular, respiratory, nervous, and circulatory systems to perform well. You will learn more about human body systems in Chapter 5.

ISTEP+ Prep

Answer the questions below. Write your answers on a separate sheet of paper.

Multiple-Choice Questions

1. What is the smallest unit of a living thing?
   A a plant
   B a cell
   C an ecosystem
   D a root

2. About how much of Indiana is covered by forests?
   A about one-third
   B about one-fourth
   C about one-fifth
   D about one-tenth

Constructed-Response Questions

3. Why do scientists measure the level of pollution along the Grand Calumet River?

4. What is an ecosystem?

5. What systems of the human body are important to athletes?

Field Trip

Glendale Fish and Wildlife Refuge

You can visit Glendale Fish and Wildlife Refuge near Washington. The refuge contains Dogwood Lake, which attracts many birds, including bald eagles. Ducks and other waterfowl also live in the refuge. Wildlife shares Dogwood Lake with humans, who enjoy using the lake for recreation.

Indiana Surveys of Bald Eagles, 1980–2000	
Year	**Number of Bald Eagles**
1980	fewer than 10
1985	more than 20
1990	more than 70
1995	between 130 and 140
2000	180

In 2001 more than 280 bald eagles were counted!

Find out more:

Research to find out more about bald eagles in Indiana. Then write a letter to a newspaper. In your letter:

- Describe some of the environmental dangers to bald eagles.
- Suggest ways that people can help increase the bald eagle population in Indiana.

EC IN 10 9 8 7 6 5 4 3 2 1

You Will Discover

- the building blocks that make up all living things.
- how scientists classify plants and animals.
- some adaptations that help animals survive.

Chapter 1

Classifying Plants and Animals

www.sfsuccessnet.com

1

What are some ways to classify living things?

cell

nucleus

genus

species

chloroplast

cytoplasm

vertebrates

invertebrates

3

Explore What are living things made of?

Materials

small piece of onion

microscope and
plastic microscope slide

forceps

dropper

water

Process Skills

You can use a
microscope and
other tools of
science to help
you **observe**
objects.

What to Do

1 Separate the layers
of an onion.

Use forceps to remove
the thin skin between
the layers.

2 Spread out the piece of skin on
the microscope slide. Put a drop
of water onto the onion skin.

3 **Observe** the onion
skin through the
microscope.

100 ×

Think About It

1. Draw what you **observed**.
2. Describe what you observed.

TARGET SKILL

Compare and Contrast

Sometimes you need to compare and contrast information to understand what you are reading. When you compare you say how things are alike. When you contrast you say how things are different.

Science Article

Onions and Their Cells

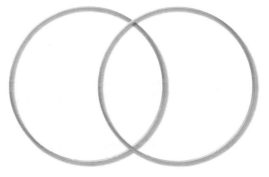

An onion has many different characteristics. An onion may be white, yellow, green, or red. Onions have layers. You can see thin lines going from the bottom to the top of the onion. Onions look very different when you study them with a microscope. You see box-like structures called cells. They are usually the same color as the onion. You can see a dot in the center of each cell.

Apply It!

Make a graphic organizer like the one at the right. In one circle, write the characteristics of the onion that you see without using a microscope. Write the characteristics of the onion cells in the other circle. Any characteristics that are the same belong in the center section.

You Are There!

When you look at a brick house, you can easily see the individual building blocks that it's made of. But have you seen the building blocks that make up a plant or animal? Without a way to magnify them, you wouldn't know that the blocks exist. Some are so small that over ten thousand could fit on the period at the end of this sentence.

Lesson 1

What are the building blocks of life?

How are a dandelion and a cat alike? Both are living things. They are both made from the building blocks of life.

What Cells Are

A cell is the building block of life. A **cell** is the smallest unit of a living thing that can perform all life processes. All living things are made of cells.

Some living things are made up of just one cell. Most living things, like plants and animals, are many-celled. Every part of a cat—from its muscles to its blood—is made of thousands, millions, even billions of cells.

A microscope helps you see cells.

Many cells have a particular role. Some cells help the living thing get energy it uses to grow, develop, and reproduce. Other cells help it get rid of what it doesn't need. Others help it move or react to its environment. Still other cells may protect the living thing or help it stay healthy. All cells come only from other living cells.

Scientists use microscopes to study cells. A microscope is a tool that makes objects seem larger than they really are. Most cells are very small and hard to see. By using a microscope, scientists are able to look at a cell and see details that help them learn about the cell.

1. ✔ **Checkpoint** Why are cells considered the building blocks of living things?

2. **Math in Science** In 1675, a Dutch scientist named Anton van Leeuwenhoek (LAY vehn hook) used a simple microscope to observe living things. How many years ago did van Leeuwenhoek observe these cells? Use mental math.

The size and shape of a cell are related to the cell's job.

A group of one type of cell is a tissue. Each kind of tissue does a certain job.

A group of tissues that work together is an organ. A heart is one of many organs in an animal.

A group of organs that work together make up an organ system. The heart, blood, and blood vessels are some parts of one system.

The Parts of a Cell

Beetles, eagles, and elephants look nothing alike. But the cells that make up these animals have many similar parts. All cells have a nucleus and a cell membrane. All cells have a gel-like liquid called cytoplasm. The different parts of a cell have special jobs.

Each part of a cell helps it carry out its life processes. The **nucleus** is the control center for the cell. The instructions for the cell's activities are stored in the nucleus. The cell membrane is the cell's outer border. It separates the cell from its environment. It also controls what substances move into or out of the cell. The **cytoplasm** contains the things that the cell needs to carry out its life processes.

Cells Working Together

If cells are the building blocks of life, what can they build? In a many-celled plant or animal, cells are organized to work together. Different types of cells do different kinds of work. Groups of the same type of cell form tissue. Groups of tissues that work together form an organ. Groups of organs that work together form systems.

An organism is the highest level of cell organization. It is a complete living thing that is made from all parts in all of the systems together.

Viruses

A virus is a very tiny particle that has characteristics of both nonliving and living things. Viruses do not make or use food. A virus can reproduce only by using plant or animal cells to create more viruses. Many scientists do not think a virus is a true living thing.

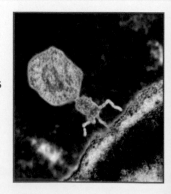

Like animal cells, plant cells have a cell membrane, cytoplasm, and a nucleus. But plant cells also have parts that animal cells do not have.

Plants make their own food. They need special parts to do this. **Chloroplasts** are the special parts in plant cells that trap the Sun's energy. The plant needs this energy to make food. Animal cells do not have chloroplasts.

The cell wall is another part of a plant cell that animal cells do not have. The cell wall is outside the cell membrane. It helps support and protect the cell.

A Plant Cell

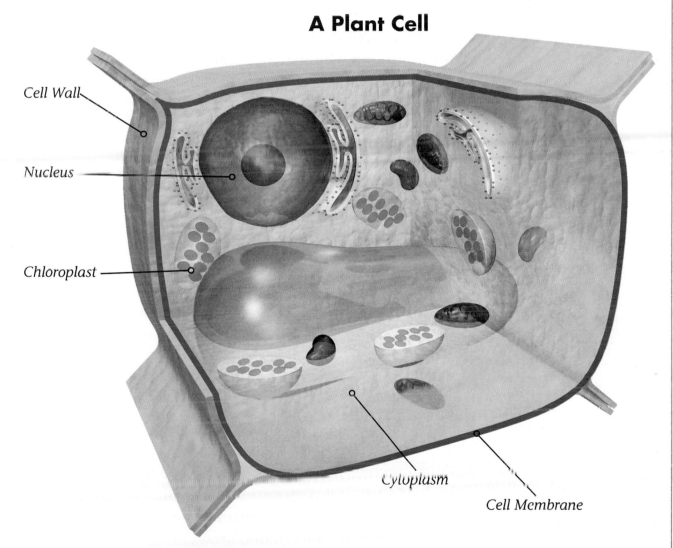

Cell Wall

Nucleus

Chloroplast

Cytoplasm

Cell Membrane

✓ **Lesson Checkpoint**

1. Describe the difference between a cell, a tissue, and an organ.
2. Can a single-celled organism contain tissue? Explain.
3. ⊙ **Compare and Contrast** Make a graphic organizer to compare and contrast animal and plant cells.

Lesson 2

How are living things grouped?

The world is filled with more than one million different kinds of organisms. How can scientists ever sort them all out?

Classification Systems

Scientists sort all living things into different groups. They ask questions about the organism they want to classify. They look at its cells and what parts the cells have. They think about where it lives and how it gets its food. All organisms in the same group have some common characteristics.

Kingdoms

The largest classification group is a kingdom. Until recently, most scientists used five kingdoms to classify organisms. Today, some classification systems have six kingdoms. All animals— from ants to elephants—belong to the same kingdom. All plants belong to another kingdom.

You would not put mushrooms in the same kingdom as sharks. But do mushrooms belong to the same kingdom as dandelions? You can decide by answering the questions that scientists ask.

- How many cells does the organism have?
- Where does it live?
- How does it get food?

A dandelion has roots, a stem, leaves, and a flower. Since it has different parts, it has more than one cell. It lives on land and grows in the soil. The mushroom has a cap and a stem. It also has more than one cell and grows on land in soil. A dandelion makes its own food. A mushroom must get its food from other living or dead things. It does not make its own food.

Both the dandelion and the mushroom have more than one cell and both live on land. But, one organism makes its own food while the other does not. They are in different kingdoms.

Dandelions need sunlight.

Mushrooms can grow in dark places without sunlight.

Kingdoms of Living Things

Ancient Bacteria
Ancient bacteria have only one cell and no separate nucleus. Scientists think ancient bacteria were the first cells to exist on Earth. These organisms may live on land or in the water. They make their own food.

True Bacteria
True bacteria are also one-celled organisms that have no separate nucleus. They live in land or water. Some of these bacteria get food. Others make their own food.

Protists
Most protists are one-celled. They have a nucleus and other cell parts. They live in water and moist environments. Many must get their food, but some make their own. Algae, ameba, and paramecia are protists.

Fungi
Fungi are mostly many-celled organisms. Each cell has a nucleus and other cell parts. Fungi live on land and need to get food from other living or nonliving things. Mushrooms, yeasts, and molds are fungi.

Plants
Plants have tissues and organs that are made of many cells. Each cell has a nucleus and cell wall. Most plants live on land, but some live in water. They use the Sun's energy to make their own food.

Animals
Animals are many-celled organisms with tissues, organs, and systems. They live in land or water environments. Animals do not make their own food. They get energy by eating plants or other animals.

1. ✅**Checkpoint** Why is a classification system important to scientists?
2. **Social Studies** in Science A scientist named Carolus Linnaeus (lin NAY us) classified about 12,000 organisms into groups based on similar characteristics. Find out when he lived and what country was his home.

Getting More Specific

Scientists divide kingdoms into smaller groups. They divide each of these groups into even smaller groups. They continue sorting into smaller and smaller groups. Each time they sort, they use the organism's features to decide whether or not the organism belongs to the group. Scientists use very specific characteristics to sort living things into the smallest groups. Once the living thing has been classified in this way, scientists name it.

Scientists use the smallest two groups to name organisms. The first part of an organism's scientific name is its genus. A **genus** is a group of closely related living things. For example, peach trees and plum trees are in the same genus. They share characteristics such as leaf shape. Both kinds of trees have flowers with parts that develop into tasty fruit. Black-footed cats and house cats are in the genus *Felis*. They share characteristics such as sharp claws and hunting behaviors.

The second part of an organism's scientific name is its species. A **species** is a group of similar organisms that can mate and produce offspring. The species name often describes a characteristic, such as where the organism lives or its color.

The ocelot is in the same family as the house cat and the black-footed cat.

Members of the Cat Family

The cats in the photos are in the same family. They all share some characteristics. In the past, some larger cats were grouped in the same genus as small cats. As scientists gathered more details, they used more specific characteristics to classify. They sorted the cat family into more groups.

The scientific name for the house cat is *Felis domesticus*.

The scientific name for the black-footed cat is *Felis nigripes*. In Latin, *nigripes* means "black feet." So this name tells something about what the animal looks like. The scientific name for a house cat tells where it lives. The Latin word *domesticus* means "of the house." The scientific name for a house cat is *Felis domesticus*.

The scientific name for the black-footed cat is *Felis nigripes*.

The common name that people in one region use for an organism might not be the same as the one used in another region. People in different regions might use the same name for different organisms. But, in all parts of the world, every living thing has only one scientific name.

The Animal Kingdom

Kingdom

Division

Class

Order

Family

Genus

Species

✓ **Lesson Checkpoint**

1. What are some of the characteristics scientists use to classify organisms?
2. In which kingdoms would you expect to find living things that can make their own food?
3. **Writing in Science** **Expository** Use the library or Internet to find the genus and species of a living or an extinct organism. Write about that organism in your science journal.

How are plants classified?

Biologists sort plants in a variety of ways, based on how they transport water and nutrients or how they reproduce.

How Plants Transport Water and Nutrients

In warm, wet regions bamboo plants can grow as tall as 30 meters (100 feet). But how can the cells at the top of such a tall plant get the water and nutrients they need from the soil? Bamboo has tubelike structures that move water and nutrients to all the organs of the plant—the leaves, stems, and roots. The tissues that make up the system of tubes connect the leaves, the stems, and the roots. Water and nutrients move up and down these tubes to all organs of the plant. Each part of the plant gets what it needs to do its job.

Plants that have these tubes are called vascular plants. You are familiar with many vascular plants. Grass, ferns, dandelions, celery, and trees are all vascular plants.

The vascular tissue does more than help the organs of the plant get the materials they need. The vascular tissue also adds support to the stems and leaves of the plant. Because of the added support, the plant can grow larger.

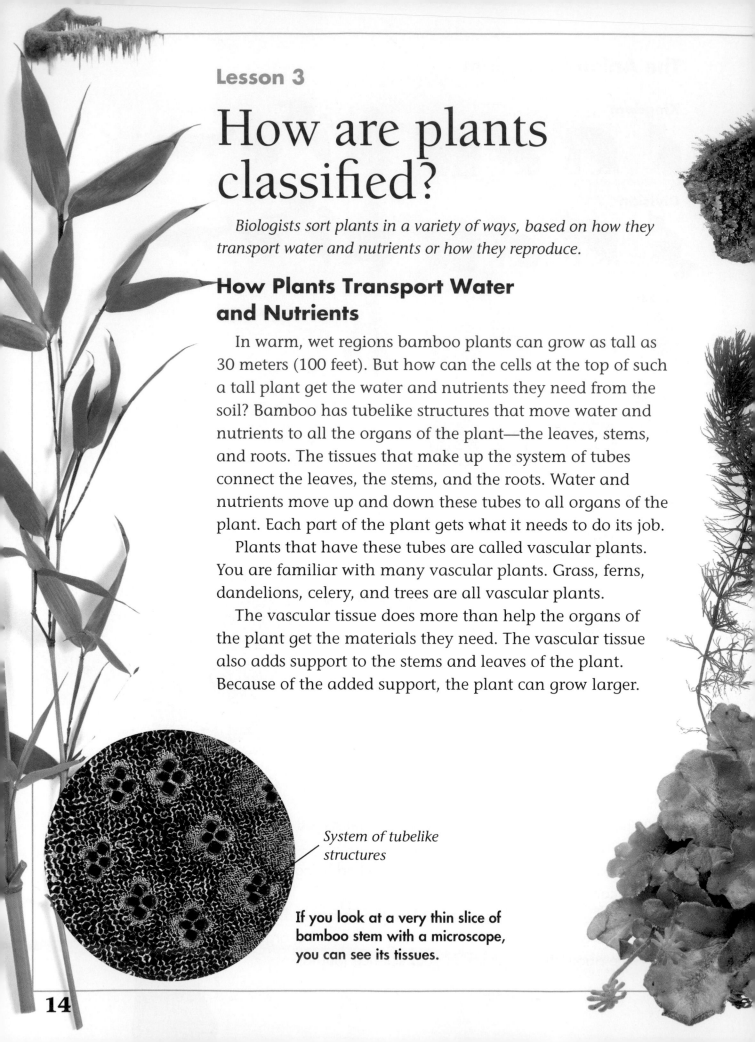

System of tubelike structures

If you look at a very thin slice of bamboo stem with a microscope, you can see its tissues.

Moss

More Down-to-Earth Plants

Not all plants have a system where water and nutrients move directly to all of its organs. Plants without this system of tubes are called nonvascular plants. Nonvascular plants do not have true roots, stems, or leaves. They can only pass water and nutrients from one cell to the cell that is next to it. That means that water and nutrients do not travel very far or very quickly. These plants are usually small.

These plants do not have a system of tubes to help support their stems and other organs. As a result, they don't grow very tall. But, sometimes they grow so close to each other that they look like one plant. Most nonvascular plants live in moist places.

Mosses

Mosses form the largest group of nonvascular plants. They often look like a velvety green mat. They sometimes live in places where other plants cannot survive because of low temperatures. Mosses do not have true stems or leaves, but they are able to make their own food.

Hornwort

Hornworts

Hornworts are another group of nonvascular plants. Do you wonder how hornworts got their name? At one stage in its life cycle, part of a hornwort looks like a cattle horn. And the old English word for *plant* is *wort*. Like mosses, hornworts don't have true stems or leaves. Hornworts prefer warm places.

Liverworts

Liverwort

The liverwort is a nonvascular plant that often grows on moist rocks or soil along the sides of a stream. Some liverworts look like flat leaves that are connected to the ground. Some have parts that look like little umbrellas. Some species have a spicy smell. And, as you may have guessed, some species are shaped like a liver.

1. ✓**Checkpoint** What are some examples of vascular plants?
2. **Math in Science** Suppose a young evergreen tree that is now five feet tall grows an average of six inches each year. About how tall will this tree be thirty years from now?

A soybean pod holds 2 or 3 seeds or beans. Soybeans are used as food or as a raw material for other products.

The seed cone is the part we usually call a "pine cone."

The spots on the underside of this fern leaf are actually groups of spore cases.

How Plants Make New Plants

Another way that scientists classify plants is by how they make new plants, or reproduce. Plants with flowers or cones produce seeds. Other plants reproduce using spores.

Flowers and Seeds

Plants in one group make seeds. A seed has many cells. It has a young plant and stored food inside a protective covering. Seeds are different shapes and sizes. You can see most seeds without using a hand lens. Flowering plants are the largest group of plants that make seeds. The seeds and other parts of flowering plants provide food for people and animals. A cactus, a fruit tree, a poppy, and wheat are examples of flowering plants.

Cones and Seeds

Pine trees belong to the group of plants that make seeds but do not have flowers. These plants are called conifers. Conifers grow two kind of cones. One cone makes pollen and the other makes seeds. Most conifers are evergreen plants. Evergreen plants keep their leaves, or needles, year-round.

Spores

Ferns and mosses are two kinds of plants that do not make seeds. They reproduce by forming tiny cells that can grow into new plants. Each tiny cell is called a spore. Spores are different sizes and shapes. Each one is a single cell surrounded by a protective cell wall. To begin growing into a new plant, a spore needs a moist, shady place where it can get nutrients.

Spore cases in most ferns form on the underside of fern leaves. They look like brown dots or streaks. In mosses, spores are in cases at the tips of short stalks. Each spore case holds hundreds of spores.

Many different flowering plants often grow close together.

Conifers live in many different habitats.

Ferns can grow in shady areas without direct sunlight.

✓ Lesson Checkpoint

1. What are conifers?
2. Name one way of classifying plants into two groups.
3. **⊙ Compare and Contrast** How are seeds and spores alike? How are they different?

How are animals classified?

Animals are classified based on their similarities and differences.

The body temperature of most reptiles depends on the temperature of their surroundings.

Animals with Backbones

Scientists divide the animal kingdom into two main groups. All the animals in one group have backbones. Animals in this group are called **vertebrates.** Vertebrates are divided into five divisions—fish, amphibians, reptiles, birds, and mammals.

| **Fish** | Fish are usually covered with scales. They live only in water. Fish breathe mostly with gills. Fish are cold-blooded and most lay eggs. |

| **Amphibians** | Amphibians are covered with a skin. They can live both on land and in the water. They breathe with lungs or gills or both. They are cold-blooded. Amphibians hatch from eggs. |

| **Reptiles** | Reptiles are covered with scales. Most reptiles live on land. Some can live in water. They breathe with lungs. Reptiles are cold-blooded. Reptiles usually lay eggs instead of having live births. |

| **Birds** | Birds are covered with feathers. They usually live on land, but many birds spend much of their time in water. Birds use lungs to breathe. They are warm-blooded. All birds lay eggs. |

| **Mammals** | All mammals have hair or fur. Most live on land, but a few live in water. They breathe with lungs. Mammals are warm-blooded, they make their own heat. Most mammals have live births. |

The python has a very long backbone.

Reptiles

Reptiles live in water and land environments. This group of vertebrates includes alligators, crocodiles, lizards, snakes, turtles, tortoises, and tuataras.

Besides having a backbone, reptiles have other characteristics in common. Reptiles breathe air with lungs. Their dry skin covered with scales or plates.

While alligators and crocodiles look similar, they differ in several ways. Even though their heads have different shapes, both alligators and crocodiles have long teeth on both sides of their lower jaws. When an alligator closes its mouth, you cannot see these teeth. Alligators live in fresh water. Crocodiles prefer salt water habitats.

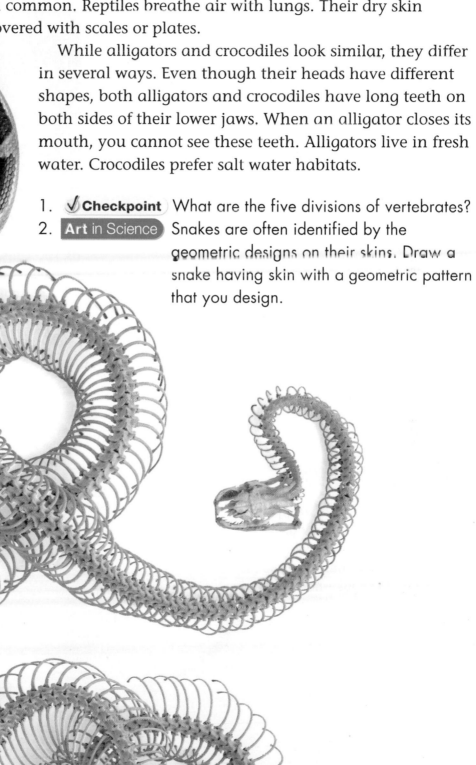

1. ✓**Checkpoint** What are the five divisions of vertebrates?
2. **Art** in Science Snakes are often identified by the geometric designs on their skins. Draw a snake having skin with a geometric pattern that you design.

Life Cycle of a Reptile

The Burmese python is a long, thick snake whose length seems to go on forever. It can grow up to 6 meters (about 20 feet) and weigh as much as a fully-grown man.

The Burmese python is not a poisonous snake. It squeezes its prey and then swallows it whole. To find its food, the Burmese python uses heat sensors along its upper lip. It also has a keen sense of smell. The python can stretch its jaws far apart. The snake is able to swallow animals with bodies that are much larger than its own head. A Burmese python is a good climber and uses its tail to wrap around things.

About three months after mating, the mother python lays as many as 100 eggs. She pushes them together into a pile and coils herself around them.

The mother python stays wrapped around the eggs while they grow. She keeps them warm by vibrating her muscles. During this time, she never leaves the eggs—not even to eat.

Six to eight weeks later, the eggs hatch. Each python hatchling is about 51 centimeters (20 inches) long and weighs about as much as two tennis balls.

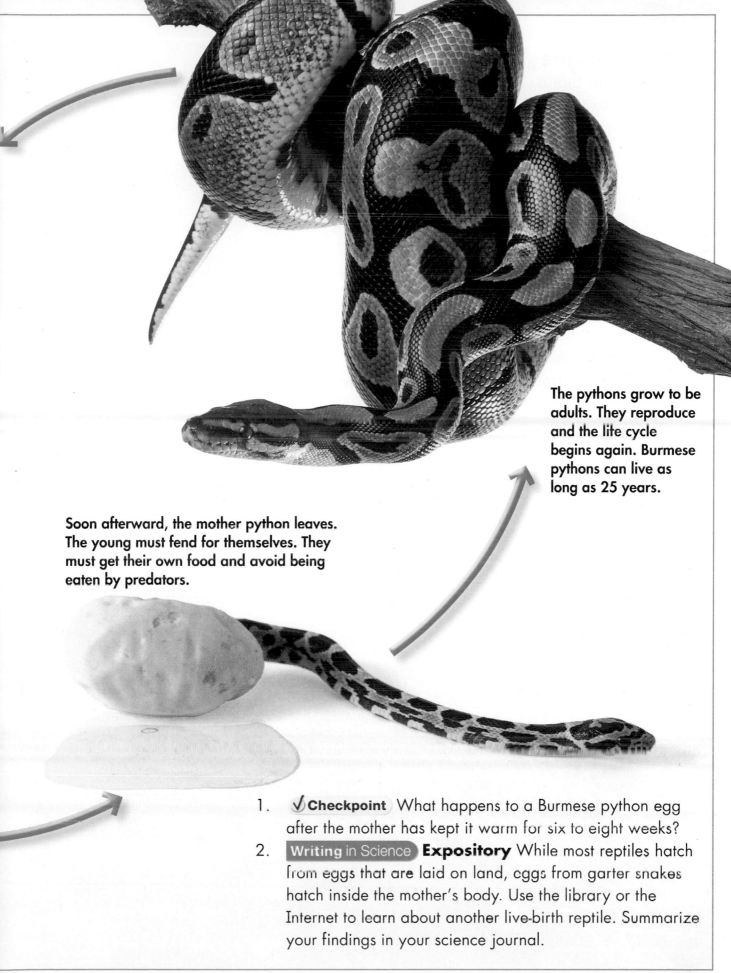

The pythons grow to be adults. They reproduce and the life cycle begins again. Burmese pythons can live as long as 25 years.

Soon afterward, the mother python leaves. The young must fend for themselves. They must get their own food and avoid being eaten by predators.

1. ✓**Checkpoint** What happens to a Burmese python egg after the mother has kept it warm for six to eight weeks?

2. **Writing** in Science **Expository** While most reptiles hatch from eggs that are laid on land, eggs from garter snakes hatch inside the mother's body. Use the library or the Internet to learn about another live-birth reptile. Summarize your findings in your science journal.

Invertebrates

Animals that do not have a backbone are called **invertebrates.** Most of the animals in the world are invertebrates. Some of these are jellyfish, worms, insects, spiders, and lobsters. Some invertebrates, like jellyfish and worms, have no protection for their soft bodies. Others, such as snails and clams, have a soft body inside a hard shell.

Arthropods and More

Arthropods are animals with jointed legs. They are the largest group of invertebrates. Insects, spiders, crabs, and shrimp are all arthropods. Their legs and bodies are divided into sections.

Arthropods are covered by a hard, lightweight outer skin, or exoskeleton. Like a suit of armor, the exoskeleton protects the animal inside.

Some other groups of invertebrates include sponges, sea stars, worms, and mollusks. Sponges are sea animals that have many pores. Some worms, such as earthworms and leeches, have bodies made of segments. Others, such as tapeworms, have simpler bodies.

Earthworm

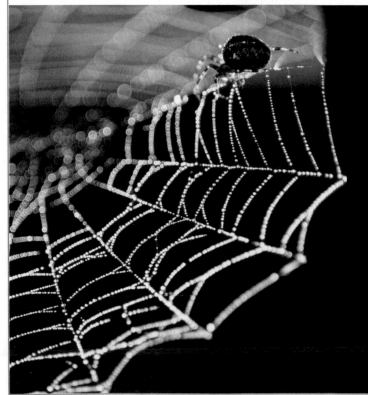

Spiders

Like all arthropods, spiders have an exoskeleton and jointed legs. Some people think spiders are insects, but spiders have eight legs. Insects have only six. Spiders have only two main body parts. They don't have feelers. Insects have three main body parts and feelers. Spiders can spin silk. The silk that spiders spin is one of the strongest natural fibers. Most spiders make webs with their silk to trap their prey.

Invertebrates

Scientists have identified more than one million species of invertebrates.

Crab

Tapeworm

Sponge

Clam

1. ✓**Checkpoint** Name some animals that are classified as arthropods.

2. **Math** in Science Snails travel at very slow speeds. Suppose a snail moves at an average speed of 8 centimeters per hour. At this rate, about how long would the snail take to travel 2 centimeters?

Mollusks

A snail is one type of mollusk. Most snails have a single, coiled shell. Like some other mollusks, snails move with a muscular structure called a foot. The foot oozes a slimy liquid, which makes moving along easier for the snail. Some snails live in water environments, while others live on land.

Most mollusks are a few centimeters long, but some can get very large. The giant squid, for example, is the largest invertebrate. It can grow up to 15 meters (about 50 feet) long. Some mollusks, such as oysters, usually don't move very far. Others, such as octopus, are fast swimmers.

The Life Cycle of the Brown Snail

The brown garden snail is a mollusk that lives on land. After mating, the mother snail digs a nest that is about 3 centimeters deep. She will lay about 85 eggs in this nest. Snails lay eggs most often during warm, damp weather.

Depending on the temperature and the amount of moisture in the soil, the eggs will hatch in two to four weeks. The tiny, newly hatched snail has a fragile shell. A newly hatched snail must find its own food. A young snail will first eat whatever is left of its own eggshell. Then, it will eat other snail eggs that have not yet hatched.

In about two years, the snails become adults. As the snail grows, its shell grows, too, into a spiral shape. The life span of a snail is about 10 years.

The snail leaves a trail of mucus as it crawls along.

The brown garden snail lays its eggs.

The eggs hatch in two to four weeks.

Newly hatched snails must find food to grow.

Adult snails reproduce, and the life cycle begins again.

√Lesson Checkpoint

1. Are there more vertebrates or invertebrates on Earth?

2. Name the largest group of invertebrates.

3. ⊚ **Compare and Contrast** the life cycles of Burmese pythons and brown garden snails.

How do animals adapt?

Animals inherit characteristics from their parents. These special physical features and behaviors help them survive.

How Animals Get What They Need

The same way human children often have the same hair color as their parents, young animals inherit traits from their parents. A trait is a physical feature. Animals have characteristics like their parents. Young animals are born knowing some behaviors that will help them survive. They learn other behaviors.

Ducks waddle because their short legs are far apart on their bodies.

An adaptation is a physical feature or behavior that helps an animal get food, protect itself, move, or reproduce. Every animal needs food, water, oxygen, and shelter to survive. Sometimes there are not enough resources to go around. Animals with excellent adaptations have a better chance of getting the resources they need. The better an animal is at getting what it needs, the better its chances of reproducing. The adaptations are passed to the next generation.

Birds' Adaptations

Birds have many adaptations that help them get what they need. Feathers are an important adaptation for birds. Without feathers, birds could not fly, no matter how light their bodies. The shapes of their beak helps birds to get food. For example, finches eat mostly seeds. Their beaks are made for cracking the shells of seeds. Herons' long sharp beaks are perfect for spearing fish. Hummingbirds poke their long, narrow beaks into flowers to gather nectar. Webbed feet help ducks and other waterfowl move around in the water. Cactus wrens live in a desert climate where there is not much water. They get all the water they need from the things they eat.

Webbed feet help make ducks and other waterfowl strong swimmers.

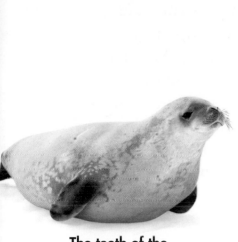

The teeth of the crab-eating seal are adapted to its diet.

A polar bear's fur coat not only blends into the cold, snowy environment, it also keeps the bear warm.

Other Adaptations

Mammals have many adaptations to help them. Polar bears have thick coats of fur that keep them warm in their frozen climate. The fat they store also helps them stay warm. Their sharp claws and teeth help them catch and eat food. The long neck of the giraffe helps it reach tree leaves that it eats.

A halibut is different from most other fish. Both of its eyes are on the same side of its body. A halibut lives on the ocean floor so an eye on the other side of its body it would be covered with sand. Fish and other animals with an eye on each side can see something coming from two directions. Humans and other animals that have both eyes in front can tell how far away things are.

The crab-eating seal of the Antarctic does not actually eat crab. Instead, it eats krill, which are small shrimp-like arthropods. The teeth of this species of seal have adapted so they can sift krill from the water. This feeding adaptation enables the seal to get enough food.

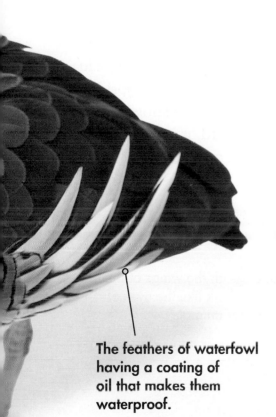

The feathers of waterfowl having a coating of oil that makes them waterproof.

1. **✓Checkpoint** What is an adaptation?
2. **Math** in Science A jumping spider can leap as much as 40 times its own body length to catch its prey. How far can a spider whose body is 2 cm long jump?

Some birds have feathers that change with the seasons.

Rock ptarmigan in summer

Rock ptarmigan in winter

This colorful Mandarin fish lives in a brightly colored coral reef. It blends into its environment and can hide from predators.

Mandarin fish

Fulgorid bug

Adaptations that Protect Animals

Some animals have adaptations that help them avoid being eaten by predators. The color of animals can help them blend in with their environment. Bright colors may warn predators that the animal is poisonous. Box turtles, hedgehogs, and other animals have hard shells or spiny skins. Some animals are protected by stingers, quills, bitter-tasting flesh, or smelly sprays.

Blending In

Some animals have adaptations that make it difficult for their enemies, or predators, to see them. Colors, shapes, and patterns of animals can keep them hidden in their surroundings.

Some birds inherit adaptations that help them hide from predators in the winter. Against the snow, the rock ptarmigan's dark, summertime feathers would make it very visible to its enemies. But, in cold weather, the rock ptarmigan sheds its darker feathers. Its winter "outfit" is made of white feathers that blend in with the snow.

Insects also use colors to trick their enemies. For example, the markings on the wings of the fulgorid bug look like the eyes of a cat. When the fulgorid bug senses an approaching predator, it shows its eyespots. A predator, such as a bird, may mistake these markings for the eyes of a cat. The fulgorid bug then has time to escape.

The markings on the wings of the fulgorid bug look like the eyes of a much larger animal.

Protected by Poison

Some frogs and toads have interesting adaptations that protect them from predators. The European green toad has a poison gland behind each eye. When this gland is pressed—such as when a predator tries to bite its head—it squirts poison.

Another poison-packing amphibian is the poison-dart frog, which lives in the South American rain forests. The bright colors of this frog warn predators, "Look out! I'm dangerous." Although each frog is just a few centimeters long, it produces enough poison to kill a human being.

Escaping Predators

Animals have different ways of moving. The faster they are, the more easily they can escape their predators. Birds' wings allow them to fly away from predators that cannot fly. Fins enable fish to swim away from their enemies. Other animals can run at top speed longer than their enemies can.

Zebras

Zebras inherit their striped pattern from their parents. Even their manes and tails are striped! But, no two zebras are exactly alike. The stripes help hide zebra babies in the middle of the herd where they will be safer from lions and other enemies. The stripes on baby zebras are sometimes brown and white.

A zebra baby has very long legs—almost as long as its mother's! The baby is able to stand shortly after it is born. Within an hour, the baby zebra can run fast enough to keep up when the herd is running to escape danger.

1. **✓ Checkpoint** Name some adaptations that animals use to avoid predators.
2. **Art** in Science Design an animal with an adaptation that would help it live in your classroom.

Animal Instincts

Instincts help animals meet their needs. Instincts are behaviors that are inherited. Ducklings, for example, are born with the instinct to follow their mother. By staying close to their mother, they will get the protection and food they need.

Migration

In places where winters are cold, many animals face a shortage of food for part of the year. Plants stop growing. Insects and other invertebrates die or bury themselves. Some animals deal with this food shortage by migrating. Migration is travelling in search of food or a place to reproduce.

During the spring and summer, Canada geese live in Canada and the upper United States, including Alaska. Flocks of these geese migrate as far south as Mexico to escape cold winter weather and find food. Canada geese are adapted to fly as fast as 60 miles per hour and as high as 8,000 feet.

Sometimes migrating animals face barriers. Some barriers are made by people. Migrating amphibians often must cross busy roads as they travel to and from their breeding ponds. Other barriers are natural. White storks must cross the Mediterranean Sea to get to their winter homes in Africa.

Hibernation and Inactivity

Migration is a natural behavior for an organism. It does not need to be learned. Another type of natural behavior that helps an animal survive is hibernation. Hibernation is a state of inactivity that occurs in some animals when outside temperatures are cold. Some mammals and many reptiles and amphibians hibernate. Some hibernating animals conserve energy by slowing down their body functions. They spend most of the time sleeping. They move only occasionally to raise their body temperature or to eat. Other hibernating animals remain totally inactive. They get their energy from stored body fat.

In the winter, as many as fifteen marmots crowd into an underground nest, or burrow. During hibernation, marmots awaken a few times a week. They may occasionally move around and nibble some stored food.

Some mammals, such as brown bears, spend several winter months sleeping in their dens. The bears do not eat during this time. Unlike true hibernators, the body temperature of these bears drops only slightly. On warmer days, they may awaken. Some bears even give birth during the winter.

During the summer, garter snakes stay warm by basking in the Sun. When the temperatures get colder, the snakes gather underground in large groups. During hibernation, the snakes move very little.

1. ✔**Checkpoint** How do the instincts of migration and hibernation help animals to survive?
2. **Social Studies** in Science Humans sometimes have to move, or migrate, to meet their needs. Describe an example from history where people moved to meet their needs.

How Animals Learn

Not all behaviors come by instinct. Some behaviors develop as a result of training or changes in experience. Young animals learn many things by observing their parents and other adult animals. Trial and error plays a major role in how animals behave. The behaviors they learn develop slowly. Over long periods of time the animal interacts with its environment and learns which behaviors work and which do not.

Bear cubs learn to fish and hunt by watching their parents. The cubs watch their mother wade into streams to grab fish.

Parents Teach Offspring

Many animals learn to get food by watching their parents. Lion cubs learn to hunt by watching their parents. A pride, or group of lions, often hunts together. Zebras are common prey for lions. A herd of zebras keeps safe from attack by staying together. When a zebra is separated from the herd, the lions will chase it toward a group of lions that is hiding. The lions will then pounce on their prey. A lion cub learns to pounce on its prey by pouncing on its mother's twitching tail.

Offspring Teach Parents

Scientists found that when monkeys learn new things, they teach other monkeys what they've learned. Scientists dropped sweet potatoes near the monkeys' home. The potatoes landed in sand. The monkeys liked the potatoes, but they did not like the sand that stuck to the potatoes. One of the younger monkeys found that she could wash the sand off in a nearby stream. She taught her mother how to wash the sand off too.

Monkeys learn that sticks are handy tools.

Learned and Inherited

Some behaviors are partly inherited and partly learned. The white-crowned sparrow inherited the ability to recognize the song its species sings. But, learning to sing the song is not inherited. Young sparrows that were separated from their parents never learned to sing the complete song.

Humans inherit the ability to learn much more than animals. We inherit the ability to learn language. We are not born speaking Spanish, English, or Chinese. We must learn the words used in our language.

✓ Lesson Checkpoint

1. Explain the difference between instinct and learned behavior.
2. How do the adaptation of body color and patterns help the Mandarin fish survive?
3. **Technology** in Science Scientists track migrations with radio tags that are attached to the animals. Find out how bird banding and satellites help scientists track migrating birds.

Guided Inquiry

Investigate How can you use a chart to classify a set of objects?

A dichotomous key is a set of rules scientists use to help classify organisms. Often these rules are in a list. Sometimes they are in a chart, such as the Classification Chart shown on page 35. This chart will help you identify a tree by its leaves.

Materials

leaf A

leaf B

leaf C

leaf D

leaf E

leaf F

Process Skills

You can use a chart to help **classify** objects.

What to Do

1 Study the leaves. Find the letter next to each leaf picture. Look for the features in the first step on the **Classification** Chart on page 35. Which leaves are wide? Which is narrow? Sort the leaves into 2 groups.

2 The Classification Chart shows that very narrow leaf D is from a pine tree. Record its identify in the Identification Chart.

Identification Chart	
Leaf	**Name**
Leaf A	
Leaf B	
Leaf C	
Leaf D	pine
Leaf E	
Leaf F	

3 Follow the Classification Chart to identify the remaining leaves.

Take It to the NET
More Activities www.sfsuccessnet.com

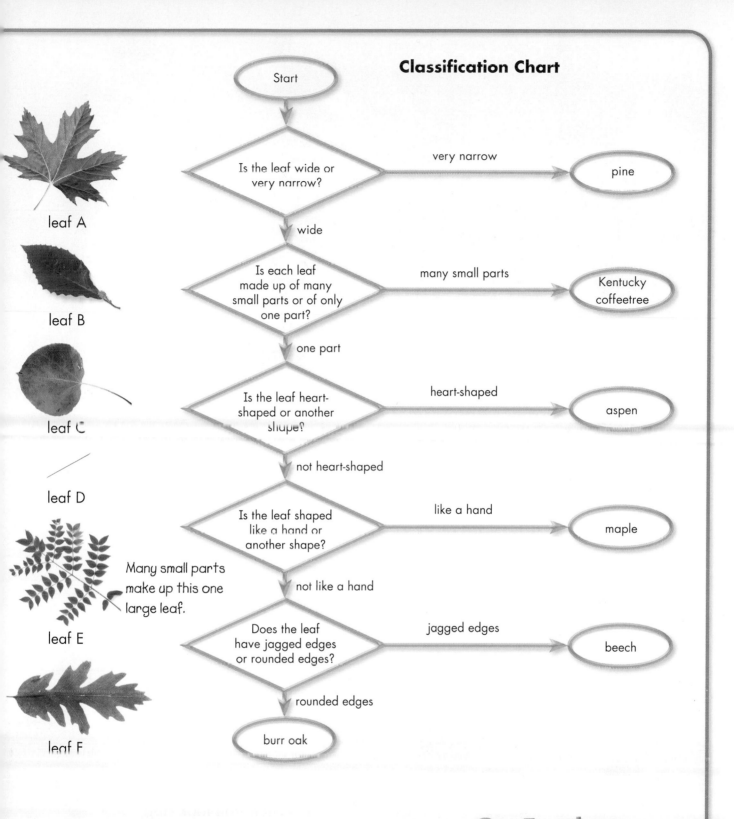

Classification Chart

Start

Is the leaf wide or very narrow? → **very narrow** → pine

wide

Is each leaf made up of many small parts or of only one part? → **many small parts** → Kentucky coffeetree

one part

Is the leaf heart-shaped or another shape? → **heart-shaped** → aspen

not heart-shaped

Is the leaf shaped like a hand or another shape? → **like a hand** → maple

not like a hand

Does the leaf have jagged edges or rounded edges? → **jagged edges** → beech

rounded edges

burr oak

leaf A

leaf B

leaf C

leaf D

leaf E

Many small parts make up this one large leaf.

leaf F

Think About It

1. List the features you used to **classify** the leaves.

2. What other features could you use to classify leaves?

Go Further

How could you use a chart to classify a group of animals? Make a plan to answer this or other questions you may have.

Symmetry in Nature

A figure is symmetric if it can be folded along a line so that both parts match exactly. The fold line is called a line of symmetry. Many plants and animals have one or more lines of symmetry.

This picture shows a line of symmetry for a dog.

When you look at a dog from the side, it has no lines of symmetry.

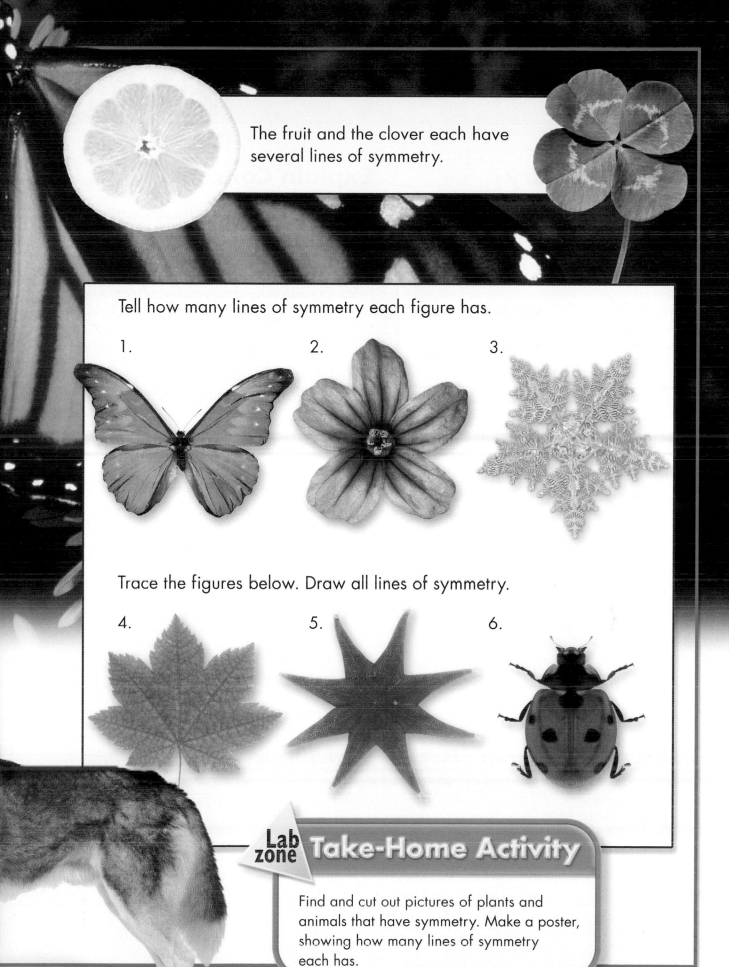

The fruit and the clover each have several lines of symmetry.

Tell how many lines of symmetry each figure has.

1.

2.

3.

Trace the figures below. Draw all lines of symmetry.

4.

5.

6.

Lab zone **Take-Home Activity**

Find and cut out pictures of plants and animals that have symmetry. Make a poster, showing how many lines of symmetry each has.

Chapter 1 Review and Test Prep

Use Vocabulary

cell (p. 7)	**invertebrates** (p. 22)
chloroplast (p. 8)	**genus** (p. 12)
cytoplasm (p. 8)	**species** (p. 12)
nucleus (p. 8)	**vertebrates** (p. 18)

Use the word from the above list that best completes each sentence.

1. Animals with backbones are called _____.

2. About $\frac{98}{100}$ of all animals are _____.

3. The basic unit of a living organism that can perform all life processes is a(n) _____.

4. A(n) _____ is a group of living things that are so much alike that they can reproduce.

5. _____ is a gel-like liquid inside a cell.

6. The _____ controls a cell's activities.

7. A(n) _____ is a cell part that plants use to make food.

Explain Concepts

8. Describe how cells, tissues, organs, organ systems, and organisms are related.

9. Explain why many nonvascular plants are small and grow low to the ground.

10. Explain how a scientific name gives information about a living thing and its close relatives.

Process Skills

11. **Infer** how animal life would be different if animal cells had chloroplasts.

12. **Classify** an invertebrate that has jointed legs, a segmented body, and an exoskeleton.

13. **Predict** If the outdoor temperature increases by 10°C, what will happen to a reptile's body temperature?

Compare and Contrast

14. Use the graphic organizer below to compare and contrast vertebrates and invertebrates.

 Test Prep

Choose the letter that best completes the statement or answers the question.

15. Scientists classify clams, squid, and octopuses as
   Ⓐ vertebrates.
   Ⓑ reptiles.
   Ⓒ mollusks.
   Ⓓ mammals.

16. Offspring inherit some behaviors and learn others. Which behavior is learned?
   Ⓕ a snake hibernating
   Ⓖ a sea turtle digging a hole on the beach for its eggs
   Ⓗ an amphibian migrating
   Ⓘ a guide dog helping a visually impaired person

17. Which is NOT true about an animal cell?
   Ⓐ A cell wall surrounds it.
   Ⓑ A thin outer membrane surrounds it.
   Ⓒ It has a nucleus.
   Ⓓ A gel-like liquid is inside the cell.

18. In the winter, the rock ptarmigan has white feathers. This is an example of
   Ⓕ hibernation.
   Ⓖ adaptation.
   Ⓗ classification.
   Ⓘ migration.

19. Explain why the answer you chose for Question #18 is best. For each of the answers you did not choose, give a reason why it is not the best choice.

20. Writing in Science **Expository**
Suppose that the only plants on Earth were nonvascular plants. Write a paragraph explaining how this would affect your life.

Biologist

Do you like snakes? Maybe, you prefer koala bears. If you like animals you might like to be a wildlife biologist. Wildlife biologists search for ways to help animals. The biologists learn about their habits, what they eat, where they go, and how long they live.

At NASA's Kennedy Space Center, biologists study the animals in the area. NASA biologists have been studying why the population of Eastern Indigo Snakes is getting smaller. With the information the biologists gather, they hope to increase the population.

Plant biologists also work for NASA. They are finding ways to grow plants in space so that astronauts on long trips will have a source of food that does not have to be stored on the spacecraft.

If you think biology is for you, you should take science classes in high school. You might volunteer to work with plants or animals. You will need to get a college degree in biology or a related science. Some biologists specialize in a group of plants or animals.

Dr. Mary Musgrave studies how plants produce seeds in space.

Lab zone Take-Home Activity

Think of other careers where people work with living things. Research two of these careers and write a short description of each one.

Energy from Plants

You Will Discover

- how plants make their own food.
- how the parts of a plant work together as a system.
- how new plants are made.
- what happens to plants as they grow and change.

Online Student Edition

What features help plants make their own food and reproduce?

photosynthesis

pistil

stamen

sepal

ovary

42

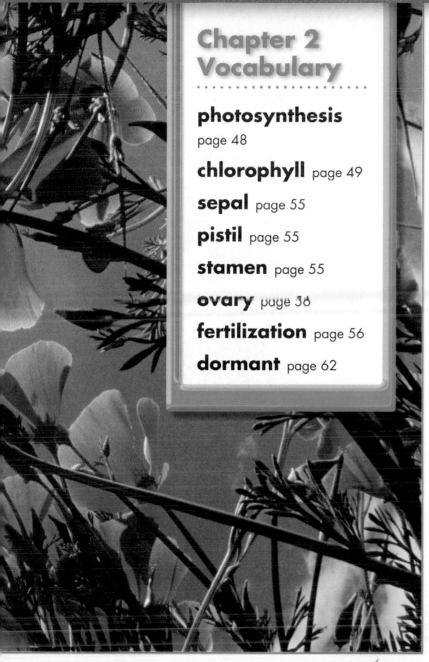

Chapter 2 Vocabulary

. . . .

photosynthesis
page 48

chlorophyll page 49

sepal page 55

pistil page 55

stamen page 55

ovary page 58

fertilization page 56

dormant page 62

chlorophyll

fertilization

dormant

43

Explore How can you show that a plant needs light?

Materials

plant

black paper

scissors and tape

water

What to Do

1 Cut 2 squares of black paper. Each square should be big enough to completely cover one side of a leaf.

Place one square on one side of a leaf and another square on the other side. Tape the squares together.

2 Place the plant in a sunny place. Water it every other day for a week.

3 Remove the squares. Record your **observations** of the covered and uncovered leaves.

Think About It

Compare your **observations** of the leaves. What do you think might cause the leaves to look different?

Process Skills

When you **observe** several objects, such as leaves, comparing and contrasting the objects can help you observe more carefully.

How to Read Science

Draw Conclusions

- A conclusion is a decision you reach after you think about facts and details.

- You can also use what you know to make a decision or form an opinion that makes sense of events.

Read part of a letter that a man sent about his sweet potato plant to the Plant Doctor column of a gardening magazine. Then look at the Plant Doctor's conclusion. The details that led to the conclusion are highlighted.

Ask the Plant Doctor

Question: I have grown a sweet potato plant in the same place in my yard for several years. Each year the plant is shaded a little more by the bushes and trees around it. This year its leaves are bronze or gold, and lately they are falling off the plant. In fact, the whole plant looks sickly. What's wrong?

Answer: Sweet potato plants grow best in full sun. They need sunlight to make food for healthy growth. Their leaves range from dark maroon to yellow-green. The plants will not survive cold winters, but the weather is still warm. Your letter said that you did not think the problem was related to water, nutrients, or insects. My conclusion is that your sweet potato plant needs more sunlight. Trim the trees and bushes around it.

Apply It!

Use a graphic organizer like the one to the right to show the facts that led to the conclusion.

Facts

Conclusion

◀») You Are There!

The bright sunlight beams on the plants around you.
Many of the plants have colorful flowers. Some are
delicate, lacy flowers. Some are clusters of tiny blooms
that look like one huge flower. The leaves are different
shapes and sizes too. Except for small brown spots on
the underside of a few of them, the leaves all have one
thing in common. They are green. Why can so many
different plants grow here?

Lesson 1

What are plants' characteristics?

Plants are made of small building blocks called cells. Different parts of a cell do different jobs. Some parts have the job of making food for the plant.

Plant Cells

How is a giant redwood tree in California like a small dandelion in your backyard? Both are living things that are made of many cells. They are multi-celled organisms. Both also belong to the plant kingdom.

The redwood tree towers 90 meters above the forest floor. The dandelion barely stands above your ankle. Yet if you looked at a tiny piece of a redwood needle and a tiny piece of a dandelion leaf under a microscope, you would see similar parts of similar size. These parts are cells.

All plants are made of cells. Plants may look different, but they have many of the same kinds of cells. The cells are organized into tissues and tissues are organized into organs. Each plant has special parts that use the water and materials that it absorbs from the soil. Some of the special parts use the energy from sunlight to change the water and materials into food for the plant. Other parts transport the food to the cells in the rest of the plant.

1. **✓Checkpoint** What is a multi-celled organism?
2. **Math in Science** Suppose a dandelion is 15 centimeters tall. About how many times greater is the height of the redwood tree? (Remember 1m – 100 cm.)

Plant Habitats

Plants live in many kinds of habitats—from cold mountain meadows to blistering hot deserts. Plants have special adaptations that help them survive in their environment. Some plants, like water lilies, grow in the soil at the bottom of ponds. The stems reach up through the water, and a flower blooms above the surface. Large leaves float on the water and trap sunlight energy. You may know these leaves as lily pads.

How Plants Make Food

Suppose you were helping take care of plants in a garden. You would make sure that they got plenty of sunlight and water. Sunlight and water are two things that plants need to live, grow, and reproduce. Plants also need carbon dioxide from the air and mineral nutrients from the soil.

Photosynthesis

Unlike animals, plants make their own food. The food they make is sugar. The process of making the sugar is called **photosynthesis.** In photosynthesis, plants use carbon dioxide that their leaves absorb from the air and water that their roots absorb from the soil. The water and the nutrients it carries travel through tubes in the stem to the leaves. The plants use sunlight energy to change these ingredients into food. Oxygen and water, the waste products of photosynthesis, pass into the air through openings in the leaves. Tubes in the stem carry sugar to other parts of the plant. The stems, roots, and leaves all store extra sugar.

Water travels through the plant's tubes to its leaves. In the leaves, tubes called veins carry water to the cells.

Tubes in the stem carry water and sugar.

The thick, nonliving outer layer protects the plant cells.

Chloroplasts

Photosynthesis takes place in the chloroplasts of leaf cells. When you look at chloroplasts through a microscope, you see stacks of dark green disks connected by thread-like materials. Chloroplasts contain **chlorophyll.** "Chloro" is a Greek word for green. Chlorophyll is the substance in plants that makes them green. But chlorophyll does a lot more than make plants green. It captures energy from sunlight. Plants use this energy to change water, carbon dioxide gas, and mineral nutrients from the soil into oxygen, sugar, and other foods.

Water, food, and gases pass into and out of each cell through the cell membrane.

Cross Section of a Leaf

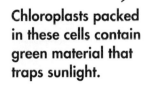

Chloroplasts packed in these cells contain green material that traps sunlight.

Tiny openings called stoma are on the underside of most leaves. Carbon dioxide, oxygen, and water pass into and out of the leaves through these openings.

✓ Lesson Checkpoint

1. Name three characteristics of plants.
2. In what part of the plant cell does photosynthesis occur?
3. **⊙ Draw Conclusions** Most plant parts that are green contain chlorophyll. What might you conclude about a plant part that is not green?

What are the parts of plants?

A plant has different parts. Each part plays a role in helping the plant survive in its environment.

The Roles of Leaves and Stems

You know that most plants are made of cells—millions of them. Similar cells are grouped to do certain jobs. For example, some cells make food, and some store it. Some cells provide support for the plant, and some help carry nutrients throughout the plant. Groups of similar cells form tissues, such as wood and the outer covering of plants. Different tissues work together to form organs, such as leaves, stems, and roots. Most plants have all these parts, whether the plant is a redwood tree or a dandelion.

Leaves

All leaves have the same role. Their job is to produce food so the plant can survive in its environment. To make that job easier, leaves are different shapes and sizes. For example, the leaves of some plants, like pine trees, are thin, sharp needles. The narrow shape prevents the tree from losing too much water. Other plants, like the banana plant, grow in places with plenty of water. Their leaves are wider than a kitchen table.

Most leaves are flat on top to catch as much sunlight as possible. The leaves use the energy of sunlight to make food.

Leaves may be different shapes and sizes, but they all produce food for the plant.

Stems

What does a tree trunk have in common with the thin stalk of a grass plant? They both are stems. Stems vary greatly in size and shape, but they all have the same two basic functions. They carry water, minerals, and food between the roots and the leaves. They also support the plant, holding the leaves up so they can get sunlight.

Some stems are soft and flexible. You can bend them in your hand. Examples include the stems of daisies, dandelions, and tomato plants. These stems are usually green and carry out photosynthesis just like leaves do.

Some stems grow strong and thick. They can support larger plants such as trees. The tree's outer layer of dead cells forms bark that protects the plant.

A waxy covering protects the stem and prevents it from drying out.

The woody stems of trees and shrubs are hard and rigid.

During the process of transpiration, water escapes from a leaf through tiny openings called stoma. The water evaporates. It becomes a gas and moves into the air.

Arranged for Advantage

Leaves are usually spread out along stems in ways that catch the most sunlight. Notice how leaves are attached to the stem so they keep out of the shade of other leaves.

Some leaves grow opposite each other, like a mirror image.

Some leaves grow staggered, forming a zig-zag pattern.

Some leaves grow in a circle around the same point on the stem.

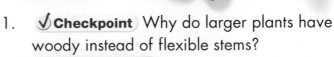

1. ✔ **Checkpoint** Why do larger plants have woody instead of flexible stems?

2. **Health** in Science Many foods that people eat are the leaves and stems of plants. Find out what nutrients these plant parts have.

Plants Without Roots

Some plants do not have true underground roots. Yet they are able to get what they need to make their own food. These air plants, as they are called, absorb moisture directly from the air. They take the nutrients they need from dust in the air. Spanish moss is an air plant that grows in many parts of the southern United States. You can see it hanging from telephone wires, walls, fences, and from other plants.

The Roles of the Roots

If you have ever tried to pull up a large weed, you know one of the main jobs that roots do—they anchor the plant firmly in the ground. Because most roots are underground, they can absorb, or take in, water and mineral nutrients from the soil around them. One thing that roots do not do is make food. Root cells do not contain chlorophyll. However, some roots store food. The plant uses this food when it cannot produce enough during photosynthesis.

Fibrous Roots

Roots grow away from the stem in search of water and nutrients. In some plants, the roots spread out in many directions, forming a fibrous root system. They are able to absorb water and mineral nutrients from a large area. The plant can take in the water before it runs off. The plant stores the extra water in its stem. The roots in a fibrous system are all about the same size. They grow longer, but they don't grow very thick or very deep. Most grasses and trees have fibrous roots. Plants that grow in hot, dry areas also have fibrous roots.

A fibrous root system has no main root. Roots and root hairs stretch out in many directions.

Onions

Daisies

Taproots

Carrots, turnips, and dandelions have a taproot system. This system is made of a large, main root called a taproot. It grows straight down. The taproot absorbs water and nutrients from the soil. As it stores food for the plant, it grows thicker. Some smaller roots grow from the side of the taproot.

Root hairs extend from the sides of the main taproot and the smaller roots. Each of the tiny root hairs also absorbs water and nutrients from the soil. They help the plant get the materials it needs to grow and to make food.

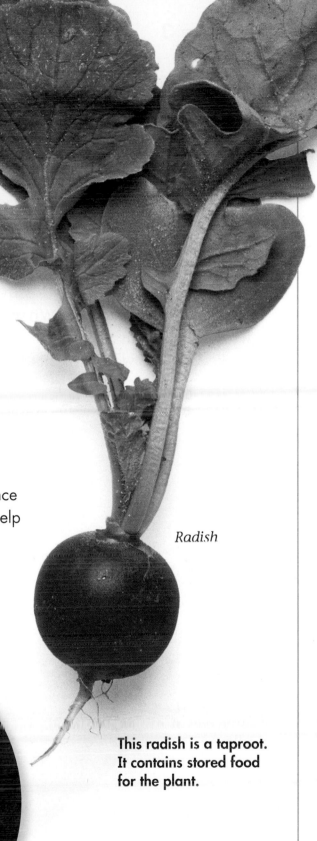

Radish

This radish is a taproot. It contains stored food for the plant.

✓ Lesson Checkpoint

1. What are two jobs of roots?
2. How do stems help a plant to survive?
3. Writing in Science **Expository** In your science journal, explain how you think fibrous roots help hold soil in place.

Tiny root hairs also take in water and mineral nutrients.

How do plants reproduce?

Flowers are the organs that make seeds in flowering plants. The seeds grow into new plants. Several processes and all parts of a flower are needed to make seeds.

Parts of Flowers

One way that scientists classify plants is by how they make new plants, or reproduce. When plants are classified in this way, they are put into one of two groups. Plants in one group make seeds. Flowering plants and conifers are in this group.

The pistil is the female organ of the plant. It produces egg cells.

These are the top parts of the pistil.

The stamen is the male part of the plant. Stamens make tiny grains of pollen at their tips.

The petal is often the most colorful part of the flower.

Sepals are the leaf-like parts that cover and protect the flower bud.

Incomplete Flowers

Most flowers have four main parts—sepals, petals, stamens, and at least one pistil. Some flowers do not have all four parts. For example, a corn plant has two kinds of flowers. The corn tassel is a male flower that has stamens but no pistils. The ear is a female flower that has pistils but no stamens. The sperm in the pollen from the stamens on one flower combine with the eggs in the pistil of another flower to make seeds.

Most flowers have four main parts. The part that you can see easily is the petals. Petals are often colorful. They are different shapes and sizes. They protect the parts of the flower that make seeds. They attract bees, butterflies, birds, and other living things.

The small green leaves below the petals are **sepals.** They cover and protect the flower as it grows inside the bud. As the bud opens and the flower spreads its petals, the sepals are pushed apart.

If you look at the center of the flower in the photos, you can see small, knoblike structures. These structures are part of the **pistil.** The smaller stalks surrounding the pistil are **stamens.** The anthers are at the tips of the stamens. The anthers make tiny grains of pollen. Sperm cells in pollen combine with the flower's eggs to make seeds.

1. **✓Checkpoint** What are the four main parts of a flower?
2. **Art** in Science Make a model or draw a picture of a flower. Label the four parts you read about on these pages.

55

A bee carries pollen grains from flower to flower.

Pollen on the Move

In order for a seed to form, pollen has to get from a stamen to a pistil. Animals play a big part in making this happen.

Flowers make a sweet liquid called nectar. This is a tasty food for bats, bees, butterflies, and birds. These and other animals move from flower to flower in search of nectar. The colors of the petals and the flower's scent attract animals and guide them to the nectar deep inside the flower. As the animal feeds, pollen from the stamens rubs off onto its body. The pollen may then rub off onto the pistil of the next flower the animal visits. This movement of pollen from stamen to pistil is called pollination.

Once a pollen grain lands on a pistil, a thin tube grows from the pollen down through the pistil. This pollen tube reaches the thick bottom part of the pistil called the **ovary.** Inside the ovary are egg cells. Sperm cells from the pollen travel down the pollen tube into the ovary. There the sperm cell and egg cell combine in a process called **fertilization.**

Bats pollinate flowers at night.

Fertilization

After fertilization, the flower goes through a lot of changes. The petals and stamens dry up and fall off. They are no longer needed for the plant to reproduce. The fertilized egg inside the ovary develops into a seed. The ovary at the base of the pistil grows large and develops into a fruit. The fruit protects the seed or seeds. Some fruits are moist and fleshy, such as apples, peaches, or grapes. Other fruits are dry and hard, such as peanut shells and pea pods. When the fruit is ripe, the seeds are ready to grow into new plants.

Animals do not pollinate all flowers. Grasses and most trees depend on the wind for pollination. The wind blows the pollen from stamens to pistils. Plants that depend on the wind for pollination don't need to attract animals. So, these plants don't have sweet smells or big flowers with colorful petals. Instead these plants produce huge amounts of pollen. The wind will deposit at least a few of the grains of pollen where they can pollinate a flower.

A single ragweed plant can release more than one million grains of pollen into the wind.

Pollen

✓ Lesson Checkpoint

1. What part of the flower makes egg cells?
2. What are some ways that pollen moves from stamen to pistil?
3. Writing in Science **Expository** Suppose while you are walking through a fragrant garden, your friend complains about all the bees flying around. Write what you might say to your friend about the bees' behavior.

What is the life cycle of a plant?

Like animals, plants have a life cycle. Whether a plant grows from a seed or a spore, it goes through several stages of growth. Plants, unlike animals, continue to grow as long as they live.

Life Cycle of a Flowering Plant

How long does a plant live? That depends on the kind of plant. Some bristlecone pine trees are over 4,000 years old. A tomato plant lives for only a few months. The life cycle of a plant includes all the changes a plant goes through during its life.

A seed needs the right conditions to begin growing. When the seed has the right amount of oxygen and water, and the right temperature, it sprouts. The young roots grow downward because of gravity. The new stem looks like it's reaching for the sunlight as it pushes up through the seed coat. Perhaps you have seen a plant that is bending toward the light.

Seed coat

Leaf

Stem

Root

When a seed begins to grow, or germinate, it absorbs water and swells. The seed coat splits open.

The young plant inside the seed uses stored food to grow. The first root and the first stem push through the seed coat.

By now, the leaves have begun to grow and make food for the plant through photosynthesis. The stem and roots keep growing. More leaves form.

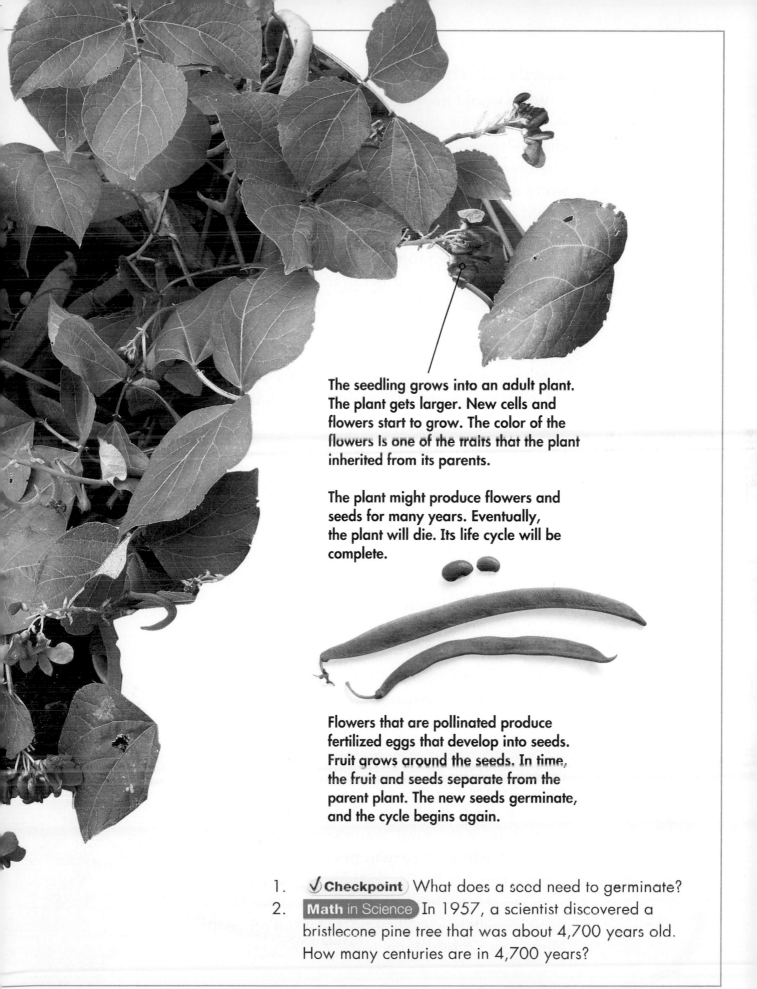

The seedling grows into an adult plant. The plant gets larger. New cells and flowers start to grow. The color of the flowers is one of the traits that the plant inherited from its parents.

The plant might produce flowers and seeds for many years. Eventually, the plant will die. Its life cycle will be complete.

Flowers that are pollinated produce fertilized eggs that develop into seeds. Fruit grows around the seeds. In time, the fruit and seeds separate from the parent plant. The new seeds germinate, and the cycle begins again.

1. ✓Checkpoint What does a seed need to germinate?
2. Math in Science In 1957, a scientist discovered a bristlecone pine tree that was about 4,700 years old. How many centuries are in 4,700 years?

Seeds on the Move

What would happen if all the cherries on a cherry tree fell to the ground and stayed near the tree? Many of the seeds in the cherries would start to grow. But roots from the parent tree had already spread over a wide area. They would absorb most of the water and nutrients from the soil. The shade of the parent tree would allow only a little sunlight through to the young plants. The fallen seeds would not have enough living space and resources to grow properly. They would grow a lot better if their seeds were scattered farther from the parent tree. That is why plants have adaptations that help them scatter their seeds.

Animal Helpers

Many animals eat fruit. Since the seeds of the fruit have a protective covering, they can pass unharmed through an animal's digestive system. The seeds can end up on the ground in the animal's droppings far from the parent plant.

Some fruits are covered with tiny hooks that catch on an animal's fur. As the animal moves, the fruits go along for the ride. When the tiny hooks break, the fruit falls to the ground. In this way, the seeds can be scattered far and wide.

You probably know that some animals gather and bury nuts and seeds for the winter. Some of those nuts and seeds start to grow after they have been buried.

Wind as a Helper

Have you ever blown on a dandelion puff? You probably noticed the small white threads that floated like parachutes. These threads catch the wind and carry the fruits and seeds far away. Milkweed plants and cottonwood trees also have "parachutes" that carry fruits in the breeze.

The wing-shaped fruits of maple trees also take advantage of the wind. You might call these fruits "whirly-birds" as they twirl through the air like a propeller.

In the southwestern United States, wind blows tumbleweeds across the land. Seeds fall off as the plant goes rolling along.

Water as a Helper

Some fruits and seeds get around by floating on water. Perhaps you've seen one drifting along in a lake or river. Coconuts, which are the fruits of one type of palm tree, can float between islands. Storms can wash the fruits from one island onto the beach where a new palm tree sprouts.

Even with all of the ways seeds can be scattered, most of the seeds that plants make never grow into new plants.

Many animals eat fruit. The seeds may be deposited far from the place the animal found and ate the fruit.

1. **✓Checkpoint** Why is it important that seeds are scattered away from their parent plant?

2. **Writing** in Science **Narrative** Suppose you are a seed. Write a letter to your parent plant explaining what happened to you from the time you left home to the time you settled on the ground to grow.

Spore Cases

Spores

Starting to Grow

When a seed drops to the ground, it may or may not begin to grow right away. It depends on whether the seed's environment has everything the seed needs to grow. A seed needs water, oxygen, and the right temperature.

A seed contains a small, young plant. Food stored in the seed gives the young plant energy to start growing. If the seed does not get what it needs, it stays **dormant,** or in a state of rest. A seed might remain dormant for days, months, or even years.

Spores

Some plants do not make flowers or cones. These plants grow from spores instead of seeds. A spore is much smaller and simpler than a seed. A spore is only one tiny cell. You need a microscope to see it. Because it is just one cell, it has very little stored food. Animals eat many kinds of seeds, but they usually do not eat spores.

Spores are very hardy. They can stay dormant in dry conditions for many years. Just like a seed, when the conditions are right, a spore grows into a new plant. In order to grow, a spore must land on wet ground. Once it germinates, it needs almost constant moisture.

A Two-Step Cycle

Mosses and certain other plants with spores actually reproduce in two steps. In the first step, the plant produces a spore. If the spore germinates, it grows into a plant that has male and female cells. The second step begins when a male and a female cell combine. The fertilized egg grows into a plant that produces the next generation of spores.

Spores grow inside spore cases. When the cases burst, the spores explode into the air. Some spores fall near the parent plant. The wind may carry others away. When the spore lands, it remains dormant until it has the right temperature and moisture. Then it swells with water. The next step in the complex life cycle begins.

Hundreds of spores head in every direction when a spore case bursts.

Other Uses of Plants

People use plants and plant parts in more ways than as food and drinks. Plants and their parts provide fibers to make cloth. The clothing you wear and the towels you use have cotton in them. The cotton fibers come from the fluffy white material that covers the seeds of the plant. Linen, another fabric, is made from fibers from flax plants.

Other everyday objects are made from plant materials, too. Paper and lumber are plant products. Leaves, plant roots, and twigs are woven into baskets and mats. Trees and certain other plants produce a milky substance that is used to make rubber.

1. ✔**Checkpoint** Describe how spores are different from seeds.
2. **Social Studies** in Science A plant called sphagnum moss becomes a material known as peat. Use library books or the Internet to find out how people use peat.

New Plots from Plant Parts

Not all plants grow from seeds or spores. Some plants grow from stems, roots, or leaves. Plants that grow this way are usually identical to the parent plant.

Have you ever planted tulips? You do not start with seeds. You start with tulip bulbs. A bulb is a type of underground stem. A bulb is made of thick, fleshy layers of leaves that store food. When these underground leaves push above the surface of the soil, they turn green and start making their own food. Other plants that grow from bulbs include lilies and daffodils. Onions are bulbs too. Their layers are actually leaves.

Sometimes new little plants begin to grow right on the leaves of the parent plant. For example, plantlets form on the leaves of a houseplant named the piggyback plant. Or, you may have seen a potato with sprouts growing from its buds. In time, the sprouts will grow into new potato plants.

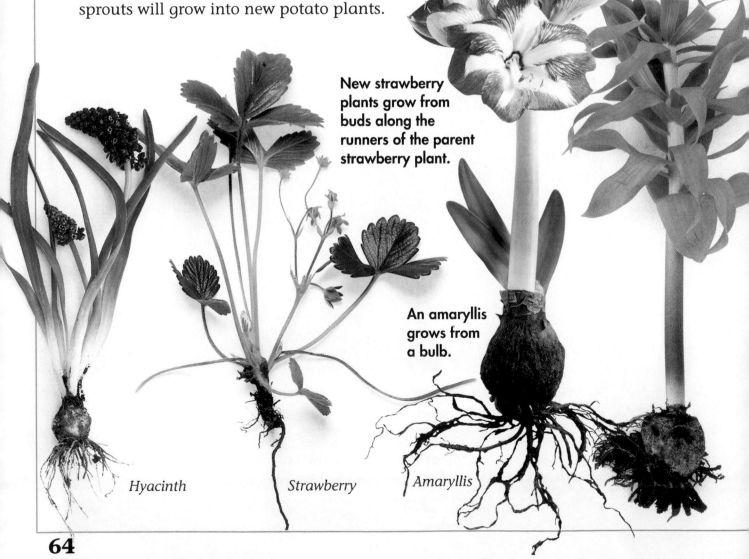

Crown Imperial Lily

New strawberry plants grow from buds along the runners of the parent strawberry plant.

An amaryllis grows from a bulb.

Hyacinth   *Strawberry*   *Amaryllis*

New Plants from Stems

Some plants, such as strawberries, have stems called runners. Runners grow along the ground. At certain points along the runners, roots grow into the soil and leaves develop. These are new plants that grow from the runner. Soon the new plant may send out runners of its own.

If you cut a section of stem from an African violet plant and place it in water, it will grow into a whole new African violet plant. These sections, or cuttings, can be taken from roots and leaves too.

Grafting

Suppose an apple grower has some apple trees that grow good apples but have weak roots. The trees might die easily because the roots are not able to absorb water and nutrients from the soil. Other trees have strong roots but do not produce very good apples. The grower can take branches from the trees with good apples and join them to branches of the trees with strong roots. This process is called grafting. Grafting works only if the tubes that carry water, mineral nutrients, and food between the two plant parts match up. Then, new tubes can grow between the two parts.

If you plant a part of the potato that contains a bud, a new potato plant will grow.

✓ Lesson Checkpoint

1. What are some ways that plants reproduce without seeds?
2. Explain why death is part of the life cycle of a plant.
3. **Draw Conclusions** A healthy plant has water on the underside of several of its leaves. What can you conclude is the source of the water?

Investigate How can you grow a potato plant without a seed?

potato field

Materials

$\frac{1}{2}$ potato

toothpicks

cup with water

What to Do

1 Push 3 toothpicks part way into a piece of potato.

Be careful!

Be careful with sharp objects.

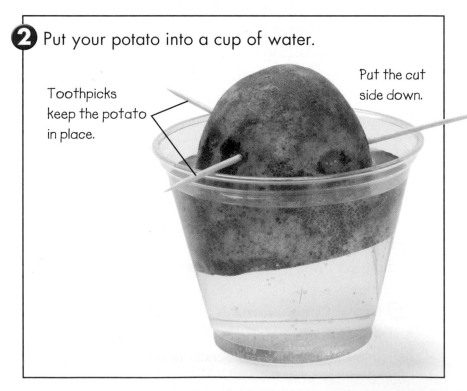

2 Put your potato into a cup of water.

Put the cut side down.

Toothpicks keep the potato in place.

Process Skills

You **observe** when you use your senses to gather information. You **infer** when, based on observations or past experiences, you make an evaluation or judgment. You **predict** when you infer an expected future result.

3 **Observe** the potato daily for 2 weeks. Add water to keep the bottom of the potato under water.

The potato's eyes are small, white growths. Stems and leaves can grow from the eyes.

4 Draw or describe what you observe.

Drawing or Description of Your Observations		
At the Start	**After 7 Days**	**After 14 Days**

Think About It

1. Based on what you have **observed**, **predict** what might happen to a potato left for 2 weeks in damp soil. Explain the evidence for your prediction.

2. **Infer** Why might a potato farmer save part of a crop?

3. How are observations, inferences, and predictions different from each other?

Go Further

How could you grow other plants such as carrots or houseplants without seeds? Make a plan to investigate this or other questions you may have.

How Plants Respond to Sunlight

Four young iris plants and four young petunia plants were exposed to different amounts of sunlight for five weeks. Their heights were measured at the end of the five weeks. The graphs show the results.

Effect of Sunlight on Irises

Height of Plant (cm)

Sunlight Conditions

Direct Sunlight 6 hours/day · Direct Sunlight 3 hours/day · Indirect Sunlight · Total darkness

Effect of Sunlight on Petunias

Height of Plant (cm)

Sunlight Conditions

Direct Sunlight 6 hours/day · Direct Sunlight 3 hours/day · Indirect Sunlight · Total darkness

Use the graphs on page 68 to answer the questions.

1. In what sunlight conditions does an iris grow best?
   A. Direct sunlight for 6 hours per day
   B. Direct sunlight for 3 hours per day
   C. Indirect sunlight
   D. Total darkness

2. Which statement is true?
   F. Petunias grow best in indirect sunlight.
   G. Petunias and irises grow best in different conditions.
   H. Petunias usually grow taller than irises.
   I. The amount of sunlight does not affect the growth of petunias and irises.

3. In what sunlight conditions does a petunia grow best?
   A. Direct sunlight for 6 hours per day
   B. Direct sunlight for 3 hours per day
   C. Indirect sunlight
   D. Total darkness

Lab zone **Take-Home Activity**

Find five kinds of plants that grow in your neighborhood. Use field guides to find out how tall each plant usually grows. List the plants in order from the shortest to the tallest.

Chapter 2 Review and Test Prep

Use Vocabulary

chlorophyll (p. 49)	**photosynthesis** (p. 48)
dormant (p. 62)	**pistil** (p. 55)
fertilization (p. 56)	**sepal** (p. 55)
	stamen (p. 55)
ovary (p. 56)	

Use the vocabulary word from the list above that completes each sentence.

1. The part of a flower that makes pollen is a _____.

2. A seed might remain _____ for years before beginning to grow.

3. A sperm cell and egg cell combine during _____.

4. The _____ is a leaflike part of a plant that protects the flower bud.

5. Plants make their own food during a process called _____.

6. The _____ is the female organ of the flower that produces egg cells.

7. Plants are green because of a green material called _____.

8. The _____ is the part of the flower that grows into a fruit that protects the seeds.

Explain Concepts

9. How do plants make food?

10. What is the job of the small openings on the underside of leaves?

Process Skills

11. **Infer** You plant some flower seeds. You observe that the seeds did not germinate. **Infer** what may be the reasons that the seeds did not sprout.

12. **Observe** the plants in your classroom, near your school, or in and around your home. Collect data about whether or not these plants produce flowers. Interpret the data. Decide which of the plants make seeds and which make spores.

13. **Predict** A friend of yours used to live in warm, moist Hawaii where she had a fern garden. Suppose your friend moves to the desert area of Nevada and tries to grow another fern garden. Predict what will probably happen to her garden.

Draw Conclusions

14. You have a plant that has one or more pistils, but no stamens. You have another plant with stamens but no pistils. Use a graphic organizer to help you draw a conclusion about how your plants will make seeds. Write a paragraph to explain.

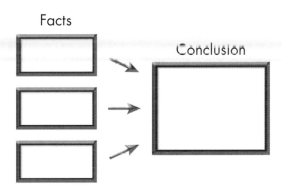

Facts

Conclusion

Test Prep

Choose the letter that best completes the statement or answers the question.

15. The root system of a plant does NOT
Ⓐ absorb water and minerals.
Ⓑ make food for the plant.
Ⓒ hold the plant in the ground.
Ⓓ store food for the plant.

16. In what part of a plant cell does photosynthesis take place?
Ⓕ nucleus
Ⓖ cell membrane
Ⓗ chloroplast
Ⓘ cell wall

17. Which part of a flower becomes the fruit?
Ⓐ ovary
Ⓑ stamen
Ⓒ pistil
Ⓓ seed

18. When a seed germinates, it gets food from
Ⓕ sunlight.
Ⓖ the soil.
Ⓗ chlorophyll.
Ⓘ energy stored in the seed.

19. Explain why the answer you chose for Question #16 is best. For each of the answers you did not choose, give a reason why it is not the best choice.

20. Writing in Science **Expository**
Explain the steps of fertilization that take place after a pollen grain lands on a pistil.

Plant Biologist

Dr. Tom Dreschel is a plant biologist at NASA. He developed a way to grow plants without soil.

Plant biologists study how plants work. They study all the parts of a plant: leaves, flowers, stems, roots. They even study plant cells. They want to know how all these parts work together.

As a plant biologist you would test plants to learn how they react to different conditions. You might test to see what happens to plants when there is no rain for months at a time. Some chemicals in the air and water can harm plants. Your tests might find out what the chemicals do to the plant. All scientists must keep detailed records of their experiments. This helps them draw conclusions and make hypotheses. They write about their work to help those who want to do similar experiments.

Some of the discoveries you make might help farmers grow bigger vegetables and fruits. You may find a way to protect plants from being eaten by insects. You might also discover a way to help plants survive long periods without water.

If working with plants sounds exciting to you, you will need to prepare. You should take math and science classes. After you graduate from high school, you will need to go to college and study plants and what they need to grow.

Lab zone Take-Home Activity

Make a list of plants that you would grow in a vegetable garden in a community plot near your home. Give reasons for your choices.

EC NTL 10 9 8 7 6 5 4 3 2 1

You Will Discover

- the living and nonliving parts of an ecosystem.
- how energy flows through an ecosystem.
- how plants and animals interact with their environment.

Chapter 3

Ecosystems

www.sfsuccessnet.com

How do organisms interact with each other and with their environment?

ecosystem

community

herbivores

carnivores

74

Chapter 3 Vocabulary

population

niche

omnivores

decomposers

Explore How can you make a model of an earthworm habitat?

Materials

earthworm bottle

spoon   cup with sand

6 earthworms

black paper and tape

foil and rubber band

Process Skills

As you watch the earthworms, you **observe** how they change their environment as they meet their needs.

What to Do

1 Get an earthworm bottle. Use a spoon to add a thin layer of sand. Add 6 earthworms.

Earthworms are living organisms. Handle with care!

2 Tape black paper around the bottle. Cover the top with foil fastened with a rubber band. Wait 24 hours.

3 Remove the paper and foil. **Observe** the sand, dirt, and earthworms.

4 Replace the paper and foil. Observe daily for 4 days.

Think About It

1. What changes did you **observe**?
2. How do you think earthworms might get the energy and water they need?

How to Read Science

 Sequence

Sequence means the order in which things happen. *Sequence* can also mean the steps we follow to do something.

- Clue words such as *first, then, next,* and *finally* can help you figure out the sequence of events.

- Some events take place at the same time. Clue words such as *meanwhile, while,* or *during* signal this.

Science Article

Life in a Grassy Field

First, a seed germinates in the ground. It gets plenty of sunlight and water. Eventually, it grows into a healthy plant. Then, a grasshopper eats the plant. Next, a toad might eat the grasshopper. Finally, a snake catches the toad and then eats it. That's one way that energy flows through a food chain.

Apply It!

Complete a graphic organizer like the one at the right to show the entire sequence of the key information from the science article.

77

🔊 You Are There!

You are walking along a dusty trail in the
Sonoran Desert. You see a nest in a giant
Saguaro cactus. A black-tailed jackrabbit runs
across your path. This harsh, dry land is still
full of life. The animals and plants that live
here get what they need to survive.

What are the parts of ecosystems?

An ecosystem is made of living and nonliving parts that all work together. Every organism in an ecosystem has a part to play.

What a System Is

A system is made of many parts that work together for a purpose. A system can have nonliving and living parts. Each part is important. If a part is missing or damaged, the system will not work as well. A bicycle with a rider is an example of a simple system. The handlebars, pedals, gears, frame, and rider work together. Like all systems, parts of the bicycle interact with other parts. For example, parts on the handlebars may control the gears or the brakes.

Most systems need inputs, or things coming into the system from outside the system. The actions of the rider are inputs of the bicycle system. Things also leave a system. The outputs of the bicycle system include dust that the spinning tires produce.

Ecosystems

An ecosystem is one kind of system. An **ecosystem** is all the living and nonliving things in an environment and the many ways they interact. An ecosystem may be large, like a desert, or small, like a rotting cactus.

Animals, plants, fungi, protists, and bacteria are the living parts of an ecosystem. These organisms interact with each other and with the nonliving parts of the system. The nonliving parts of an ecosystem include air, water, soil, sunlight, climate, and landforms.

1. **✓Checkpoint** What are some nonliving parts of an ecosystem?

2. **Writing** in Science **Expository** Give an example of a system from your everyday life. In your science journal, write about the parts that work together.

79

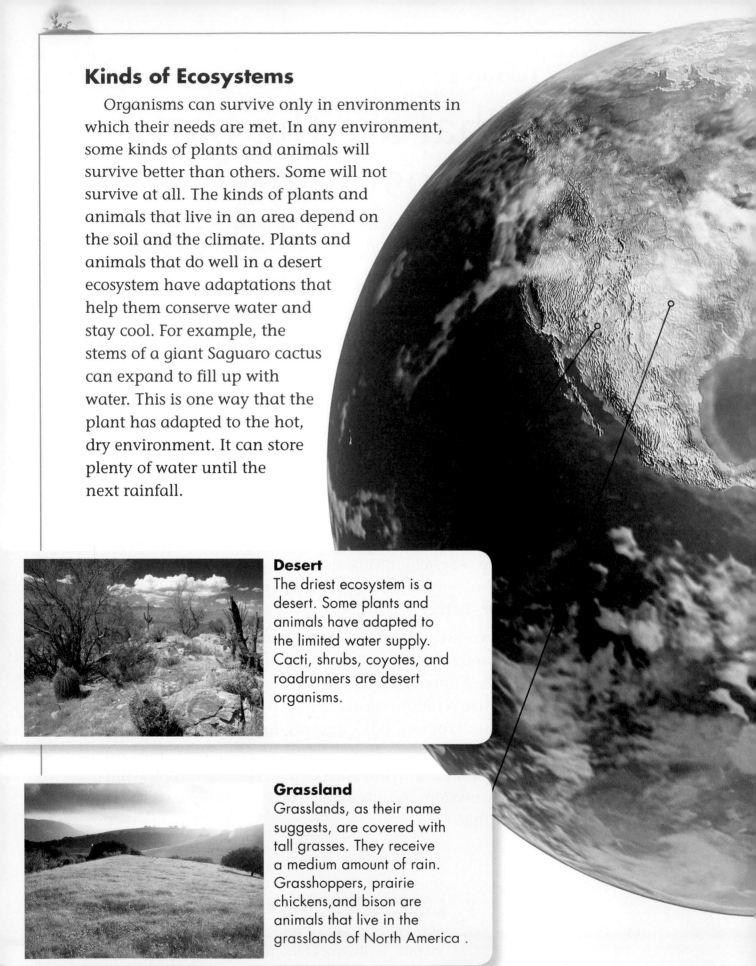

Kinds of Ecosystems

Organisms can survive only in environments in which their needs are met. In any environment, some kinds of plants and animals will survive better than others. Some will not survive at all. The kinds of plants and animals that live in an area depend on the soil and the climate. Plants and animals that do well in a desert ecosystem have adaptations that help them conserve water and stay cool. For example, the stems of a giant Saguaro cactus can expand to fill up with water. This is one way that the plant has adapted to the hot, dry environment. It can store plenty of water until the next rainfall.

Desert
The driest ecosystem is a desert. Some plants and animals have adapted to the limited water supply. Cacti, shrubs, coyotes, and roadrunners are desert organisms.

Grassland
Grasslands, as their name suggests, are covered with tall grasses. They receive a medium amount of rain. Grasshoppers, prairie chickens,and bison are animals that live in the grasslands of North America .

Tundra

A tundra is a cold, dry region. The ground beneath the surface is frozen all year long. Some grasses can grow in a tundra, but trees cannot. In the spring and summer, arctic foxes, caribou, and other animals thrive in these areas.

Forest

Forests are filled with trees, wildflowers, and animals. They usually get more rain than grasslands. Deer, foxes, raccoons, and squirrels often live in forests.

Tropical Rainforest

Rainforests are always wet. They get rain year-round. A rainforest supports thousands of species of plants and animals. Colorful birds like the toucan and beautiful flowers like the orchid live in rainforests.

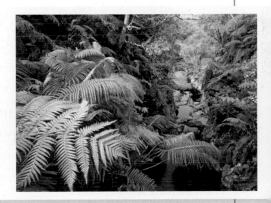

1. ✔**Checkpoint** Describe three ecosystems.
2. **Math** in Science A roadrunner's top speed is about 25 kilometers per hour. A black-tailed jackrabbit's top speed is about 56 kilometers per hour. A jackrabbit can run about how many times as fast as a roadrunner?

Populations of desert bighorn sheep like dry, rough, and rocky land. If the water holes in the area dry up, the sheep move to search for new sources of water.

The Lucifer Hummingbird uses its long, tubelike bill to get nectar from deep, narrow flowers.

Organisms and Their Environment

A **population** is all the members of one species that live within an area of an ecosystem. In a desert ecosystem, there are many different populations. All the prairie dogs make up one population. Among the plants, barrel cacti make up another population. The size of each population may change depending on the amount of food, water, and space that is available.

The different populations that interact with each other in the same area form a **community.** All the organisms in a desert ecosystem form a community.

The area or place where an organism lives in an ecosystem is called a habitat. You can think of a habitat as an organism's "address." In the Sonoran desert, the habitat of the Gambel's quail is near shrubs where it can hide from predators. The habitat of a Saguaro cactus seed is a shrub that provides a shady environment. A habitat contains all the living and nonliving things that an organism needs.

Special Roles

If an organism's habitat is its address, its niche is its job. Each organism in an ecosystem has a different job, or role. The specific role an organism has in its habitat is called its **niche.** A niche includes the type of food the organism eats, how it gets its food, and which other species use the organism as food. Adaptations also help to determine an organism's niche.

Each population in a habitat has a different niche. For example, a hummingbird and a roadrunner share the same desert habitat. However, they do not have the same niche. A Lucifer hummingbird eats spiders, small insects, and nectar from various plants. It will perch on the branches of tall plants to avoid one of its enemies, the roadrunner. The roadrunner's niche as a predator includes chasing scorpions, lizards, and snakes for food. Its niche as prey also includes running to escape enemies, like the coyote.

Ecosystem

Community

Populations

Habitats

✓**Lesson Checkpoint**

1. Describe the living and nonliving parts of an ecosystem.
2. Explain the difference between an organism's habitat and its niche.
3. **Social Studies** in Science Compare and contrast the science and social studies uses of the word *community*.

A Plantlike Protist

Euglena is a special one-celled organism. It is found in ponds and lakes. Like other plant-like protists, the euglena has chloroplasts and is a producer. If sunlight is not available, the euglena absorbs nutrients from decaying organisms.

How does energy flow in ecosystems?

Every living thing needs energy. Energy in an ecosystem is passed from one organism to another.

Energy in Plants and Animals

Sunlight is the main energy source for life on Earth. Energy from sunlight affects both the living and nonliving parts of an ecosystem.

In the process of photosynthesis, green plants change sunlight energy into chemical energy. The plants use this chemical energy to stay alive. Since plants make, or produce, their own food they are called producers.

Many organisms cannot make their own food, so they eat other organisms. Organisms that eat, or consume, other living things are called consumers. There are different types of consumers. Consumers that get energy by eating only plants are **herbivores.** Consumers that eat only animals are **carnivores.** Consumers that eat both plants and animals are **omnivores.** Some consumers, called scavengers, feed on dead plants and animals. Scavengers that eat only meat are carnivores.

Organisms often have adaptations that help them in their niche. Mountain lions and other carnivores have claws for catching their prey and sharp teeth for eating meat. Deer and other herbivores that do not catch their food have teeth that rip leaves off plants and four stomachs that help digest the plants. Scavengers like the turkey vulture use their sharp beaks to tear meat.

1. ✓ **Checkpoint** Describe three types of consumers.
2. **Math** in Science About every 4 months, the teeth of the great white shark are replaced with new teeth. About how many times will a tooth be replaced in 1 year?

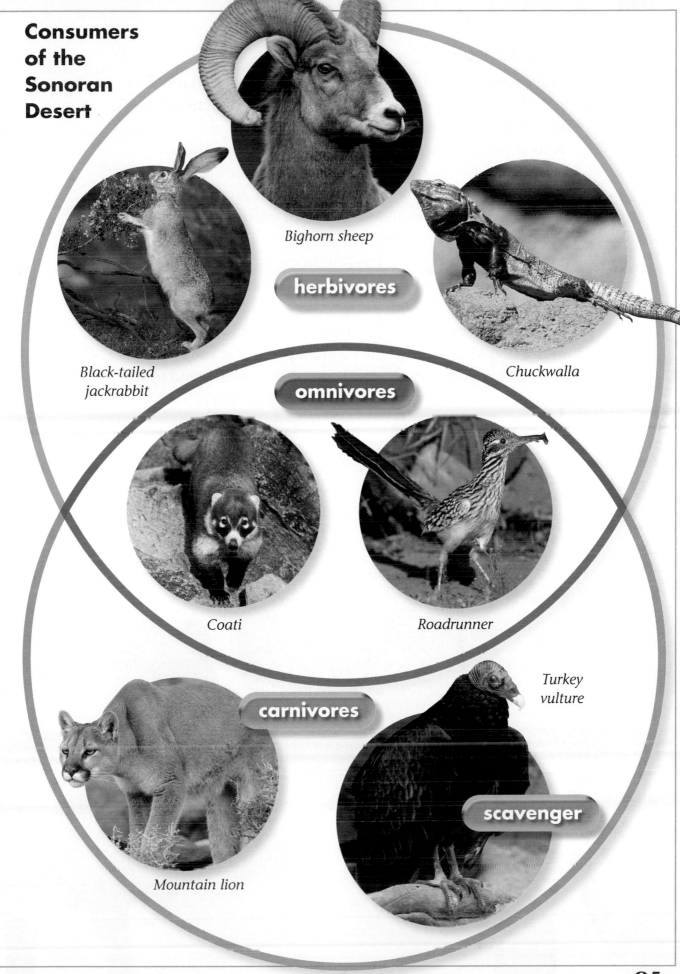

Consumers of the Sonoran Desert

Bighorn sheep

herbivores

Black-tailed jackrabbit

Chuckwalla

omnivores

Coati

Roadrunner

carnivores

Turkey vulture

scavenger

Mountain lion

A Food Chain

The energy stored by producers can be transferred along a food chain. In a food chain, organisms transfer energy by eating and being eaten.

A food chain always begins with energy from sunlight. Producers are the next link in the chain. The flow of energy through the chain happens in one direction. In the diagram of a food chain, arrows show the flow of energy. Arrows point from the "eaten" to the "eater."

In a desert ecosystem, a food chain might consist of a producer, such as the prickly pear cactus, that is eaten by an omnivore, such as the collared peccary.

Coyotes are predators. Predators get the energy they need by hunting and killing prey. The collared peccary is prey for the coyote. The coyote uses the food energy that was stored in the prickly pear cactus, and then passed to the peccary.

The prickly pear cactus gets its energy from the Sun.

Collared peccaries get energy from the plants and animals they eat.

Small Things That Make a Big Difference

What would happen if there were only producers and consumers in an ecosystem? Before long, plants would use up all the minerals in the soil. They would die. Herbivores would then starve. If nutrients and minerals were not replaced, new organisms would not be able to grow.

Decomposers digest the waste and remains of dead plants and animals. These remains still have food energy stored inside them. Some bacteria, fungi, and insects are decomposers. Decomposers break down dead plant and animal tissues into minerals and nutrients that are put back into the soil, air, and water. Living plants use these materials. When animals eat the plants, the minerals and nutrients are passed from the plants to the animals.

Whatever affects the decomposers of an ecosystem affects the health of the soil. The producers that grow in the soil, and all the consumers that eat them, would be affected too.

Decomposers are breaking down this cactus.

The coyote uses the energy it gets from the animals it eats.

1. ✓**Checkpoint** Why are decomposers important in the food chain?
2. ⊙ **Sequence** A sequence of events is modeled by the food chain below. In your science journal, explain how the food energy stored by the grass is transferred to the hawk.
   grass ⟶ grasshopper ⟶ mouse ⟶ snake ⟶ hawk

A Food Web

An ecosystem has many food chains. The same food source can be part of more than one food chain. As a result, one food chain often overlaps other food chains. A system of overlapping food chains is called a food web. In a food web, the flow of energy branches out in many directions.

In any ecosystem, producers and consumers can be eaten by more than one kind of organism. Some predators eat more than one prey.

In one desert ecosystem, the coyote competes for food with the mountain lion. They both hunt collared peccaries, Gambel's quails, and black-tailed jackrabbits.

Black-tailed Jackrabbit

Prickly Pear Cactus

Collared Peccary

You may have been surprised that the food web shows that roadrunners eat rattlesnakes. A roadrunner can run as fast as 25 kilometers per hour. Because of its speed, it is one of the few animals that can catch a rattlesnake.

Anything that affects the size of a population of organisms also affects the food web. Disease, storms, pollution, and hunting are events that can affect a food web.

Desert Bighorn Sheep

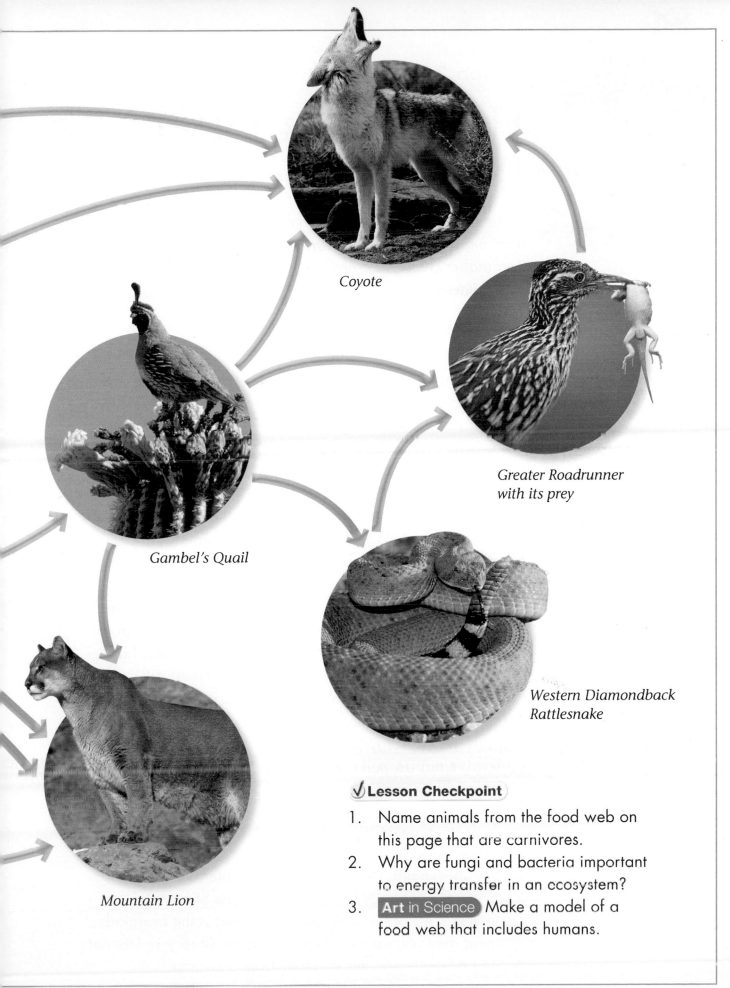

Coyote

Greater Roadrunner
with its prey

Gambel's Quail

Western Diamondback
Rattlesnake

Mountain Lion

✓ **Lesson Checkpoint**

1. Name animals from the food web on this page that are carnivores.
2. Why are fungi and bacteria important to energy transfer in an ecosystem?
3. **Art** in Science Make a model of a food web that includes humans.

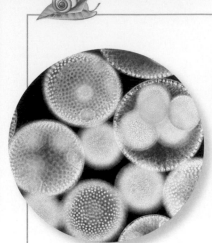

Algae cells clump together on rocks and stems in the water.

How does matter flow in ecosystems?

All organisms need more than energy to survive. They also need matter in the form of minerals, oxygen, and carbon dioxide. This matter is then returned to the ecosystem when organisms die and decay.

Water Ecosystems

Since almost three-fourths of Earth's surface is covered with water, many organisms live in water ecosystems. Some water ecosystems are in wetlands where the water level is close to the surface of the soil. Some are deep in the ocean. Different organisms live in the saltwater habitats of oceans than in freshwater habitats.

In some wetland ecosystems, like swamps, the water level is at or above the surface of the soil year-round. The Okefenokee Swamp is a wetland that is home to many organisms. The producers in this ecosystem are as large as bald cypress trees, or as small as single-celled algae.

Bald cypress trees are deciduous trees with needle-like leaves. They have very wide bases and "knees" that grow from their roots and stick up out of the water. Some bald cypress trees are more than 30 meters (100 feet) tall.

Single-celled algae are plantlike protists. Since they carry out photosynthesis, they are producers in a swamp ecosystem.

Matter and energy flow through an ecosystem. Plants use minerals from the soil and gases in the air. Herbivores get the matter and energy they need from the plants they eat. Carnivores get the matter and energy they need from the animals they eat.

The freshwater snail is a consumer in a swamp ecosystem. It feeds on algae.

1. ✔**Checkpoint** Describe some freshwater ecosystems.
2. **Social Studies** in Science Another type of wetland is a marsh. One of the most famous marshes is the Everglades, near the southern tip of Florida. Use the library or Internet to find out how a marsh differs from a swamp.

The Okefenokee Swamp is a freshwater ecosystem. It is home to many plants, fish, water birds, and other animals.

Everglades National Park is a brackish, or saltwater, swamp. Much of the Everglades is covered with sawgrass. Alligators, fish, water birds, and other animals live here.

Coral reefs are in shallow ocean areas. All ocean water is salty. Coral reefs have many different organisms. The fish that live in this ecosystem are very colorful.

The deep sea is another saltwater ecosystem. The organisms here must live without light.

How Matter Flows Through a Food Web

A food chain shows one possible path along which energy and matter can move through an ecosystem. Many of the producers and consumers of a swamp ecosystem are part of more than one food chain. In the food web shown here, the blue-spotted sunfish is part of three different food chains.

In this food web, the algae use energy from sunlight and matter from its environment to live. The freshwater snail uses matter from the algae to grow. The sandhill crane and the great blue heron get some of the matter they need by eating snails.

When danger threatens a freshwater snail, it draws the soft part of its body inside its shell.

Algae use nutrients in the water. Algae are at the bottom of many food chains in the Okefenokee Swamp.

The blue-spotted sunfish makes its home among beds of algae. It feeds on zooplankton and small invertebrates, such as insects.

Zooplankton are tiny organisms that feed on single-celled algae.

The sandhill crane is an omnivore. This long-legged, long-necked bird feeds on seeds, grains, berries, invertebrates, reptiles, amphibians, and fish.

The osprey's diet is mainly fish, but it alos eats snakes and amphibians. It usually flies over water when searching for prey. Ospreys build their nests at the top of cypress trees.

The great blue heron is a consumer. It eats fish, mollusks, and amphibians. The heron stabs its prey with its long, sharp bill. Then, it quickly swallows the prey whole.

1. ✓**Checkpoint** The producer in this Okefenokee Swamp food web is not a plant. Explain how this is possible.

2. **Writing** in Science
Narrative Choose one consumer for this Okenfenokee Swamp food web. In your journal, write a story the consumer might tell about its experiences. Base the story on the consumer's position in the food web.

Map Facts

The Okefenokee Swamp

The Okefenokee Swamp covers parts of Georgia and Florida. Much of the swamp is always boggy. In drier areas, alligators dig holes that collect water. Many animals drink from the "gator holes."

Decay in Ecosystems

All living things eventually die and rot, or decay. Decaying plants make up a large part of the Okefenokee Swamp. Decay is a very important process. Without decay, dead organisms and wastes would pile up and interfere with the habitats of living things.

During the process of decay, scavengers feed on the remains of the dead organisms. Then, decomposers, like fungi and bacteria, break down the dead organisms and return minerals and nutrients to the ecosystem.

Rate of Decay

Dead organisms can decay slowly or quickly. How fast an organism decays depends on temperature. You put food in a refrigerator because organisms decay more slowly in colder temperatures. In warmer temperatures, decay happens quickly.

You cover the food in your refrigerator because organisms decay more quickly when they are in contact with oxygen. Fungi and some bacteria need oxygen to live and grow. In many ecosystems, green plants are an important source of oxygen.

The amount of moisture can also affect decay. Many decomposers grow better and work faster when there is more moisture.

Things that were once alive change much quicker than things that were never alive. Suppose you put a dead insect and a pebble that are about the same size in a hole. You put a leaf and a piece of plastic bag that's about the size of the leaf in the same hole.

You won't see it happen, but the decomposers go to work immediately. They begin breaking down the remains of the insect and the leaf. Soon, the minerals and nutrients in the decomposing material will return to the soil, air, and water. But, many years will pass before the plastic bag and the pebble change.

Most organisms use oxygen from the air to break down food. Organisms get their energy from food and release carbon dioxide into the air or water.

Green plants take in carbon dioxide. During photosynthesis, plants take carbon dioxide from the air or water and release oxygen into the air.

Carbon dioxide is also a part of the decay process. When decomposers break down the tissues of dead organisms, carbon dioxide is released into the air.

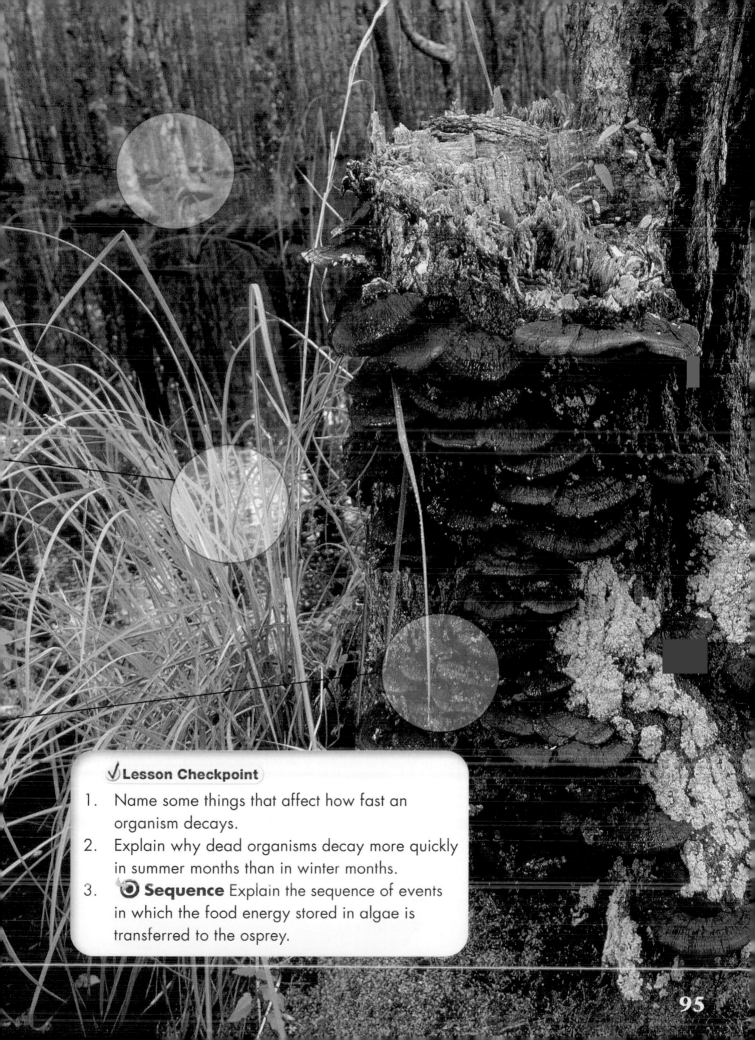

✓ Lesson Checkpoint

1. Name some things that affect how fast an organism decays.

2. Explain why dead organisms decay more quickly in summer months than in winter months.

3. **◑ Sequence** Explain the sequence of events in which the food energy stored in algae is transferred to the osprey.

Guided Inquiry

Investigate What do decomposers do?

Molds help break down many things, including bread. To make bread last longer, some breads have preservatives that help keep mold from growing. For this activity use bread that does not have preservatives.

Materials

bread

spoon and water

2 resealable plastic bags

masking tape and hand lens

What to Do

1 Put 2 slices of bread on a table. Leave them uncovered overnight.

2 Put a spoonful of water on one slice.

3 Place each slice in a plastic bag. Seal and label the bags.

Process Skills

Observations and past experiences can help you make **inferences**.

Take It to the NET
More Activities www.sfsuccessnet.com

4 Look at the bread every day for 10 days. Record what you **observe**.

Keep the bags sealed!

damp

dry

Day	Observations	
	Damp Bread	**Dry Bread**
Day 1		
Day 2		
Day 3		
Day 4		

Think About It

1. Which slice had more mold? What changes did you **observe**?

2. **Infer** How does water affect the growth of mold? Where does the mold get the matter and energy it needs?

Go Further

How does mold grow in other conditions, such as cold or dry environments? Make a plan to investigate.

Graphing Populations

Scientists sometimes conduct studies on how the size of a certain population changes over a period of time. You can see an example of changes in a population of rabbits in the line graph below. The graph shows how the size of a rabbit population changed over a 10-year period.

Changes in Rabbit Population

Number of Rabbits

Year of Study

Take It to the NET Graphs www.sfsuccessnet.com

Use the graph on page 98 to answer the following questions.

1. During which group of years did the population of rabbits increase each year?
   A. year 0 to year 4
   B. year 0 to year 5
   C. year 4 to year 7
   D. year 7 to year 10

2. What was the size of the population in year 9?
   F. 300
   G. 3,000
   H. 30,000
   I. 300,000

3. During which group of years did the population of rabbits decrease each year?
   A. year 2 to year 4
   B. year 3 to year 5
   C. year 4 to year 8
   D. year 8 to year 10

4. What are some possible reasons for the decrease in the rabbit population?

Lab zone Take-Home Activity

The people that live in a certain area make up a population. Use the Internet or other sources to find data about population changes in your city or state over the last 50 years. Make a graph like the one on page 98.

99

Chapter 3 Review and Test Prep

Use Vocabulary

carnivores (p. 84)	**herbivores** (p. 84)
community (p. 82)	**niche** (p. 82)
decomposers (p. 87)	**omnivores** (p. 84)
ecosystem (p. 79)	**population** (p. 82)

Use the vocabulary word from the list above that completes each sentence.

1. _____ get food energy by eating only plants.

2. All the organisms that live in an ecosystem form a(n) _____.

3. _____ are consumers that get food energy from plants and other animals.

4. Living and nonliving things interact in a(n) _____.

5. _____ are consumers that eat only animals.

6. Each organism in a habitat has a different role, or _____.

7. _____ recycle matter from dead plants and animals.

8. All the members of one species that live within an area of an ecosystem make up a(n) _____.

Explain Concepts

9. Not all living things eat plants, but all living things depend on plants for their energy. Explain why this is true.

10. The blue-spotted sunfish is the prey of the sandhill crane and the osprey. This sunfish is also a predator. Explain how an animal can be both a predator and prey.

11. In most food chains, $\frac{9}{10}$ of the energy that an animal gets from its food is used by the animal or is lost as heat. What fraction of the food energy can be passed on to another consumer?

Process Skills

12. **Infer** which part of a food web has the most available energy?

13. **Classify** each of the following organisms as a consumer or producer: fish, bean plant, housefly, grass, algae, hummingbird, human.

14. Predict In a garden, caterpillars that eat the leaves of the plants are eaten by beetles. **Predict** what would happen to the population of plants if the beetle population decreased.

 Sequence

15. An animal takes in and then returns nutrients and minerals to the ecosystem. Complete a graphic organizer like the one shown to describe the sequence of events that take place.

 Test Prep

Choose the letter that best completes the statement or answers the question.

16. The energy in an ecosystem comes from
Ⓐ predators.
Ⓑ decomposers.
Ⓒ sunlight.
Ⓓ prey.

17. Which of the following is NOT part of an organism's niche?
Ⓕ the place that it lives
Ⓖ the food that it eats
Ⓗ the species that eat the organism
Ⓘ the way it gets its food

18. In a simple food chain, a frog eats insects, and a snake eats the frog. The primary role of the frog in this food chain is to
Ⓐ be a source of food energy.
Ⓑ find a space to live.
Ⓒ start a new species.
Ⓓ make a habitat.

19. Explain why the answer you chose for Question #18 is best. For each of the answers you did not choose, give a reason why it is not the best choice.

20. Writing in Science **Persuasive** Suppose your city council is planning to build a shopping mall in the middle of a forest preserve. Write a letter to your council representative explaining how building the mall might affect food webs in that forest ecosystem.

Ecosystems in Space

Astronauts need the same things in space that they do on Earth. They need food, water, and oxygen. None of these things are in space. Astronauts must take enough of these necessities with them to last until they return home.

But what if you want to stay in space for a long time? The space station does not have enough room to store several years' supply of food and water.

At the Biomass Production Chamber, NASA scientists are working to solve this problem. Their goal is to make an ecosystem that can continually recycle energy and matter in space. Plants are being used to create this ecosystem.

Plants provide food. Because they keep producing food, less food needs to be stored. Two plants that have been tested are wheat and potatoes. These plants provide many nutrients people need to live.

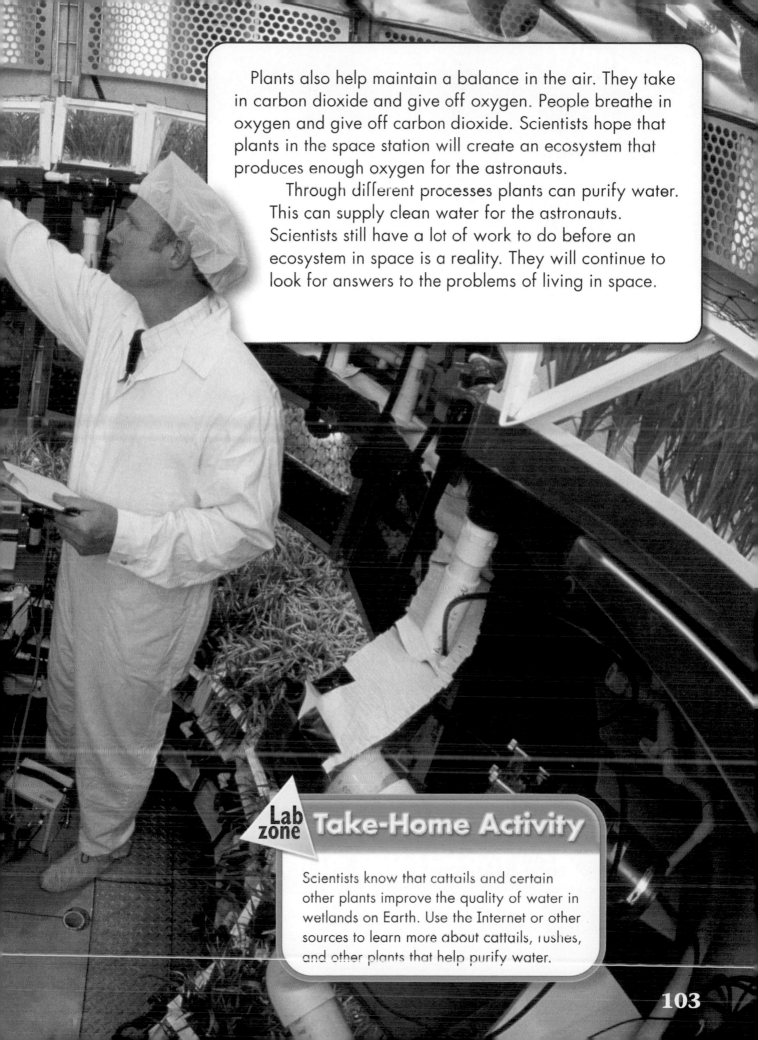

Plants also help maintain a balance in the air. They take in carbon dioxide and give off oxygen. People breathe in oxygen and give off carbon dioxide. Scientists hope that plants in the space station will create an ecosystem that produces enough oxygen for the astronauts.

Through different processes plants can purify water. This can supply clean water for the astronauts. Scientists still have a lot of work to do before an ecosystem in space is a reality. They will continue to look for answers to the problems of living in space.

Lab zone Take-Home Activity

Scientists know that cattails and certain other plants improve the quality of water in wetlands on Earth. Use the Internet or other sources to learn more about cattails, rushes, and other plants that help purify water.

Rachel Carson

In the 1950s, people used a chemical called DDT to poison harmful insects. Farmers sprayed on their fields. In cities and towns, it was used on the plants in parks.

Rachel Carson was a scientist and a writer. She began to notice that every spring, there were fewer and fewer songbirds. She wondered what was happening to the bird populations. After making careful observations, Carson learned that DDT was building up on land and in lakes and streams. The chemical had entered the food chains and the webs of many ecosystems. For example, a worm would take in DDT from the soil. A robin would then eat the worm. A hawk would eat the robin. Soon, DDT was poisoning the consumers in many food chains.

Through her observations, Carson could see that all of nature is interdependent. She wanted to warn as many people as possible about the dangers of using DDT. In 1962, she wrote a book titled *Silent Spring.* She wanted people to realize that modern technology could destroy habitats and food chains. Almost immediately laws forbidding the use of DDT were passed. Society has been more aware of ecosystems ever since.

Lab zone Take-Home Activity

Use the Internet or other sources to find information about pesticides that are labeled "Garden Safe."

EC NTL 10 9 8 7 6 5 4 3 2 1

Chapter 4
Changes in Ecosystems

You Will Discover

- how living things depend on each other and their environment.
- how living things interact in an ecosystem.
- how ecosystems change.
- how changes to the environment affect living things.

www.sfsuccessnet.com

How do changes in ecosystems affect our world?

competition

succession

hazardous waste

106

Chapter 4 Vocabulary

parasite

host

extinct

endangered

Explore What is the effect of crowding on plants?

Materials

small paper cups

pencil

spoon

potting soil

90 radish seeds

water

Process Skills

By **observing** the plants as they grow, you **collect data** about the effects that crowding has on plants.

What to Do

1. Use a pencil to make 4 small holes in the bottom of each cup. Half fill each cup with potting soil.

2. Sprinkle 10 radish seeds in one cup. Sprinkle 80 seeds in the other cup. Cover the seeds in both cups with potting soil.

3. Add 5 spoonfuls of water to both cups. Put them in a bright place. Add 1 spoonful of water to both cups daily.

4. Every few days for 3 weeks **collect data** about the radish plants in each cup. **Observe** carefully. Record their number and appearance.

Label the cups.

Think About It

Based on your **observations**, which cup has healthier plants after 3 weeks? Explain.

How to Read Science

 Cause and Effect

A **cause** is why something happens. An **effect** is what happens. Sometimes clue words such as *because* and *since* signal a cause and effect. Sometimes there are no clue words or the author does not tell why something happened. The student who wrote the lab report observed the effects of having too many plants growing close together.

Lab Report

Procedure

Day	Procedure	Observations
1	We planted radish seeds in two small milk cartons. We filled each milk carton with garden soil. We planted 3 radish seeds in carton A, and 20 radish seeds in carton B.	The cartons are the same size and contain the same amount of soil. The only difference is the number of seeds.
7	We watered the seeds in each carton every few days.	The seeds are beginning to grow. We can see a few plants in carton A. We see more plants in carton B.
14	The plants have been growing for two weeks.	The plants in carton A are very tall and full. The plants in carton B are much smaller and look crowded.

Apply It!
Make a graphic organizer like the one at the right. Use it to show what happened to the carton with more seeds and why it happened.

Cause
A cause is why something happens.

Effect
An effect is what happens.

A chipmunk pops out of its burrow and scampers across the forest floor. You hold your breath and stand very still. Unaware of your presence, the chipmunk stops in front of a mushroom that is only a few feet from where you stand. The interaction between the chipmunk and the mushroom is just one of many interactions that take place in a balanced ecosystem.

Lesson 1

How are ecosystems balanced?

All living things depend on one another and their environment to live and grow. Interactions among living and nonliving things help maintain balance in ecosystems.

Needs of Living Things

The Eastern American chipmunk is just one of more than 10,000 animal and plant species that live in the Great Smoky Mountains.

Each day, the chipmunk depends on the living and nonliving things in the forest to survive. It gets food from the fungi and plants that grow in the forest environment. The plants also provide oxygen, which the chipmunk needs to breathe. It drinks rainwater that collects in nearby puddles and streams. It digs its burrow in the rocky ground near the base of a tree. The burrow protects the chipmunk from cold weather and predators, such as hawks and foxes.

All plants and animals need food, water, living space, shelter, light, and air to grow and be healthy. Each kind of organism also needs the right soil and weather conditions. Living things get what they need from the environment in which they live. Living things can survive only in environments where their needs are met.

The forests of the Great Smoky Mountains meet all the needs of the Eastern American chipmunk.

1. **✓Checkpoint** What do all plants and animals need to live and grow?
2. **Writing** in Science **Expository** In your science journal, write about an ecosystem near your school. List at least two plants and two animals in that ecosystem. Identify three things each plant and animal needs.

A Balancing Act

Ecosystems are healthy when all their parts are in balance. All the living things in an ecosystem are interrelated, so what happens to one population affects the entire community.

In a way, balancing an ecosystem is like balancing a seesaw. Suppose one side of the seesaw holds the food supply, living space, and shelter for a group of animals. If the number of animals that the food and space will support is on the other side, the seesaw is in balance. If many animals were to get on, there would not be enough food or room to go around. The animal side of the seesaw would drop, and the seesaw would no longer be balanced.

The seesaw example is also true for plants. They need water, sunlight, and minerals from the soil. Plants also need space. Many seedlings might sprout from tree seeds that are planted close together. But many of the seedlings will not become trees because they did not have enough living space.

All organisms help keep the balance of an ecosystem. For example, rabbits eat grasses. This helps keep grass from taking over the space that other plants might need. Red foxes eat rabbits. The foxes help keep the rabbit population from getting too large and eating all the grass. The grass and other plants provide oxygen and moisture that the animals need.

Balanced ecosystems are constantly changing. Organisms are born. They live, die, and then decompose. Constant change helps keep ecosystems in balance. Many changes cancel each other out and the system remains balanced. For example, water evaporates from a pond, but water is replaced when it rains. Animals use oxygen in a system. But new plants continue to grow. The plants put oxygen back into the ecosystem through the process of photosynthesis.

Populations of these animals live in and use the resources of the Great Smoky Mountains. Each animal also needs space in which to raise its offspring and hide from predators.

✓ **Lesson Checkpoint**

1. What happens when the number of organisms in a population increases?
2. What are two things that might prevent a plant population from growing in size?
3. **Math in Science** Suppose 40 foxes live in a forest community.If hunters capture $\frac{1}{5}$ of the fox population, how many foxes would be captured?

How do organisms interact?

Organisms in an ecosystem compete for and share resources. They have other relationships too.

Change in Ecosystems

Populations in ecosystems change naturally as the amount of resources changes. Think about the chipmunk at the beginning of the chapter. A population of chipmunks will grow where food is plentiful. As the population increases, more food, more water, and more living space are needed. Eventually, the population may use up these resources.

Then, as resources decrease, each chipmunk will have less food to eat, less water to drink, and less space in which to live. Some chipmunks will die or move out of the area. As the population decreases, more resources will be available for the remaining chipmunks. The population begins to grow, and the cycle starts again.

Competing

Populations grow when their needs are met. But populations that share an ecosystem may need the same resources. When two or more species must use the same limited resources, **competition** occurs. Every organism has adaptations that help it compete for resources. An organism that competes successfully is more likely to survive and reproduce.

Living space is one cause of competition. Plant species compete for light and water. Bird species compete for the same nesting site. Predators compete for prey.

Sharing Resources

Certain behaviors help animals avoid or reduce competition. For example, both owls and hawks feed on some of the same animals. Because hawks hunt during the daytime and owls hunt at night, competition is reduced.

Living in groups can make it easier to obtain food or stay protected. Wolves are predators that usually hunt large herbivores, such as deer. Several wolves will work together to hunt a deer. Deer protect themselves from wolves by traveling in groups. With many deer bunched together, it is hard for a pack of wolves to attack any individual deer.

1. ✓ **Checkpoint** What are two behaviors that help animals avoid or reduce competition?
2. **Cause and Effect** Identify the cause and effect of deer traveling in groups.

Helping Each Other

Two different organisms can live closely together for most or all of their lives. This relationship may be helpful to both organisms, or it may help one organism but not the other. These special relationships exist between animals, plants, fungi, protists, and bacteria.

Lichens are two organisms that help each other. Lichens are combinations of fungi and algae that live together, often on the surface of rocks. The algae supply the fungi with sugar, nutrients, and water. The fungi protect the algae from too much sunlight and very warm temperatures. Neither organism could survive in its habitat without the other.

Living Side by Side

Moss and oak trees, as shown in the picture, also live together. The tree provides the moss with a sheltered living space, but the moss does not help or harm the oak tree.

Some animals also have this kind of relationship. Beetles, silverfish, and other insects sometimes travel with army ants. They eat whatever food is left as the ants march along. They have no effect on the army ants.

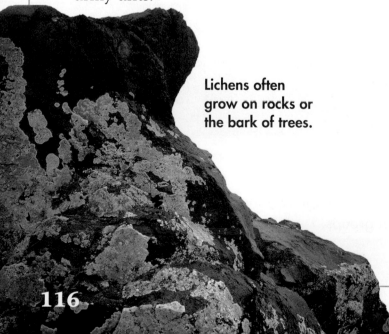

Lichens often grow on rocks or the bark of trees.

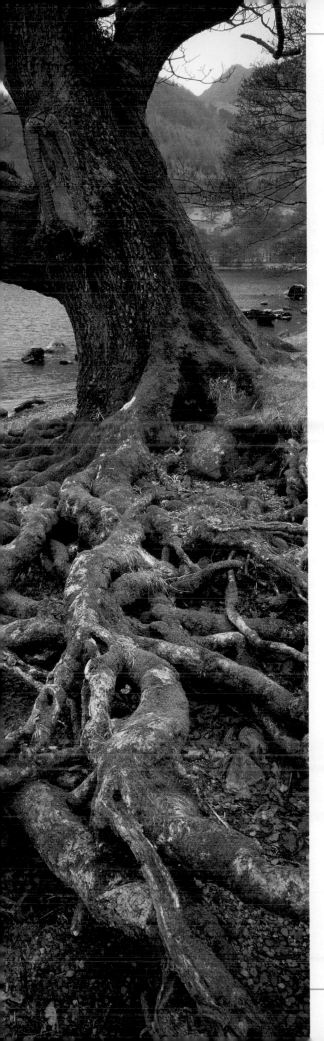

Mistletoe is a parasite plant that takes away water and nutrients from its host tree.

Causing Harm

Sometimes a close relationship between two organisms helps one but harms the other. The organism that is helped is called a **parasite.** Parasites are organisms that live on or in another organism. The organism that is harmed by the parasite is called the **host.** Both plants and animals can act as parasites and as hosts. A parasite uses its host as a source of food.

An insect called the balsam woolly adelgid is a parasite that kills Fraser fir trees of the Appalachian Mountains. As the insects feed, they harm the trees.

The larvae of the Asian long-horned beetle burrow deep into a tree, eventually killing the tree.

✓ Lesson Checkpoint

1. What is a parasite?
2. What might happen to the parasite if its host were to die?
3. Social Studies in Science Use a map to locate the Appalachian Mountain system. Which states contain this mountain system?

117

Lesson 3

How do environments change?

Environments naturally change over time. These changes can occur very slowly or very quickly. Changes to an environment can affect ecosystems and the species that inhabit them.

The Process of Change

Thousands of years ago, a forest may have been a lake filled with fish and water plants. Over many years, the lake dried up and was replaced by a marsh. And later still, trees began to grow, replacing the marsh grass and bushes.

This process of gradual change from one community of organisms to another is called **succession.** Succession occurs as the environment changes. Changes in an environment affect the communities within it. As communities change, conditions might change also. New conditions allow different communities to grow.

At first, the newly formed lake has no living things. In time, rivers carry soil into the lake. Algae, bacteria, and spores from fungi are in the soil.

The algae and other organisms add nutrients to the lake. The lake can now support small plants. Insects that eat the plants enter the ecosystem. Herbivores also become part of this new community.

One Step at a Time

In most cases, succession occurs in stages. If conditions are right, bare land might become grassland. Grassland will give way to shrubs. Shrub land will become a forest. Communities grow and replace one another until there is a stable community with few changes.

Changes in climate may also affect ecosystems. Climate is the average temperature, winds, and rainfall for an area over many years. Climates change very slowly over a long period of time. More than 15,000 years ago, snow and ice covered parts of North America. Trees, grasses, and many flowering plants could not grow. As the climate became warmer, plants and animals moved in. Eventually the plants and animals formed the forest communities we see today.

1. ✓ **Chookpoint** Whut Is succession?
2. **Art** in Science Draw pictures or make models of the stages of succession described in the first paragraph of this lesson.

Birds, insects, reptiles, fish, and mammals live and interact in the lake community. As time passes, the lake slowly fills with soil, fallen leaves, and material from decomposed organisms. The lake gradually changes into a marsh.

After many years, the marsh has filled with sediments. It dries up. Pine, oak, and hickory trees begin to grow. The marsh has gradually changed into a forest community.

119

Changing Species

In the 1800s and early 1900s, settlers watched huge flocks of passenger pigeons fly over the Great Smoky Mountains. By 1915, not a single passenger pigeon was alive. The passenger pigeon had become **extinct.** The entire species had died out and was gone forever.

Species sometimes become extinct because they cannot adjust to changes in the Earth's environment. Climate changes, volcanoes, and even meteors have caused extinction throughout Earth's history. In modern times, human activities like habitat destruction and hunting are the main reasons species become extinct. Once a population drops below a certain number, the species may not be able to recover.

Populations of some species have been reduced so much that they are in danger of becoming extinct. These species are called **endangered** species. Species that may soon become endangered are threatened species. Both endangered and threatened species sometimes leave an area to search for a more suitable environment.

Hunting, poisoning, and habitat destruction caused red wolves to become extinct in the wild during the 1980s. Red wolves bred in captivity are slowly being returned to their natural communities.

Habitat destruction and hunting killed the passenger pigeon.

In 1970, the peregrine falcon was an endangered species. People worked hard to save the species. By 1999, it was no longer endangered.

Species Then and Now

Fossils show us that life on Earth has not always been the same as it is now. Over long periods of time, changes in the environment have caused species to change or adapt as well. Scientists can compare fossils of organisms that lived long ago to organisms that are alive today.

Woolly mammoths lived long ago. They have since become extinct, but many are preserved as fossils. Some mammoths have been frozen solid. Scientists compare these frozen mammoths with modern elephants. They both have large tusks and long noses. Their skeletons are also very much alike. Both the woolly mammoth and modern elephants are classified in the same family.

Fossils can also tell us about the environment long ago. Sometimes fossils of marine creatures are found in dry climates. This tells scientists that long ago shallow seas must have covered the area where the fossils were found.

In ancient times, many kinds of sea lilies filled the oceans. Many sea lilies have been preserved as fossils.

1. ✓Checkpoint When are species considered threatened?

2. ◎ **Cause and Effect** Why do organisms become extinct?

Today only a few species of sea lilies remain. These flower-like animals attach themselves to the ocean floor.

Rapid Changes

A hurricane's strong winds rip up trees and flatten plants. Heavy rains and huge waves flood a coastal community. Lightning strikes a tree, starting a forest fire that burns almost everything in its path.

Hurricanes, floods, and fires, along with volcanic eruptions and earthquakes, are natural events that can quickly change the landscape. These rapid changes may force species to leave the area because the resources they need are no longer available.

Before the Fire
Fire can spread quickly with fuel from dead branches, dry leaves, and rotting plants. During periods with little rain, a fire can spread even faster.

Although some rapid events are destructive, they also play an important part in keeping an ecosystem balanced. Fires help clear away dead and dying plant matter, making more room for new plants to grow. Some trees, like the Table Mountain pine, have sealed cones that open when they come in contact with the heat of a fire. The ash from a volcanic eruption enriches the soil.

Natural Disasters

In the spring and summer of 1993, huge amounts of rain caused the Mississippi and Missouri Rivers to overflow. Some areas were flooded for almost 200 days. The floods left thousands of acres of land covered with sand and mud.

The floods affected many plants and animals. Grasses and trees died because of too much water. Birds had fewer offspring because many nesting places were destroyed. But the populations of some fish increased. They used the flooded areas to feed and reproduce.

Forest Ablaze
Lightning, earthquakes, and human carelessness can start forest fires. The temperature of a forest fire can reach 700°C.

After the Fire
Forest fires leave only the charred remains of trees and brush. They destroy many habitats. But they clear land, and very quickly new plants begin to grow.

✓ **Lesson Checkpoint**

1. Name two processes that change an environment over a very long period of time.
2. What are two events that change an environment very quickly?
3. **Writing in Science** **Descriptive** Suppose that you live for 75 years in the same location. Write a paragraph in your science journal describing how the environment might change during your lifetime.

123

Lesson 4

How do people disturb the balance?

Human activities change environments. When ecosystems change, some organisms die or leave the area. Other organisms adapt to the changes and survive.

People and the Environment

Like all organisms, humans interact with their environment. We get our food, shelter, and water from the land and organisms that surround us. Unlike other organisms, we can change large parts of the environment to meet our needs. We cut down trees to provide us with lumber and land for houses. We clear prairies to plant crops or build roads. When we change the environment, however, we sometimes upset the balance of ecosystems.

We also affect ecosystems with wastes from the products we make and use. These waste products can pollute the air we breathe and the water we drink. Many of the things we do release dust, dirt, and harmful gases into the air. Automobiles and factories can release harmful chemicals into the air. These chemicals in the air can harm plants. Animals that depend on these plants may lose their source of food or shelter.

Natural Air Pollution Detector

Lichens grow just about everywhere—in soil, on tree trunks and branches, on rocks, roofs, and walls. These organisms are sensitive to the air pollutant known as sulfur dioxide. The air surrounding some cities is so polluted that lichens cannot survive. Whether or not lichens can grow is one indicator of the air pollution in an area.

124

Polluted Water

Water becomes polluted when wastes and chemicals get into rivers, lakes, and oceans. Some of these substances enter the water through sewer systems. Other chemicals are used on land to help plants grow or to kill insects. Rain washes these chemicals off the land and into the water. Some of these chemicals can harm or kill fish and other plants and animals that live in or near the water.

Some of the pollutants in rivers and streams may end up in Earth's oceans. Oil is a pollutant that can harm the ocean's plants and animals. Sometimes, spills and leaks occur during the drilling and shipping of oil. Algae, plants, mollusks, and fish become coated with oil and die. Birds that are coated with oil often drown.

Fire on the Water

In 1952, the Cuyahoga River caught fire. The river was heavily polluted with oil, logs, and other wastes. The fire burned because of the oil floating on the water. This event led to the Clean Water Act, which made it illegal for anyone to put pollutants into water.

1. ✓**Checkpoint** Why do humans have a great impact on the environment?
2. **Technology** in Science When an oil spill occurs, members of the International Bird and Rescue Research Center (IBRRC) carefully wash any oil-soaked birds with a dishwashing liquid. Research other technologies that are used to help animals survive oil spills.

125

Land Pollution

Garbage, litter, and other substances can pollute the land. Humans produce huge amounts of garbage. Every day, each person throws away about 2 kilograms of garbage. Most of this trash is dumped into landfills and then covered with soil.

Disposing of hazardous wastes can cause another kind of land pollution. **Hazardous wastes** are substances that are very harmful to humans and other organisms. These substances may be poisonous, disease-causing, fire-starting, or they may react dangerously with other substances. Until recently, most hazardous wastes were put into containers and buried in the ground. Some of these containers leaked. The hazardous wastes seeped into the ground or water and damaged nearby habitats.

Stripping Away the Land

Many valuable substances lie under Earth's surface. One of these substances is coal. Strip mining has been one way to get coal from the Earth. At one time, huge machines dug up and cleared away the top layers of soil. Large holes were left behind. The land surrounding the holes began to erode. Piles of soil and rock were washed into ponds and rivers. The nearby ecosystems were greatly affected.

Restoring the land is important for the environment. Habitats are restored and animals can return to the area. If this is not possible, crops are planted so that the land is useful.

Birds and other animals may look for food in a landfill.

Land Reclamation

Federal law requires land disturbed by mining must be reclaimed. Reclaiming means that mining companies must replace rock and soil that were removed. They must replant the area with crops or native trees and grasses. Mining companies must submit a plan to reclaim the land they use before the first shovel ever touches the ground.

Coal mining in some states began in the 1840s. For more than 100 years, no repairs were made to lands that had been strip-mined. Then, beginning in the 1970s, laws were passed to regulate strip-mining. For example, the Surface Coal Mining Law requires that coal companies study the ecosystems before any digging begins. The companies would then plan how to restore the land after they finished mining.

California is one state that has reclaimed some mining areas. An area in Sacramento County where gravel was dug has now been restored to its natural water habitat. Other areas grow alfalfa, corn, and other crops. A field of strawberries now covers one mining area.

A young tree is being protected as it grows.

1. ✓**Checkpoint** What human activities damage the environment?
2. **Art** in Science Make a brochure or poster that tells about ways to reduce different types of pollution.

Preserving the Environment

Our nation has many natural treasures. You can watch millions of gallons of water cascade over Niagara Falls or look out over the breath-taking Grand Canyon. The United States has established the National Parks system to preserve nature's beauty, historic sights, and the habitats of many plants and animals.

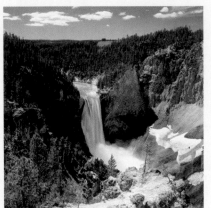

Yellowstone National Park

In 1872, Yellowstone became the world's first national park. Most of the park is in Wyoming. Many kinds of trees and other plants and animals, such as bears and moose, live there. Yellowstone's most unusual features are bubbling mud pots and geysers that shoot boiling water high into the air.

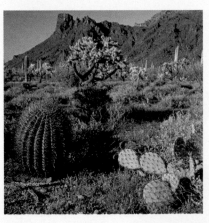

Saguaro National Park

Saguaro Natinal Park is in the Sonoran Desert in Arizona. The Sonoran Desert is home to more species of plants and animals than any other American desert. It is the only region in the world where giant Saguaro cacti grow. This monument preserves ancient villages as well as modern wildlife.

Okefenokee National Wildlife Refuge
This refuge in Georgia is the home of many plants and animals. Cranes, herons, egrets, and other waterfowl wade in the marshy areas. Bobcats, deer, otters, and other animals roam in the grassy areas. They are protected from poachers, people who hunt without a license. Decaying vegetation sometimes makes the water in the Okefenokee brown.

Everglades National Park
Everglades National Park in Florida is a subtropical area. It is a refuge for the wildlife that lives in wet habitats. The park is only a portion of the area called the Everglades. Big Cypress Swamp and many islands off the coast are also in the Everglades.

✓ **Lesson Checkpoint**

1. What are some of the effects of habitat destruction?
2. What are some things people have done to protect the environment?
3. **Social Studies in Science** On the Internet or at the library, find out more about how the National Park system was started. Write about what you find in your science journal.

Investigate How can a change in the environment affect plant growth?

Changing conditions can change which plants can grow in a place. In some farming areas, irrigation has led to a build up of salt in the soil. This can affect which plants are able to grow there.

Materials

paper cups

pencil

plastic spoon

potting soil

30 radish seeds

tap water

salty solution

very salty solution

Process Skills

When you record information you have **observed**, you are **collecting data**.

What to Do

1 Use a pencil to make 3 small holes in the bottom of each cup. Use a spoon to fill the cups $\frac{2}{3}$ full of potting soil.

2 Place 10 radish seeds on top of the potting soil in each cup. Add a thin layer of potting soil.

Label the cups.

3 Add 5 spoonfuls of water to each cup. Use tap water in cup A, salty water in cup B, and very salty water in cup C. Every day put 1 spoonful of water into each cup.

Put the cups in a bright place.

4 **Observe** the cups every day for 10 days.

5 **Collect data**. Every day record how many radish plants are in each cup.

Effect of Salt on Radish Plants			
Day	**Number of Radish Plants**		
	Cup A (tap water)	**Cup B (salty water)**	**Cup C (very salty water)**
Day 1			
Day 2			
Day 3			
Day 4			

Think About It

1. How did salt in the environment change how radish plants grew?

2. **Infer** How might a build up of salt in the soil affect a farmer?

Go Further

Are there plants that can grow in salty soils? Make a plan to investigate this or other questions you may have.

Recycling a Fraction

Since 1990, Americans have thrown out about 2 kg of garbage per day for every person in the country. That's about 56 kg per week for a family of 4! This garbage doesn't just disappear. Most of it is buried in landfills, some of it is burned, and a fraction of it is recycled. The pictures below show how this fraction has changed, as recycling has become more popular with Americans.

Recycled

Landfill or Burned

What fraction of the garbage was recycled in 1990?

The picture for 1990 shows 6 equal parts.

One part represents the recycled garbage.

$$\frac{1}{6}$$

← One part is recycled

← Six equal parts in all

In 1990, $\frac{1}{6}$ of the garbage was recycled.

1990   1995   2000

Take It to the NET
Fractions www.sfsuccessnet.com

Use the pictures on page 132 to answer the questions.

1. In 1995, what fraction of the garbage was recycled?

    A. $\frac{1}{4}$ B. $\frac{1}{3}$ C. $\frac{1}{2}$ D. $\frac{3}{4}$

2. In 1995, what fraction of the garbage was put into landfills or burned?

    F. $\frac{1}{4}$ G. $\frac{1}{3}$ H. $\frac{1}{2}$ I. $\frac{3}{4}$

3. In 2000, what fraction of the garbage was recycled?

    A. $\frac{7}{10}$ B. $\frac{3}{10}$ C. $\frac{1}{3}$ D. $\frac{1}{7}$

4. In 2000, what fraction of the garbage was put into landfills or burned?

    F. $\frac{7}{10}$ G. $\frac{3}{7}$ H. $\frac{3}{10}$ I. $\frac{7}{3}$

5. About how much garbage (in kg) does a family of 8 throw out each day? In 1995, how much of this garbage (in kg) was recycled? Remember: $\frac{1}{4}$ of n = n ÷ 4

Lab zone Take-Home Activity

Find out how much garbage your family would throw out in a day, in a week, and in a year at the rate of 2 kg per person per day. Find how many kilograms of garbage would be recycled in one year if your family recycled $\frac{1}{10}$ of the garbage they throw out.

Chapter 4 Review and Test Prep

Use Vocabulary

competition (p. 114)	**hazardous waste** (p. 126)
endangered (p. 120)	**host** (p. 117)
extinct (p. 120)	**parasite** (p. 117)
	succession (p. 118)

Use the vocabulary term from the list above that completes each sentence.

1. An organism that feeds on and harms a living thing is called a(n) _____.

2. A species that is _____ has no living members.

3. _____ is the struggle between organisms to meet their needs.

4. A species that is at risk of dying out is a(n) _____ species.

5. _____ can be very harmful to organisms and the environment.

6. The process of one community gradually replacing another community is _____.

7. A(n) _____ is an organism that provides energy or an environment for another organism.

Explain Concepts

8. Animals carry away seeds that stick to their fur. Explain how this relationship helps one organism but does not help or harm the other.

9. Suppose an ant colony lives on a tree. What is the effect of chopping down the tree?

10. In 2003, 316 mammals, 258 birds, 78 reptiles, 20 amphibians, and 82 fish were listed as endangered. About how many times as great was the number of endangered mammals than the number of reptiles?

Process Skills

11. **Infer** Suppose you find the fossil skull of an animal with sharp teeth like those of a wolf. What might you infer about what this animal ate?

12. **Observe** What observations could you make that would help you determine that living things in an area interact with other living things?

13. **Predict** A tree in a forest was struck by lightning, causing a large fire. The grasses, bushes, and trees in the forest all burned. Predict how the ecosystem will change.

Cause and Effect

14. Make a graphic organizer like the one shown below. Fill in two more possible causes of the effect that's described.

Causes
1. Number of predators increases.
2.
3.

→

Effect
Rabbit population decreases in number.

Test Prep

Choose the letter that best completes the statement or answers the question.

15. A pet-store gerbil has lived alone in a cage. Suppose you were to put it in a cage with two other gerbils. How can the pet-store gerbil survive in its new environment?
Ⓐ It must wait to eat until the other gerbils have finished.
Ⓑ It must build a new home.
Ⓒ It must compete with the other gerbils for resources.
Ⓓ It must hide in the cage.

16. One result of two different species living in the same area and using the same limited resources is
Ⓕ succession.
Ⓖ learned behavior.
Ⓗ pollution.
Ⓘ competition.

17. Nonliving things that affect organisms in an ecosystem include soil, temperature, and
Ⓐ plants.
Ⓑ water.
Ⓒ decomposers.
Ⓓ parasites.

18. Suppose you found a rock that had imprints of water plants and shells. What does this tell you about the area in which you found the rock?
Ⓕ It was once under water.
Ⓖ It was once a forest.
Ⓗ Dinosaurs once lived there.
Ⓘ Many predators lived there.

19. Explain why the answer you chose for Question #15 is best. For each of the answers you did not choose, give a reason why it is not the best choice.

20. Writing in Science **Expository**
Explain how predators and parasites are different and alike.

Ecologist

Ecologists explore the world of living things and how they interact with the environment. Ecologists are scientists who help us understand the connections between an organism and everything around it. They work in many environments—cities, suburbs, forests, farms, freshwater habitats, and oceans.

Ecologists do different jobs for different organizations. Sometimes they work indoors, and sometimes they work outdoors. Parks, nature centers, wildlife refuges, government research labs, museums, zoos, aquariums, conservation organizations, and field stations are some of the places where ecologists study living things. NASA's Kennedy Space Center is a national wildlife refuge. More than 200 species of birds and several endangered species live there. NASA ecologists work to protect the ecosystems.

People with different training work as ecologists. They are high school or college graduates. Some have even more education. They all like being outdoors and exploring the world around them. They all are curious about how the environment works and how it changes.

Rebecca Bolt Smith is a wildlife ecologist at NASA. Her work at the Space Center provides information about ecosystems on Earth.

Lab zone Take-Home Activity

Many boys, and girls, clubs have ecology programs. Some communities also have ecology activities in parks. Look in your local library or on the Internet to find an ecology activity that you and your friends can do in your community.

Chapter 5

Systems of the Human Body

www.sfsuccessnet.com

You Will Discover

- how similar cells form structures.
- how organs carry out life processes.
- how organs and organ systems work together.
- how the human body defends itself against disease.

How do the body's smallest and largest parts work together?

voluntary muscles

neuron

pathogens

infectious disease

138

Chapter 5 Vocabulary

involuntary muscles

Muscles that you cannot control are **involuntary muscles.**

immune system

vaccine

A **vaccine** is a kind of medicine that protects you from a disease.

139

Directed Inquiry

Explore How does shape affect bone strength?

Long bones are round like pipes, but filled with a soft material.

Materials

construction paper

tape

books

What to Do

1 Fold a piece of construction paper to make a square tube. Fasten completely with tape.

2 Roll another piece of paper to form a round tube. Fasten completely with tape.

3 Stand the tubes on a table. Place a book on top of each tube. Add books to each tube, one at a time, until a tube collapses.

tape

square tube

tape

round tube

Process Skills

You can make an **inference** based on observations and experiences.

Think About It

1. Which tube held more books?

2. **Infer** Which is a stronger shape for bones?

How to Read Science

 Draw Conclusions

- A conclusion is a decision you reach after you think about facts and details.

- Sometimes writers present facts and details and draw conclusions for the reader.

- Sometimes readers must draw their own conclusions based on the facts and details presented.

Read the science article. Some of the facts and details are highlighted for you.

Science Article

Build Strong Bones

A baby's body has about 300 "soft" bones. These grow together to form the 206 bones that adults have. Some of a baby's bones are made of a soft, flexible material called cartilage. As the baby grows, this material also grows and slowly hardens into bone. You can strengthen the bones in your skeleton by drinking milk and eating dairy products like cheese and yogurt. These foods contain the mineral calcium that helps bones become strong.

Apply It!

Make a graphic organizer like the one shown. Write each fact from the article in a fact box. Then draw a conclusion. Add it to the graphic organizer.

141

You focus the lens of your microscope and bring the tissue sample into view. The many open spaces and holes you see make you think of a sponge. You increase the magnification. Now you are able to see individual cells. What you first thought was a sponge is actually a network of living cells.

142

What are the skeletal and muscular systems?

Complex organisms are made of many organ systems. The skeletal and muscular systems work together to support and move your body.

Parts of Organ Systems

Like all complex organisms, your body is made of many kinds of cells. Similar cells work together to form tissues.

Tissues work together to form organs. These organs carry out all the processes that are needed for life. Each organ in your body has a different job. For example, your heart is an organ that is made up of muscle, nerve, and connective tissues that work together to pump blood.

A group of organs that work together makes up an organ system. The heart and blood vessels are organs that make up the circulatory system. Each part of an organ system is important. If one organ is damaged, the other organs in the system will be affected.

Different organ systems work together and depend on one another. When you rollerblade, you use your skeletal and muscle systems to stand and skate. You use your nervous system to control the movement in your arms and legs. Your respiratory and circulatory systems work together to give your muscles the energy they need.

1. **✓ Checkpoint** Order the following from smallest to largest: organs, cells, organ systems, tissues.
2. **Social Studies in Science** The postal system helps people deliver letters and packages. What is another system in your community? Describe how its parts work together.

Types of Joints

Joints hold your bones together and allow them to move. The photos show examples of two types of joints.

Ball-and-socket joints allow the most movement of any type of joint. Your shoulder and your hip have ball-and-socket joints. The end of one bone fits into a bowl-shaped area in another bone. The ball-and-socket joint allows your bones to have circular movement, like swinging your leg.

A hinge joint lets your bones move backward and forward, the way a door moves. You can bend or straighten your leg because of the hinge joint at your knee.

The Skeletal System

Can you touch your backbone, your ankle bone, and your knee? These are bones that are all part of your skeleton. Your skeleton is made mostly of a tissue called bone.

Without the support of your skeleton, you would fall into a blob-like heap. Just as a house could not stand without its wooden frame, your body cannot stand without its skeletal system.

Your skeleton also protects organs inside your body, like your brain, heart, and lungs. Your skeletal system also helps you move. Muscles that move your body are attached to your skeleton.

Building Strong Bones

Your skeletal system needs certain minerals to help it stay healthy. Minerals, like calcium, help to build bone tissue and keep bones strong. Calcium also helps muscle and nerve tissues to work properly. The bones of your skeleton store calcium and other minerals your body needs.

In addition to supporting the body and storing calcium, many bones produce different kinds of blood cells. Some of these blood cells carry oxygen to cells in other systems. Others fight bacteria that cause disease. Some cells help stop the bleeding from a cut.

One bone attaches to another bone at a joint. Joints can be classified by the type of movement they allow. Tissues around joints protect them. The tissues also help hold the bones together at the joint.

The Human Skeleton

There are 206 bones in the adult human skeleton. Some of these bones are labeled in the picture. Bones have different shapes. The shape of a bone is related to the job it does.

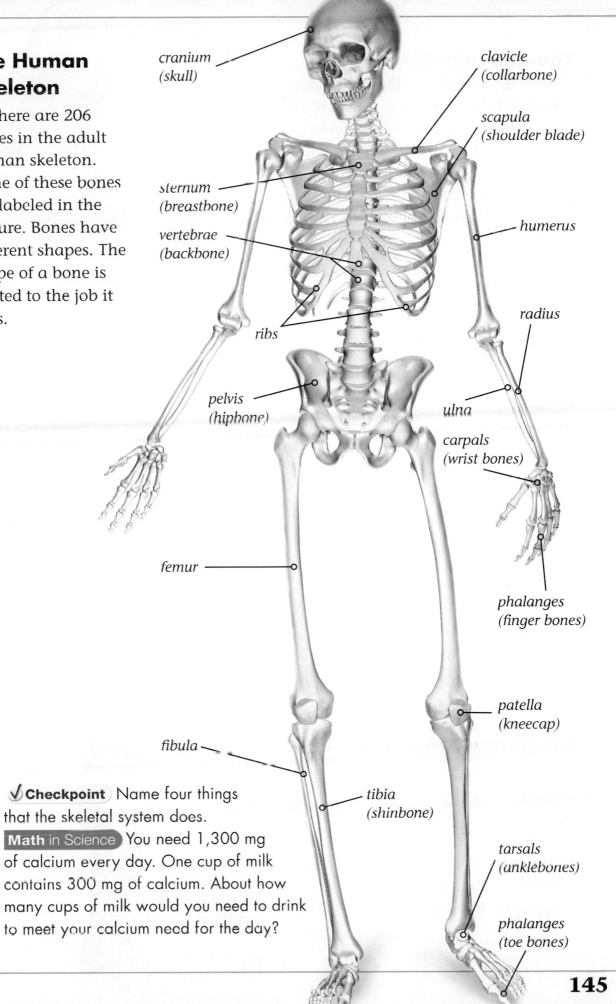

cranium (skull)

clavicle (collarbone)

scapula (shoulder blade)

sternum (breastbone)

vertebrae (backbone)

humerus

ribs

radius

pelvis (hiphone)

ulna

carpals (wrist bones)

femur

phalanges (finger bones)

patella (kneecap)

fibula

tibia (shinbone)

tarsals (anklebones)

phalanges (toe bones)

1. ✓**Checkpoint** Name four things that the skeletal system does.
2. **Math** in Science You need 1,300 mg of calcium every day. One cup of milk contains 300 mg of calcium. About how many cups of milk would you need to drink to meet your calcium need for the day?

145

The Muscular System

Muscles that move your body are attached to your skeleton. Without your muscular system, bones could not move at their joints. Because your muscles shorten, or contract, you can walk, run, smile, or sing. Without muscles, you could not breathe or swallow food.

Voluntary Muscles

Muscles that you control are **voluntary muscles.** You choose when you want voluntary muscles to work. Smiling, running, and chewing are actions controlled by voluntary muscles.

Most of the muscles in your body are skeletal muscles. Skeletal muscles are voluntary. They are different shapes and sizes. They help your skeleton move. Skeletal muscles work in pairs. For example, a pair of muscles works together in your arm. When you first bend your arm, one of the muscles contracts and the other relaxes. Then when you straighten your arm, the first muscle relaxes and its partner contracts.

Involuntary Muscles

Muscles that you cannot control are **involuntary muscles.** You use involuntary muscles to breathe or digest food. They keep blood flowing through your blood vessels. They help your eyes adjust to light that gets brighter or dimmer.

chest muscles
(pull arm
toward chest)

biceps
(bend arm)

abdominal
muscles
(flatten
abdomen)

inner thigh
muscles
(turn leg)

Your body has more than 600 different skeletal muscles.

146

back muscles
(draw arm up and back)

triceps
(straighten
arm)

trapezius
(raises the shoulder)

gluteus
maximus
(extends leg)

calf muscles
(bend leg)

Muscle Tissue

The photos show each type of muscle under a microscope.

Skeletal muscles are attached to your bones. They seem to have stripes.

Smooth muscles are involuntary. They work automatically in different organ systems.

Cardiac muscle is involuntary. It is found only in the heart. Like skeletal muscle, cardiac muscle looks striped.

✓ Lesson Checkpoint

1. How do your skeletal and muscular systems work together?
2. What type of muscle tissue would you find in the heart? blood vessels? toes?
3. **Draw Conclusions** Why is it important that involuntary muscles work without your control?

147

What are the respiratory and circulatory systems?

The respiratory and circulatory systems work together to deliver oxygen and nutrients to cells throughout the body.

The Respiratory System

Your body cells need a constant supply of oxygen to use the nutrients in the food you eat. The cells get that oxygen from the air you breathe. Air enters your body through your nose and mouth. It passes through several organs on its way to your lungs.

Air moves from your nose and mouth to your pharynx, or throat. Both air and food move through your pharynx, but only air moves on to your trachea, or windpipe. The walls of the trachea are made up of a stiff connective tissue called cartilage. The trachea divides into two branches. Each branch, or bronchial tube, connects to a lung. The bronchial tube inside each lung divides into many tiny branches. Each tiny branch leads to an air sac.

Tiny blood vessels are wrapped around each air sac. Oxygen from the air sacs passes into the blood through the walls of these tiny blood vessels. Blood in the blood vessels carries the oxygen to every cell in your body.

Take a Breath!

When your body cells use oxygen, they give off carbon dioxide. The carbon dioxide leaves your body when you breathe out. The respiratory system helps move these substances into and out of your body.

The lungs are the main organs in the respiratory system. But the lungs have no muscles, so how are they able to move? A dome-shaped muscle called the diaphragm is just below the lungs. As the diaphragm contracts and then relaxes, air is forced in and out of your lungs. Muscles in your chest help too. You breathe in and out.

Parts of the Respiratory System

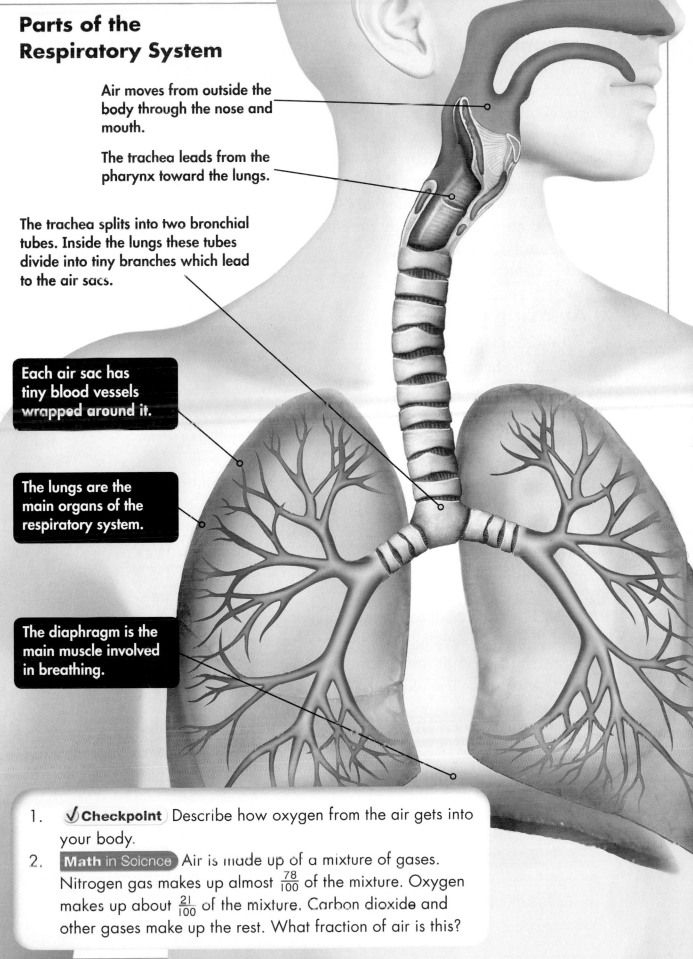

Air moves from outside the body through the nose and mouth.

The trachea leads from the pharynx toward the lungs.

The trachea splits into two bronchial tubes. Inside the lungs these tubes divide into tiny branches which lead to the air sacs.

Each air sac has tiny blood vessels wrapped around it.

The lungs are the main organs of the respiratory system.

The diaphragm is the main muscle involved in breathing.

1. **✓Checkpoint** Describe how oxygen from the air gets into your body.
2. **Math in Science** Air is made up of a mixture of gases. Nitrogen gas makes up almost $\frac{78}{100}$ of the mixture. Oxygen makes up about $\frac{21}{100}$ of the mixture. Carbon dioxide and other gases make up the rest. What fraction of air is this?

How Pumps and Passages Work Together

Your respiratory and circulatory systems work together to bring oxygen to cells and carry carbon dioxide away from cells.

Each breath you take brings oxygen into your respiratory system. Oxygen passes from the air sacs in your lungs into your blood. Then blood vessels carry the blood with the oxygen to your heart. Your heart pumps the blood to the rest of your body. The blood brings oxygen to the body's cells.

The circulatory system has the special job of moving blood through your body. Your heart, blood vessels, and blood make up your circulatory system.

An Amazing Pump

The right and left sides of the heart each work as a pump. The right side of the heart collects blood from the body. This blood is full of carbon dioxide from the cells. The heart pumps the blood to your lungs. The carbon dioxide will leave your body when you breathe out. The left side of the heart collects the blood from the lungs. This blood is full of oxygen. The heart pumps it to the body. A muscular wall separates the two pumps so that the blood coming in does not mix with blood leaving the heart.

Each side of the heart has two chambers, an atrium and a ventricle. Each atrium receives blood coming into the heart. The right atrium receives the oxygen-poor blood returning from the body. The left atrium receives the blood filled with oxygen from the lungs. On each side of the heart, the blood passes from the atrium through a one-way valve into the ventricle. The blood that moves from the right atrium into the right ventricle is pumped to the lungs. The blood that moves from the left atrium into the left ventricle is pumped to the rest of the body.

✓ Lesson Checkpoint

1. Name the three main parts of the circulatory system.
2. Explain why it is important to move blood through the body.
3. Math in Science Suppose that during the time you are sitting in your classroom, your heart beats 70 times per minute. Using mental math, calculate the number of times your heart would beat in one hour.

150

The Heart

Blood returning from the body enters the right side of the heart.

The left pump moves blood filled with oxygen into the body.

The right pump sends blood to the lungs. In the lungs, carbon dioxide leaves and oxygen enters the blood.

Blood from the lungs enters the left side of the heart.

Large blood vessels called veins bring oxygen-poor blood from the body to the right side of the heart.

Large blood vessels called arteries carry oxygen-rich blood from the left side of the heart to the body.

Lesson 3

What are the digestive and nervous systems?

The digestive system makes nutrients available to all body cells. The nervous system controls all other systems in the body.

The Digestive System

One of your favorite foods might be pizza. It contains many nutrients your body needs. But a whole pizza, or even a thin slice, could not travel through your body. Even the tiniest piece of food is too large to be used by your cells.

Any food you eat must be broken down into nutrients that your cells can use. Your digestive system does this job, which is called digestion. Digestion is the process that breaks food into forms that your cells can use.

Digestion begins as soon as you bite into food. It continues as the foods you eat travel through the organs in your digestive system. The food changes into nutrients that your body can use. The nutrients pass into your blood through the thin wall of blood vessels in the lining of your intestines. Your circulatory system carries blood with the nutrients to the cells throughout your body.

The Ice Man's Last Meal

In 1991, the frozen body of a man was discovered in the Alps. Scientists studied the clothing and tools that were found near this man. They concluded that he was a hunter who had died about 5,300 years earlier. Scientists also removed a tiny sample of the man's large intestine and looked at the sample under a microscope. From this sample, they learned that the man had eaten bread, meat, and a kind of plant about 8 hours before he died.

Parts of the Digestive System

Digestion begins in your mouth. Your teeth and chemicals in your saliva start to break down the food.

The food you swallow enters a tube called the esophagus. The esophagus is about 25 centimeters long. Smooth muscles in its walls contract and move the food toward your stomach.

Next, the partly digested food enters your stomach. Smooth muscles in the walls of your stomach mash the food. They mix it with juices from your stomach walls until it is a thick liquid. Muscles then push the food into the small intestine.

The small intestine is a twisted, folded tube that is about 7 meters long and 2.5 centimeters wide. Most digestion takes place during the three to six hours that food stays in your small intestine. Juices made in the small intestine and other organs break the food into nutrients.

Anything that cannot be digested and some liquid move into the large intestine. The large intestine removes much of the liquid and stores the solid waste until it leaves the body.

1. ✔ **Checkpoint** Where does the process of digestion begin?
2. **Writing** in Science **Narrative** Write a story about the journey of a piece of bread through the digestive system.

Neurons

The basic working unit of the nervous system is the nerve cell, or **neuron.** All parts of your nervous system contain neurons. A nerve is a bundle of neurons, and many bundles of neurons make up the spinal cord. Neurons are specialized cells. They carry information in the form of electrical signals. A signal to or from the brain goes through many neurons.

Every neuron has a cell body with a nucleus. The cell body has two types of extensions. One type carries nerve signals away from the cell body. The other type sends them toward it.

The Central Nervous System

Your central nervous system is the control center of your body. It links all body systems and carries signals from one system to another. Your brain and spinal cord make up your central nervous system. Your central nervous system controls your breathing, heart rate, and the movements of skeletal and smooth muscles.

The central nervous system also handles information about what is happening outside your body. It gets much of this information from your sense organs, like your eyes, ears, nose, and tongue. The system then sends messages to different body systems so you can respond. Suppose a friend yells, "Catch!" You see the ball, reach out, and grab the ball in midair. All these actions depend on the central nervous system sending signals between many body parts.

The Spinal Cord

The spinal cord is the main communications path that connects the parts of the central nervous system. Three layers of connective tissue cover and protect the spinal cord. Signals pass along it between your brain and the rest of your body. Sometimes the spinal cord decides what your body does. Your body reacts before you think for even a split-second about what to do. The action is quick and automatic. Reflexes such as blinking or pulling your hand away from a hot surface are controlled by your spinal cord.

The Brain

The brain is a very complex organ that is made up of billions of nerve cells. It is the central nervous system's main switching area. The same three layers of connective tissue that cover the spinal cord also cover the brain. The space between the outermost layer and the middle layer is filled with a watery fluid. The skull, layers of connective tissue, and fluid all help protect the brain from injury.

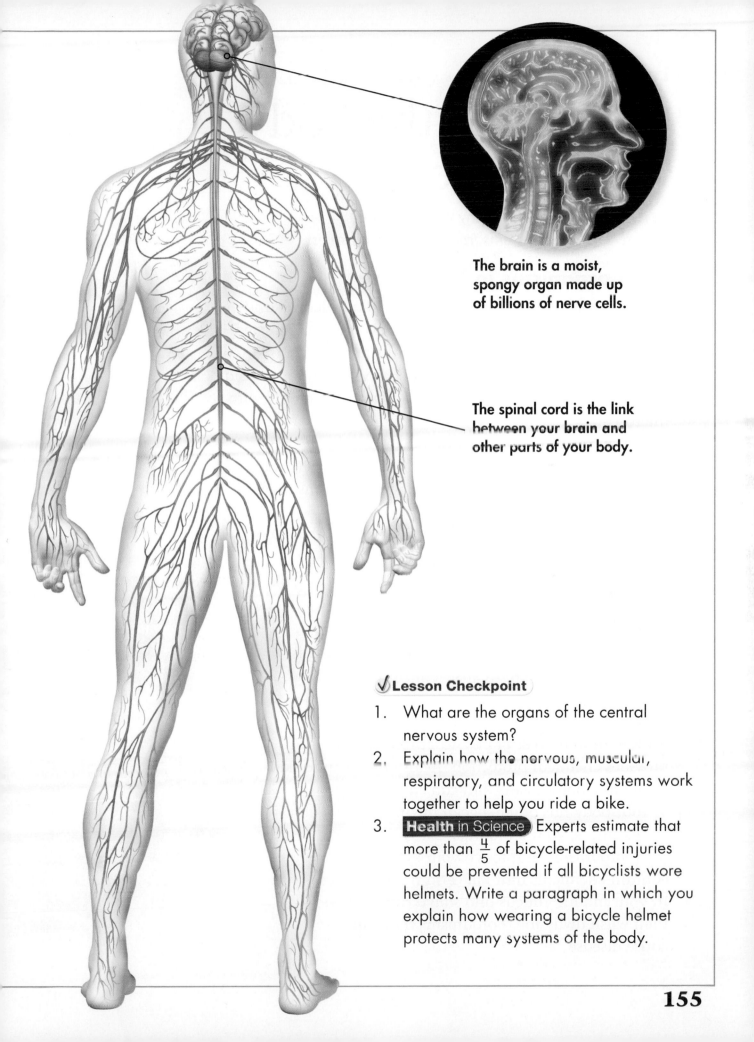

The brain is a moist, spongy organ made up of billions of nerve cells.

The spinal cord is the link between your brain and other parts of your body.

✓ Lesson Checkpoint

1. What are the organs of the central nervous system?

2. Explain how the nervous, muscular, respiratory, and circulatory systems work together to help you ride a bike.

3. **Health** in Science Experts estimate that more than $\frac{4}{5}$ of bicycle-related injuries could be prevented if all bicyclists wore helmets. Write a paragraph in which you explain how wearing a bicycle helmet protects many systems of the body.

How does the body defend itself?

The human body has many ways to prevent disease-causing organisms from getting into tissues.

Microorganisms in Your Body

When you get a cut or scrape, you should clean it and cover it with a bandage so the wound will not get infected. You get an infection when disease-causing organisms enter, live in, and multiply within your body. Most organisms that cause diseases are so small that they can be seen only with a microscope. That's why they are called microorganisms.

Not all microorganisms that live in your body cause disease. In fact, many microorganisms are in your body all the time and cause no problems. Microorganisms are on your skin, in your mouth, and in your digestive system. Most of them are harmless as long as they stay where they belong.

Your Body's Defenses

Your body uses special cells, tissues, organs, and chemicals to keep disease-causing microorganisms from causing harm. Your skin, breathing passages, mouth, and stomach are just some of your body's defenses against invading microorganisms.

Your skin is your body's first defense. Your skin is more than a layer of physical protection, it also provides chemical protection. Acids in your sweat kill many microorganisms that can cause disease.

Your body has other special means of protection. For example, your tears wash away disease-causing microorganisms that touch your eyes. Your tears contain chemicals that kill certain micro-organisms. In your mouth, mucus and saliva can trap and then wash away microorganisms that can cause disease.

If you swallow disease-causing organisms, acids in your stomach will kill many of them.

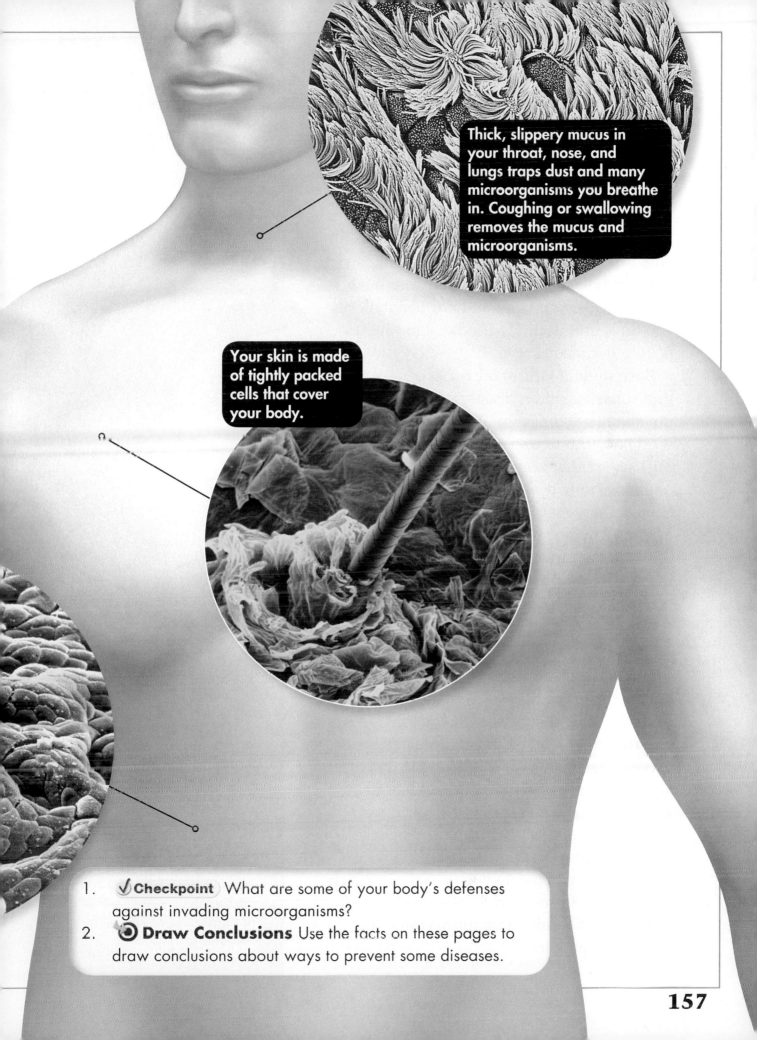

Thick, slippery mucus in your throat, nose, and lungs traps dust and many microorganisms you breathe in. Coughing or swallowing removes the mucus and microorganisms.

Your skin is made of tightly packed cells that cover your body.

1. ✔**Checkpoint** What are some of your body's defenses against invading microorganisms?

2. **⊙ Draw Conclusions** Use the facts on these pages to draw conclusions about ways to prevent some diseases.

Bacteria and Viruses

Organisms that cause some diseases are called **pathogens.** Pathogens do not belong in your body. If they enter your body and multiply, they create an infection and you develop a disease.

Diseases caused by pathogens are infectious. An **infectious disease** is a disease that can pass from one organism to another. When you have an infectious disease, pathogens have gotten inside your body and harmed it. If you have an infectious disease, you can pass it to someone else.

Bacteria and viruses are pathogens that cause infectious diseases. Viruses are about 100 times smaller than most bacteria. Viruses have no nucleus or other cell parts. They can reproduce only by using living cells to create more viruses. Different types of viruses invade different types of cells. For example, viruses that invade the cells of your nose, mouth, or throat can give you a cold.

Staying Healthy

Some microorganisms travel through the air. So, if you are sick, cover your mouth and nose when you sneeze or cough. Many diseases are spread by direct contact between two people or between a person and an object. You can do a few simple things to reduce your chance of catching diseases by direct contact. Wash your hands before you eat. Make sure that utensils and objects have been properly cleaned before you use them. Objects like towels, glasses, and silverware can pass disease-causing microorganisms from one person to another.

Sometimes people are infected by food that carries harmful bacteria. Many cases of food poisoning are caused by bacteria known as *E. coli.*

All these photographs were taken through special microscopes that magnified these images many thousands of times.

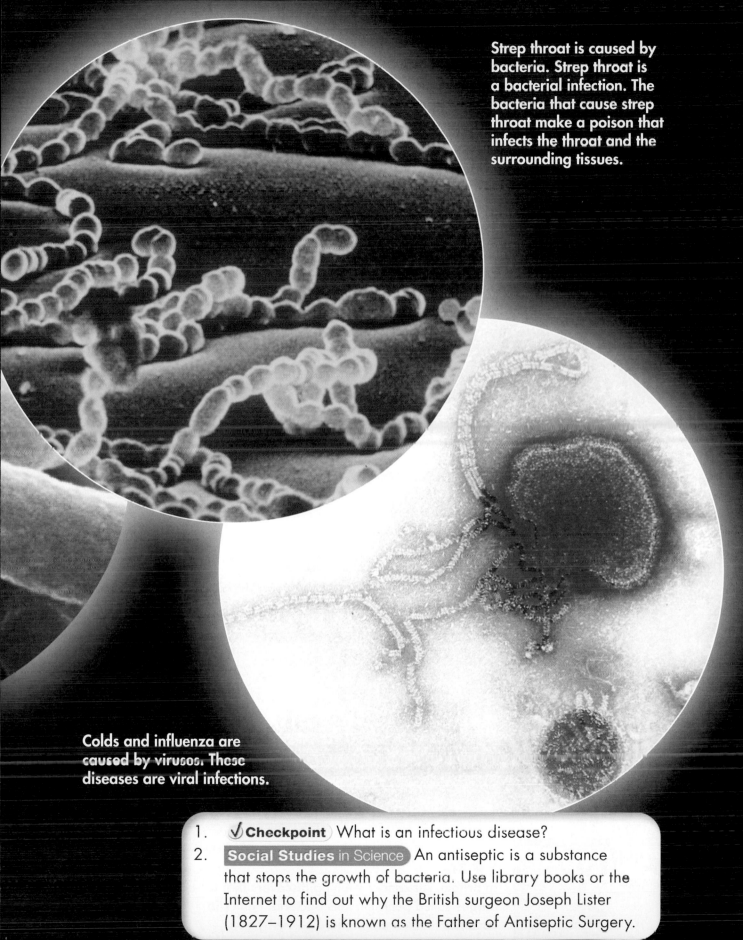

Strep throat is caused by bacteria. Strep throat is a bacterial infection. The bacteria that cause strep throat make a poison that infects the throat and the surrounding tissues.

Colds and influenza are caused by viruses. These diseases are viral infections.

1. ✓ Checkpoint What is an infectious disease?
2. Social Studies in Science An antiseptic is a substance that stops the growth of bacteria. Use library books or the Internet to find out why the British surgeon Joseph Lister (1827–1912) is known as the Father of Antiseptic Surgery.

How Your Body Fights Infections

About 200 years ago, people began to learn much more about the causes of infectious disease and how to protect against them.

1796
Edward Jenner, a doctor in England, uses material from a sore to make a vaccine against smallpox.

1854
Florence Nightingale, an English nurse, demands that army hospitals be kept clean to save lives.

1868
Louis Pasteur, a French scientist, shows that microorganisms cause disease. He develops a way to kill certain microorganisms.

1882
Robert Koch, a German scientist, identifies a kind of pathogen. He hypothesizes that an infectious disease is caused by one specific pathogen.

1928
In Britain, Alexander Fleming discovers that a fungus called penicillin kills bacteria. Penicillin becomes the first antibiotic.

Attacking the Invaders

Microorganisms called pathogens can cause disease if they get past your body's defenses. Your **immune system** helps protect you from many pathogens. Your immune system is made of blood cells and other tissues.

Special white blood cells join together to destroy pathogens that have begun to damage other cells. These blood cells also make antibodies that attach to pathogens. An antibody is a chemical that the body makes to stop pathogens from infecting other cells. A different antibody is made for each kind of pathogen.

Your immune system uses antibodies that your body already has. If you have antibodies to a pathogen, your immune system will attack whenever it enters your body. If the antibodies prevent you from getting sick, you are immune to the disease.

Preventing the Disease

A **vaccine** is a kind of medicine that protects you from a disease. The vaccine signals your immune system to make antibodies to a certain pathogen. You develop immunity without you ever having the disease.

Vaccines are not available for all infectious diseases. You can help protect yourself by eating healthy foods, getting plenty of rest and exercise, and washing your hands often.

Sometimes a person's own immune system produces antibodies that attack a pathogen very quickly. For example, once you have chicken pox, you will probably never get it again. The first time you have chicken pox, your body produces antibodies that attack the disease. The next time the chicken pox virus enters your body, the antibodies will attack it before you ever become sick.

✓ **Lesson Checkpoint**

1. What are antibodies?
2. Explain how a vaccine causes immunity.
3.   **Technology** in Science Many products claim to kill pathogens. Make a list of products found in your home or a nearby store that claim to kill bacteria.

Investigate How can some diseases be spread?

Pathogens that cause disease can be spread from person to person. This can happen when one person touches another, such as when shaking hands. Hand washing can help prevent pathogens from spreading.

Materials

4 sheets of dark paper

masking tape

container with flour

hand lens

What to Do

1 Letter the sheets of paper from **A** to **D**.

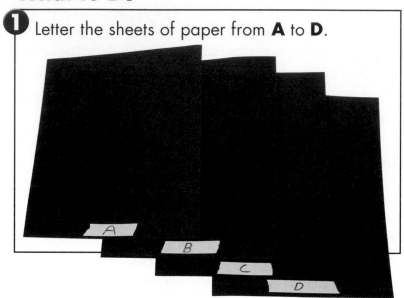

2 **Make a model** of how some pathogens spread. Dust your right hand with flour. Use this hand to shake hands with someone. Then slap your hand on sheet **A**.

Process Skills

You can **make a model** to help you **infer** how a process works.

3 Have the second person shake hands with someone, and then slap his or her hand on sheet **B**. The third student should shake hands with a fourth and slap his or her hand on sheet **C**. Have the fourth student slap his or her hand on sheet **D**.

Suppose the grains of flour were germs.

4 Look at the sheets through a hand lens. Draw what you **observe**.

How Pathogens Can Pass from Hand to Hand

Sheet	Drawing of Observations
Sheet A	
Sheet D	

Think About It

1. What can you **infer** from your **model** about how pathogens pass from person to person?

2. Why do you think doctors wash their hands in between seeing different patients?

Go Further

How could washing your hands affect the spread of some diseases? Make a plan using your model to answer this or other questions you may have.

Units of Measure and the Human Body

In science you often work with units of length, area, and volume. Length can be thought of as unit lengths joined together, end-to-end. Area can be thought of as a collection of unit squares joined together side-to-side. Volume can be thought of as a set of unit cubes that would fill a certain space.

If all the blood vessels in an average human could be placed end-to-end, the total length would be about 90 million meters. That is long enough to go around the Earth more than twice!

The average adult human has about 2 square meters of skin. That's about the area covered by a beach towel.

Take It to the NET
Units of Measure www.sfsuccessnet.com

Your heart pumps about 60 to 90 cubic centimeters of blood with each beat.

Choose the most appropriate unit to complete each sentence.

1 Each hair on your head grows about 12.7 _____ per year.
- A. centimeters
- B. meters
- C. square centimeters
- D. square meters

2 The tissue covering the brain of an average human has an area of 2,300 _____.
- F. centimeters
- G. meters
- H. square centimeters
- I. square meters

3 The volume of blood pumped by the human heart each day is about 9,500,000 _____.
- A. meters
- B. centimeters
- C. square centimeters
- D. cubic centimeters

Lab zone Take-Home Activity

The width of your index finger is about 1 centimeter. Using your index finger, estimate the length and width of a small box you have at home. Then, estimate the area the box covers and its volume.

Chapter 5 Review and Test Prep

Use Vocabulary

immune system (p. 161)	neuron (p. 154)
infectious disease (p. 158)	pathogens (p. 158)
	vaccine (p. 161)
involuntary muscles (p. 146)	voluntary muscles (p. 146)

Use the vocabulary term from the list above that completes each sentence.

1. A(n) _____ can be passed from one organism to another.

2. Skeletal muscles are _____.

3. Organisms that cause some diseases are _____.

4. A(n) _____ can make you immune to a disease without having the disease.

5. The _____ is made up of cells in your blood and other tissues.

6. _____ are muscles that you are not able to control.

7. A(n) _____ receives and sends electrical messages.

Explain Concepts

8. Explain how your circulatory system finishes the work of your digestive and respiratory systems.

9. Would digestion take more or less time if you did not chew your food? Give reasons that explain your answer.

10. A signal passes through a nerve cell at a speed of more than 92 meters per second. Some high-speed trains travel this fast. About how many seconds would it take for a train traveling at this speed to go 1 kilometer? Remember, 1 km = 1,000 m.

Process Skills

11. **Infer** Some kinds of vaccines are given more than once. The second shot is called a booster shot. What effect do you think a booster shot has on your immune system?

12. **Predict** Your biceps and triceps are skeletal muscles that work together when you bend your elbow. When one muscle contracts, the other relaxes. Predict what would happen if the biceps of your arm were damaged.

13. Make a graphic organizer like the one shown below. In the box, write the name of any organ system. In each pie section, write the name of an organ in that system and the job that organ does.

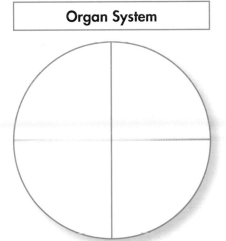

Organ System

 Draw Conclusions

14. Your skull and your ribs protect some of your body's systems. Which systems do they protect and why do these systems need extra protection?

Test Prep

Choose the letter that best completes the statement or answers the question.

15. Cells that destroy pathogens are
    Ⓐ neurons.
    Ⓑ white blood cells.
    Ⓒ viruses.
    Ⓓ skin cells.

16. Which structure is the link between the brain and the rest of the body?
    Ⓕ the vertebrae
    Ⓖ the trachea
    Ⓗ the esophagus
    Ⓘ the spinal cord

17. Muscles that help your bones move are
    Ⓐ cardiac muscles.
    Ⓑ smooth muscles.
    Ⓒ skeletal muscles.
    Ⓓ involuntary muscles.

18. Most food is digested and absorbed in the
    Ⓕ small intestine.
    Ⓖ mouth.
    Ⓗ stomach.
    Ⓘ large intestine.

19. Explain why the answer you chose for Question #17 is best. For each of the answers you did not choose, give a reason why it is not the best choice.

20. **Writing** in Science **Expository**
    Explain how your circulatory and immune systems work together to keep you healthy.

Two Early Doctors

Dr. Rebecca Lee Crumpler and Dr. Rebecca J. Cole were the first two African American women in the United States to graduate from medical school and become doctors.

Dr. Rebecca Crumpler was born around 1833 in Delaware. After working as a nurse in Massachusetts, she entered the New England Female Medical College. She graduated in 1864. After the Civil War, Dr. Crumpler moved to Virginia to provide medical care for newly freed slaves.

Later, Dr. Crumpler returned to Boston. She dedicated her time to caring for women and children.

Rebecca J. Cole was born in 1846. In 1867 she became the first African American woman to graduate from the Woman's Medical College in Pennsylvania.

After graduation, Dr. Cole went to New York to work with Dr. Elizabeth Blackwell. In 1849, Dr. Blackwell had become the first American woman to receive a medical degree. Dr. Cole visited poor families in their homes. She taught mothers how to care for their families, especially for infants and young children.

Then Dr. Cole practiced medicine in South Carolina. She returned to Philadelphia. In 1873, she and another doctor opened a center to provide medical and legal help for poor women and children.

Both Dr. Crumpler and Dr. Cole dedicated their lives to caring for and educating women and children. They inspired many people to help others.

Lab zone Take-Home Activity

Doctors who treat children are called pediatricians. Use the Internet or other sources to learn more about pediatricians.

Unit A Test Talk

Find Important Words

You can organize information by making a concept map that uses important words in a passage that you read. Or, you can underline the important words as you read the passage. Some important words about the work of the central nervous system are underlined.

The Central Nervous System

The central nervous system reacts to changes inside and outside the body. It is the link between all the systems of the body. Nerve endings gather and carry messages from all parts of the body to the <u>brain</u>. Nerve endings are tiny branches of nerve cells called <u>neurons</u>. The brain changes the messages and sends information back through the <u>spinal cord</u> to the parts of the body. For example, after your brain receives a message from nerve endings in your skin, it may tell <u>voluntary</u> <u>muscles</u> that you want them to move. <u>Involuntary</u> <u>muscles</u> will begin to work without your control.

Use What You Know

Use the underlined words to help you answer the question or complete the statement.

1. _____ are part of the central nervous system.
   (A) Voluntary muscles
   (B) Involuntary muscles
   (C) Skin cells
   (D) Neurons

2. Messages travel _____.
   (A) only between the brain and the spinal cord.
   (B) only from all parts of the body to the brain.
   (C) only from the brain to all parts of the body.
   (D) both to and from the brain and all parts of the body.

3. What is the link between all systems of the body?
   (A) the voluntary muscles
   (B) the involuntary muscles
   (C) the central nervous system
   (D) the nerve endings

4. Most of the information the brain receives is gathered by
   (A) neurons.
   (B) muscles.
   (C) the skin.
   (D) the spinal cord.

Unit A Wrap Up

Chapter 1

How are plants and animals classified?
- Cells make up all living things. Some of the cells have special jobs.
- Plants and animals are sorted by their characteristics.
- Living things have adapted to survive in their environments.

Chapter 2

How do plants use energy from the Sun?
- Plants make their own food.
- The parts of a plant work together to meet the plant's needs.
- Plants reproduce in different ways.

Chapter 3

How do plants, animals and their environments interact?
- Ecosystems have living and nonliving parts.
- The flow of energy and matter through an ecosystem is a complex path.

Chapter 4

How do changes in ecosystems affect living things?
- Living things depend on one another and upon their environment.
- Change affects living and nonliving things in an ecosystem.

Chapter 5

How do the parts of the human body work together?
- Cells in the human body are organized into structures that form systems that work together.
- The systems have different jobs.
- Parts of the human body help fight disease.

Performance Assessment

How Seeds Travel

Find out how seeds might travel. Use an assortment of fruits and seeds. Place each fruit and seed on a table or other flat surface. Use a piece of cardboard to vigorously fan each seed for 30 seconds. Record how far each seed moves. Put the fruits and seeds back on the table. Press a piece of cloth or fake fur onto each fruit and seed. Record which fruit or seeds stick to the cloth or fur. Finally, drop each fruit and seed into a container that is half filled with water. Record whether each fruit or seed sinks or floats. Based on your observations, describe how each type of seed or fruit travels.

Read More About Life Science

Look for books like these in the library.

Experiment Do mealworms prefer damp or dry places?

A mealworm can sense whether the environment is damp or dry. Sometimes conditions change. The mealworm's body helps it react to the changes.

Materials

small tub and cup with sand

2 sponges and plastic spoon

water

10 mealworms and food

Ask a question.

Do mealworms prefer to live in a damp place or a dry place?

State a hypothesis.

If mealworms can move to either a damp place or a dry place, then to which place will they move? Write your **hypothesis**.

Identify and control variables.

In this experiment, the **variable** you will change is moisture. The variable you will observe is the place to which the mealworms move. Other conditions, such as light and temperature must be **controlled**, or kept the same.

The variable you change is called the independent variable. The variable you observe is called the dependent variable. Controlled variables are things that must not be changed if the experiment is to be a fair test. Identify each of these variables in this experiment.

Process Skills

When you plan an experiment and figure out what you will change and what must not be changed, you are **identifying and controlling variables**.

Take It to the NET
More Activities www.sfsuccessnet.com

Test your hypothesis.

1 Cover the bottom of a tub with a layer of sand.

2 Wet 1 sponge. Squeeze out any extra water.

3 Place the damp sponge at one end of the tub. Place the dry sponge at the other end.

4 Put 1 spoonful of food in the center. Use a plastic spoon to place 10 mealworms in the middle of the tub, between the 2 sponges.

Wash your hands after handling mealworms.

damp sponge

dry sponge

5 After 30 minutes, **observe** where the mealworms are located. Record your observations in a chart.

They are alive! Handle with care!

6 Observe the mealworms every day for 5 days. Record their location in your chart. Put more water on the damp sponge every day.

Collect and record your data.

	Number of Mealworms				
	Day 1	Day 2	Day 3	Day 4	Day 5
Damp sponge					
Dry sponge					

Take It to the NET
More Activities www.sfsuccessnet.com

Interpret your data.

Record your data in the bar graphs.
Compare what you see in the 2 graphs.

The height of each bar should show how many mealworms were at a sponge.

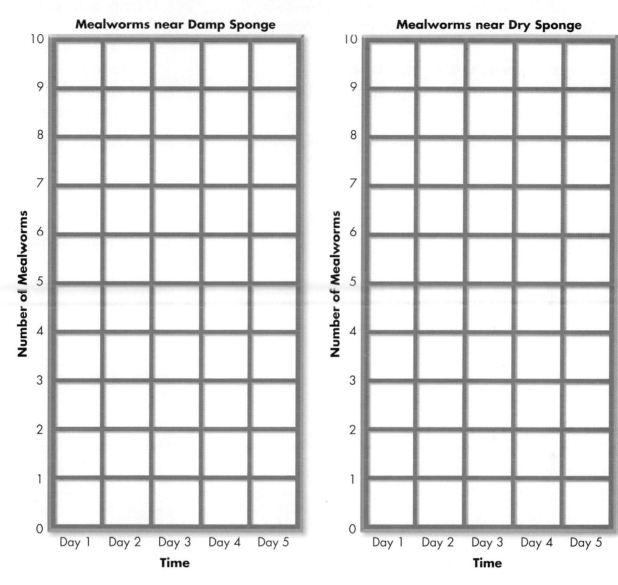

Mealworms near Damp Sponge

Number of Mealworms: 0–10
Time: Day 1, Day 2, Day 3, Day 4, Day 5

Mealworms near Dry Sponge

Number of Mealworms: 0–10
Time: Day 1, Day 2, Day 3, Day 4, Day 5

State your conclusion.

What conclusion can you draw from your graphs? Does it agree with your hypothesis? **Communicate** your conclusion.

Go Further

Mealworms are a young stage of a small beetle. Do the adult beetles prefer damp or dry places? Let the mealworms grow to be adults. Design and carry out a plan to investigate this or other questions you may have.

Science Fair Project

Using Scientific Methods
1. Ask a question.
2. Make a hypothesis.
3. Plan a fair test.
4. Do your test.
5. Record what happens.
6. Tell your conclusions.
7. Inquire further.

Home Sweet Home

Idea: Make a pond or bog terrarium. Use library resources or go to a pet store to learn about the types of organisms you might include and what those organisms need. Make a diagram of one or more food chains in your terrarium.

Different Types of Plants

Idea: Grow a corn plant and a bean plant. Make a poster that describes the difference between the two types of plants.

What's Under that Rock?

Idea: Design an experiment to find out the type of moisture and/or light conditions a pill bug *(also called a sow bug or wood louse)* prefers. Look for pill bugs under logs and rocks. Keep the pill bugs in a container that has a layer of sand and moss.

Inside Information

Idea: Create a model of the digestive or circulatory system. Label the parts of the system and describe what they do. Indicate places where problems in the system may occur as a result of poor diet or lack of exercise. You can make your model from materials such as clay, cut paper, or papier maché, or you can draw your model.

Take It to the NET
Science Fair www.sfsuccessnet.com

EC NTL 10 9 8 7 6 5 4 3 2 1

Unit B

Earth Science
in Indiana

Did you know that limestone from Indiana is considered "the nation's building material"? To build and repair the Pentagon, a building in Washington, D.C., builders have used Indiana limestone. Exporting limestone is important to Indiana's economy.

Earth Science in Indiana

What do water, fossils, plains, and soil have in common? They all provide opportunities for learning about earth science in Indiana. You will learn more about the science behind them in Unit B.

Water

Indiana's Office of Water Quality in Indianapolis reports on the condition of Indiana's streams and lakes. The office pays special attention to groundwater and other sources of drinking water. Precipitation such as rain and snow keep Indiana's water refreshed. You will learn more about weather and the water cycle in Chapter 6.

Average Number of Days of Precipitation, January through June		
Month	Indianapolis	Evansville
January	12	11
February	11	9
March	12	12
April	13	12
May	13	12
June	11	10

Fossils

A geologist in Martin County discovered fossil tracks left in the mud by a primitive amphibian. A geologist is a scientist who studies the earth and its processes. The picture below shows fossilized tracks. You will learn more about fossils in Chapter 8.

Tipton Till Plain

A glacier once covered Indiana's Tipton Till Plain. Glaciers advanced into Indiana thousands of years ago. When the ice melted, thick layers of sand and gravel filled the valleys and covered the hills of northern Indiana to produce a gently rolling landscape. Large boulders were also left behind when the glaciers melted. You will learn more about landforms in Chapter 9.

Soil

Soil is one of Indiana's most valuable natural resources. Because farming is so important to Indiana's economy, Indiana farmers protect their soil from pollution and erosion. You will learn more about soil in Chapter 10.

Answer the questions below. Write your answers on a separate sheet of paper.

Multiple-Choice Questions

1. Which the following produced northern Indiana's gently rolling landscape?
  A fossils
  B erosion
  C glaciers
  D precipitation

2. In which month shown on the chart did Indianapolis and Evansville have the SAME number of days of precipitation?
  A January
  B March
  C April
  D June

Constructed-Response Questions

3. What is a geologist?

4. What purpose does Indiana's Office of Water Quality serve?

5. Why is soil a valuable resource in Indiana?

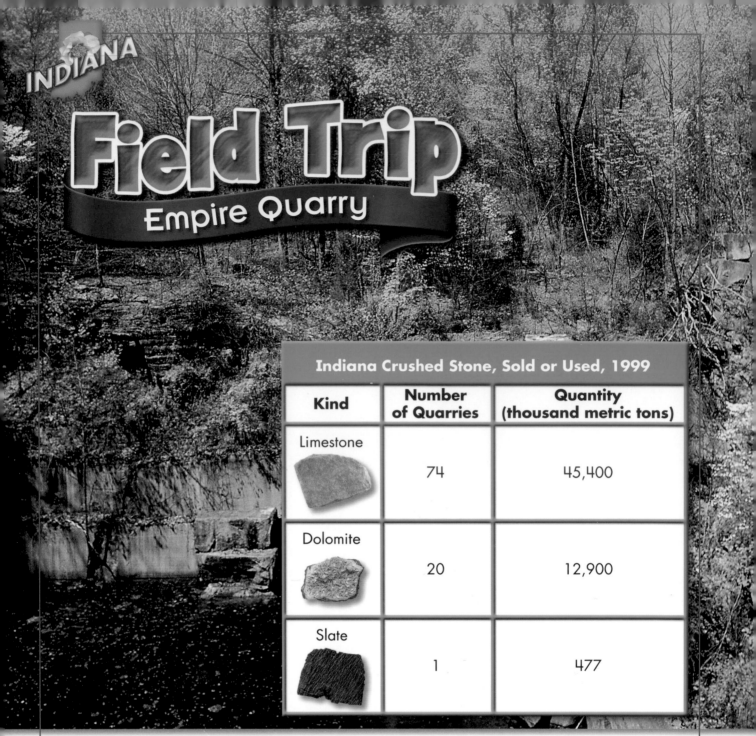

Field Trip
Empire Quarry

Indiana Crushed Stone, Sold or Used, 1999		
Kind	**Number of Quarries**	**Quantity (thousand metric tons)**
Limestone	74	45,400
Dolomite	20	12,900
Slate	1	477

Is the Empire State Building in Indiana? No, but the limestone used to build the Empire State Building was taken from the Empire Quarry in Bedford County. Quarries are pits from which stone is cut or blasted. Indiana's limestone formed long ago when dissolved minerals cemented tiny bits of ancient skeletons and shells together. Limestone in Indiana is mined mostly from quarries near Bedford and Bloomington.

Find out more:

Research to find out more about other buildings around the United States that have been built with Indiana limestone.

- Make a poster showing the properties of limestone that make it such a good material for building.
- Draw a map of the United States. Show locations of buildings built with Indiana limestone.

You Will Discover

- how ocean water and fresh water are different.
- how the water cycle gives us fresh water.
- what causes weather.
- how we predict weather.

Chapter 6
Water Cycle and Weather

Online Student Edition

How does Earth's water affect weather?

- evaporation
- condensation
- precipitation

wind vane

178

humidity

DRY   WET

Chapter 6 Vocabulary

anemometer

barometer

front

meteorologist

Scientists called meteorologists study weather conditions.

179

Explore How can you make fresh water from salt water?

Some countries without enough fresh water make fresh water from salt water.

Materials

salt water and spoon

small cup and bowl

plastic wrap and tape

marble

What to Do

1 Pour 5 spoonfuls of salt water into a bowl. Set a small cup in the middle of the bowl.

Place a marble above the small cup.

Plastic wrap should not touch cup.

Tape plastic wrap to bowl.

2 Place in sunlight for several hours.

3 Remove the marble, plastic wrap, and cup. Put the bowl and cup in a warm place. Let the water evaporate for about 3 days.

4 **Observe** the bottom of each container.

Think About It

1. **Communicate** What did you find in the bottom of each container? Explain your results.
2. Think about the variables that affect evaporation. **Predict**. How could you speed up evaporation? Describe how you could test your prediction.

Process Skills

You can write, speak, or draw pictures to **communicate** information.

Cause and Effect

Linking causes and effects can help you better understand what you read. Writers sometimes signal cause and effect with words such as *because, since, so,* and *as a result.*

- A cause may have more than one effect. An effect may have more than one cause. Sometimes an effect leads to another event, which creates a chain of causes and effects. Some causes and effects are marked in the article below.

- You can use a graphic organizer to show cause and effect.

Newspaper Article

Skating on Thin Ice

A skater was rescued from icy waters in Lily Pond today. Last night temperatures dropped, causing the ice on the pond to thicken. In the chilly dawn, the skater glided over the ice. But the temperature rose, so the ice began to melt. As a result, the ice was much thinner at noon when the skater returned. Since the thin ice could not support his weight, the skater fell through the ice and into the water near the edge of the pond. He recovered quickly, because he was rescued right away.

Apply It!

Make a graphic organizer like the one shown below for each cause and effect from the newspaper article. If an event is BOTH a cause and an effect, you should write it in both boxes.

Cause ⇒ Effect

You Are There!

You are gazing at the Earth from space. The giant blue ball turns slowly. Huge chunks of brown and green with splashes of white creep into view, cross the blue ball, and disappear behind it. The chunks are Earth's continents and islands. The vast expanse of blue is the world's great ocean. Masses of white clouds drift across the lands and ocean. Your radio breaks the silence with a squawk. Earth is calling.

Where is Earth's water?

Any ocean that you might step into is linked to all the oceans in the world. The world's oceans connect to form one huge mass of salty water, with large and small areas of land.

Earth—The Water Planet

Throughout history, people have used bodies of water to travel from place to place. Because almost $\frac{3}{4}$ of Earth's surface is covered with water, they had very little choice. Water provides a home and food for millions of Earth's organisms. In turn, these organisms are food for people.

Earth's water is always in one of three states. At a temperature of 0°C, water freezes into a solid called ice, and ice melts into water. At a temperature of 100°C, water becomes an invisible gas called water vapor.

Some of the water near Earth's surface is water vapor in the atmosphere. But more than $\frac{97}{100}$ of Earth's water is in the oceans and the seas. The seas are smaller areas of the ocean. Most of the rest of Earth's water is frozen in glaciers and polar ice caps. Less than $\frac{1}{100}$ is in rivers and lakes.

People have named sections of Earth's great ocean. The chart lists the names and areas of some of the sections.

Approximate Areas of the Oceans of the World					
Ocean	Pacific	Atlantic	Indian	Southern	Arctic
Area (km²)	165 million	82 million	73 million	20 million	14 million

1. **✓Checkpoint** About how much of Earth's water is frozen in glaciers and ice caps?
2. **Math** in Science Look at the chart above. About how much greater is the area of the Pacific Ocean than the area of the Atlantic Ocean?

Salty Water

"Water, water, everywhere, Nor any drop to drink." These lines in a famous poem describe a crew on an ocean ship that has run out of drinking water. Water is all around them. How could they run out of drinking water?

If you have ever tasted ocean water, you know the answer. It tastes very salty. But, taste is not the main problem. Ocean water is not healthy for drinking. Your body cannot use water that is saltier than your blood.

But why is the ocean salty? Water is a liquid made up of hydrogen and oxygen. Ocean water is a mixture of water and many dissolved solids. Most of the salt in ocean water comes from rocks and soils on the land. Rivers carry dissolved salts and minerals to the ocean. The most common salt in the ocean is sodium chloride, the same salt that's in your saltshaker. The ocean supplies much of our table salt and some of our minerals.

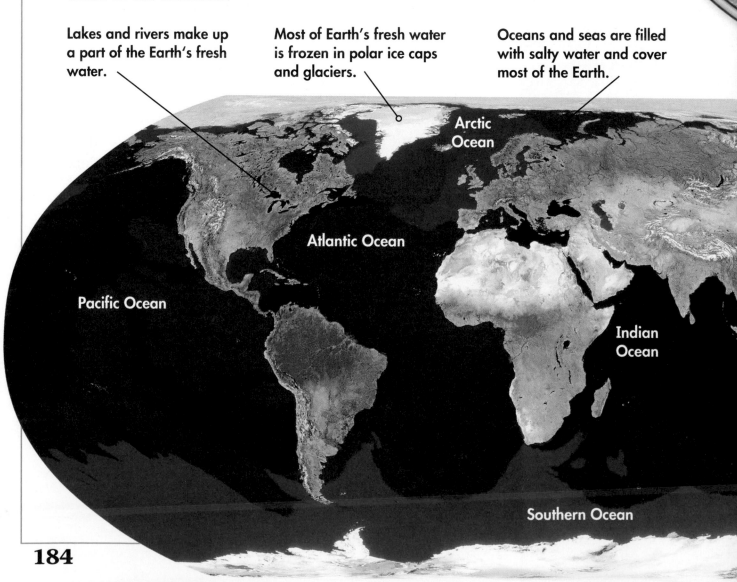

Lakes and rivers make up a part of the Earth's fresh water.

Most of Earth's fresh water is frozen in polar ice caps and glaciers.

Oceans and seas are filled with salty water and cover most of the Earth.

Arctic Ocean

Atlantic Ocean

Pacific Ocean

Indian Ocean

Southern Ocean

Earth's Water

$\frac{1}{100}$
Usable Fresh Water

$\frac{2}{100}$
Frozen Fresh Water

$\frac{97}{100}$
Salt Water

Differences in Saltiness

Saltiness of the water near the ocean's surface varies from place to place. In warm, dry places, ocean water turns rapidly into water vapor in the air. The salt that's left behind makes the water even saltier. Some of the saltiest water on Earth is located in the Red Sea, which has deserts on three sides.

Ocean water is less salty near the North and South Poles. Less salt dissolves in the cold water. And water turns to vapor more slowly in the lower temperatures. The ocean is also less salty in areas where rivers, melting ice, or heavy rains add plenty of fresh water. For example, many rivers flow into the Baltic Sea. Its water is less salty than most ocean water.

Most of the Earth's water is salty ocean water. Most of Earth's fresh water is frozen in glaciers and ice caps. People cannot use it for drinking. They cannot use it to keep land plants and animals alive. Earth's liquid fresh water is underground or in lakes, rivers, and streams. The water vapor in the air and the liquid and frozen water that fall through the atmosphere are all fresh water.

✓ Lesson Checkpoint

1. Why is the water in the Baltic Sea less salty than most ocean water?
2. Is the water in the Red Sea more or less salty than average?
3. ⊙ **Cause and Effect** What causes ocean water to be more salty than average in warm places?

Lesson 2

How do water and air affect weather?

Why do some places get lots of rain while other areas get very little? The way water moves in and out of the atmosphere affects our lives.

How Water Is Recycled

Earth's water is always being recycled. The never-ending movement of water from Earth's surface to its atmosphere and back again is called the water cycle. You can see an example of the water cycle as puddles disappear after a rain. Some water runs into drains that flow into lakes, rivers, or the ocean. The rest is in the air. Water is made of small particles that are constantly moving. As the Sun's energy warms the water, the particles move faster. They fly away from the liquid water and change into a gas called water vapor.

The process of changing liquid water to water vapor is called **evaporation.** The higher the temperature, the faster water changes from liquid to gas.

Condensation

When moist air rises, it cools. The water vapor in it condenses in the atmosphere. These tiny droplets of liquid water form clouds and fog.

Evaporation

Water is stored in lakes, oceans, glaciers, marshes, soil, and spaces in rock. It evaporates in the Sun's warmth. Some water vapor also comes from the leaves of plants.

To understand the next step in the water cycle, think of what happens when you breathe on a cold window. The cold glass cools the water vapor in your warm breath. The water vapor turns into a liquid that fogs up the window. The process of water vapor becoming liquid water when it cools is called **condensation.**

Like the fog from your breath, a cloud is made of tiny drops of water or ice crystals. The drops and crystals combine with others until they become so large and heavy that gravity pulls them downward. Then they fall as **precipitation,** which is any form of water that falls to Earth. The cycle begins again.

Temperature, air movement, and how much water vapor is in the air affect how quickly water evaporates and condenses. Because land features affect temperature, they affect the water cycle too. When wind blows moist air up one side of a mountain, clouds form there. More precipitation falls than on the other side of the mountain.

So, the Sun's energy powers the water cycle that provides fresh water from the ocean. Earth's total amount of water never changes.

1. ✔**Checkpoint** What is the water cycle?
2. **Technology** in Science Old desalinators used evaporation and condensation to remove salt from ocean water. Use the Internet to find out how modern desalinators work.

Precipitation
Depending on air temperatures and wind conditions, the water may fall as rain, snow, or hail. If the air temperature in or below the cloud is above freezing, the water vapor will condense and fall as rain. If the air temperature is below freezing, water falls as snow, sleet, or hail. Most precipitation falls on oceans.

Storage
The water from precipitation over land sinks into soil and underground pores in rock. Some water runs off the land into streams, rivers, and lakes. Most of it falls, flows, or seeps into the ocean.

The Earth's Atmosphere

When you look up on a clear day, you seem to see a high, blue ceiling. You are really looking through 9,600 km (about 6,000 mi) of air. The blanket of air that surrounds Earth is its atmosphere. Like other matter, air has mass and takes up space.

Air is made up of a mixture of invisible gases. Almost $\frac{4}{5}$ of the Earth's atmosphere is nitrogen. Most of the rest is oxygen, but small amounts of carbon dioxide gas are also present. The part of the atmosphere closest to Earth's surface contains water vapor. The amount of water vapor depends on time and place. For example, air over an ocean or a forest has more water vapor than air over a desert.

Gravity pulls the mass in air toward Earth's surface. The pushing force of air is called air pressure. Air pushes with equal force in all directions. At any moment, many kilograms of gas press down on your school building. They do not crush it because the air inside the building exerts pressure too. Air pushing down is balanced by air pushing up and sideways. Air pressure decreases as you go higher in the atmosphere.

Air Pressure

Air pressure also changes with temperature. As the air near Earth's surface warms, its particles move farther apart. The air can rise, and then it pushes down with less pressure. An area of low pressure forms. If the air near Earth's surface cools, the particles in the air become more closely packed. This denser, cooler air sinks. An area of high pressure forms.

Air moves from a place with high pressure to a place with low pressure. The moving air is called wind. The name of a wind is the direction from which it comes. A north wind comes from the north and moves toward the south. Winds near the ocean are sometimes named differently, as you can see in the diagram.

Land Breeze

A land breeze blows from the land toward the sea. At night, the water is warmer than the land. The air above the land is cooler, so it sinks. This creates high pressure at the surface of the land. The air above the land moves toward the water.

Sea Breeze

A sea breeze blows from the sea toward the land. During the day, the air above the land is warmer than air above the water. The air rises, creating low pressure at the surface of the land. The air above the water moves toward the land.

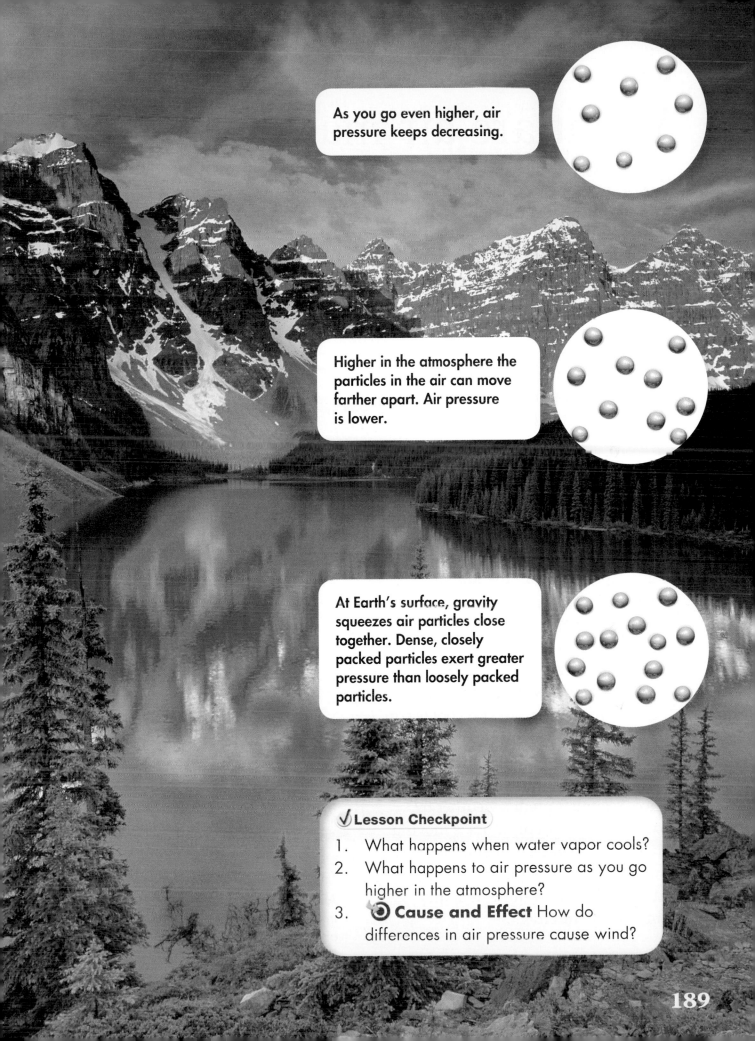

As you go even higher, air pressure keeps decreasing.

Higher in the atmosphere the particles in the air can move farther apart. Air pressure is lower.

At Earth's surface, gravity squeezes air particles close together. Dense, closely packed particles exert greater pressure than loosely packed particles.

☑ **Lesson Checkpoint**

1. What happens when water vapor cools?
2. What happens to air pressure as you go higher in the atmosphere?
3. 🎯 **Cause and Effect** How do differences in air pressure cause wind?

189

What are air masses?

Air masses affect weather all over the world. As they move, so does the type of weather they carry.

Air Masses

An air mass is a huge body of air that has nearly the same temperature and humidity. **Humidity** is the amount of water vapor in the air. The way air masses move and interact causes most weather. Air masses form over large areas of land or water. For several days or weeks, an air mass is heated or cooled by the area over which it forms. An air mass that forms in the polar areas will be cool or cold. An air mass that forms in a tropical area will be warm or hot.

An air mass has water vapor that evaporates from the land or water below it. So, air masses that form over water have greater humidity than those that form over land. An air mass that forms over a tropical ocean will probably be both warm and humid. If the air mass forms over a cool ocean, it will be cool and moist.

As an air mass moves, it takes its temperature and humidity to another place. Scientists predict weather by tracking where an air mass is moving, what other air masses it will meet, and how it will meet them. Weather is the result of how air, water, and temperature interact.

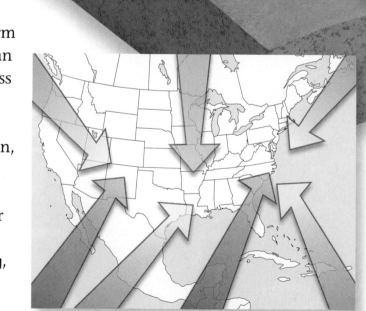

Air masses bring weather into the United States. Moist air forms over the ocean. Dry air forms over land.

Rapidly rising air causes clouds to build upward.

Direction of front

Air cools and the water vapor in it condenses into clouds.

Cold air slides under the warm air and forces the warm air up.

When Air Masses Meet: Cold Front

Global winds usually blow air masses from west to east. As an air mass moves, it collides with air masses with different temperature and humidity. The different air masses do not mix. The area where the two different air masses meet is called a **front.** Two types of fronts are cold fronts and warm fronts.

A cold front forms when a cold air mass bumps into a warm air mass that is moving more slowly or not moving at all. The density of cold air is higher than the density of warm air. The denser cold air sinks under the warm air. The warm air along the front cools as it is pushed upward. Water vapor in the cooling air condenses into clouds. You can usually see a line of clouds along a cold front.

Cold fronts often cause strong winds and brief, heavy precipitation. In fact, thunderstorms may develop along the front. But cold fronts usually move faster than warm fronts, so the precipitation and other weather conditions they bring do not usually last long. The front often passes quickly, the skies clear, and the colder air mass replaces the warmer one. The weather turns fair and cooler.

1. ✓**Checkpoint** Why does an air mass that forms over a desert have low humidity?
2. **Art in Science** Draw an outdoor place you like as it would look when a cold front passes. Be sure to include the sky and the clouds.

When Air Masses Meet: Warm Front

When a warm air mass runs into a cold air mass that is moving more slowly, a warm front develops. The warm air is lighter and has less pressure than the cold air mass. The warm air moves forward and creeps over the trailing edge of the cold air mass. As the warm air rises, it cools. The water vapor in it condenses into clouds.

Warm fronts usually move more slowly than cold fronts do. The air is lifted more slowly and spreads out more so it affects weather over a larger area. Warm fronts usually bring steady, long-lasting precipitation. Air temperatures are usually higher after a warm front passes.

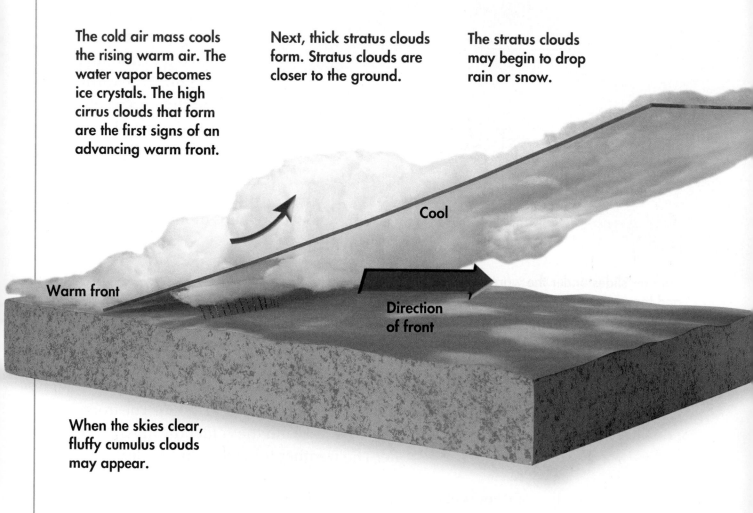

The cold air mass cools the rising warm air. The water vapor becomes ice crystals. The high cirrus clouds that form are the first signs of an advancing warm front.

Next, thick stratus clouds form. Stratus clouds are closer to the ground.

The stratus clouds may begin to drop rain or snow.

Cool

Warm front

Direction of front

When the skies clear, fluffy cumulus clouds may appear.

Clouds

Cloud formation begins as the Sun's energy warms water in oceans, lakes, rivers, and the ground. The heated water evaporates. The Sun's energy warms the air holding the water vapor. The air rises and cools. The water vapor becomes the tiny water droplets and ice crystals that make up clouds.

Clouds with many shapes, sizes, and colors move across the sky. Conditions in the atmosphere determine what a cloud is like. Since 1803, scientists have classified types of clouds. Today, the ten names given to types of clouds are combinations of three basic types: cumulus, stratus, and cirrus. Scientists add *alto* to the name if the clouds are very high or *nimbo* if they are rain-bearing.

Cumulus clouds are thick, white, and puffy, like piles of cotton. They sometimes appear in fair or good weather and may reach very high in the sky. Stratus clouds are flat layers of clouds that form close to Earth's surface. Cirrus clouds are feathery clouds that form high in the atmosphere when water vapor turns to tiny crystals of ice. They are sometimes called "mare's tails."

✓ Lesson Checkpoint

1. What is an air mass?
2. Weather is caused by variations in what three basic ingredients?
3. **⊙ Cause and Effect** How does the Sun cause clouds to form?

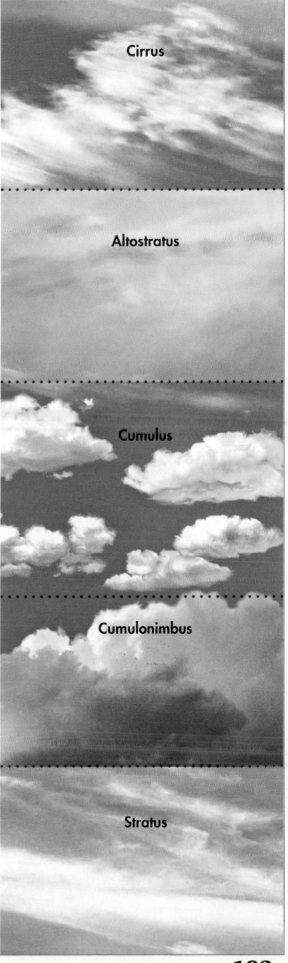

Cirrus

Altostratus

Cumulus

Cumulonimbus

Stratus

Lesson 4

How do we measure and predict weather?

Weather is much of the day-to-day changes in temperature, winds, precipitation, and other conditions in the atmosphere. Climate is the usual year-after-year weather in an area.

Aneroid Barometer

Measuring Weather

Temperature, air pressure, and water are three basic weather factors that affect weather conditions. The ocean also affects weather and climate around the world. Ocean currents move warm water to cold lands and cold water to warm lands. So, temperatures of land areas near coasts might be milder than those farther from the ocean. Water heats and cools more slowly than land does. The land and sea breezes that result affect temperature on land.

Scientists called **meteorologists** study weather conditions. They also look at temperature, water, and air movement. Today, almost all of the measurement data that meteorologists use are collected automatically at weather observation stations.

You probably know that a thermometer measures air temperature. Air pressure is measured with a tool called a **barometer.** Air pressure can be measured in units called millibars (mb). For example, a reading of 1000 mb means higher air pressure than a reading of 900 mb. The first tool to measure air pressure was the mercury barometer, invented in 1643 by Evangelista Torricelli. Today air pressure is also measured with an aneroid barometer.

Wind Vane

Mercury Barometer

Air Pressure and Weather Conditions

Even without a measuring tool, you can tell something about air pressure by looking outside. When air pressure is low, the weather is often damp and cloudy. When air pressure is high, the weather is usually dry and clear. So on a sunny day with a bright blue sky, you know the air pressure is probably high.

Wind also affects weather. Wind speed is measured with a tool called an **anemometer.** Most anemometers have three or four cups that are shaped like halves of small, hollow balls. The faster the cups spin in the wind, the higher the wind speed shown on the anemometer. A **wind vane** shows the direction from which the wind is blowing. The pointer on the wind vane points into the wind. You may have seen wind vanes on rooftops.

Meteorologists use a rain gauge to measure the amount of rainfall. The top of the rain gauge collects rain and directs it into a small tube with numbered markings. The numbers show in inches or centimeters how much rain has fallen. Meteorologists measure the humidity with a tool called a hygrometer.

Anemometer

Hygrometer

1. **✓ Checkpoint** What does a barometer measure?
2. **Social Studies** in Science In the newspaper or on the Internet, look up daily high and low temperatures for Boston, Oklahoma City, Miami, Santa Fe, San Francisco, and your city. Which cities have the greatest difference between the high and the low? How do you explain the difference?

195

Predicting Weather

You usually know what weather will be like in each season. For example, you know most summer days will be warmer than most winter days. Predicting day-to-day changes is more of a challenge.

A weather forecast is a prediction of what the weather will be like for the next few days. Meteorologists measure temperature, precipitation, air pressure, and wind over a large area. They use the measurements to find high and low pressure areas and fronts. They use data from current weather conditions to make the forecast.

To forecast weather for tomorrow, most meteorologists compare computer models. Weather radar is one source of data for the models. With radar pictures, forecasters can see how the atmosphere is changing. Weather radar can track precipitation. Meteorologists can see where rain is falling. They can predict where and when it is likely to fall next.

Tracking Weather

Meteorologists use charts and maps to record measurements and information from weather satellites and radar. Then they analyze the data and use computer models to predict the weather.

Charts are used to record daily weather conditions. For example, this chart shows high and low temperatures and precipitation.

WEATHER FOR MAY 26			
City	Temperature (°F)		Precipitation (inches)
	High	Low	
Albuquerque, NM	78	59	0
Indianapolis, IN	72	62	0.15
Juneau, AK	54	41	0.12
New York City, NY	61	56	0.74
Tallahassee, FL	94	68	0

Newspapers often have weather information for larger cities.

LEGEND	
Warm Front	●●●●
Cold Front	▼▼▼
Stationary Front	●▼●▼
High Pressure	**H**
Low Pressure	**L**

A weather map shows fronts and how they are moving. A stationary front is standing still.

Reading Weather Maps

A weather map uses symbols to show fronts and weather conditions in different places. A key on the map explains the symbols. Curving lines connect locations with the same air pressure. The letters H and L are used to show high and low pressure systems. Triangles and half circles stand for cold and warm fronts. Some maps show more weather information as well.

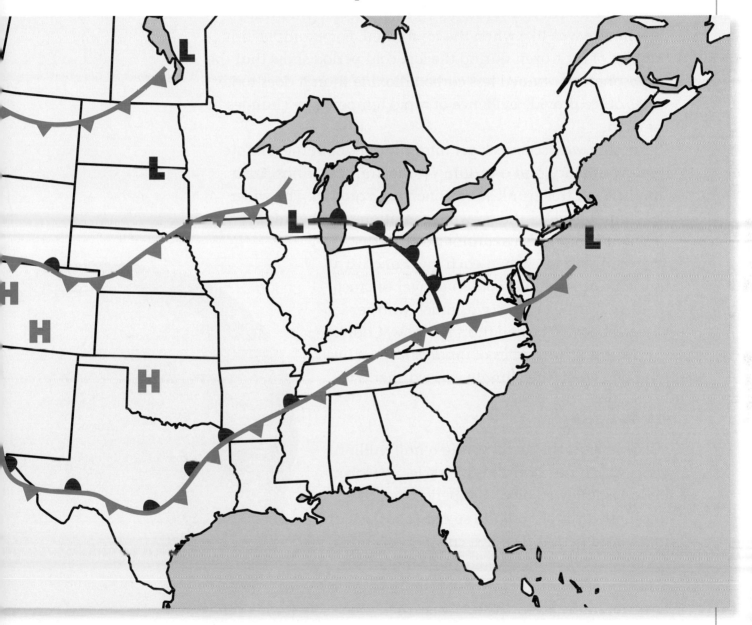

1. ✓ **Checkpoint** How are curving lines used on a weather map?
2. **Math** in Science On the Internet or in a newspaper, look up the daily high and low temperatures in your area for five days in a row. Use the data to make a line graph. Use one color for the highs and another color for the lows.

How Weather and Climate Have Changed

About four billion years ago, the Earth cooled. Its atmosphere formed. Since then, Earth's climate has had dramatic changes from very cold periods to warm periods. During the last cold period, thick ice sheets stretched from the poles to cover almost a third of the Earth.

Scientists have different ways of learning about Earth's past climate. They drill into ice from glaciers to find what the climate was like when the ice formed. For example, tiny bubbles of air frozen during the last cold period show that the atmosphere contained less carbon dioxide than it does today. Cores of ice provide evidence of rapid temperature changes in the area.

Another way scientists get information about the climate in a given place and a certain year is from tree rings. Each ring in a cut tree trunk shows one year's growth. The wider the ring, the better the growing conditions for the tree.

Scientists can also examine Earth's crust. They can estimate when each layer of crust formed. For example, coal in a layer of crust means that the climate was much warmer when the layer formed than it is now. Coal is formed from the bodies of organisms that lived long ago when the climate was warmer.

At Present

For at least the last two and a half million years, Earth has had climatic cycles. A warm period is followed by a cold period and then another warm period and so on. Today, we are in a warm period. The last cold period ended about 10,000 years ago. Earth's temperature and climate change slowly during these cycles. Even so, many scientists are concerned that people are causing some changes in Earth's temperature to happen too quickly.

If the ring is wide, the weather was warm and the tree grew well. If the ring is narrow, the weather was cold.

In the Future

When people burn fossil fuels, they add carbon dioxide and other pollutants to the atmosphere. Water vapor and carbon dioxide are common "greenhouse gases" in our atmosphere. In the right amounts, greenhouse gases help keep Earth warm. But extra greenhouse gas can cause Earth's temperature to increase. If Earth becomes just a few degrees warmer, climates may change. For example, the southern polar ice cap could melt, putting more water into the oceans. Higher ocean levels might cause flooding in low areas near coasts.

Government leaders and scientists all over the world are looking for ways to replace fossil fuels with cleaner energy forms. They are looking for ways that people will need less energy to power their activities.

✓ Lesson Checkpoint

1. Where can water be found on Earth?
2. Describe the formation and type of clouds along a warm front.
3. **Writing in Science** **Persuasive** Suppose you are mayor of your town or city. Write a notice for a public meeting. Explain how burning fossil fuels can affect global climate. Ask people to come to the meeting and discuss ways to reduce the use of fossil fuels in your town or city.

Guided Inquiry

Investigate How does water change state?

Materials

cup and thermometer

metric ruler

water

computer or graphing calculator (optional)

What to Do

1 Fill a cup with water to a height of about 30 mm. Accurately record the height and temperature.

Your teacher will put your cup in a freezer.

2 Freeze the water overnight. Then record the height and temperature.

3 When the ice just begins to melt, record the height and temperature.

4 When all the ice has melted, record the height and temperature.

ice

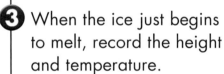

	When Readings Were Made			
	Day 1 Start	**Day 2** After freezing	**Day 2** When ice began to melt	**Day 2** When all was melted
Height (mm)				
Temperature (°C)				

5 Leave the cup at room temperature. Record the height and temperature for 3 more days.

6 Make a bar graph showing how the height you **measured** changed.

Height of Ice and Liquid Water

Height (mm): 36, 34, 32, 30, 28, 26, 24, 22, 20

| Day 1 Start | Day 2 After freezing | Day 2 When ice began to melt | Day 2 When all ice was melted | Day 3 | Day 4 | Day 5 |

When Height Readings Were Made

Think About It

1. How did the height of the water change? Explain.

2. **Interpret Data** As the temperature changed, what changes of state occurred? Was thermal energy added or removed during each change?

3. Based on your graph, **predict** how long it will take for the water to evaporate completely.

Go Further

What would happen if you added salt to the water before freezing? Make a plan to find out.

Graphing Temperatures

In the area where you live, how much does the temperature change within a few hours or within a day?

A line graph shows how data changes over time. The line graph below for August 21, 2003 shows how the temperature in one city changed during an 18-hour period on that date.

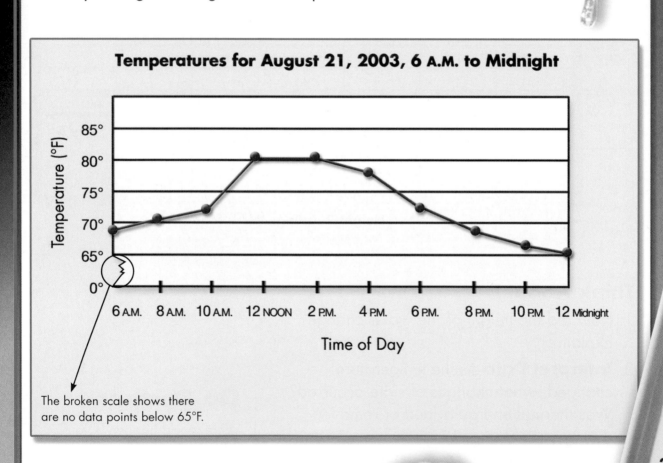

Temperatures for August 21, 2003, 6 A.M. to Midnight

The broken scale shows there are no data points below 65°F.

Use the line graph on page 202 to answer the questions.

1. What was the highest temperature in this city on August 21, 2003? How do you know?

2. On the line graph, the line between 12:00 and 2:00 does not go up or down. What does this tell you?

3. Does the line graph tell you what was the lowest temperature in this city for August 21, 2003? Explain.

4. For the same city, the record high temperature on August 21 is 87°F. The normal high temperature for that date is 76°F. Make a bar graph comparing the highest temperature on August 21, 2003, with the record high and the normal high.

Lab zone Take-Home Activity

Find a weather report in your daily newspaper, on the Internet, or on television or the radio. Make a bar graph comparing yesterday's highest temperature with yesterday's lowest temperature.

Chapter 6 Review and Test Prep

Use Vocabulary

anemometer (p. 195)	**humidity** (p. 195)
barometer (p. 194)	**meteorologist** (p. 194)
condensation (p. 187)	**precipitation** (p. 187)
evaporation (p. 186)	**wind vane** (p. 195)
front (p. 190)	

Use the term from the list above that best completes the sentence. You will not use all of the terms. Use each term only once.

1. A(n) _____ is the area where one air mass meets another.

2. A(n) _____ points into the direction from which the wind is blowing.

3. A weather forecast is a prediction made by a scientist called a(n) _____.

4. _____ is the amount of water vapor in the air.

5. A(n) _____ measures air pressure.

6. A(n) _____ measures wind speed.

7. Water vapor changes to liquid water in a process called _____.

Explain Concepts

8. Use as many vocabulary words as possible to explain the role the Sun plays in the water cycle.

9. What type of front is approaching if you see cirrus clouds high in the sky? Explain how you know.

10. Why do clouds almost always cover the tops of some mountains?

Process Skills

11. **Interpret Data** Interpret the data on the chart. Which month had no rainy days?

Monthly Rainfall	
Month	**Rainfall**
August	0 cm
September	1 cm
October	5 cm
November	3 cm

12. **Infer** what tool was used to gather the data on the chart.

13. **Communicate** You are taking a balloon ride high in the atmosphere. Describe how the air changes as the balloon rises higher in the atmosphere.

Cause and Effect

14. Make a graphic organizer like the one shown below. Complete it to show how a cold front forms.

| Cause | ➡ | Effect |

Test Prep

Choose the letter that best completes the statement or answers the question.

15. Which is an example of precipitation?
Ⓐ evaporation
Ⓑ condensation
Ⓒ snow
Ⓓ clouds

16. Which does NOT affect how quickly water evaporates or condenses?
Ⓕ air movement
Ⓖ humidity
Ⓗ temperature
Ⓘ wind direction

17. Most of Earth's water is
Ⓐ in the oceans.
Ⓑ underground.
Ⓒ frozen in glaciers.
Ⓓ in the clouds.

18. To predict the weather in your area tomorrow, you would need all of the following tools except
Ⓕ a barometer.
Ⓖ a rain gauge.
Ⓗ an anemometer.
Ⓘ a thermometer.

19. Explain why the answer you select for #18 is best. For each of the answers you do not select, give a reason why it is not the best choice.

20. Writing in Science **Expository** Write a weather prediction for a TV news show. Use a weather map from a newspaper to get information for your report.

Eye in the Sky

Observing Weather from Space

Where do scientists find the information they need to understand and predict weather? NASA provides much of the information. NASA uses special tools and spacecraft to gather information about the atmosphere, ocean currents, polar ice caps, and the global water cycle. Scientists use the data to learn about how the air, water, and temperature changes interact.

NASA scientists share what they learn with other scientists to help all people understand what happens to the Earth's air and water. An international program called Earth Observing System (EOS) is one source of information. EOS uses satellites, scientists, and special tools to gather data that measure climate and environmental change on all parts of Earth.

An important satellite of EOS is named *Terra*. The name, *Terra*, means "Earth." This name was the winner of NASA's "name the satellite" contest for students of all grades. *Terra* gathers data about how Earth's lands, oceans, air, ice, and actions of people act together in the global environment.

In 1999 *Terra* began to carry a special NASA tool that measures the height and motion of clouds. As *Terra* circles Earth, its cameras collect information about each point in the atmosphere or on Earth's surface.

If you have watched television weather reports, you have seen pictures of clouds taken by satellites. Meteorologists use data about cloud height and motion to get information about winds. They use the information to forecast the weather in the clouds' path. Even if the winds are high in the atmosphere, their direction and speed affect local weather. High winds called the jet stream move weather systems around the world.

Clouds, winds, rainfall, and the melting or freezing of sea ice all affect weather and climate around the world. By collecting pieces of data about each, NASA scientists can put together the big picture they need in order to understand and predict global weather and climate.

Lab zone Take-Home Activity

In library books or on the Internet, find some photographs of Earth taken from space. What can you tell about weather or atmospheric conditions from the photographs?

Weather Modification Pilot

Knowing what kind of weather to expect is very important to us. We want to know what the weather will be like when we travel or plan activities. Weather reports warn us of storms, too. Dr. Joanne Simpson is the chief scientist for meteorology at NASA's Goddard Space Flight Center. Her research on weather helps to warn us of severe storms.

In 1949, Joanne Simpson became the first woman to receive a doctoral degree in meteorology. She has studied models of cloud systems, cyclones, and the way the ocean and the atmosphere affect each other. Dr. Simpson tested some of her ideas by flying through clouds and even hurricanes.

Before joining NASA in 1979, she was a university professor. She also worked at the National Oceanic and Atmospheric Administration (NOAA) in Washington, D.C. One of her first projects at NASA was studying severe storms. She was the project scientist for the Tropical Rainfall Measuring Mission Observatory before she became the chief scientist for Meteorology.

Dr. Simpson has received many honors for her work in meteorology. Recently she was given the Charles F. Anderson Award by the American Meteorological Society. She has helped many young scientists be successful in their careers.

Lab zone Take-Home Activity

Suppose you met Dr. Simpson. Write three questions that would you ask her about predicting the weather or about becoming a meteorologist.

EC NTL 10 9 8 7 6 5 4 3 2 1

You Will Discover

- how hurricanes form.
- why you can't always see a tornado.

Chapter 7

Hurricanes and Tornadoes

www.sfsuccessnet.com

How do storms affect Earth's air, water, land, and living things?

SEA-CLUSION
MIAMI, FLA.

hurricane

storm surge

210

Chapter 7 Vocabulary

tropical depression

tropical storm

tornado

vortex

Explore How can you make a model of a hurricane?

Materials

bowl with water

spoon and food coloring

newspaper

What to Do

1 **Make a model** of a hurricane. Be neat. Put newspapers on the table.

2 Stir water in a large bowl. Move the spoon around the side of the bowl. Make the water move fast.

3 Stop stirring. Right away, have a partner add several drops of food coloring to the center.

4 Watch as the food color moves out from the center. It makes a spiral.

The spiral looks like the pattern made by the clouds in a hurricane. The clouds swirl around the center of the hurricane.

Think About It

Compare and contrast your model and a real hurricane.

Process Skills

Making a model of a real thing can help you learn about the real thing, even if the model is different from the real thing in some ways.

Take It to the NET
More Activities www.sfsuccessnet.com

Reading Skills

Main Idea and Details

The **main idea** is what a paragraph or map is about. It is the most important idea that the writer wants to share with the reader.

- Sometimes the main idea is stated in the first sentence of the paragraph. The title of the map tells the main idea.

- Other times you must state the main idea in your own words. Details make the main idea clearer.

- Some details explain the main idea. Other details give examples to support the main idea.

Hurricane Andrew
16 August – 28 August 1992

A Science Map

This map tells about Hurricane Andrew. Look for details shown in the map, such as where the hurricane started, how many days it lasted, and where it ended.

Apply It!

Make a graphic organizer like the one shown. List the main idea of the map. Then write in the details shown in the map.

Main Idea

Detail   Detail   Detail

🔊 You Are There!

It's a day late in the summer. You hear the sounds of pounding hammers and buzzing saws. Some people are fixing roofs. Others are cutting up fallen trees. Still others are replacing broken windows. What happened here? A hurricane struck last week. Wind ripped at the town for hours. It lifted heavy objects and sent them flying. Rain poured down. Streets flooded. Fortunately, people paid attention to weather forecasts. Most of them left town before the hurricane arrived. Now they are back. They are rebuilding.

SEA-CLUSION
MIAMI, FLA.

Lesson 1

What are hurricanes?

A hurricane is a type of storm that has lots of energy. It gets this energy from warm ocean water. Hurricanes develop as part of a system that includes tropical storms.

How Tropical Storms Become Hurricanes

In August 1992, an area of low pressure formed over the Atlantic Ocean. It gained strength and grew. It became a tropical storm. People gave it a name—Andrew. Then the storm grew even more powerful. It became Hurricane Andrew.

Tropical storms form in the tropics, the part of Earth near the equator. A **hurricane** is a dangerous storm with wind speeds of at least 119 kilometers per hour. Many bands of thunderstorms make up a hurricane. The bands wrap around the hurricane's center.

Hurricane Andrew moved to the west across the ocean. It smashed into the Bahamas. The United States was next. On August 24, the hurricane slammed into Florida. Winds near the storm's center may have reached 250 kilometers per hour. How fast is that? Moving at that speed, you could run a mile in less than 30 seconds!

In about 4 hours, Hurricane Andrew swept across southern Florida. It weakened over land, but it regained strength as it moved across the warm water in the Gulf of Mexico. It crashed into Louisiana. Then, Andrew moved northward over land. Its winds quickly weakened. But its rains still flooded many areas.

Andrew caused many deaths. It damaged businesses and destroyed neighborhoods. More than 160,000 people lost their homes. Andrew became the United States' most costly natural disaster.

1. ✓**Checkpoint** How fast are a hurricane's winds?
2. Social Studies in Science In what direction was Hurricane Andrew heading when it traveled from the Bahamas to Florida? Use a map to help.

Thunderstorms grow out of a tropical depression.

Air pressure at the ocean's surface drops. Surface winds blow faster and begin to swirl. A tropical storm develops.

Thunderstorms begin to move in spiral bands. Air pressure drops lower, and surface winds blow faster. The tropical storm is now a hurricane.

Stages of Tropical Storms

A tropical storm needs special conditions before it can form. It needs a large area of warm ocean water. It needs an area of low air pressure at the ocean surface. Winds blow from all directions toward the area of low pressure. They get heat and water vapor from the ocean. The warm, moist air rises. Clouds build as water vapor condenses. A tropical disturbance develops.

Sometimes the towering clouds in a tropical disturbance become thunderstorms. As the water vapor condenses, it releases heat energy. Air in the thunderstorms gets warmer, causing the storms to grow. Air high above the ocean moves away from the thunderstorms. As the winds increase and begin to swirl, the storms become known as a **tropical depression.** The wind speeds can reach 61 kilometers per hour. Then, as winds blow even faster, a **tropical storm** forms. The winds are now blowing more than 62 kilometers per hour. The air pressure in the storm has dropped even lower.

Direction of Storm

Hurricane as a System

Thunderstorms move in spiral bands toward the area of lowest air pressure. More air moves out from the top of the storm than moves in at the ocean's surface. Air pressure drops even lower. Surface winds blow even faster toward the center. When the winds reach 119 kilometers per hour, the tropical storm becomes a **hurricane.**

A system is made up of parts that affect each other or that work together. Two of Earth's systems are the atmosphere and the ocean. The two systems work together to produce a hurricane. Hurricanes are systems that form in the atmosphere and get their energy from the ocean.

A hurricane can cause changes to many of Earth's systems. The land and living things are systems that hurricanes can affect. A hurricane's winds create large ocean waves. A hurricane that moves over land can change the shape of the coast. A hurricane can uproot trees and destroy people's houses.

The Eye

The spot in the middle of the hurricane is its eye. Winds in the eye are gentle. The eye has no rain and few, if any, clouds. It usually has the lowest air pressure of the storm. The entire hurricane spins around its eye.

The Hurricane's Eye

The bands of thunderstorms around the eye have the strongest winds and constant, heavy rains. The eye of a typical hurricane is about 20 to 50 kilometers across. Winds on one side of the eye blow in the opposite direction of the winds on the other side of the eye.

People in the area under the eye may be fooled into thinking that the hurricane has passed. If they go exploring too soon, they can be caught outside when the other half of the hurricane roars in.

1. **✓ Checkpoint** What is the source of a hurricane's energy?
2. **Social Studies** in Science Prepare a television news report about hurricanes. Make a map showing areas that have been hit by hurricanes in the past several years. Give the report to your class. Describe the hurricanes' effects on Earth's systems.

The Effects of Winds and Water

When a hurricane moves over land, it can destroy many things. Its winds can break tree trunks or lift roofs from houses or completely flatten buildings. Winds pick up and hurl objects. All hurricanes have strong thunderstorms and fast, swirling winds. As you can see in the table, hurricanes are classified by their wind speed.

Rating Hurricanes	
Category of Hurricane	**Wind Speed (kilometers per hour)**
Category 1	119 to 153
Category 2	154 to 177
Category 3	178 to 209
Category 4	210 to 249
Category 5	Greater than 249

High above the surface, winds blow out and away from the hurricane.

When the hurricane moves over land, the bands of thunderstorms can produce violent winds called tornadoes.

Fast-moving ocean currents carry sand away from dunes and beaches.

Thunderstorms move in spiral bands toward the eye.

Strong winds push ocean water in front of the hurricane onto land in a storm surge.

High waves move farther onto land on top of the storm surge.

218

This lighthouse is on Key Biscayne, Florida. The photograph shows how the area looked in 1992 before Hurricane Andrew.

After Hurricane Andrew, the lighthouse stands above a wrecked shore and broken forest.

In many hurricanes, water causes the worst damage. The slower the hurricane moves, the more rain can fall on an area. Rain can mix with soil and cause mudslides. A hurricane loses strength quickly after it moves over land or colder water. But it can still cause deadly floods.

When the hurricane is near land, its winds push large waves of ocean water onto shore. This rise in sea level caused by the storm's winds is called a **storm surge.** A storm surge can carry large boats onto land. At high tide, the storm surge can cause even worse flooding. In 1900, a hurricane swept over Galveston, Texas. The storm surge killed more than 6,000 people. Fortunately, modern weather reports give people time to move to safety.

In some ways, a hurricane may be helpful. The rains add water that plants need. Wildfires are less likely. Some rainwater soaks deep into the ground and keeps wells flowing. A hurricane may damage some habitats and create others. It can remove non-native plants so native plants can return.

1. ✓**Checkpoint** What are three ways in which a hurricane can cause damage?
2. **Math** in Science A tropical storm's winds are blowing at 63 kilometers per hour. How much must the speed increase for the storm to be a hurricane?

A Natural Disaster with a Name

To tell listeners about several different storm systems, the National Hurricane Center uses a list to name the storms. Female and male names follow one another in alphabetical order. A tropical storm gets a name when its winds reach 63 kilometers per hour. If the storm becomes a hurricane, it keeps that name. The name may be used again unless the storm causes severe damage. Then another name that starts with the same letter is used. The table lists the first few names for Atlantic storms.

2005	2006	2007
Arlene	Alberto	Andrea
Bret	Beryl	Barry
Cindy	Chris	Chantal
Dennis	Debby	Dean
Emily	Ernesto	Erin
Franklin	Florence	Felix

Instruments on the Quik Scat satellite collect wind speed data.

How Scientists Predict Hurricanes

In the past, people did not know that a hurricane was coming until it was very close. Today, meteorologists make weather forecasts to tell people about hurricanes that are far from land.

Meteorologists use data from instruments all over the world to track hurricanes. Satellites far above Earth's surface send data such as a hurricane's rainfall. Special planes that pilots fly into hurricanes gather data too. Scientists use these data for computer models. A model represents a system or set of events. People study models of things that may be too big or too dangerous to study directly.

Computer models predict a hurricane's strength, direction, and speed. The models use data such as wind speed and water temperature. Meteorologists compare forecasts from the models to real events. Then they adjust the models to make them better. When they make a forecast, these scientists also use their own knowledge and experience.

Data for wind speeds are used to predict which storms may grow into hurricanes.

Sensors in satellites measure temperature of ocean water beneath hurricanes.

Hurricane Models

Hurricane models predict the storm's path. The forecast shows where the hurricane is. It also shows where the hurricane might be heading. The forecast shows Hurricane Isabel's most likely path. As you go farther into the future, the area that the storm might affect gets bigger.

Teamwork of Scientists

Many scientists work together to forecast hurricanes. Some scientists might study how heat moves. Others might study the best ways to write computer programs for models. Still others might study how winds high in the atmosphere affect a hurricane's path. Scientists in different parts of the world share information. They all work together to make better forecasts.

✓ **Lesson Checkpoint**

1. How do weather satellites help people study hurricanes?
2. What are three types of information that a computer model might give in a hurricane forecast?
3. 🌀 **Main Idea and Details** Give the main idea of how computer models help scientists forecast hurricanes. Include supporting details.

What are tornadoes?

A tornado is part of a thunderstorm. A group of thunderstorms can produce many tornadoes. Most of the world's tornadoes form over the Midwest United States.

How Tornadoes Form

The day began with bright sunshine. In the afternoon, though, the sky turned stormy. Rain poured down. People saw flashes of lightning and heard booms of thunder. Winds sent things flying through the air. Then people heard a new noise—a roar like that of an approaching train. They could barely see a whirling column of air through the rain. A tornado was coming!

A funnel cloud is a rapidly spinning column of air that comes down out of a thunderstorm. It becomes a **tornado** when it touches the ground. The center of a tornado has low air pressure. Tornadoes form in strong thunderstorms. Most tornadoes occur in the spring and summer. The winds of most tornadoes have speeds that are less than 200 km per hour. However, a tornado's winds can reach speeds of 500 km per hour—the fastest winds on Earth.

Before a tornado can form, an area inside a thunderstorm must be spinning. Then a narrower column of air must start spinning faster. This column may become a tornado. Sometimes tornadoes develop when the bands of thunderstorms in a hurricane move onto land.

Before thunderstorms form, winds change direction and increase in speed. Winds begin to spin.

As the thunderstorm forms, air within it rises. The spinning air begins to tilt upward.

The area of spinning grows wider.

Inside the spinning storm, a smaller column of spinning air becomes shaped like a funnel.

The funnel grows longer and narrower. It spins even faster as it moves along picking up things in its path.

The Vortex

What do a sink and a thunderstorm have in common? A vortex can form in each of them. A **vortex** is an area where air or liquid spins, or spirals, in circles. Watch as water drains from a sink. You might see a small vortex of swirling water. A tornado is a vortex that forms in a thunderstorm. Air spirals upward along the outside of a tornado.

Air rushes into the low pressure area at the center of a tornado. Water vapor condenses in the rising air along the outside. A funnel cloud may appear below the storm base. As the funnel cloud picks up dust and other objects, the vortex may get darker and may be easier to see. But, sometimes you cannot see a tornado. Heavy rain, dust clouds, or nighttime can hide it.

1. ✔**Checkpoint** What are three ways in which a tornado is different from a hurricane?
2. **Writing in Science** **Expository** Find out where and when strong tornadoes have hit your state. Write a newspaper article about the tornadoes.

The funnel cloud stretches downward. After it touches the ground, it is called a tornado.

Dust Devil

A dust devil is a column of whirling air. It is not a tornado nor is it part of a thunderstorm. It can form when the sky is clear. A dust devil's winds are much slower than a tornado's. They reach only about 95 kilometers per hour. Dust devils are common in places like deserts where columns of hot air rise.

Waterspout

A waterspout is a rapidly spinning column of air over a lake or ocean. It does not pull large amounts of water high into its vortex. But it does lift a spray of water droplets. All waterspouts are linked with clouds. A waterspout may form over water. Or, it may be a tornado that formed over land and then moved over water. Waterspouts are usually weaker than tornadoes.

Forecasting Tornadoes

In parts of the Midwest, warm moist air masses often clash with cold air masses. Strong thunderstorms form. A few of them produce tornadoes. So, scientists do not give tornado warnings for every thunderstorm. But, if a tornado is likely, people need to move to a safe place. A tornado is difficult to forecast. It can form and move quickly. Once a tornado is seen, there is little time to warn people.

Tornadoes destroy weather instruments and everything else in their path. Some scientists have taken great risk by getting close to tornadoes to learn more about them. Today, meteorologists can look inside a thunderstorm. They use an instrument called Doppler radar. It detects things like the direction and speed of wind – and the vortex of a tornado.

Some Doppler equipment is moved from storm to storm.

Classifying Tornadoes

The strong winds of tornadoes cause incredible damage. The kind of damage they cause gives scientists an idea of just how strong the winds were. They use the actual damage and the wind speed to classify the tornado. The scale was developed by scientist T. Theodore Fujita.

Fujita Scale		
Strength of Tornado	Wind Speed (km/hour)	Damage caused
F0 Gale	64–116	Tree branches broken, chimneys damaged
F1 Moderate	117–180	Tree trunks broken, cars pushed off roads
F2 Significant	181–253	Trees knocked down, weak buildings destroyed
F3 Severe	254–332	Cars and trains turned over, roofs torn off buildings
F4 Devastating	333–419	Sturdy wooden buildings destroyed, cars thrown
F5 Incredible	420–512	Houses shattered, cars thrown more than 100 meters

Safety

Tornado watches and warnings from the National Weather Service are on radio and television. A watch means that tornadoes are likely to form within a few hours. A warning means that a person or a weather forecasting tool like radar has detected a tornado. Some towns alert people with a loud siren.

When your area has a tornado warning, go into a basement and take cover under a sturdy table. If the building does not have a basement, go into a small room such as a bathroom, closet, or hallway. Keep away from the outside walls of the building. Keep away from windows. If you are caught outside, lie flat in a low area. Cover your head. If you are in a car, get out. A tornado can move faster than a car. Also, it can pick up a car and smash it against the ground.

Comparing Tornadoes and Hurricanes

Hurricanes and tornadoes are strong storms. Both types of storms spin around a center of low air pressure. Both have high winds and can cause great damage. Both can affect all of Earth's systems.

However, hurricanes and tornadoes are different in several ways. A hurricane can be hundreds of kilometers across. It has many thunderstorms. A hurricane forms over the ocean. It can last for many days. A tornado is usually hundreds of meters across. It forms within a single thunderstorm. Almost all tornadoes form over land. Most tornadoes last only a few minutes. A tornado's winds can be much faster than a hurricane's winds.

✓ Lesson Checkpoint

1. How does Doppler radar help scientists know what is happening inside of a thunderstorm?
2. What are the safest parts of a building when a tornado warning is given for your area?
3. Ⓞ **Main Idea and Details** Give the main idea of how a tornado forms in a thunderstorm. Include supporting details.

Investigate Where is the hurricane going?

Weather forecasters record where a hurricane was and where it is. They look at other things too. They predict a hurricane's path and warn people in the path that a hurricane might be coming.

Materials

Storm Map

What to Do

1 Look at the Storm Map. Find where the hurricane was on day 1 and day 2. Think about its direction. **Predict** where it will go. What places would you warn that a hurricane might come? Record in your first prediction.

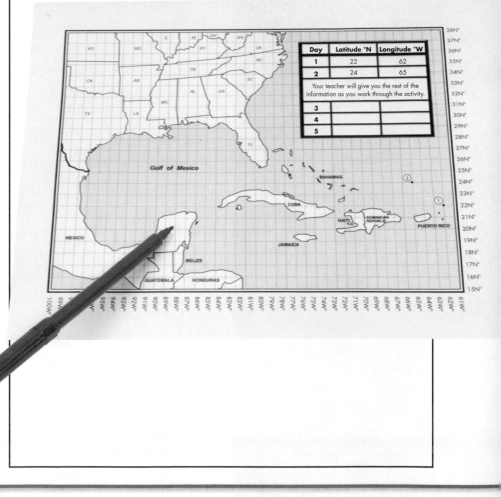

Day	Latitude °N	Longitude °W
1	22	62
2	24	65
Your teacher will give you the rest of the information as you work through the activity.		
3		
4		
5		

Process Skills

To help **predict** where a hurricane might go, you **make inferences** based on what you already know (where the hurricane has been and where it is currently).

2 Your teacher will tell you the location of the hurricane on day 3. Mark this position on the map. Make a new prediction. Predict where the hurricane will go next. What places would you warn? Record your second prediction.

3 Your teacher will tell you the location of the hurricane on day 4 and day 5. Mark the positions on the map. Complete the Predictions Chart.

Predictions Chart

	Prediction What places would you warn that a hurricane might be approaching?	**Accuracy** How accurate was your prediction?
1st prediction (step 1)		
2nd prediction (step 2)		

Think About It

1. How did you **predict** where the hurricane might go?

2. How might people be affected by an accurate prediction? by a prediction that is not accurate?

Go Further

Hurricanes are a type of severe weather. Think about the weather in your area. How could you track the weather in your area over the course of three weeks? Make and carry out a plan. Decide what weather data you will collect and what weather tools you will need.

Math in Science

Ranking Hurricanes

The Saffir-Simpson scale uses three measurements to rate a hurricane. The three measurements are its highest continuous wind speed, its storm surge, and its lowest air pressure.

Category	Sustained Wind Speed (km per hour)	Storm Surge (meters)	Lowest Air Pressure (millibars)
1	119–153	1.2–1.7	Above 980
2	154–177	1.8–2.6	965–980
3	178–209	2.7–3.8	945–964
4	210–249	3.9–5.4	920–944
5	Over 249	Over 5.4	Under 920

Remember that when a group of numbers is given in the form of 119–153, the group includes the least number, 119, the greatest number, 153, and all numbers between them.

Use the Saffir-Simpson Hurricane Scale to answer the questions.

1. Hurricane Camille, which struck in 1969, had a sustained wind speed of 288 kilometers per hour and a storm surge of 7.5 meters. What category was Hurricane Camille?

2. How much faster is the least wind speed in Category 2 than the least wind speed in Category 1?

3. Suppose a hurricane had a sustained wind speed of 165 kilometers per hour and a storm surge of 2.2 meters. Its lowest air pressure was 968 millibars. What category is it?

Lab zone Take-Home Activity

Use the Internet or other resources to find information about 3 different hurricanes from the past 25 years. Make a chart showing the name of the hurricane, the year it occurred, and its category.

Chapter 7 Review and Test Prep

Use Vocabulary

hurricane (p. 215)	**tropical depression** (p. 216)
storm surge (p. 219)	
	tropical storm (p. 216)
tornado (p. 222)	
	vortex (p. 223)

Use the vocabulary term from the list above that best completes the sentence.

1. A _____ has wind speeds of at least 119 kilometers per hour.

2. The ocean water that a hurricane can push onto land is a _____.

3. A low pressure air mass with storms that have winds that begin to spin over warm ocean water is a _____.

4. A hurricane keeps the name it was given when it became a _____.

5. A rapidly spinning column of air that comes out of a thunderstorm and touches the ground is a _____.

6. Particles of air can spin in a spiral pattern called a _____.

Explain Concepts

7. Explain what kinds of information scientists need to make a model to predict a hurricane or tornado.

8. Explain how a hurricane gets energy from warm ocean water.

9. How is a dust devil different from a tornado?

10. A tornado passes across a field without any trees, cars, or buildings. The tornado is rated F0 on the Fujita scale. Explain why this tornado was not rated higher.

Process Skills

11. Use the graph to **infer** whether a tornado or a hurricane caused the high winds. Explain your answer.

Wind Speed

12. Suppose ocean waves caused by a hurricane mix warm water with colder, deeper water. **Write a hypothesis** describing how the strength of the hurricane will change.

13. A low pressure system forms over Lake Michigan. Explain why you think a hurricane could or could not form there. **Use a map model** to help.

Main Idea and Details

14. Make a graphic organizer like the one below. Fill in details or give examples that support the main idea.

Hurricanes can affect Earth's systems—air, water, land, and living things

Detail	Detail	Detail

Test Prep

Choose the letter that best completes the statement or answers the question.

15. What indicates that a tornado warning should be given?
Ⓐ Thunderstorms develop.
Ⓑ A dry cold front moves quickly.
Ⓒ A tornado is reported.
Ⓓ Moist air moves over land.

16. One way that tornadoes are different from hurricanes is
Ⓕ tornadoes do less damage.
Ⓖ tornadoes last longer.
Ⓗ tornado winds are more violent.
Ⓘ only tornadoes produce rain.

17. Hurricanes often
Ⓐ occur in the Midwest.
Ⓑ contain many thunderstorms.
Ⓒ form from one thunderstorm.
Ⓓ last for only a few minutes.

18. A tornado always
Ⓕ begins as a vortex.
Ⓖ creates a storm surge.
Ⓗ forms over the ocean.
Ⓘ is hundreds of kilometers wide.

19. Explain why the answer you selected for Question #18 is best. For each answer you did not choose, give a reason why it is not the best choice.

20. [Writing in Science] **Narrative**
Suppose you are in a basement during a tornado. Research other first-hand accounts to help you gather details of the experience.

Colonel Joseph B. Duckworth

Pilots did not always use all of their instruments while flying planes. Colonel Joseph B. Duckworth changed the way pilots were trained. His influence saved many lives.

In 1940, Colonel Duckworth developed a system of flying. He trained pilots to use all of the instruments.

On July 25, 1943 a hurricane formed off the coast of Texas. The planes at Bryan Field had to move before the hurricane destroyed them. Colonel Duckworth claimed that he could fly one of the planes right into the hurricane. He and Lieutenant Ralph O'Hair flew through the winds and rain into the eye of the hurricane. They returned safely.

Their observations proved what many scientists thought. The air temperature in the eye of a hurricane is warmer than the surrounding storm. The two pilots found that the eye of the hurricane was nearly 10 miles across and shaped like a cone. Colonel Joseph B. Duckworth and Lieutenant Ralph O'Hair were the first men to fly into a hurricane on purpose.

Lab zone Take-Home Activity

Make a list of questions to help you learn about these hurricanes and tornadoes. Interview someone you know who has experienced one of these storms.

Flying in the eye of a hurricane

EC NTL 10 9 8 7 6 5 4 3 2 1

Chapter 8

Minerals and Rocks

You Will Discover

- what rocks are made of.
- how the three types of rocks form.
- how the type of rock can change.

www.sfsuccessnet.com

How can rocks tell us about Earth's past, present, and future?

sediment

igneous rock

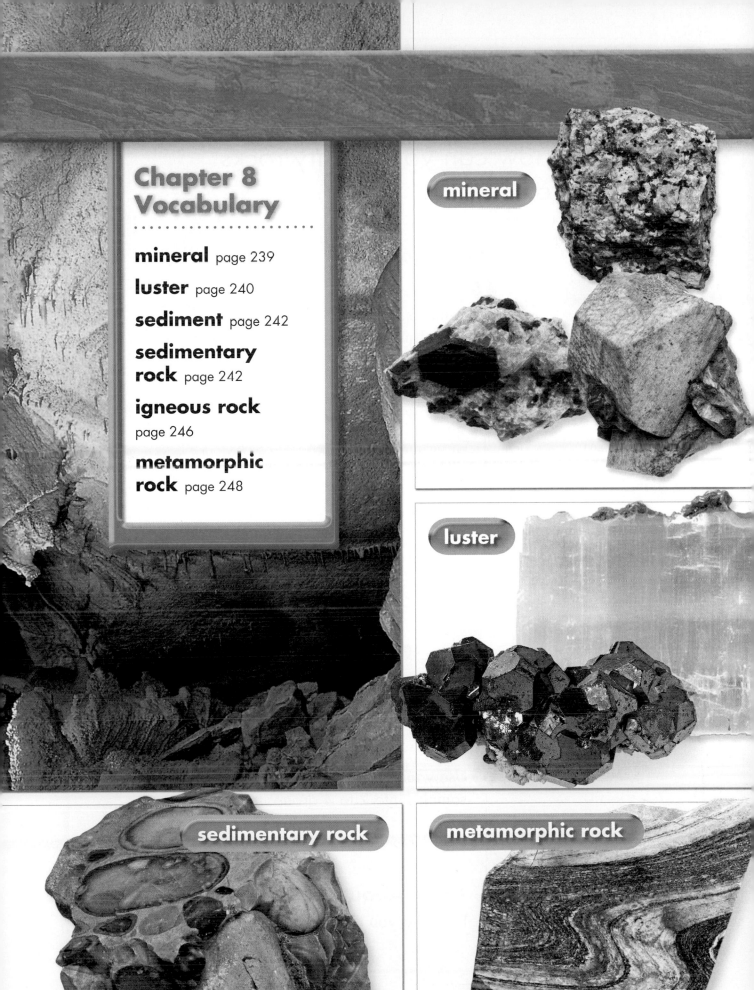

Chapter 8 Vocabulary

mineral

luster

sedimentary rock

metamorphic rock

235

Explore How can you classify rocks and minerals?

Materials

8 rocks and minerals

hand lens

What to Do

1 **Observe** the rock and mineral samples. Examine them with a hand lens. Think of ways to describe them.

2 Tell how the samples are alike and different. List words you could use to describe and sort the samples.

3 Use your ideas to **classify** the samples into 2 to 4 groups.

Process Skills

Observing objects carefully can help you **classify** them.

Think About It

How did you **classify** the samples?

Reading Skills

Summarize

A summary is a short retelling of something you have read. When you write a summary, include only the most important ideas and details. Leave out most other details, and do not add any new ideas. Use your own words when you summarize. A graphic organizer can help you organize the information for your summary.

Gem Guide

Amethyst

Throughout history, sparkling amethysts have been favorite gems of kings and queens. Gems are minerals that are very beautiful. Amethyst is the purple form of the mineral quartz. This mineral is found in colors ranging from transparent to very dark. Amethysts are often cut into different shapes and made into rings, necklaces, bracelets, and other jewelry.

Apply It!

Read the magazine article. Use a graphic organizer like the one at the right to choose ideas for your summary. Then write a one- or two-sentence summary about amethyst.

Detail	Detail	Detail

Summary

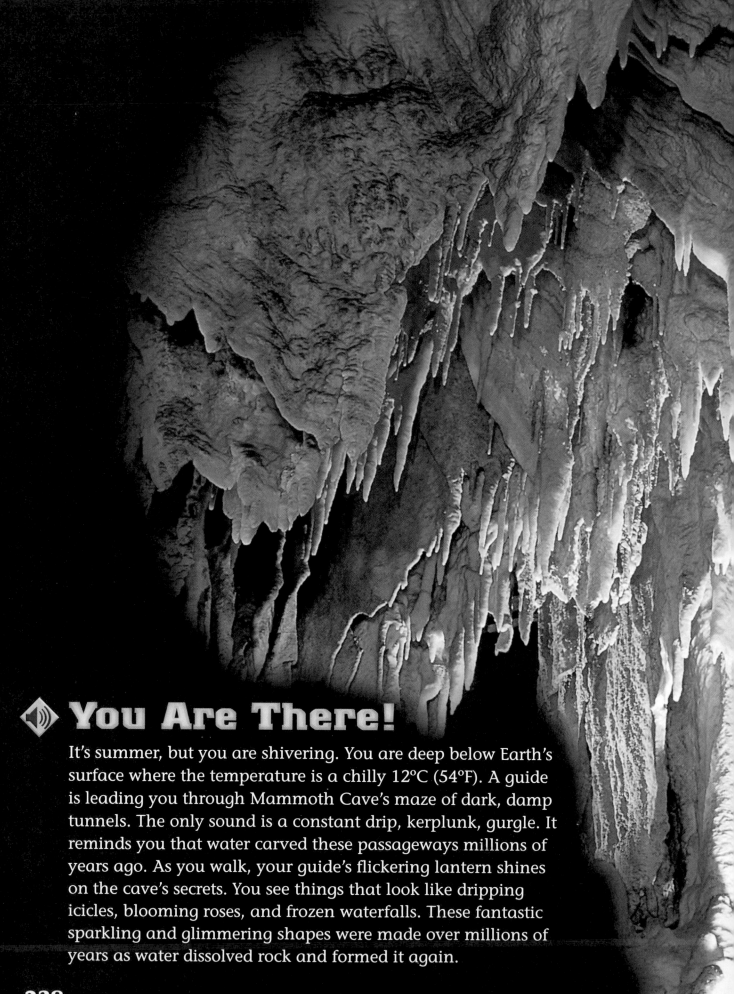

◈ You Are There!

It's summer, but you are shivering. You are deep below Earth's surface where the temperature is a chilly 12°C (54°F). A guide is leading you through Mammoth Cave's maze of dark, damp tunnels. The only sound is a constant drip, kerplunk, gurgle. It reminds you that water carved these passageways millions of years ago. As you walk, your guide's flickering lantern shines on the cave's secrets. You see things that look like dripping icicles, blooming roses, and frozen waterfalls. These fantastic sparkling and glimmering shapes were made over millions of years as water dissolved rock and formed it again.

Lesson 1

What are minerals?

Earth's crust is built of rocks. All rocks are made of minerals. Minerals can be identified by the way they look and by testing their physical properties.

Granite is one of the most common rocks on Earth.

Mineral Crystals

The salt you sprinkle on your food is a mineral. The metal fork you use to eat with is made from minerals. The ceramic plate you eat from is made of minerals. **Minerals** are natural, nonliving solid crystals that make up rocks.

Each mineral has crystals that are a particular shape. For example, fluorite has cube-shaped crystals. Corundum crystals look more like hexagons. All over the world, each mineral also has the same chemical makeup. A grain of the mineral quartz from a beach in Australia has the same chemicals in it as a chunk of quartz chipped from the Ouachita Mountains in Arkansas.

Scientists have identified over 3,000 minerals. But most of the rocks in the Earth's crust are made from only about 30 of them. These are often called the "rock-forming" minerals. Most rocks are made of different combinations of minerals. Each type of rock always has the same combination. Granite always contains crystals of quartz and feldspar. A few other types of rock consist of only one or two minerals. White marble is made only of the mineral calcite.

Quartz is hard and glassy.

Many micas form rocks that are usually brown or black.

1. ✓**Checkpoint** What are minerals?
2. ◑ **Summarize** Each mineral has the same chemical makeup no matter where it is found. Which details support this summary of the second paragraph?

Feldspar is often white or pink.

10
Diamond

9
Corundum

8
Topaz

7
Quartz

6
Feldspar

5
Apatite

4
Fluorite

3
Calcite

2
Gypsum

1
Talc

How to Identify a Mineral

How can you tell one mineral from another? To identify a mineral, scientists test some of its physical properties. Some of these properties are color, luster, hardness, streak, and cleavage.

One of the easiest things to see is color. Feldspar minerals make up more than half the minerals in Earth's crust. They are often pink or white. The color of mica, another common mineral, ranges from tan to almost black. So, color alone is usually not enough to identify the mineral. To narrow things down, scientists may look at luster. A mineral's **luster** is the way its surface reflects light. The luster may be dull, metallic, pearly, glassy, greasy, or silky.

Satin spur gypsum has a silky luster.

The shiny piece of galena has a metallic luster.

Hardness

Scientists may also do some hands-on tests. They test a mineral's hardness by finding out how easily it can be scratched. They use a special chart called the Mohs Scale for Hardness. This scale ranks minerals from 1 to 10. A mineral with a greater number can scratch all minerals with lesser numbers. For example, the mineral topaz is an 8. Quartz is a 7. If a piece of topaz is rubbed against some quartz, the topaz will leave a scratch on the quartz.

Cinnabar has a bright red streak.

Orpiment has a pale yellow streak.

Pyrite has a green-black streak.

Streak

Another hands-on test is the streak test. Streak is the color of the powder that a mineral leaves when it is scratched on a special plate. Streak is useful because even though a mineral might come in several colors, its streak is always the same color. For example, halite can be colorless to white, with bits of yellow, red, or sometimes blue. But its streak is always white.

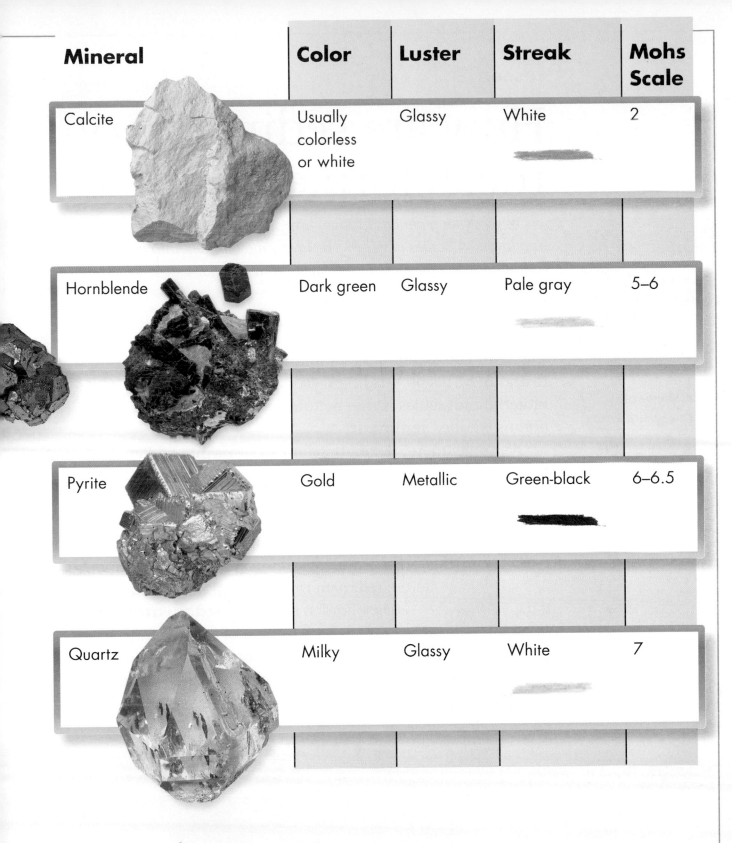

Mineral		Color	Luster	Streak	Mohs Scale
Calcite		Usually colorless or white	Glassy	White	2
Hornblende		Dark green	Glassy	Pale gray	5–6
Pyrite		Gold	Metallic	Green-black	6–6.5
Quartz		Milky	Glassy	White	7

✓ **Lesson Checkpoint**

1. What are rocks made of?
2. Why is the streak test useful?
3. ↻ **Summarize** What would happen if you scratched a piece of quartz against a piece of hornblende? Explain your answer.

Lesson 2

How are sedimentary rocks formed?

Over very long periods of time, tiny pieces of weathered rock settle into layers in bodies of water. The layers may harden into new rock that holds clues about living things from long ago.

Layers of Rock

Water, ice, wind, and gravity sweep bits of rock, soil, shells, and dead plant and animal matter from one place to another. This process is known as erosion. The eroded material that settles on the bottoms of lakes, rivers, and oceans is called **sediment.**

Over time, more and more sediment flows into bodies of water. The flowing water deposits particles of different sizes and shapes. Some particles are smooth and round. Others have sharp corners. New layers of particles settle on top of old layers. The newer layers press the older layers together. The weight of the layers and sticky clay minerals in the sediment cement the particles together. They harden and form **sedimentary rocks.** The type of sedimentary rock that forms depends on the materials in the sediment.

Conglomerate forms where water carries rounded pieces of rock.

Types of Sedimentary Rock

One type of sedimentary rock forms from sediment made of materials that were once living things. Limestone, for example, is made of hard skeletons and shells of sea animals that lived long ago. The remains settled in layers that dissolved minerals cemented together.

You can probably tell what type of sediment makes up another sedimentary rock. Sandstone is made up of bits of quartz that are each about the size of a grain of sand.

Mudstone is a third type of sedimentary rock. Mudstone forms in lakes or oceans where very tiny particles of clay minerals settle. It is similar to shale, another sedimentary rock.

How Rocks Change into Soil

Over time, loose rocks at Earth's surface and beneath it take a beating. Water that drips into cracks in rock freezes and thaws again and again. This makes the cracks larger and weakens the rock. Eventually this causes pieces of the rock to break apart. Even plant roots can force their way down into a rock and break it into smaller pieces. These natural Earth processes, known as weathering, take their toll. Even the tallest mountains wear down over millions of years.

The little pieces of weathered rock are ingredients in soil. Soil is full of dead and decaying plant and animal remains too. But soil is also full of life! Tiny life-forms such as bacteria, fungi, worms, and insects make their home in soil. They break the plant and animal remains into nutrients that plants can use.

Limestone forms from tiny bits of skeletons and shells.

Sandstone forms from quartz sands.

Mudstone forms from very tiny particles of clay minerals.

1. **✓ Checkpoint** How does water freezing and thawing cause weathering?
2. **⊙ Summarize** What makes up soil?

After an animal dies, its skin, muscles, and other soft body parts decay. Its skeleton, shell, or other hard parts are left.

Sediments such as sand or mud settle on top of the remains.

More layers form. Eventually, materials in the remains are replaced with minerals in the sediment that harden into rock.

Over many years, the rock layers weather. The fossil appears at the surface.

How Rocks Tell a Story

Scientists who study sedimentary rocks often get a glimpse of what life on Earth was like millions of years ago. They may uncover a set of footprints that a dinosaur made as it stomped through mud 100 million years ago. Or they may discover a perfect stone copy of a set of teeth that belonged to a dog-sized horse that became extinct, or died out, about 50 million years ago.

The footprints and the teeth are both examples of fossils. Fossils are evidence, or clues, of ancient plant and animal life on Earth. Many fossils can be found in sedimentary rock. Sometimes you can see fossils of shells in limestone.

Fossils give scientists information. For example, a set of dinosaur tracks can provide evidence that the dinosaur walked on two legs or on four legs. Fossils of bones, shells, teeth, leaves, and tree trunks give clues about which types of animals and plants lived at a certain time in Earth's history. The fossils also give scientists an idea of what the animals and plants looked like.

Fossils also show that the Earth's features and environment have changed. For example, fossils of giant sea turtles that lived about 70 million years ago have been found in South Dakota. Such fossils provide evidence that a shallow sea once covered what is now South Dakota.

Scientists use fossils to make models of extinct animals.

Fossils help scientists estimate the age of plants and animals that lived long ago.

How a Fossil Forms

Fossils help scientists form hypotheses about Earth's history. Many plants and animals lived during a certain time before becoming extinct. Fossils can help scientists figure out the age of the layer of rock in which they were found. For example, ammonoids, sea creatures that looked like snails, are estimated to have lived only from about 408 to 66 million years ago. An ammonoid fossil found in a layer of rock means the layer formed between 408 and 66 million years ago. As they study fossils in various layers of rock, scientists learn more about how living things have changed.

Geologic Time Scale

Scientists have divided their estimates of Earth's history into periods of time. They put these time periods into a geologic time scale. The earliest period is at the bottom. The most recent period is at the top. This order matches the ages of layers of sedimentary rock. The layers with the oldest fossils are at the bottom. Newer layers of rock form on top of the older layers.

The geologic time scale is divided into four major time periods from bottom to top: the Precambrian era, the Paleozoic era, the Mesozoic era, and the Cenozoic era.

✔ Lesson Checkpoint

1. What kinds of materials end up as sediments?
2. Describe how an organism becomes a fossil.
3. ↺ Summarize how fossils help scientists.

Present

Flowering plants began to appear at the beginning of the Cenozoic era. Fossils of bees also date back to this time.

65 million years ago

The first fossils of birds were found in rocks from the Mesozoic era.

The Mesozoic era was the Age of the Dinosaurs. Fossil evidence shows that dinosaurs appeared and then became extinct during this period.

248 million years ago

Fossils of fish, simple plants, insects, and the first animals to live on land are in rocks from the Paleozoic era.

544 million years ago

over 544 million years ago

Rocks from the late Precambrian era have fossils of jellyfish.

245

Obsidian looks like glass. It forms when lava cools very rapidly following the eruption of a volcano.

Pumice is formed from lava that has lots of gas bubbles. Some pumice is so full of gas that it floats on water!

Basalt is the most common quickly cooled igneous rock. Most of the ocean floor is basalt.

What are igneous and metamorphic rocks?

Rocks can form below or above Earth's surface. Heat and pressure can change rock from one type to another. Rock is constantly changing form. Usually change takes a long time.

Igneous Rocks

You know that rocks are hard and that they can break apart and crumble into soil. But did you know that rocks also can melt? A layer of rock below Earth's crust is so hot that it is partially melted. This molten rock is called magma. **Igneous rocks** form from this molten rock. In fact, the word *igneous* means "fire" in the Latin language.

Igneous rocks may form above Earth's surface or below it. If you have ever seen pictures of a volcano erupting, you have seen magma exploding onto Earth's surface. The molten rock, which is called lava after it reaches the surface, may ooze out of the volcano like a red-hot river. Or it may be hurled out of the volcano in hot, gooey globs. Either way, the lava on the surface cools quickly. It may harden into solid igneous rock in just a few days. An igneous rock that cools quickly does not have much time to form crystals. Any crystals that do form are tiny and not very easy to see.

Most igneous rocks do not make such a dramatic entrance. Instead the magma slowly rises toward Earth's surface. As it rises, it fills in cracks and hollow spaces in the crust. The magma slowly cools. As it hardens, crystals of minerals form in the rocks. These crystals are large. Magma cooling and hardening into igneous rock below Earth's surface is a very slow process. It can take more than a million years!

Granite is a slowly cooled igneous rock. Its large crystals of quartz, feldspar, and mica are easy to see.

Pegmatite contains the same minerals as granite. It cools and hardens very slowly. It often has very large crystals.

A piece of gabbro cools slowly. The minerals in it may separate into layers.

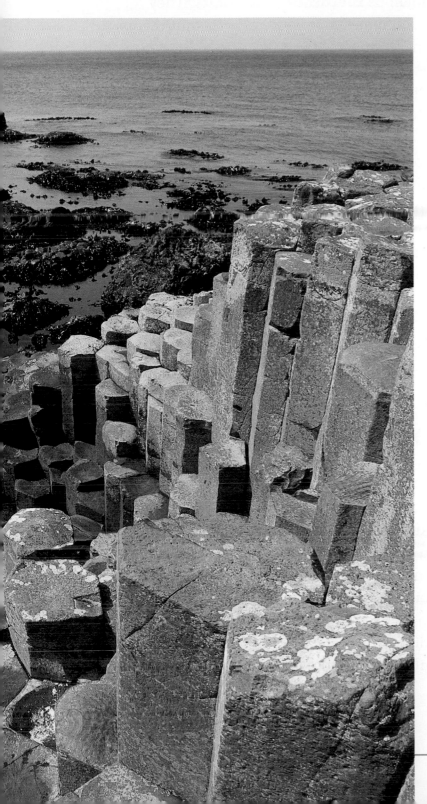

The Giant's Causeway

A causeway is a road that is built above water. Pillars usually hold up the road. Why do you think these basalt pillars are called the Giant's Causeway? The tops of these pillars form a path of stepping stones to the sea. About 40,000 of these columns are near the coast of Northern Ireland. They formed between 50 and 60 million years ago by lava rapidly cooling when it reached the sea. As it cooled, the lava became squeezed together. Cracks developed in the rock from top to bottom and formed the huge pillars. Scientists are not sure why so many of the columns have six sides.

1. **✓ Checkpoint** Which igneous rock will have larger crystals, one that cooled slowly or one that cooled quickly?

2. **Math in Science** When the Hawaiian volcano Mauna Loa erupted in 1950, the lava flowed out of it at a speed of 9.3 kilometers per hour. The lava reached the sea in about 3 hours. Estimate how many kilometers the sea is from the source of the lava.

247

Slate forms from the sedimentary rock shale. The minerals in slate are arranged so that it splits quite easily into layers.

Gneiss can form from sedimentary or igneous rock. It forms at very high pressures and temperatures.

Phyllite forms from sedimentary rock. Layering of the minerals mica and chlorite make it shiny.

Metamorphic Rocks

Powerful forces are at work below Earth's crust. As you already know, temperatures can be hot enough to melt rock. Rock is also under a lot of pressure. It is being squeezed by the weight of other rocks. These natural forces can cause rocks to completely change form. Rocks that have changed as a result of heat and pressure are known as **metamorphic rocks.** They have gone through a *metamorphosis,* a word that means "change of form."

Metamorphic rocks can form from sedimentary, igneous, and other metamorphic rocks. Limestone, a sedimentary rock, becomes the metamorphic rock marble. The igneous rock granite can become the metamorphic rock gneiss. Rock that has already been changed sometimes goes through even more changes.

As metamorphic rocks form, they can change in several ways. The heat and squeezing may cause the mineral crystals in the rock to change. They might form again as new crystals that are a different size or shape. Sometimes the chemicals in the rock will form new types of minerals. Heat and pressure can also cause the minerals to settle in parallel layers. As a result, some metamorphic rock often chips into flat sheets and slabs.

The Rock Cycle

The recycling of old rock into new is an ongoing process known as the rock cycle. Heat, pressure, chemical reactions, weathering, and erosion are some of the forces that drive this cycle. As you can see in the diagram on the next page, all three types of rock can change from one type to another at some point in the cycle. Not all rocks complete the entire cycle. For example, rocks deep in the crust may never get to the surface. Sedimentary rock may melt and become igneous rock without ever becoming metamorphic rock.

How Rocks Change

Lava, gas, rocks, and ash erupt from a volcano.

 Ash from volcanoes and bits of weathered rock form layers of sediments.

Over time, rain and wind wear away igneous rock.

Magma cools slowly beneath Earth's surface and hardens into igneous rock.

Some sedimentary and metamorphic rock wears away to form new layers.

Igneous rock forms when lava cools quickly and hardens.

Layers of sediment harden into rock.

Heat and pressure can change igneous or sedimentary rock into metamorphic rock.

Heat can cause metamorphic rock to melt into magma.

Sedimentary rock that is heated enough can melt to make new magma.

✓ Lesson Checkpoint

1. Compare and contrast the two ways igneous rock can form.
2. What causes sedimentary or igneous rock to turn into metamorphic rock?
3. **Art in Science** Draw a diagram that shows how the minerals in metamorphic rock might be arranged.

Lab zone

Guided Inquiry

Investigate What properties can you use to identify minerals?

The rock in the picture is made of minerals.

Materials

6 minerals

hand lens

streak plate

What to Do

1 Use a hand lens. **Observe** the properties of each mineral.

2 Look at each mineral. Record its color in your Table of Observed Properties (p. 251). Record its luster.

3 Rub each mineral across a streak plate. Record the color of the streak.

Put the streak plate on the table during testing. If you hold it, it could break and cut you.

D

Process Skills

When you **observe** objects you can **classify** them by their properties.

Table of Diagnostic Properties				
Mineral	**Properties**			
	Color	Luster (glassy or metallic)	Streak	Hardness
Rose quartz	pink	glassy	white	7
Calcite	white/clear	glassy	white	3
Feldspar	varied	glassy	white	6
Mica (muscovite)	varied	glassy	white	2.5
Hornblende	dark green to black	glassy	pale gray to gray	5.5
Pyrite	gold	metallic	green to brown to black	6.5

Take It to the NET
More Activities www.sfsuccessnet.com

4 The hardness scale ranks minerals from 1 to 10. The softest is 1. The hardest is 10. Scratch mineral A against mineral F. Harder minerals will scratch softer ones.

Is mineral A harder than mineral F? Does your result agree with the numbers in your Table of Observed Properties?

5 Compare the properties you observed with the Table of Diagnostic Properties (p. 250). Identify each mineral.

Table of Observed Properties

Mineral	Observed Properties				Identity of Mineral
	Color	Luster (glassy or metallic)	Streak	Hardness	
Mineral A				6	
Mineral B				not measured	
Mineral C				not measured	
Mineral D				not measured	
Mineral E				not measured	
Mineral F				2.5	

Think About It

1. What is mineral E? Which of its properties did you **observe**?

2. What properties did you use to describe and identify the minerals?

Go Further

How could you test the hardness of the minerals by scratching them with different objects? Make a plan to investigate this or other questions about minerals.

Math in Science

Large Numbers in Science

When you study Earth and its history, you will often see large numbers. For example, the chart on the next page shows that some rock samples have been estimated to be billions of years old.

Numbers with many digits are quite easy to read, write, and use. The chart below shows the a large number written in standard form.

Our number system is a place-value system. The value of each numeral, or digit, is determined by its place in the number. To show the number 4 billion, 500 million, the 4 must be written in the billions place and the 5 in the hundred millions place. Zeros are used to show that there are no ten millions, no millions, no hundred thousands, and so on.

hundred billions	ten billions	billions	hundred millions	ten millions	millions	hundred ththousands	ten thousands	thousands	hundreds	tens	ones
		4,	5	0	0,	0	0	0,	0	0	0

The table below shows the estimated ages of rock samples from four different locations. Use the table to answer the questions.

Rock Sample	Estimated Age in Years
White Mountains in New Hampshire	180 million
Pike's Peak in Colorado	1 billion, 30 million
Gneiss from Finland	2 billion, 700 million
Granite from Minnesota	3 billion, 600 million

1. How old is the sample from the White Mountains?
   A. 180,000 years
   B. 180,000,000,000 years
   C. 180,000,000 years
   D. 100,000,080 years

2. How old is the granite from Minnesota?
   F. 3,600 years
   G. 3,600,000 years
   H. 360,000,000 years
   I. 3,600,000,000 years

3. How old is the Pike's Peak sample?
   A. 1,030,000,000 years
   B. 1,030,000 years
   C. 1,030 years
   D. 130 years

4. Which sample is the oldest?
   F. Granite from Minnesota
   G. Gneiss from Finland
   H. Pike's Peak Sample
   I. White Mountains Sample

Lab zone Take-Home Activity

Use library resources to find more information about the age of rocks in other parts of the world. Make a chart like the one above.

Chapter 8 Review and Test Prep

Use Vocabulary

igneous rock (p. 246)	**mineral** (p. 239)
luster (p. 240)	**sediment** (p. 242)
metamorphic rock (p. 248)	**sedimentary rock** (p. 242)

Use the vocabulary term from the list above that best completes the sentence.

1. A _____ is a natural, nonliving solid crystal that is found in rocks.

2. Weathered rock, soil, and dead plant and animal matter form _____ when they settle in a body of water.

3. Heat and pressure may change another type of rock into _____.

4. Cooled lava becomes _____.

5. Fossils are sometimes found in the layers of _____.

6. A mineral's _____ describes how it reflects light.

Explain Concepts

7. Do you think that most animals and plants that once lived on Earth have left fossil evidence? Explain your answer.

8. Explain how metamorphic rock can change into igneous rock.

Process Skills

9. **Infer** why fossils are not found in igneous rock.

10. Suppose you have three minerals: a piece of sylvanite, a piece of millerite, and a piece of marcasite. The marcasite leaves a scratch on both the sylvanite and the millerite. The millerite leaves a scratch on the sylvanite. **Classify** the minerals in order of their hardness.

11. Mount St. Helens is a volcano in the state of Washington that erupted in 1980. **Predict** which kind of rock would be most common near the volcano: sedimentary, igneous, or metamorphic rock.

12. The table shows five minerals and their Mohs rating. **List** the minerals **in order** from softest to hardest.

Mineral	Mohs Rating
Augite	5.5
Cinnabar	2.5
Emerald	7.5
Magnetite	6
Sapphire	9

Summarize

13. Use the ideas in the graphic organizer to write a summary.

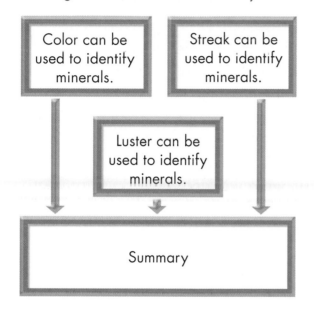

| Color can be used to identify minerals. | Streak can be used to identify minerals. |

Luster can be used to identify minerals.

Summary

Test Prep

Choose the letter that best completes the statement.

14. A physical property that scientists use to identify a mineral is
  Ⓐ color.
  Ⓑ smell.
  Ⓒ age.
  Ⓓ temperature.

15. Weathering causes
  Ⓕ storms.
  Ⓖ sediments to harden.
  Ⓗ rock to wear away.
  Ⓘ volcanoes to erupt.

16. Rocks are
  Ⓐ combinations of one or more minerals.
  Ⓑ classified by their sizes.
  Ⓒ soil mixed with sediment.
  Ⓓ sediments that have hardened over a few years.

17. Magma that slowly cools below Earth's surface forms igneous rocks that have
  Ⓕ large crystals.
  Ⓖ very tiny crystals.
  Ⓗ no crystals.
  Ⓘ crystals that settle in layers.

18. The ongoing process in which old rock is broken down and formed into new rock over millions of years is known as
  Ⓐ weathering.
  Ⓑ erosion.
  Ⓒ the rock cycle.
  Ⓓ metamorphosis.

19. Explain why the answer you selected for Question #16 is best. For each of the answers you did not select, give a reason why it is not the best choice.

20. **Writing in Science** **Descriptive**
Suppose you have discovered a new mineral. You want to classify it. Write a paragraph describing your mineral's physical properties and how you would test them.

Doug Ming

Dr. Douglas Ming is a NASA scientist who studies soils. He is a member of the Mars Exploration Rover team at the Johnson Space Center in Houston, Texas.

Dr. Douglas Ming is a NASA soil scientist. For 15 years Dr. Ming and his team studied ways that different watering methods affect plant systems. One of the team's goals was to grow plants in conditions like those on the Moon or Mars. As part of his research, Dr. Ming lived in an enclosed environment for a month. He was able to see what living, working, and conducting experiments on Mars would be like. At the same time, the NASA rover Sojourner was on Mars testing technologies that led to the robot rovers Spirit and Opportunity.

Even before Spirit and Opportunity landed on Mars in 2004, NASA scientists were working on ways to protect explorers from the harsh Martian atmosphere and radiation levels. The rovers sent new data that help Dr. Ming and others identify materials in the Martian soil that future explorers can use. The rovers also measure chemicals in the dust that might harm equipment.

Another instrument is looking for evidence of water in the soil and rocks of Mars. The mineral hematite is in one of the rocks that Spirit has examined. On Earth, hematite is sometimes linked to a watery environment. Measurements from this rock will help scientists learn about the link between water, hematite, and past environments on Mars. These data also show that weathering occurs on Mars.

The work of Dr. Ming and his team will be used in planning the spacesuits, habitats, and vehicles of the first human visitors on Mars.

Hematite makes Mars appear red.

Lab zone Take-Home Activity

Use the Internet or other sources to find more about hematite. Write a paragraph in your science journal that summarizes what you learn.

Chapter 9
Changes to Earth's Surface

You Will Discover

- how rock on Earth's surface is broken apart.
- why some landforms get larger while others get smaller.
- what causes volcanoes and earthquakes.

Online
Student Edition

www.sfsuccessnet.com

How is Earth's surface shaped and reshaped?

landform

landslide

volcano

258

Chapter 9 Vocabulary

weathering

erosion

deposition

fault

epicenter

earthquake

Explore How can you observe a mineral wear away?

Model the wearing away of a mineral. The chalk represents the mineral. The wearing away is caused by rocks and water.

Materials

plastic jar with lid

chalk

rocks

timer or stopwatch
(or clock with
second hand)

water

What to Do

1 Shake chalk and rocks in a jar for 1 minute. Look for changes in the chalk. Shake for 3 minutes more. **Observe** the chalk.

Put on lid!

8 rocks
4 pieces of chalk

2 Empty the jar. Fill the jar $\frac{1}{2}$ full with water. Repeat step 1 using the same rocks, 4 new pieces of chalk, and water.

Put on lid!

water ($\frac{1}{2}$ full) —
4 pieces of chalk
8 rocks

Think About It

1. How did the chalk change after being shaken with rocks for 1 minute? for 3 minutes?

2. **Infer** Compared to shaking chalk with only rocks, what effect did shaking chalk with both rocks and water have on the chalk?

How to Read Science

Reading Skills

Compare and Contrast

We compare when we say how things are alike. We contrast when we say how things are different.

- Writers use words to signal likenesses and differences. The most common clue word for likenesses is *like*.

- Clue words such as *however*, *yet*, and *but* signal differences.

Likenesses and differences have been highlighted in the article.

Science Article

Weathering, Erosion, and Deposition

Several processes work to shape Earth's surface. The process of weathering wears away rocks and particles. However, during another process, erosion, the weathered material is moved away. Various forces remove the weathered material. Yet some of the same forces may work together to carry the rocks and particles to a new location. This process is called deposition.

Apply It!

Make a graphic organizer like the one shown. List ways that the processes are alike and different.

Different   Different

Alike

261

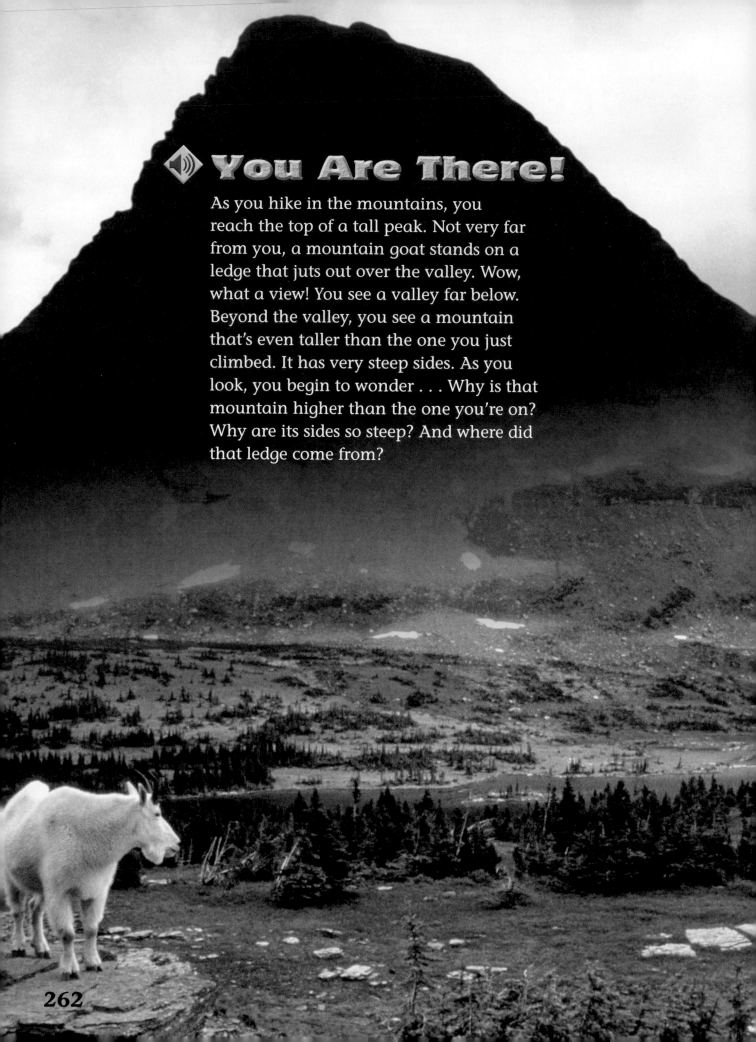

🔊 You Are There!

As you hike in the mountains, you reach the top of a tall peak. Not very far from you, a mountain goat stands on a ledge that juts out over the valley. Wow, what a view! You see a valley far below. Beyond the valley, you see a mountain that's even taller than the one you just climbed. It has very steep sides. As you look, you begin to wonder . . . Why is that mountain higher than the one you're on? Why are its sides so steep? And where did that ledge come from?

Lesson 1

How does Earth's surface wear away?

Earth's surface is constantly changing. It is worn away by many things. These include water, ice, temperature changes, wind, chemicals, and living things. Sometimes these forces work quickly, and sometimes they take a long time.

Earth's Crust

The outer surface of Earth is a layer of rock called the crust. The crust covers all of the Earth. In places such as the oceans, the crust is under water.

A mountain is one of many different shapes of Earth's crust. Earth's surface also has many other natural features or **landforms.** Landforms are different sizes and shapes. Plains are flat landforms on low ground, and plateaus are flat landforms on high ground. Along coasts, landforms such as peninsulas extend into the water. Valleys and canyons are also landforms. What others can you name?

Some landforms take shape quickly, while others form over a long time. A mountain may take millions of years to form. But rocks rolling down the side of that mountain can change it in a hurry. Think of what happens to the large amounts of soil that a flood carries from one place to another. Or think about the dust you may have seen blowing across an unplanted area on a windy day.

1.   ✔**Checkpoint** List five examples of landforms.
2.   **Writing** in Science **Descriptive** In your science journal, write about landforms you have seen and how you think they might have been formed.

How Weathering Affects Landforms

Earth's landforms are constantly changing. Rocks in the Earth's crust are slowly being broken into smaller pieces in a process called **weathering.** Water, ice, temperature changes, chemicals, and living things cause weathering. There are two types of weathering, physical weathering and chemical weathering.

Physical Weathering

In physical weathering, only the size of rocks is changed. Large rocks are broken into smaller pieces of the same kind of rock. Water is one cause of physical weathering. Water flowing in rivers and streams and in ocean waves carries particles of rock, soil, and sand. The particles scrape against each other, and they gradually become smaller and smaller.

Ice is another cause of physical weathering. Water from rain or melting snow can seep into cracks in rocks. If this water freezes, it forms ice. Have you ever compared an ice cube in an ice tray to the water that it came from? What did you notice? Just like in the ice tray, ice in rock takes up more space than the water did. The ice forces the sides of the crack outward. The crack goes deeper into the rock. Each time this process repeats, the crack gets larger. Eventually, the rock can split.

Temperature changes to the rock's surface may also cause weathering. When the rock's surface gets hotter, it expands or grows larger. When it gets colder, the surface contracts or gets smaller. Some scientists think that many temperature changes can weaken the surface of rock.

Living things can cause weathering too. You have probably seen weeds growing in cracks in sidewalks. Plants also can sprout in a crack in a rock. As these plants and their roots get bigger, they can cause the rock to split.

Weathering weakened the rock of the Old Man of the Mountain in New Hampshire. In spite of efforts to save it, the rock fell to the bottom of the cliff in 2003.

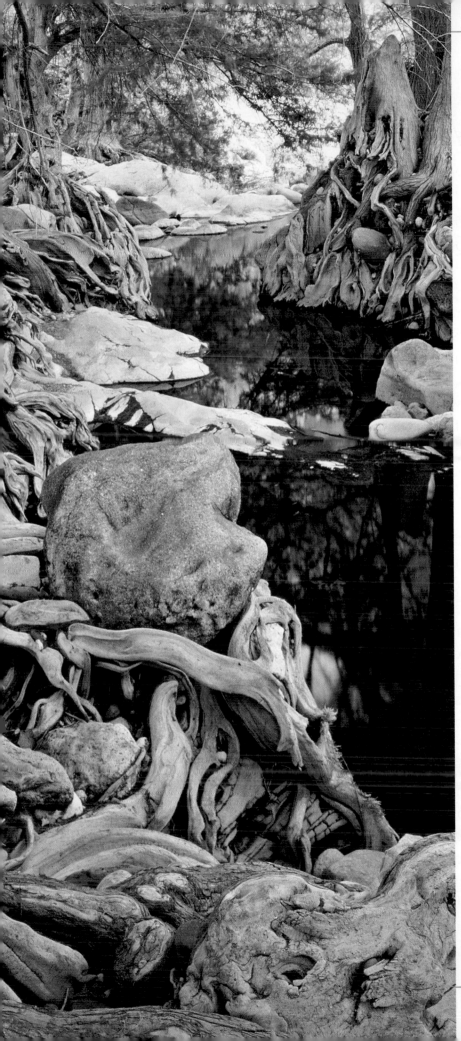

Chemical Weathering

In the second type of weathering, rock is again broken into smaller pieces. But, the material that makes up the rock or soil also changes.

In chemical weathering, chemicals cause rocks to form into different materials. The new materials can break into smaller pieces. For example, rainwater mixes with carbon dioxide in the air to form a weak acid. When it rains, the acid combines with the rock material to form a new chemical. Gradually the new chemical breaks down the rock.

Animals and plants give off chemicals that can cause weathering. Sometimes the activities of people add chemicals to the environment too.

Flowing water weathers rock and moves it to a new place.

✓ **Lesson Checkpoint**

1. List 4 causes of weathering.
2. Why do cracks in a rock get larger because water has frozen in them?
3. ⟳ **Compare and Contrast** How are physical weathering and chemical weathering alike? How are they different?

Lesson 2

How do weathered materials move?

Materials that are removed from rock by weathering can be carried to a new place, where they become part of another landform.

Effects of Erosion

Water, ice, gravity, and wind often work together to move weathered pieces of rock. This process is called **erosion.**

Moving water erodes, or carries away, materials from landforms. Falling rain picks up loose material from the surfaces of rocks. As the rainwater runs into streams, it takes loose, weathered material with it. The stream may carry that material a long way.

Water running downhill wears away rocks and soil. After many years, the grooves that the water carves in the land become canyons or valleys.

Waves constantly change the shape of the shoreline. They carry grains of sand away from a beach. They pound against cracks in rocks on the shore. Gradually pieces of rock break off. The waves carry the pieces away. As parts of the shoreline erode, new landforms, such as new beaches, develop.

In colder parts of Earth, moving ice erodes landforms. More than two million years ago, huge ice sheets called glaciers covered vast areas of Earth's surface. For thousands of years, these sheets crept back and forth. When Earth's climate cooled, they grew. During warmer times, as they began to melt, they would shrink. Glaciers still cover some of Earth's surface. For example, valley glaciers form in valleys of cold mountain regions where snow and ice pile up faster than they melt.

Most glaciers move very slowly. Ice melts into a thin layer of water at the bottom of the glacier. As the glacier slides along on this water, it wears away bits of rock and soil. Even small glaciers are so powerful that they can easily rip rocks apart and carry large chunks for long distances.

Deposition

Pieces of rock and soil are carried by wind or flowing water. The pieces that start at one place end up someplace else. As parts of Earth's surface are broken down, other parts are built up. **Deposition** is the laying down of pieces of Earth's surface. Sometimes deposition happens slowly, and at other times it happens very fast.

As moving water slows, the larger pebbles settle on the bottom first. Then smaller particles, like sand, sink. Finally, the smallest bits of soil, called silt, sink too. Rivers deposit large amounts of material where they flow into the ocean. The deposited material forms a fan-shaped area called a delta.

Wind can carry only small particles. Wind deposits silt that forms a layer on top of the soil. In deserts, wind deposits grains of sand in mounds called sand dunes. Without plants or something to keep the sand from blowing, wind will continue to shape the dunes.

1. ✓ **Checkpoint** Which particles are the first to settle as moving water slows?
2. **Art** in Science Draw a diagram that shows how particles travel in a river and become deposited near an ocean.

Gravity and Landslides

No part of Earth's surface is perfectly flat. The force of Earth's gravity pulls all objects from higher places down to lower places. It causes loose, weathered material to roll downhill. Bits of rock and soil may travel slowly downhill a little at a time. But sometimes they travel rapidly. Heavy rains or earthquakes may loosen material on a steep slope. Gravity then pulls the loosened material downward and into piles at the bottom. The rapid downhill movement of a large amount of rock and soil is a **landslide.** Buildings, cars, trees and other objects are sometimes carried along with the sliding soil.

Gravity and Avalanches

In colder areas, an avalanche is the name for large amounts of snow and ice that fall rapidly down a mountain. Strong winds, earthquakes, and explosions can trigger avalanches. One way people try to prevent avalanches is by clearing away snow before too much builds up. Landslides and avalanches can cause a great deal of damage, especially if they occur on large mountains.

Controlling Erosion and Deposition

Erosion and deposition are likely to happen when the land does not have trees or other plants. There is nothing to stop wind and water from eroding rocks and soil.

However, people can control erosion in various ways. People can grow plants on hills to slow erosion. The roots will hold the soil in place. The leaves will stop some raindrops from hitting the ground and washing away soil. Farmers can plow hilly fields in steps, called terraces. The rainwater forms puddles on the terrace instead of running down the hill and carrying the soil with it. Crops have more time to absorb the water.

Along the seashore, people can build barriers that stop large waves from carrying sand away from a beach. The barriers also help limit erosion of the land around the roads and buildings near the coast.

Sometimes people want to limit deposition. For example, they may dig deposited material out of waterways so ships can pass.

Terraces slow the speed of the water running downhill.

Without a barrier to stop them, oceans crash onto the shore. Over time, the waves will carry eroded material away.

✔ Lesson Checkpoint

1. List three things that cause both erosion and deposition.
2. How is a landslide different from other kinds of erosion and deposition?
3. **Compare and Contrast** erosion and deposition caused by running water with erosion and deposition caused by a glacier.

Lesson 3

How can Earth's surface change rapidly?

Volcanoes and earthquakes cause large, rapid changes to Earth's surface.

Volcanoes

A volcano is a landform that can bring about a rapid change to Earth's surface. Before a volcano forms, things happen deep underground. At 80 to 160 kilometers (50 to 100 miles) underground, very hot rock, called magma, is partially melted into liquid. Gas in the magma forces it upward. A **volcano** forms at a weak spot in Earth's crust where magma reaches the surface. Volcanoes are usually cone-shaped.

When the magma boils onto the surface, the volcano erupts. When magma flows out of the volcano, it is known as lava. Lava is still very hot, perhaps more than 1,100°C (2,000°F).

Sometimes, the pressure builds up so the gases in the magma explode. Hot rocks, gases, and ashes burst from the openings called vents. Not all volcanic eruptions are violent, though. The temperature and the kind of rock that makes up the magma determine the type of eruption. In some volcanoes, magma oozes upward and flows from the volcano. A bowl-shaped area, or crater, may form around the main opening.

Effects of Eruptions

Volcanic eruptions can produce incredible amounts of rock and ash. The rock and ash from the eruption of Mount St. Helens in 1980 could have formed a block about 1 km (3,300 ft) on each side! Ash flew more than 24 km (15 miles) into the air. The ash covered the surrounding areas, killing trees and wildlife. Nearby cities were also covered with a layer of ash.

Active and Dormant Volcanoes

An active volcano is one that has frequent eruptions or shows signs of future eruptions. For example, Kilauea in Hawaii began its most recent eruption in 1983. Since then, it has continued to erupt.

Before erupting in May 1980, Mount St. Helens was more than 2,950 m (9,600 ft) high.

A volcano that has not erupted for a long time is dormant. Mount Rainier in the Cascade Mountains in Washington has not had a major eruption in over 500 years. However, scientists consider it to be very dangerous. Several glaciers are near Mount Rainier. If magma inside Mount Rainier were to heat up enough to melt just some of these glaciers, floods and landslides could result.

A volcano is classified as extinct if no eruptions have been recorded. Mount Kenya in Africa is an extinct volcano. Scientists do not believe it will ever erupt again. There are extinct volcanoes all over the world.

On May 18, 1980, magma started to rise beneath Mount St. Helens. The pressure from this hot magma blasted the top off the volcano. Rocks, ash, and gases exploded into the air.

1. ✔**Checkpoint** What causes magma to rise to the surface beneath a volcano?

2. **Social Studies** in Science Look in library books or the Internet to find the locations of volcanoes in the United States. Name the states in which each is found and find their locations on a map.

After the eruption blew off the upper parts, Mount St. Helens was 400 m (1,314 ft) shorter.

Earth's Moving Plates

Earth's outer layer, or crust, rests on top of another layer called the upper mantle. These two layers, together, are divided into very large pieces called plates. The plates move all the time. Most volcanoes are along or near the places where plates come together.

The Cause of Earthquakes

A **fault** is a break or crack in rocks where Earth's crust can move. Sometimes rocks along a fault get stuck. The plates, however, continue their slow movement. They put pressure on the rocks. If the pressure gets strong enough, the rocks can break and the plates move suddenly. The sudden movement that causes the Earth's crust to shake is an **earthquake.** Like volcanoes, earthquakes often cause major, rapid changes to Earth's surface.

The focus is the place underground where the plates start to move and the earthquake begins. The point on Earth's surface that is directly above the focus is the **epicenter.**

Plate movement along a fault causes most earthquakes. But, some smaller earthquakes are caused by a strain to a weak area in the plate. As the plates slide along a fault, they give off a large amount of energy. This energy moves in the form of vibrations, or waves. Underground, the energy travels away from the focus in all directions. So, even though people farther away may feel the earthquake, the damage it causes is usually greatest near the epicenter.

Epicenter

Focus

Fires can result from earthquakes.

Tons of ash and rock can explode from volcanoes.

Effects of Earthquakes and Volcanoes

Earthquakes and volcanoes can affect many places on Earth's surface. In 1815, Mount Tambora in southeast Asia erupted. The ash from the volcano filled the sky. Less sunlight could reach Earth. Snow fell in the northeastern United States in June. In many parts of the world, 1816 was called the "year without a summer."

In 1991, Mount Pinatubo in the Philippines erupted, sending out huge amounts of ash. What effect do you think Mount Pinatubo's eruption had on the climate? The cloud of gases and ash from the eruption did indeed reduce the sunlight that reached Earth. Temperatures were cooler around the world.

In 1883, tsunamis, or huge ocean waves, traveled around the Earth following the eruption of Krakatau, a volcano in Indonesia. Earthquakes can also cause tsunamis. In 1998, an earthquake caused a great underwater landslide off the coast of New Guinea. The tsunamis that followed the landslide destroyed four villages.

Two plates meet in California along the San Andreas Fault. This fault runs from north to south through California. Many earthquakes happen in this area. Most of the earthquakes are small. You might feel a slight tremor or see the water in a fish bowl start to move. A few earthquakes are powerful enough to damage buildings, roads, and bridges.

In 1906 and 1989, strong earthquakes broke power lines in San Francisco. The broken power lines caused fires. The fire in 1906 burned for three days and destroyed 500 city blocks.

✓ Lesson Checkpoint

1. Why are some volcanic eruptions more powerful than others?
2. Explain how the actions around a fault can result in an earthquake.
3. **Writing in Science** **Narrative** Suppose that you are living in the northeastern United States in the summer of 1816. Write a diary entry that describes the strange summer.

Guided Inquiry

Investigate How does distance change earthquake effects?

Is there usually more damage near the epicenter of an earthquake or far away? **Make a model** to find out.

Materials

box

cup with popcorn

spoon and metric ruler

timer or stopwatch
(or clock with
second hand)

What to Do

1 Place the box upside down on the floor.

This activity works best on carpet or on a rug.

2 Place 1 spoonful of popcorn at each end of the box. Place 1 spoonful at the center of the box. Label the locations A, B, and C.

Label each location.

Process Skills

You used the **observations** you made and prior knowledge to **infer** why popcorn at one location moved more than the popcorn at the other locations.

Take It to the NET
More Activities www.sfsuccessnet.com

3 Tap as shown. **Observe** what happens to the popcorn at each location. Record your observations in a chart.

Hold this end of the box.

Lightly tap here for 30 seconds.

Location of Popcorn	Effects of Tapping on Popcorn
Location A (nearest epicenter)	
Location B	
Location C (farthest from the epicenter)	

Think About It

1. **Infer** Why do you think the popcorn at different locations moved different amounts?

2. How would knowing where earthquakes might occur help you decide where to put a building?

Go Further

Does how long an earthquake lasts change its effects? Make a plan to investigate this question or one of your own.

Math in Science

Comparing Sizes of Earthquakes

One way to estimate the strength of an earthquake has to do with the size of the vibrations, or waves, that go out from the focus. An earthquake scale is a way of comparing the size of these waves by giving the earthquake a number, usually between 0 and 10. This number, called the magnitude, depends on the size of the earthquake's waves.

STRONGEST EARTHQUAKES IN THE US, 1811-2002			
Earthquake	Location	Year	Magnitude
A	New Madrid, MO	1811	8.1
B	New Madrid, MO	1812	7.8
C	New Madrid, MO	1812	8.0
D	Fort Tejon, CA	1857	7.9
E	Ka'u District, Island of Hawaii	1868	7.9
F	Imperial Valley, CA	1892	7.8
G	Yakutat Bay, AK	1899	8.0
H	Near Cape Yakatoga, AK	1899	7.9
I	San Francisco, CA	1906	7.8
J	East of Shumagin Islands, AK	1938	8.2
K	Andreanof Islands, AK	1957	9.1
L	Prince William Sound, AK	1964	9.2
M	Rat Islands, AK	1965	8.7
N	Andreanof Islands, AK	1986	8.0
O	Gulf of Alaska, AK	1987	7.9
P	Gulf of Alaska, AK	1988	7.8
Q	Andreanof Islands, AK	1996	7.9
R	Denali Fault, AK	2002	7.9

Take It to the NET
Comparing Decimals www.sfsuccessnet.com

1. Copy the number line below. Mark and label points
   A through R to show the magnitude of each earthquake
   in the table. When two or more earthquakes have the
   same magnitude, write the letters above each other.
   The labeling for magnitude 7.8 has been done for you.

P
I
F
B

7.5   8.0   8.5   9.0   9.5   10.0

2. List the magnitudes from the table in order from least to
   greatest. Write each magnitude only once.

3. There were two big earthquakes in New Madrid, MO,
   in 1812. What was the magnitude of the stronger one?

4. What is the range of the magnitudes listed? (Remember,
   the range is the difference between the highest value
   and the lowest value.)

Lab zone Take-Home Activity

Refer to the table's dates telling when very
large earthquakes occurred in the United
States. Make a chart of the number of very
large earthquakes that happened during
each 10-year period. Begin with the period
1810–1819 and continue with 1820–1829
and so on, up to the present.

Chapter 9 Review and Test Prep

Use Vocabulary

deposition (p. 267)	**landform** (p. 263)
earthquake (p. 272)	**landslide** (p. 268)
epicenter (p. 272)	**volcano** (p. 270)
erosion (p. 266)	**weathering** (p. 264)
fault (p. 272)	

Use the vocabulary word from the list above that best completes each sentence.

1. During a(n) _____, underground rock suddenly shifts and the Earth's crust shakes.

2. Hot magma moves upward and erupts from a(n) _____.

3. The _____ is the place on Earth's surface directly above the focus of an earthquake.

4. Gravity causes the rapid downhill movement of rocks and particles known as a(n) _____.

5. An example of _____ is glaciers dragging rock and soil.

6. _____ occurs when acid in rainwater changes rock.

7. Sand dunes may result from _____ by wind.

8. A plateau is one kind of _____.

9. Many earthquakes are caused by plate movement along a(n) _____.

Explain Concepts

10. How does flowing water sort particles?

11. Why do trees or plants growing on a hill help control erosion?

Process Skills

12. **Classify** Name two ways that volcanoes are classified.

13. **Infer** Many volcanoes are located near the Pacific Ocean—on the east coast of Asia and on the west coasts of North and South America. What can you infer about Earth's crust in these areas?

Compare and Contrast

14. Make a graphic organizer like the one below. Show how erosion by moving water and erosion by glaciers are alike, and how they are different.

Different Different

Alike

Test Prep

Choose the letter that best completes the statement or answers the question.

15. One cause of physical weathering is
Ⓐ ice.
Ⓑ wind.
Ⓒ chemicals.
Ⓓ gravity.

16. Which of these is the result of deposition?
Ⓕ a delta
Ⓖ a valley
Ⓗ a river
Ⓘ a fault

17. Which statement is true?
Ⓐ Waves in the ocean cause erosion but not deposition.
Ⓑ Wind causes most landslides.
Ⓒ Thunderstorms can cause earthquakes.
Ⓓ Volcanic eruptions can affect the climate.

18. Weathering is
Ⓕ caused only by living things.
Ⓖ what scientists do to make weather forecasts.
Ⓗ something that happens gradually.
Ⓘ most often seen before earthquakes.

19. Explain why the answer you selected for #18 is best. For each of the answers you do not select, give a reason why it is not the best choice.

20. Writing in Science **Descriptive** Suppose that you are in Hawaii and you are watching Kilauea erupt. Write what caused the eruption and describe what you see and feel.

Oceanographer

Evan B. Forde is an oceanographer for the National Oceanic and Atmospheric Administration (NOAA).

Hot springs, or "black smokers," appear near volcanoes on the ocean floor. Black smokers shoot out water that is rich in chemicals. Very unusual forms of life live near black smokers. Some of these living things are not found anywhere else on Earth.

People who study black smokers and other physical features and life forms on the ocean floor are called oceanographers. Actually, oceanographers study many parts of the ocean, not just what's near the bottom. They are concerned with how the living and non-living parts of the ocean interact.

Perhaps you are interested in the tides. Or you may want to know more about the different rocks and minerals found in the sea. You may want to discover new kinds of fish, plants, or other organisms found in the ocean. If so, you can study any of these things by becoming an oceanographer.

Oceanographers also study how hurricanes form. They find ways to detect when hurricanes are just beginning to form so that they can predict where the hurricanes might hit. NASA satellites help them get more information about the ocean.

To prepare to be an oceanographer, learn all you can about life science and earth science.

Lab zone Take-Home Activity

Scientists need special equipment to explore the ocean floor. Use resources from the library and the Internet to learn about the special tools that oceanographers use. Write about what you find.

Chapter 10
Using Natural Resources

You Will Discover

- what natural resources are.
- which energy sources are renewable and which are nonrenewable.
- how we can conserve energy.

Online
Student Edition

www.sfsuccessnet.com

How can living things always have the natural resources they need?

solar energy

ore

282

petroleum

fossil fuels

Chapter 10 Vocabulary

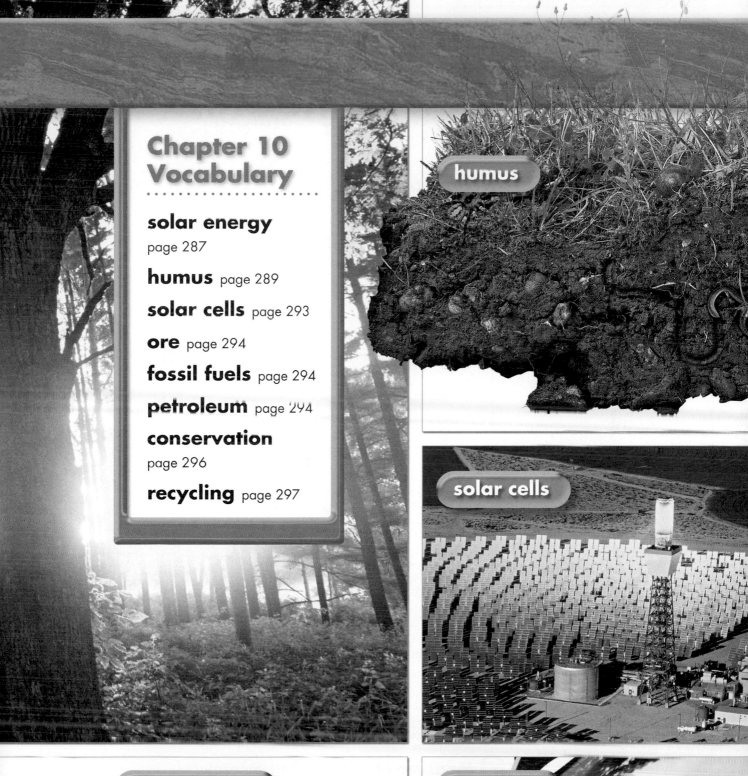

humus

solar cells

conservation

Conservation means using only what you need as efficiently as possible.

recycling

Explore How can you collect sunlight?

Materials

round-bottom bowl

aluminum foil

$\frac{1}{2}$ stick of clay

2 thermometers

tape

clock with secondhand
(or timer or stopwatch)

Process Skills

You made **inferences** based on your measurements.

What to Do

1 Line the bowl with foil. If needed, use loops of tape to hold the foil on the bowl.

2 Tilt the bowl so the sun shines into it. Use clay to hold the bowl in place

Use clay to prop up one thermometer.

Put one thermometer near the bowl.

Use clay under the bowl to hold it in place.

3 **Measure** and record the temperatures after 1 minute and after 3 minutes.

Think About It

1. Compare how the temperatures changed?
2. **Infer** Why were the temperatures different?

How to Read Science

Cause and Effect

A **cause** is a reason something happens. An **effect** is what happens.

- Sometimes writers use clue words and phrases such as *because, so, since, thus,* and *as a result* as signal words.

- A cause may have more than one effect. An effect may have more than one cause.

Read the following instructions in a handbook. Causes are highlighted in orange and effects are highlighted in blue.

Camper's Handbook

Reflective Ovens

Can you bake cookies using energy from the Sun? The answer is yes. A reflective oven can be used to collect the Sun's energy. You can make a simple reflective oven from cardboard and foil. The shiny side of the foil should face out, so that the sunlight will be reflected onto the cookies. The heat from the sunlight causes the cookies to bake. A reflective oven does not get as hot as a regular oven, so the cookies will take longer to bake. The cookies will still taste great!

Apply It!

Make a graphic organizer like the one shown. Fill in the causes and effects from the article above.

Cause	→	Effect

You Are There!

You're walking with your class in the forest. It's pretty dark in the shady areas. Sunlight strikes the trees, but it hardly reaches the ground. Sunlight is a resource that the forest—and all living things—depend on. But there are many other important resources here too. You're walking on one of them right now!

Lesson 1

What are natural resources?

Living and nonliving things support life on Earth. Soil is an important renewable resource. So is the solar energy that we capture and use.

How Resources Are Used

Are you wearing jeans? Are you holding a pencil? Do you have an apple in your lunch? Have you sipped some water today? You're using natural resources! We use natural resources to make products and to provide energy.

Natural resources are supplies that nature provides. Living things, such as fungi, plants, and animals, are natural resources. So are nonliving things such as water, soil, minerals, sunlight, and other sources of energy. Take a deep breath. You just used another natural resource—air.

All living things depend on natural resources. Plants need air, sunlight, soil, and water to live. People need air and water too. They use plant and animal resources for food. Earth's resources also provide the raw materials that we use to make the products we need. Everything we eat, use, or buy has been made from or is a natural resource.

Renewable Natural Resources

Earth has two types of natural resources, renewable and nonrenewable. Renewable resources can be replaced. **Solar energy,** which is energy the Sun gives off, is one renewable resource. Other renewable natural resources are water, oxygen in the air, trees in a forest, and soil in which food grows.

1. ✓**Checkpoint** What are three natural resources?
2. Writing in Science **Narrative** Write a journal entry that tells how you use natural resources in your daily activities.

Why Soil Is a Renewable Resource

A big clump of dirt is actually an important renewable resource—soil. Soil covers most of Earth's land surface. Many animals, such as chipmunks, rabbits, and woodchucks, make their homes in soil. Trees and other plants need soil to live, too. The plants and animals provide food for other animals, including people. Like water, soil is a nonliving natural resource that Earth renews.

How Soil Is Renewed

The processes of weathering, erosion, and deposition work together to form soil. Over time, loose rock that is at Earth's surface takes a beating. Water that drips into cracks in the rock freezes and thaws again and again. Ice pushing against the sides makes the cracks in the rock get larger. As the cracks get larger, the rock gets weaker. Eventually bits of the rock break apart. Wind containing rock and sand particles slowly scrubs away bits of loose rock.

Water breaks apart rock beneath Earth's surface too. Plant roots also force their way into rock and break it into smaller pieces. Over millions of years, this natural Earth process known as weathering wears down even the tallest mountains. Then, erosion deposits the weathered pieces in a new place.

Ingredients in Soil

Pieces of different kinds of weathered rock are a key ingredient in soil. Soil is full of other things, too, such as decaying plant and animal remains. The decomposing material called **humus** is a rich dark brown color. Air and minerals are nonliving ingredients in soil. But, as you can see in the picture above, soil is also full of life! Certain burrowing animals such as prairie dogs build elaborate towns underground. Tiny organisms such as bacteria, fungi, worms, and insects also make their homes in soil. They break down the plant and animal remains into nutrients that plants can use as food.

Different soils are made from different kinds of rocks and minerals. How much humus is in the soil also affects the way it feels. The minerals that are in the soil may affect its color. Soil samples that are taken just a few kilometers apart can look and feel very different!

1. ✓**Checkpoint** What are three key ingredients in soil?
2. **Social Studies** in Science In which region of the United States do you live? Find out about the types of soil that are often found in your region. Write about them in your science journal.

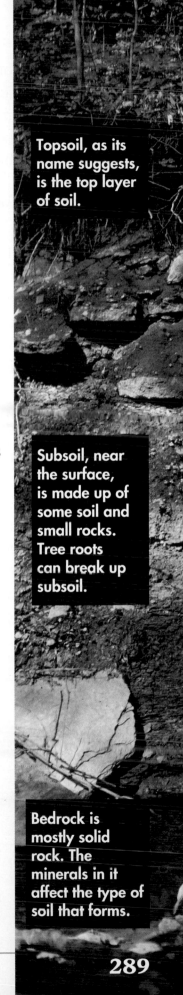

Topsoil, as its name suggests, is the top layer of soil.

Subsoil, near the surface, is made up of some soil and small rocks. Tree roots can break up subsoil.

Bedrock is mostly solid rock. The minerals in it affect the type of soil that forms.

Properties of Soil

Each type of soil has certain qualities. Topsoil contains rotting plant and animal materials. It also has particles of weathered rock. Remember that ice, water, and decomposing animals and plants cause rock to weather. As rock weathers, it breaks into particles of various sizes.

Clay

Clay, Silt, and Sand

Clay soil is made mostly of the very smallest particles. Clay may be different colors because of the materials in it. Clay with iron particles looks red, for example. Some clay feels sticky. Soil with slightly larger particles is called silt. Most particles in silty soil are slightly larger than those in clay. Silt particles feel smooth. Soil with still larger particles is called sand. Sandy soil contains particles from different materials. The most common mineral in sand is quartz. Sand also contains feldspar and other minerals. Broken shells are in sand that is near oceans. Like other soils, the color of sand depends upon the materials in it. Some sand is very light colored. Sand that forms from mostly volcanic rock can be black.

Silt

Sand

Look at the close-ups of clay, silt, and sand. What differences do you notice? How do you think each would feel if you touched it?

Soil for Growing Plants

Plants grow best in soil that has many nutrients. But, if the soil has too much sand or too much clay, plants are not able to soak up the nutrients. For example, water runs right through sandy soil, taking nutrients with it! Clay can hold lots of water, but it is so hard that plant roots can't spread very easily. Good soil for plants is the right mix of clay, silt, sand, and humus.

Soil as a Renewable Natural Resource

Soil is renewable. Good farming can replace its nutrients naturally. Farmers can plant certain crops that put nutrients back into the soil. Plants that are plowed under also add nutrients and organic material to the soil. But, the soil itself takes longer to replace. Only a few centimeters of the rich topsoil layer are renewed every 1,000 years. That's slow—especially since a few centimeters of topsoil can wear away in just ten years. Conserving soil is important to all of us. Many groups are working to reduce soil erosion to protect this natural resource.

Other Uses of Soil

When you think of soil, you may think of growing plants. You may think of the fertile silt in river sediment. But, soil can be used in other ways too. For example, clay is used to make tile, bricks, and pottery. When paper is being made, clay particles are sometimes added to make it strong and shiny. Sand is used as a raw material for making concrete, glass, and other things.

Bricks made from soil harden in the Sun.

Jars made of soil have been used for centuries.

✓ **Lesson Checkpoint**

1. Soil is a renewable resource. What keeps it from renewing easily?

2. **Cause and Effect** How do the amounts of sand, silt, and clay in soil affect plant growth?

291

Solar cells have generated electricity for NASA.

Lesson 2

How are resources used for energy?

Almost all of the energy we use is from the Sun. We also use the powerful forces of wind and moving water for energy. The Sun, wind, and moving water are sources of renewable energy.

Renewable Energy Sources

Green plants need sunlight for photosynthesis. The solar energy is transferred to animals through the food chain. Animals use chemical energy stored in plants they eat.

We use energy in many ways too. We use it to run machines, heat our homes, and help grow our food. Solar energy is a renewable energy source. Sometimes we use the Sun's energy without knowing it. How does sunlight streaming through windows change the temperature of a room?

Solar energy affects Earth's temperatures. Sunlight warms the Earth. Then the air that is closest to Earth's surface is heated when it touches the warm ground. The cycle of heating and cooling the air creates wind energy. Energy from the Sun powers the water cycle by causing water to evaporate.

Fields of solar panels absorb energy from the Sun and convert it into electricity.

How We Use Solar Energy

Is your calculator or watch solar powered? Inside your solar-powered device is a **solar cell** that changes energy from the Sun into electrical energy. Groups of solar cells form solar panels. Solar energy can be changed to electric energy to do many big jobs too. It is used to power satellites. On solar farms, fields of solar panels collect the Sun's energy. The solar energy can be changed into electric energy or into heat energy.

In a solar heat system, for example, the Sun's energy heats the water that flows through the solar panels. The heated water is stored in a tank until a pump forces it into the system of pipes. The piped water can then be used to heat homes and for activities, such as washing clothes. What are some other possible uses?

Wind Energy

Wind is a source of renewable energy. Wind energy has been used for thousands of years. Windmills can be used to run machinery, pump water, and produce electric power.

Energy from Flowing Water

Water flows from a high place to a lower place. Long ago, people built water wheels to use falling water to do work. They knew that moving water has energy. Today, people use the energy in flowing water to power the machines that produce electricity. In some places, dams are built to control the flow of water. Water is stored in a lake that forms behind the dam. The water is released when its energy is needed.

1. ✓ **Checkpoint** How do we capture and use solar energy?
2. **Writing** in Science **Persuasive** Suppose your school district is building a new school. List reasons the school should use solar power. Use your list to write a letter to your community to persuade them to share your view.

Millions of years ago, swamps covered the land.

Thick layers of dead plants were buried. Over years and years, the layers hardened into sedimentary rock.

Now, we remove the coal that formed.

Nonrenewable Energy Sources

Nonrenewable resources are supplies that exist in limited amounts or are used much faster than they can be replaced in nature. People use ores and other nonrenewable resources to make products and to provide energy. An **ore** is a mineral-rich rock that can be removed from the Earth. Nonrenewable mineral resources are commonly found in ores.

Fossil Fuels

Coal, natural gas, and oil are nonrenewable energy sources. They are fuels, which means that they are burned to produce useful heat. Coal, natural gas, and oil are called **fossil fuels** because they were made from organisms that lived long ago. Do you realize that all the energy stored in fossil fuels can be traced to the Sun? It's true!

Oil is the everyday name for **petroleum.** Fossil fuels like petroleum are the products of organisms that lived in the sea long ago. The bacteria, algae, and other organisms changed the energy in sunlight to produce energy for their lives. Their bodies stored whatever energy they didn't use. After they died, their remains and the unused stored energy settled on the seabed.

As more and more organisms settled, thick layers called sediments formed. Over millions of years, pressure from the weight of the upper layers squeezed the lower layers. The pressure, heat, and the decaying action of the bacteria gradually changed the energy-rich remains. The chemicals stored in the bodies of these tiny organisms became oil and other fossil fuels.

Impact of Fossil Fuels

Mining fossil fuels can harm the environment. Some of the richest oil deposits in the world are under the ocean floor. Getting to the oil can be risky.

The chance of an oil spill is one of the greatest dangers of drilling deep under the ocean. Oil spills cause pollution and other serious problems that kill marine organisms. Spills can also kill or harm plants and animals that live along coasts. Companies are working on ways to reduce the damage that might result from drilling and spills.

Using fossil fuels also has harmful effects. When fossil fuels burn, different substances are released into the air. Smoke and particles of ash, for example, make air unhealthy for living things to breathe. Increasing the amount of carbon dioxide gas in the atmosphere may lead to global warming. Sometimes gases break up in rainwater and create a weak acid. The acid falls to Earth in rain. This rain can damage buildings and harm plant and animal life on land and in water.

Offshore oil rigs tap into petroleum deposits that are deep beneath the ocean floor.

1. ✓ **Checkpoint** How are Earth's resources reduced?
2. 🔄 **Cause and Effect** What are some possibly harmful results from using fossil fuels?

How Resources Can Last Longer

For many years, the world has used nonrenewable resources to meet most of its energy needs. As people need more and more energy, fossil fuels will be used up faster and faster. Fuel costs will rapidly increase.

Fresh water, air, soil, and trees are resources that help all living things. But like Earth's nonrenewable resources, they will be reduced if we use them wastefully or destroy them on purpose or by accident. Restoring soil, forests, or fishing areas can be very difficult and costly! Cleaning up polluted air, water, and soil is expensive.

We can conserve energy to help our fossil fuels last longer. But, we should also try to use solar energy, wind power, water power, and other renewable energy sources.

Old tires can be used in construction, for fences, and for crash cushions. They can be used to make equipment for sports and playgrounds.

Methods of Energy Conservation

Conservation means using only what you need as efficiently as possible. You can reduce energy use in many ways. For example, to travel a short distance, you can walk or ride a bike. For longer distances, you can share rides with others. Turn off lights that you don't need, and do not leave water taps running. Use only what you need, and then shut them off!

Energy-efficient cars and appliances use less energy to do the same amount of work. Less energy is used to heat or cool buildings with good insulation. Conserving energy will help our supply of fossil fuels last longer.

Is your notepad made of recycled paper? Used paper can be recycled into new paper!

The rubber in old tires can be ground up into small pieces called crumb rubber. The crumb rubber is added to the mixture that is used to pave roads and airport runways.

Instead of sand, ground glass can be used in concrete.

Recycling

Recycling is saving, collecting, or using materials again instead of treating them as waste. Glass, cardboard, newspaper, paper, aluminum, tin, steel, and some plastics can be recycled. You may have noticed a symbol marked on plastic objects that can be recycled. The recycling symbol looks like three arrows chasing each other around a triangle. A number inside the triangle tells what materials were used to make the kind of plastic in the object.

Many products that are made from natural resources should be recycled! Many cans are made from aluminum, which is made from an ore. Paper comes from wood. Plastics come from petroleum. And glass is made from sand. By recycling, we can reuse raw materials. Some products and materials are easier to recycle than others.

More than half of the aluminum cans sold are recycled.

Some plastics are melted, shredded, formed, and recycled into T-shirts, quilted jackets, and sleeping bags!

✓ Lesson Checkpoint

1. How can we conserve energy?
2. **Writing** in Science **Persuasive** Create a poster to persuade students in your grade to conserve energy.

Investigate How can you observe a "fossil fuel" being formed?

Natural gas, a type of fossil fuel, can form when some materials decay.

Materials

2 liter plastic bottle with meat (prepared by teacher)

4 lettuce leaves

funnel, graduated cylinder, water

sand

small balloon, string, tape

What to Do

① Tear 4 lettuce leaves into small pieces. Add them to the bottle with meat. Pour 40 mL of sand over them. Do not shake the bottle.

Use the funnel when measuring the sand, when adding the sand, and when adding the water.

② Pour 20 mL of water into the bottle so it runs down the side in the bottle.

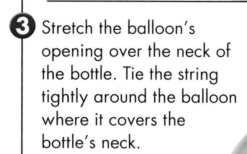

③ Stretch the balloon's opening over the neck of the bottle. Tie the string tightly around the balloon where it covers the bottle's neck.

④ Put tape over the string and around the edge of the balloon to seal it to the bottle.

tape

5 Put the bottle in a warm place for 5 days. Each day observe the balloon and the contents of the bottle. Try to detect *any* change. Record what you observe. You have made a **model** of the process of decay.

Natural gas should be produced very slowly. The balloon will not expand, but after 5 days enough natural gas may have been produced to cause the balloon to stand straight up.

Day	Balloon	Contents of Bottle
Day 1		
Day 2		
Day 3		
Day 4		
Day 5		

Think About It

1. Did the balloon and the contents of the bottle change? How?
2. **Infer** What made the balloon change?

Go Further

What would happen to the formation of natural gas if you changed the conditions, such as the temperature or the presence of water? Make a plan to find out.

Math in Science

Water Use

Water is a renewable natural resource. But, did you know just how renewable it is? Nearly every single drop of water we use trickles back to a lake, sea, or ocean. The Sun's heat causes it to evaporate and then return to Earth in the form of rain, snow, sleet, or hail. This cycle goes on and on—so water is never used up! But that doesn't mean it's OK for us to use it carelessly.

The circle graph shows how much water an average American family of four uses each day in three different rooms. The average household uses about 1,150 liters of water per day.

Daily Water Use

Laundry: 140 L

Kitchen: 125 L

Bathroom: 885 L

1 In which room is the greatest amount of water used?
   A. Kitchen
   B. Dining Room
   C. Laundry
   D. Bathroom

2 How much water does the average American household use each week?
   F. 8,050 liters
   G. 770 liters
   H. 157 liters
   I. 77 liters

3 In a family of four, about how much water does each person use per day?
   A. 4,600 liters
   B. 2,870 liters
   C. 287 liters
   D. 28.7 liters

4 How much more water is used in the bathroom each day than in the kitchen and laundry combined?
   F. 885 liters
   G. 620 liters
   H. 265 liters
   I. 125 liters

Lab zone Take-Home Activity

For one day, estimate the amount of water you use in the bathroom at home. Use a timer and the table below to help you. If your family has information about the water usage of your sink, shower, and toilet, use those figures instead of those in the table.

Fixture	Average Water Used
Sink	11 liters per minute
Shower	8 liters per minute
Toilet Flushing	12 liters per flush

Use Vocabulary

conservation (p. 296)	**recycling** (p. 297)
fossil fuels (p. 294)	**solar cells** (p. 293)
humus (p. 289)	**solar energy** (p. 287)
ore (p. 294)	
petroleum (p. 294)	

Use the term from the list above that best completes each sentence.

1. To use only what you need as efficiently as possible is _____.

2. To save, collect, or use materials again instead of treating them as waste is _____.

3. The energy given off by the Sun is _____.

4. A nonrenewable energy source also known as oil is _____.

5. Fuels made from the remains of living things that died millions of years ago are _____.

6. The dark brown part of soil made up of rotting plants and animals is _____.

7. A mineral-rich rock deposit that can be removed from the Earth is _____.

8. _____ convert the Sun's energy into electricity.

Explain Concepts

9. The Sun is the major source of energy on Earth. Explain how all living things capture and use the Sun's energy.

10. Explain why our need for fossil fuels can harm the environment.

Process Skills

11. Conserve with your class! Figure out how many sheets of paper you dispose of in one week. Then try to reduce, reuse, or recycle. Collect data over a three-week period. Compare the before-and-after figures in a diagram, chart, graph, or drawing.

12. The Environmental Protection Agency estimates that 1 billion juice boxes are thrown away each year. Using what you've learned, develop a plan to reduce that number. Investigate a possible solution that your class could use.

Cause and Effect

13. When we misuse our natural resources, we can affect all living things. Copy the graphic organizer below. Complete it by adding four causes. The effect is filled in for you.

Cause	→	Effect
		Harmful things happen to plants, animals, and people.

Test Prep

Choose the letter that best completes the statement.

14. A nonrenewable natural resource is
Ⓐ coal.
Ⓑ soil.
Ⓒ oxygen.
Ⓓ trees.

15. Subsoil is mostly made up of
Ⓕ solar energy.
Ⓖ petroleum.
Ⓗ small rocks.
Ⓘ solid rock.

16. The smallest particles of sediments are found in
Ⓐ humus.
Ⓑ silt.
Ⓒ sand.
Ⓓ clay.

17. All of the energy that is stored in fossil fuels can be traced to
Ⓕ the Sun.
Ⓖ humus.
Ⓗ swamps.
Ⓘ offshore drilling.

18. Coal that has formed over millions of years can be traced back to organisms living in
Ⓐ silt, sand, and clay.
Ⓑ eroded soil.
Ⓒ swamps.
Ⓓ strip mines.

19. Explain why your answer for Question #14 is the best choice. For each answer you did not select, give a reason why it is not the best choice.

20. **Writing in Science Descriptive**
Suppose you have invented a machine that runs on energy sources from the Sun, wind, or moving water. Write a paragraph that describes what your invention does. Don't forget to tell what it looks like and how it uses renewable energy.

Auto Engineer

Would you like to build a car that uses renewable energy? You could become part of a team that designs a solar-powered car. Each year, the United States Department of Energy sponsors the American Solar Challenge (ASC). The ASC is a solar car competition. Students from colleges and universities in the United States and Canada design solar-powered cars and race them across the country.

The students work in teams. The teams put their cars through vigorous tests and inspections to be sure they are safe. Then the race is on!

The solar cars are flashy, but they have some problems. They only seat one or two people. There's not much space to carry things, and, as you may have guessed, they only run during the day! Even so, solar cars help us learn more about solar energy and how it can be used.

Most of the students who build the cars are mainly studying science, math, and engineering. Many will become mechanical engineers and design other kinds of cars or find other ways to use solar energy. They study in colleges or universities for four or more years to get a degree in engineering.

Lab zone Take-Home Activity

Hybrid vehicles can use two or more different kinds of power. Use the Internet or other sources to learn about vehicles that use both solar power and another source of energy.

Unit B Test Talk

Choose the Right Answer

To answer a multiple choice test question, you need to choose an answer from several choices. Read the passage and then answer the questions.

Although precipitation falls all over Earth, most of it falls into the oceans. Rain is the most common form of precipitation. Sometimes raindrops pass through a layer of cold air as they fall from a cloud to the ground. If the temperature of the air is colder than 0°C, the raindrops freeze into small pieces of ice, called sleet. If the pieces are larger than 5 mm across, the little balls of ice are called hailstones.

As a hailstone begins its trip toward the ground, strong winds may carry it back up into colder air. When it starts to fall again, the winds may carry it up a second time. Each time the hailstone moves back into a colder region of the cloud, another layer of ice is added to it. This cycle may repeat many times before the hailstone becomes so heavy that it falls to the ground. If you cut a hailstone in half, you can see rings of ice. Each ring represents an up-and-down trip through the cloud.

Like snow and sleet, hail is the result of moisture that freezes. But most hailstorms occur in summer! Hail is formed in the same type of clouds that produce thunderstorms, and thunderstorms usually happen in warm weather.

Use What You Know

In order to choose the right answer, you might first eliminate answer choices that you are sure are incorrect. As you read each question, decide which answer choice you can eliminate.

1. In which month is a hailstorm most likely to occur?
   Ⓐ December
   Ⓑ February
   Ⓒ June
   Ⓓ November

2. When a hailstone is cut in half, you see
   Ⓐ rings of ice.
   Ⓑ a snowflake.
   Ⓒ a small pebble.
   Ⓓ a raindrop.

3. Hail and snow are similar because
   Ⓐ both are common in cold weather.
   Ⓑ both happen in hot climates.
   Ⓒ both form when moisture freezes.
   Ⓓ both form in temperatures above 0°C.

4. Most precipitation falls in the form of
   Ⓐ hailstones.
   Ⓑ rain.
   Ⓒ sleet.
   Ⓓ snow.

Unit B Wrap Up

Chapter 6

How does the water cycle affect Earth's weather?

- The water cycle changes salty ocean water into the fresh water we need for our daily activities.
- Weather depends on the way air masses move and interact.
- Scientists use many measurements to predict the weather.

Chapter 7

How do violent storms affect both living and nonliving things on Earth?

- A hurricane is formed by bands of strong thunderstorms swirling around an area of calm.
- Tornadoes are violent, swirling winds that can appear with little warning.

Chapter 8

What do rocks tell us about how the Earth was formed and how it continues to change?

- Rocks are classified by how they formed.
- Fossils in rock are clues to Earth's past.

Chapter 9

What changes Earth's surface?

- Erosion and deposition of weathered rock change landforms over long periods of time.
- Volcanoes, earthquakes, and other natural forces change Earth's surface quickly.

Chapter 10

How can living things always have the resources they need?

- Natural resources are both living and nonliving.
- Some natural resources are renewable and some are not.
- Some sources of energy are renewable and some are not.

306

Performance Assessment

Wind Vane

Make a wind vane. Make sure that whatever materials you use are sturdy enough to last in the wind. You want to make especially sure that that the pointer turns but does not bend. Take your wind vane outside. Use it to determine the direction of the wind. Describe how you made the wind vane and how it showed the direction of the wind.

Read More About Earth Science

Look for books like these in the library.

Full Inquiry

Experiment What affects how rain erodes soil?

Moving water can change the land.
It can carry soil from one place to another.

Materials

gloves and masking tape

3 containers and soil

small paper cup and 3 books

small paper clip and foam cup

water and graduated cylinder (or measuring cup)

metric ruler

Process Skills

Scientists sometimes make **estimates** when exact **measurements** are not needed.

Ask a question.

How does the way water falls on soil change the amount of soil the water moves?

State a hypothesis.

You will conduct 2 experiments. You will make and test 2 hypotheses. Scientists sometimes conduct 2 experiments together. Why do you think they do so?

If more water falls on soil, then will more, less, or about the same amount of soil be eroded? Write your **hypothesis**.

If water falls on soil faster, then will more, less, or about the same amount of soil be eroded? Write your hypothesis.

Identify and control variables.

In these **experiments**, the variable you observe is the amount of soil the water moves. Other conditions, such as the slope of the soil, the amount of soil, and the type of soil, must stay the same. Water is the **variable** you will change. In one test you use more water (container B). In a second test you let the water fall faster (container C). You compare both to the control (container A).

Take it to the NET
More Activities www.sfsuccessnet.com

Test your hypothesis.

1 Empty 1 small paper cup of soil into one end of each container. Put a book under each container to raise the end with the soil.

Be careful!

Wear gloves.

Label the containers A, B, and C.

2 **Measure** 50 mL of water with a graduated cylinder. Unbend the end of a small paper clip. Use the tip to poke 2 small holes in the bottom of a foam cup. Hold the cup 6 cm above the soil in container A. Pour the water into the cup with holes. Let it drip onto the soil.

3 Let 100 mL of water drip from the cup onto the soil in container B.

4 Use the paper clip to make the holes in the cup 3 times as wide. Let 50 mL of water pour from the cup onto the soil in container C.

6 cm

A

5 **Observe** the soil in each container. How has it changed? Record your **observations** in the chart. **Estimate** the fraction of the soil that was moved, or eroded.

Take it to the NET
More Activities www.sfsuccessnet.com

Collect and record your data.

Container	Amount of Water Added (mL)	Amount of Erosion Observed (Estimate the fraction of the soil that moved.)
Container A (control)		
Container B (more water)		
Container C (faster water)		

Interpret your data.

Analyze your data. Make circle graphs to show your data. Explain your data to another group. Compare your data with the data from other groups.

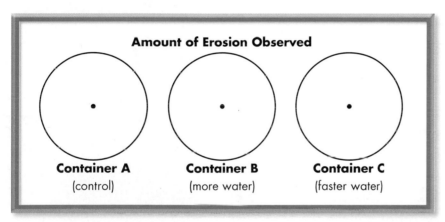

Amount of Erosion Observed

Container A (control)   Container B (more water)   Container C (faster water)

For each circle graph, find the fraction of soil that was eroded. Then shade in that fraction of circle.

State your conclusion.

Remember that you conducted 2 experiments. Think about your first hypothesis. What conclusion can you draw from your chart? Does it agree with your hypothesis? **Communicate** your conclusion. Repeat for your second hypothesis.

Go Further

You observed how soil was eroded. Would your results change if you tested sand, mud, or rocks instead? How would changing the slope of the soil affect your results? Design and carry out a plan to investigate these or other questions you may have.

Science Fair Project

Using Scientific Methods

1. Ask a question.
2. Make a hypothesis.
3. Plan a fair test.
4. Do your test.
5. Record what happens.
6. Tell your conclusions.
7. Inquire further.

The Answer Is Blowing in the Wind

Idea: Design and conduct an experiment to see if wind conditions affect the rate of evaporation from a body of water. Be sure to have adult supervision if you use an electric fan when you complete your experiment. Write a summary to explain the results of your experiment.

Acid Rain

Idea: Test what effect acid ran has on buildings and statues. Place a piece of chalk in a cup of water. Place an identical piece of chalk in a cup of vinegar. (Vinegar is an acid.) After 24 hours, compare the pieces of chalk. Infer what effect acid rain has on materials such limestone and marble that are similar to chalk.

Please Pass the Salt Water

Idea: Use the Internet or other sources to research ways to remove the salt from sea water. Use your research to design a way to make fresh water from salt water by either evaporation and condensation or by freezing.

The Last Straw

Idea: Model how ice can weather rock. Freeze a drinking straw that you've filled with water. The next day, remove it from the freezer. Write a summary to explain what happened and why.

EC NTL 10 9 8 7 6 5 4 3 2 1

Unit C
Physical Science in Indiana

Did you know that Indiana is called the "Crossroads of America"? With its central location and key role in farming and manufacturing, Indiana depends on highways and railroads to transport goods.

North St

Physical Science in Indiana

What do asphalt, steel mills, electric power plants, and canoes have in common? They all provide opportunities to learn about physical science in Indiana. You will learn more about the science behind them in Unit C.

Asphalt

Many interstate highways intersect in Indiana, giving the state its claim as the "Crossroads of America." Some Indiana roads are paved with asphalt. To make asphalt, petroleum is boiled until the asphalt separates out. Refining finishes the process. You will learn more about states of matter in Chapter 11.

Steel Town

The steel mills at Gary helped give the city its name. Elbert H. Gary was president of the U.S. Steel Works, and the city was named after him. Steel mills use heat to change iron ore and other materials into steel. You will learn more about how matter changes in Chapter 12.

Power Plants

Indiana's power plants generate electricity that is used in many different ways. Coal-fired power plants generate most of Indiana's electric power. Power plants cause charged particles to flow, producing electric current. You will learn more about electric charges in Chapter 13.

Indiana's Energy Consumption by Section, 1999

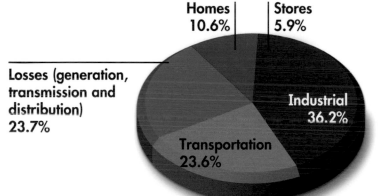

Homes 10.6%

Stores 5.9%

Losses (generation, transmission and distribution) 23.7%

Transportation 23.6%

Industrial 36.2%

Hoosier Canoe Club

Members of the Hoosier Canoe Club know that canoes with smooth sides move easily through water. Canoes can be sanded or painted to prevent friction, or resistance to motion. You will learn more about friction and motion in Chapter 14.

ISTEP+ Prep

Answer the questions below. Write your answers on a separate sheet of paper.

Multiple-Choice Questions

1. What process produces asphalt?
   A friction
   B boiling and refining petroleum
   C convection
   D electricity

2. Which section consumed the greatest percentage of Indiana's energy?
   A residential
   D commercial
   C industrial
   D transportation

Constructed-Response Questions

3. How do steel mills use heat?

4. How do power plants create electric current?

5. What is friction?

Field Trip
Hoosier Valley Railroad Museum

You can visit the Hoosier Valley Railroad Museum in North Judson to learn about steam engines. A steam engine has a furnace in which coal, oil, wood, or another fuel is burned to produce heat energy. The heat from the burning fuel changes water into steam. The steam expands. This energy of expansion pushes the steam engine's pistons back and forth. The steam engine can then do work.

Find out more:

Research to find out more about steam engines.

• Make a timeline showing machines that used steam engines, and the year in which each was invented.

EC IN 10 9 8 7 6 5 4 3 2 1

Chapter 11
Properties of Matter

You Will Discover

- what makes up matter.
- that all matter has mass, weight, volume, and density.
- how the properties of substances change.
- ways that substances combine to form new substances.

Online Student Edition

www.sfsuccessnet.com

How can matter be compared, measured, and combined?

physical change

density

mixture

Chapter 11 Vocabulary

chemical change

solvent

solution

solubility

solute

315

Explore What properties cause liquids to form layers?

Materials

corn syrup

dishwashing liquid

water (with red food coloring)

corn oil

cup

small paper clip
piece of Styrofoam®
piece of rubber band

What to Do

1 Pour in each liquid in the order they are listed in the materials section.

2 **Observe** that the liquids form layers.

3 Gently drop in a small paper clip. Watch until it stops sinking. Next, drop in a piece of Styrofoam.® Wait until it stops. Then drop in a piece of rubber band.

Because of their different properties, you can stack these liquids.

Think About It

1. **Infer** Which liquid has the highest density? the lowest density? How do you know?

2. Which object has the highest density? the lowest density? How do you know?

Compare and Contrast

Comparing and contrasting information will help you understand some kinds of writing. We compare when we say how things are alike and contrast when we say how they are different.

- Writers use words to signal likenesses and differences. The most common clue word for likenesses is *like*.
- Clue words such as *yet, but,* and *however* signal differences.

In the lab report below, the student made observations that compare and contrast the water and ice in the activity.

Lab Report

Day	Action	Observations
1	We put water in the freezer.	Water was liquid.
2	The water was frozen into ice. We put the ice into a glass of water.	The ice floated on the water.

Ice is the same substance as water. But, the temperature of ice is lower. That's why it's a solid instead of a liquid. So we were surprised that the ice floated on the water. Later, the ice was beginning to melt. It was smaller than before but still floated on the water.

Apply It!

In the graphic organizer, write two ways ice and water are alike and two ways they are different.

Alike	Different

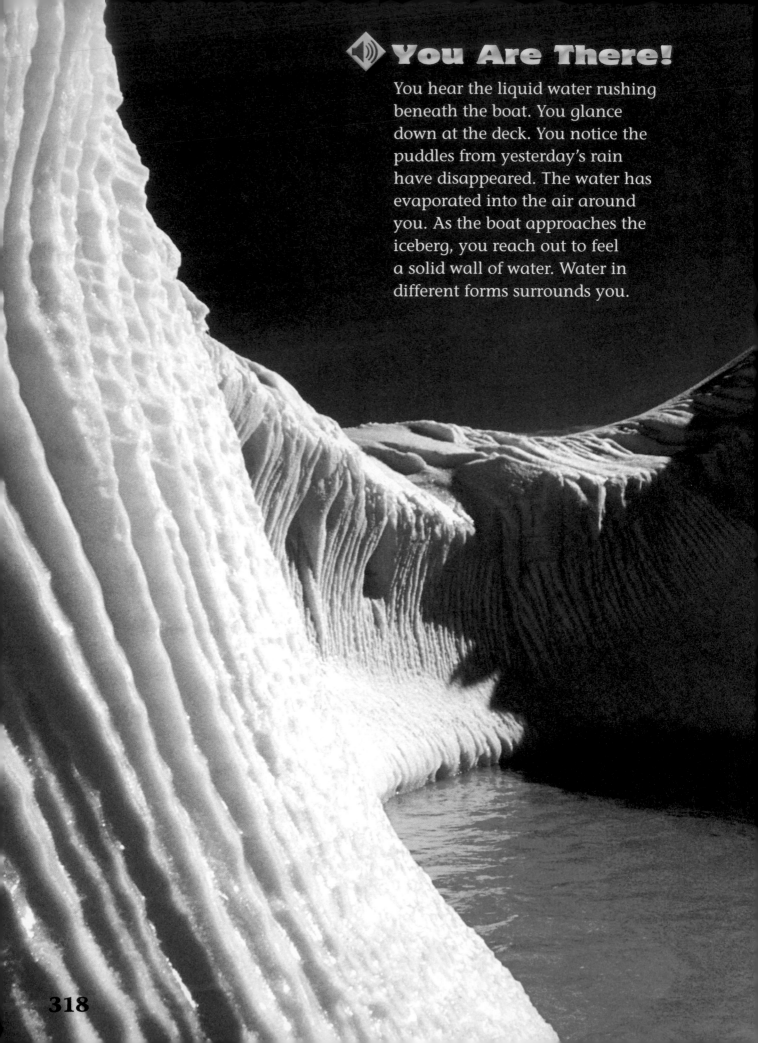

You hear the liquid water rushing beneath the boat. You glance down at the deck. You notice the puddles from yesterday's rain have disappeared. The water has evaporated into the air around you. As the boat approaches the iceberg, you reach out to feel a solid wall of water. Water in different forms surrounds you.

Lesson 1

What is matter?

All forms of matter are made up of tiny particles that are too small to see. The way these particles are arranged and move determines whether the matter is a solid, liquid, or gas.

Properties of Matter

Like ice, water, and air, you are made of matter. All living and nonliving things are made of matter. Matter is anything that has mass and takes up space. Scientists use different ways to identify matter. One way is by its properties. You can identify many properties of matter by using your senses. For example, you can look at the color, size, and shape of some matter. You can touch matter to decide if its texture is rough or smooth, soft or hard. You can recognize some matter by its smell and taste.

Testing Matter

Simple tests can show other properties of matter. You can see how matter reacts if you heat or cool it, for example. You can see if matter is affected by a magnet or if it allows electricity to pass through it. You can hit matter with a hammer to see if it is shattered or not even dented. You can see how flexible it is. Does it break or does it simply bend wherever you move it? You can observe what happens when you place matter into water. Does it float or does it sink to the bottom? You can try to mix it with other matter. Does some matter disappear? Or does something new seem to take its place?

1. **✓Checkpoint** Group five different objects in your classroom by properties. Describe the properties.
2. **Art** in Science Collect pictures or small objects that show different textures of matter. Make a collage with the pictures or objects you collect.

States of Matter

Using different instruments, scientists have learned that all matter is made up of tiny particles. These particles are arranged in different ways. These particles also move. The arrangement and movement of the particles in matter determine its form, or state. The three most familiar states of matter are solid, liquid, and gas.

Usually substances on Earth exist naturally in just one state. Can you name the only substance that you can find naturally in all three states? If you said water, you are right. You can find water naturally in all three forms. Liquid water is the same substance as a solid that we call ice and a gas called water vapor.

You can't see the particles in a solid. This drawing shows how the tightly packed particles are arranged.

You can't see the particles in a liquid either. The particles are close to each other, but they are not held tightly together.

The particles in a gas are far apart. Even if you could see them, you would not see the particles arranged in any special way.

Solids

At temperatures of 0°C or below, the shape of an ice cube is the same whether it is on a plate or in a container. A solid is matter that has a definite shape and usually takes up a definite amount of space. Its particles are closely packed together. The particles have some energy. They move back and forth, but they do not change places with each other.

Liquids

Water takes the shape of any container into which you pour it. If you pour the water in the container onto a table, its shape changes, but the amount of water stays the same. Matter that does not have a definite shape, but takes up a definite amount of space, is a liquid. In a liquid, the particles are not held together as tightly as in a solid. The particles of a liquid are able to slide past one another.

Gases

In the gas state, water is called water vapor. It is invisible. Water vapor and several other gases make up the air that is all around us. Like a liquid, a gas takes the shape of its container. Unlike a liquid, a gas expands to fill whatever space is available. A gas always fills the container it is in. The particles in a gas are very far apart from one another and move in all directions. Particles in a gas move around more easily and quickly than those in a solid.

✓ Lesson Checkpoint

1. Name the solid and gas forms of water.
2. Draw a diagram to show the arrangement and movement of particles for one state of matter.
3. 🌀 **Compare and Contrast** the movement of particles in solids, liquids, and gases.

How is matter measured?

You can use metric rulers, balances, and graduated cylinders to measure some properties of matter.

Mass

Did you know that your weight on Earth is about six times as much as your weight on the Moon? That's because your weight depends upon the force of gravity. Your weight on another planet might be much greater than your weight on Earth, but your mass is the same. While your weight on the Moon might be less than your weight on Earth, your mass is the same wherever you go.

Scientists use mass because they want a measurement that will not change if the object is moved to a different location. Mass is the measure of the amount of matter in an object. The mass of an object does not change unless matter is added to or removed from it.

Using a Pan Balance

You can use a pan balance to compare a mass that you know with one that you do not know. When the pans are level, the two masses are equal.

Suppose you found the mass of the toy in the picture and then took it apart. Next you measured the mass of each part separately and added them together. What do think the total would be? The total mass of all the parts is the same as the mass of the assembled toy. The pan balance shows that the toy has a mass of 23 grams.

The pan balance shows that the mass of the toy, 23 grams, is equal to the total mass of its parts.

23 grams

Suppose someone who did not see the toy takes all of the parts and makes a toy that looks very different from the one you see. What do you think is the mass of this new toy? That's right, 23 grams. The only way to change the toy's mass is to add parts or not use all of them. This is because the only way to change the total mass of an object is to either add matter or take it away.

Metric Units of Mass

Scientists use metric units when they measure and compare matter. The gram is the standard unit of mass in the metric system. Some of the metric units that are used to measure mass are milligram (mg), gram (g), and kilogram (kg).

Like our place-value system, the metric system is based on tens. Prefixes change the standard unit to larger or smaller units. For example, 1 gram is equal to 1,000 milligrams, and 1,000 grams is equal to 1 kilogram. The mass of a grape is about 1 gram and the mass of a cantaloupe is about 1 kilogram.

The mass of a large paper clip is about 1 g.

The mass of a nickel is about 5 g.

23 grams

The mass of this carton of milk is about 1,000 g, or 1 kg.

1. ✓ **Checkpoint** Explain why your mass is the same wherever you go.
2. **Math in Science** The mass of a nickel is about 5 g. About how many nickels are needed for a mass of 1 kg? Remember, 1 kg = 1,000 g.

323

Volume

Take a deep breath. As your lungs fill with air, you can feel your chest expand. This change in your lung size is an increase in volume. Volume is the amount of space that matter takes up.

Like mass, volume is a property of matter that can be measured. One way to measure the volume of a solid like a box, is to count the number of unit cubes that fill it. Another way to find the volume is to use a metric ruler to measure the length, width, and height of the box. Then, multiply the measurements. If a box measures 5 cm long, 2 cm wide, and 8 cm high, then the volume of the box is 5 cm $\times$ 2 cm $\times$ 8 cm, or 80 cubic centimeters.

Scientists often use metric units when they measure and compare the volume of a solid. The table below shows how the units of length in the metric system are related. Some metric units that are often used to measure volume are cubic centimeters (cm^3) and cubic meters (m^3).

Comparing Metric Units of Length

Metric Unit	Equivalent
1 millimeter	0.001 meter
1 centimeter	10 millimeters
1 decimeter	10 centimeters
1 meter	100 centimeters or 1,000 millimeters
1 decameter	10 meters
1 hectometer	100 meters
1 kilometer	1,000 meters

The water level in this graduated cylinder rose from 50 mL to 55 mL when the ball was added. The volume of the ball is 55 mL − 50 mL = 5 mL or 5 cm³.

Volume of Liquids

Liquids do not have a definite shape. To measure a liquid, you use a measuring container, such as a graduated cylinder.

A graduated cylinder is marked with metric units. Some metric units used to measure volume are milliliter (mL) and liter (L). Each liter is equal to 1,000 milliliters. The units marked on this graduated cylinder are milliliters (mL).

Volume of Other Objects

A graduated cylinder can be used to find the volume of solids that sink in water. To measure the volume of a ball, for example, put some water into a graduated cylinder. Record its height. Then place the ball into the cylinder and record the height of the water again. The ball has pushed away some of the water. The water level has risen the same number of milliliters as the volume of the ball. A volume of 1 mL is the same as 1 cm³.

Examples of Metric Lengths

What Was Measured	Measurement
Thickness of a CD	1 mm
Length of a paper clip	32 mm
Thickness of a CD case	1 cm or 10 mm
Height of a doorknob from the floor	1 meter
Length of a school bus	12 meters
Length of 40 blue whales placed end to end	11 km or 11,000 m
Distance from the North Pole to the equator	10,000 km

1. ✓ **Checkpoint** What metric units are used to measure the volume of solids? of liquids?
2. **Math in Science** Express 2 L in milliliters.

Density

Sometimes you need to know how much mass is in a certain volume of matter. Suppose a friend asked you, "Which has more mass, a piece of wood or a piece of steel?" Your first response might be, "How big is each piece?" In order to compare the masses of two objects, you need to use an equal volume of each. The amount of mass in a certain volume of matter is a property called **density.** For example, if the pieces of wood and steel are the same size, the piece of steel has more mass and a greater density than the wood.

Finding Density

You find the density of a substance by dividing its mass by its volume. The units often used for the density of solids are grams per cubic centimeter. You write density as a fraction $\frac{\text{mass in grams}}{\text{volume in cubic centimeters}}$. The density of water is 1 because 1 gram of water has a volume of 1 cubic centimeter.

An object's density determines whether it floats or sinks in a liquid. You can see in the picture at the right that liquids can float on top of other liquids. For example, water floats on top of corn syrup because its density is less than the density of the corn syrup.

cooking oil

water

syrup

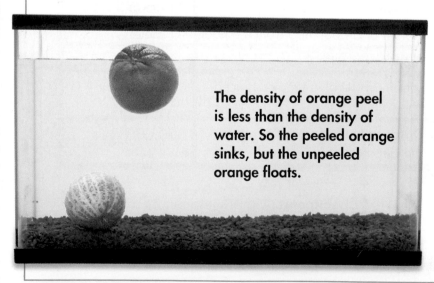

The density of orange peel is less than the density of water. So the peeled orange sinks, but the unpeeled orange floats.

Comparing Densities

The substances with the greatest densities are near the bottom of the cylinder. The substances with the least densities are near the top.

You can also compare the densities of the objects that are floating. The density of the grape is less than the density of the syrup but greater than the density of water. The density of the block is greater than that of the cooking oil but less than the density of the water. The cork has the least density of the liquids and the other objects in the picture.

An ice cube floats in water because the density of ice is less than the density of water. But it's just a little less! So, most of a floating ice cube is below the surface.

✓ Lesson Checkpoint

1. Explain why steel sinks in water and cork floats.
2. An unpeeled orange floats in water, but a peeled orange sinks. What can you conclude about the density of an unpeeled orange?
3. **Technology** in Science Scientists use submersibles (submarines) to explore oceans. Use library books or the Internet to find out more about how submarines sink or float.

Life Jacket

Life jackets or life preservers are much smaller than you are. But they help you stay floating in water. They are filled with foam or other materials that have densities less than water. A life jacket pushes some of the water out of the way just like the ball in a graduated cylinder. You can keep your head above the surface of the water.

Lesson 3

How do substances mix?

Mixtures are made by physically combining two or more substances. The solids, liquids, or gases in a mixture are not chemically combined. They can be easily separated.

Mixtures

You may have eaten a snack made from a mixture of nuts, dried apricots, and raisins. Each ingredient in this mixture keeps its own taste and shape.

A **mixture** is a combination of two or more substances. Substances in a mixture can be separated. This means that they are not chemically combined. Peas, carrots, and corn can be combined in a mixture. In fact, you can buy a bag of frozen mixed vegetables at the store. Each vegetable can be sorted into separate piles. The peas, carrots, and corn taste the same whether they are separated or mixed together. All substances in a mixture that are separated out have the same properties as before they were mixed.

Some mixtures, like salt and water, can be separated by evaporation. After the water evaporated, salt was left behind.

Some substances can mix physically with other substances. The makeup of a mixture can vary. A mixture does not necessarily contain a specific amount of each substance. They are not joined together chemically, so each substance in the mixture keeps its own properties. You can easily see the properties of each substance that makes up the bead, sand, safety pins, and salt mixture shown here.

You can easily separate the ingredients in many mixtures. Since safety pins are attracted to a magnet, you can use a magnet to separate them from the rest of the mixture. Then, you can put the rest of the mixture in water. You can use a spoon to skim off the floating beads. If you pour the water through a filter, you can remove the sand and the glass beads. Then, after the water evaporates, the salt will be left.

You separated the substances of this mixture, but you did not change the properties of any of the individual substances.

1. ✓Checkpoint When the bead, sand, and salt mixture is put into water, the yellow beads float. What does this tell you about the density of a yellow bead?

2. Writing in Science **Expository** In your science journal, write a numbered set of instructions for separating a mixture of paper clips, wood chips, gravel, and sugar.

329

Solutions

If you stir salt and water together, you make a mixture. You cannot see the salt in this mixture because it has broken into very small particles. It has dissolved in the water. The salt and water is a special kind of mixture called a solution.

In a **solution,** one or more substances are dissolved in another substance. The most common kind of solution is a solid dissolved in a liquid, such as salt in water. In this kind of solution, the substance that is dissolved is the **solute.** In a solution of salt and water, the salt is the solute. A **solvent** is the substance that takes in, or dissolves the other substance. Usually the solvent is present in the greater amount. In salt water, the solvent is water.

The salt is dissolved in this solution.

Common Solutions

In the oceans, salt and other minerals are dissolved in water. Ocean water is a solution. But a solution does not have to be a liquid. The air you breathe, for example, is a solution made up of gases. The steel used for buildings and cars is a solution. During the process of making steel, carbon and iron, two solids, are melted into liquid form. Then the carbon is dissolved in the iron.

Salt dissolves in water.

salt

Club soda is a solution made up of a gas dissolved in a liquid. The solubility of the gas decreases as the temperature of the solvent increases. That is why a club soda "goes flat" faster when it gets warm. As the water becomes warmer, more gas leaves the solution.

Instant cocoa dissolves quicker in a cup of hot water than in a cup of cold water.

Sand does not dissolve in water.

sand

Solubility

No matter what you do, you cannot make sand dissolve in water. The ability of one substance to dissolve in another is called its **solubility.** Solubility is a measure of the amount of a substance that will dissolve in another substance. Since sand does not dissolve in water, the solubility of sand in water is zero.

Sometimes you can speed up the process of dissolving the solute by raising the temperature of the solvent. This is true for most solutes that are solids. For example, you can dissolve more sugar in warm water than you can in cold water.

Another way to make a solute dissolve quicker is to crush it. If you drop a sugar cube into a cup of water it will dissolve, but it may take a while. If you crush the sugar cube into tiny crystals, the crystals will dissolve very quickly. The reason for this is that more of the sugar is touching the water when it is in tiny crystals than when it is in a sugar cube.

✓Lesson Checkpoint

1. What are the parts of a solution?
2. What factors affect the solubility of a substance?
3. Social Studies in Science During the Gold Rush, many people panned for gold. Panning separates gold from a mixture of gold and sand. Use books or the Internet to find out about the California Gold Rush.

A knitter uses a ball of yarn.

The yarn is knitted into a long strip.

The knitted strip can unravel into the same amount of yarn as the original ball.

How does matter change?

Matter undergoes physical and chemical changes. In a physical change, the size, shape, or state of the substance changes. A change that forms a new substance with new properties is a chemical change.

Physical Changes

If you cut and fold a piece of paper to make an origami sculpture, you change only the size and shape of the paper. You have not changed the particles that make up the paper.

A change in the size, shape, or state of matter is an example of a **physical change.** A physical change does not change the particles that make up matter. The arrangement of the particles, however, may be moved around during a physical change.

Are you causing a physical change when you mix salt and water? A solution of salt and water can be compared to a mixture of nuts and raisins. You can separate the nuts and raisins by hand. If you make a mixture of salt and water, the particles are too small for you to separate by hand. However, if you allow the water to evaporate, the salt will be left behind. Because the particles in a mixture do not change and can be separated, making a mixture is an example of a physical change.

Breaking a pencil is a physical change. The pieces of the pencil are still made of wood and graphite. If you sharpen the broken ends you can keep using the pencil.

Another physical change is tearing. If you tear a sheet of paper into tiny pieces, it still is made of the same kind of matter.

Have you ever made a bowl out of clay? You start with a big blob of clay and form it into the shape of a bowl. The bowl is made of clay and has most of the same properties. But it is a different shape. It has changed physically.

An origami sculpture begins with a plain square of paper.

The paper is folded many times.

The sculpture is finished.

If you unfold the sculpture, you will have the same piece of paper you started with.

1. **Checkpoint** Sawing wood, shredding paper, and crushing a sugar cube are physical changes. Give examples of three other actions that are physical changes.

2. **Math** in Science A chunk of cheese has a mass of 450 g. Suppose you grate this entire chunk. What do you expect the mass of the grated cheese will be?

Phase Changes

Suppose you freeze water into an ice cube and then let it melt. The liquid that results is still water. Ice and liquid water are the same substance in different states. These states are called phases.

What causes the particles of a substance to be in one phase rather than another? The answer has to do with energy. Energy can cause the particles in a substance to move faster and farther apart. Substances change phase when enough heat energy is added or taken away. For example, you put liquid water into a freezer to remove heat and make ice. You add energy to water when you heat it. If you boil water in a pot, some of the water becomes water vapor. Phase changes are examples of physical changes that can be reversed by adding or removing energy. Every substance changes phases at a different temperature.

Effects of Temperature on Matter

250°C
Some wood burns.

184°C
Paper starts burning.

100°C
Water boils.
Water vapor condenses.

0°C
Water freezes into ice. Ice melts into water.

328°C
Lead melts.

1535°C
Iron melts.

The melting point is a physical property that helps to identify a substance. The temperature at which a substance melts is the same temperature at which it freezes.

This is also true when a substance evaporates, or changes from a liquid to a gas. The boiling point is the temperature at which a substance changes from a liquid to a gas. The temperature at which the substance evaporates is the same temperature at which it condenses. Condensation is the changing of a gas into a liquid.

1.   ✔**Checkpoint** How does adding or taking away heat energy cause changes in matter?

2.   **Writing in Science** **Descriptive** Suppose you are a drop of water. Describe what happens to you when heat energy is added or taken away.

Energy and Water

These phase changes are examples of physical changes. Whether water is solid, liquid, or gas, it is still water.

In a solid, the particles are attracted to each other. They are close together and do not move very much.

Adding heat increases the energy of the particles. The particles move faster and farther apart. Solid ice changes phase by melting into a liquid.

Boiling water adds even more heat energy. The particles move even faster and farther apart. Liquid water changes phase to the gas water vapor.

Chemical Changes

If you leave an iron nail in a damp place, it will rust. Suppose you compare the rust with the iron nail. You will find that the nail and the rust have different properties. The color and hardness of rust and iron are different. Rust is a different substance that results from a chemical change in the iron nail. Unlike a physical change, a **chemical change** produces a completely different kind of matter. In a chemical change, particles of one substance are changed in some way to form particles of a new substance with different properties.

You can see evidence of a chemical change, like the bubbles in the picture. Or, the new substance may be a different color. It may have a different smell or temperature. Many chemical changes give off heat. In each case, the chemical properties of the materials that were mixed have changed.

The acid in vinegar reacts with baking soda and forms bubbles of carbon dioxide. The bubbling and fizzing show that a chemical change is occurring.

Rust forms slowly as oxygen from the air combines with the iron in the gear.

Tarnish, like rust, results from a chemical change when certain metals, such as silver, react with air.

Burning wood reacts very quickly with oxygen in the air. The new substances formed by this change are ashes, carbon dioxide gas, and water vapor.

Elements

In a pure substance, particles are alike. The simplest pure substances are called elements. There are more than 100 known elements. Scientists have organized information about these elements in a chart called the Periodic Table. Each element is in a particular row and column in the table. The position in the Periodic Table gives information about the make up and properties of each element. Each element has its own symbol. The letter or letters in the symbol are sometimes from the element's name in Latin.

The Periodic Table

Phase at room temperature
- Gas
- Liquid
- Solid
- Not found in nature

✓ **Lesson Checkpoint**

1. What is a chemical change?
2. When you chew food, are you causing physical or chemical changes to the food?
3. **Compare and Contrast** How are rusting and burning different? How are they alike?

337

Investigate How can you change the properties of glue?

Mixing glue with another substance can change its properties. The properties of the new substance are different from the properties of the original substances.

Materials

safety goggles

small measuring cup

glue and food coloring

cup and spoon

water

borax solution

Process Skills

After you make, **observations**, you can **collect** your **data** in a chart.

What to Do

1 Measure 30 mL of glue into a small measuring cup. Pour it into a larger cup. For fun, add food coloring.

Be careful!

Wear safety goggles.

2 Add 15 mL of water to the cup. Stir the glue. **Observe** its properties.

3 Add 15 mL of borax solution. Stir.

4 Observe what happens.

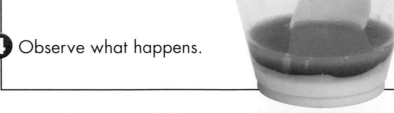

Could you do this with glue?

5 Play with the new mixture. **Investigate** its properties.

6 Record the **data** you **collect** about the properties of the glue and of the new substance.

Property	Observations	
	Glue	**New Substance**
Color		
Texture		
State of Matter (solid, liquid, gas)		
Odor		

Think About It

1. How are the physical properties of the new substance and the glue alike? What differences did you **observe**?

2. Would the new substance be a good glue? Explain.

Go Further

If you used a different amount of borax solution, would the substance have the same properties? Develop a plan for a safe, simple investigation to answer this question or one of your own. With teacher permission, carry out the plan you designed.

Math in Science

Comparing Densities

The table lists some common liquids and their densities. Each density is rounded to the nearest tenth.

	Substance	Density ($\frac{grams}{cubic\ centimeters}$)
A	Corn Syrup	1.4
B	Cooking Oil	0.9
C	Ethyl Alcohol	0.8
D	Gasoline	0.7
E	Water	1.0

Density is written as a decimal number. You can use a number line to compare and order decimals. On a number line, the values increase as you move to the right and decrease as you move to the left. For example, on the number line below, 0.7 is less than 0.9, so 0.7 is to the left of 0.9.

Take It to the NET
Ordering Decimals www.sfsuccessnet.com

Use the table and number line on page 340 to answer the following questions.

1. Which point on the number line represents the density of cooking oil?
   A. Point E
   B. Point B
   C. Point C
   D. Point D

2. Where on the number line would you plot the point for the density of corn syrup?
   F. to the left of Point D
   G. to the left of Point E
   H. at Point E
   I. to the right of Point E

3. How many liquids in the table have a greater density than gasoline has?
   A. 1
   B. 2
   C. 3
   D. 4

4. Suppose you poured liquids A–E into a graduated cylinder. Which is the correct order of liquid layers from **bottom** to **top**?
   F. D, B, C, E, A
   G. D, C, B, A, E
   H. A, D, C, B, E
   I. A, E, B, C, D

Lab zone Take-Home Activity

An object with a density that is less than 1.0 $\frac{grams}{cubic\ centimeters}$ floats in water. List ten items from your home. Predict whether each item will float or sink. Record your predictions. Then, test each item. Indicate which items have a density that is less than 1.0 $\frac{grams}{cubic\ centimeters}$.

Chapter 11 Review and Test Prep

Use Vocabulary

chemical change (p. 336)	**solubility** (p. 331)
density (p. 326)	**solute** (p. 330)
mixture (p. 328)	**solution** (p. 330)
physical change (p. 332)	**solvent** (p. 330)

Use the vocabulary term from the list above that completes each sentence.

1. _____ is the ability of one substance to dissolve in another substance.

2. The property that compares the mass of an object to its volume is _____.

3. In a solution, the _____ is the substance that takes in, or dissolves the other substance.

4. A change in size, shape, or state of matter is a _____.

5. The substance in a solution that is dissolved is called the _____.

6. The quarters, dimes, nickels, and pennies in a coin purse are a _____.

7. New substances with different properties are formed by a _____.

8. In a _____, substances are dissolved in other substances.

Explain Concepts

9. What does it mean to say that a liquid has a definite volume but no definite shape?

10. Suppose you have 50 mL of water in a graduated cylinder. After you place a marble in the cylinder, the water level rises to 78 mL. What is the volume of the marble? Explain how you know.

Process Skills

11. **Infer** A balloon filled with helium gas rises in the air. What might you infer about the density of helium compared to the density of air?

12. **Classify** Tell whether each of the following involves a physical change or a chemical change.
    - frying an egg
    - breaking a balloon
    - boiling water
    - making toast

13. Observe Suppose you put a substance in a glass of water and stir the mixture. Then you observe that all of the substance settles to the bottom of the glass. From your observation, what might you conclude about the solubility of the substance?

Compare and Contrast

14. Explain how physical and chemical changes are different. How are they alike? Use a graphic organizer like the one shown.

Alike	Different

Test Prep

Choose the letter that best completes the statement or answers the question.

15. Matter is anything that has mass and
Ⓐ is living.
Ⓑ takes up space.
Ⓒ is not broken.
Ⓓ holds water or air.

16. When most liquids are cooled to the freezing point, the tiny particles of matter that make up the liquid
Ⓕ move quickly in all directions.
Ⓖ move out into the air.
Ⓗ come closer together.
Ⓘ move farther apart.

17. A chemical change results in a
Ⓐ loss of matter or energy.
Ⓑ solution.
Ⓒ phase change.
Ⓓ different kind of matter.

18. You make a solution when you mix
Ⓕ salt and water.
Ⓖ sugar and cinnamon.
Ⓗ vegetables in a salad.
Ⓘ macaroni and cheese sauce.

19. Explain why the answer you chose for Question #16 is best. For each of the answers you did not choose, give a reason why it is not the best choice.

20. Writing in Science **Expository** Since ice is less dense than liquid water, it floats. Explain what you think would happen to the plants and animals living in a Minnesota pond if ice were more dense than liquid water.

343

Analytical Chemist

Dionne Broxton Jackson is an analytical chemist at NASA. She works with metals.

What if your pencil bent every time you tried to write with it? What if your pillow were made of metal? All of the properties of matter are important in how it is used. Matter can be hard or soft, rough or smooth. It can be sticky, stretchy, spongy, or slick. Some chemists who work for NASA make matter that can be used on space vehicles.

Metals used for space shuttles must not be damaged by a lot of heat. Some metals are better than others at handling heat. Chemists can also mix metals to make a material that can stand more heat than either metal could on its own. The Kennedy Space Center is close to the ocean. There is so much salty water nearby that metals often rust. The metals NASA uses cannot rust easily.

Plastics are also important materials used in space. They may need to be hard and slick, or soft and rubbery. Chemists can make plastics that have many different properties.

Analytical chemists need to understand math and science well. They must graduate from a college or university. They can work in many different places.

Lab zone Take-Home Activity

Gather different materials in your home, such as kitchen utensils, toothbrushes, and food containers. Make a list of which products you think might be useful in space.

EC NTL 10 9 8 7 6 5 4 3 2 1

You Will Discover

○ the difference between heat and temperature.

○ three ways heat is transferred.

Chapter 12

Heat

www.sfsuccessnet.com

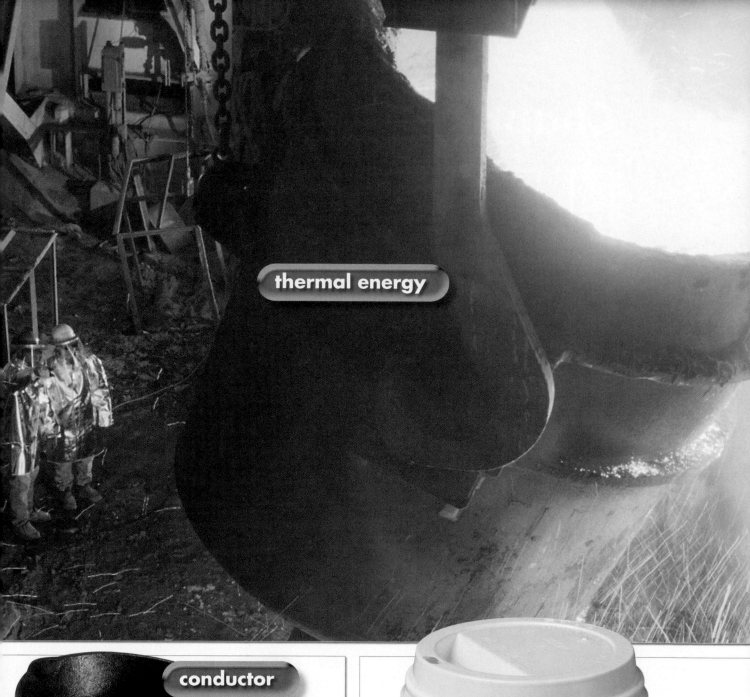

How does heat energy move from one object to another?

thermal energy

conductor

insulator

346

Chapter 12 Vocabulary

conduction

convection current

radiation

347

Explore How can you make things warmer?

Materials

safety goggles

paper clip

eraser

sheet of paper

clock with a second hand
(or timer or stopwatch)

What to Do

1 Touch a paper clip. **Observe**. Does it feel warm?

Be careful!

The paper clip could break.

2 Bend one end back and forth 4 times quickly. Quickly touch the bent part. Observe.

3 Touch an eraser. Rub it on paper for 1 minute. Quickly touch the surface you rubbed on the paper. Observe.

4 Rub your hands together for 15 seconds. Observe.

Process Skills

You can use what you learn by **observation** to help you make accurate **inferences**.

Think About It

1. How did bending change the paper clip?
2. What happened when the eraser rubbed against the paper? What happened when you rubbed one hand against the other?
3. What can you **infer** about what happens when one object rubs against another?

Take It to the NET
More Activities www.sfsuccessnet.com

How to Read Science

Cause and Effect

- Writers may use clues such as *because, so, since, thus,* and *as a result* to signal cause and effect.

- A cause may have more than one effect. An effect may have more than one cause. An effect may cause something else to happen.

Think about what you know about hot-air balloons and heat transfer as you read the interview with a balloonist. Cause and effect are highlighted.

Magazine Interview

Extreme Sports for Kids!

Extreme Sports for Kids: I understand that you enjoy riding in hot-air balloons. Just what causes a hot-air balloon to rise?

Balloonist: It all results from heat transfer. A balloon is like a huge plastic bag. To inflate the bag, I fill it with air. Then I heat that air with a burner. A flame reaches into the plastic bag.

ESK: Then does heat transfer take place?

Balloonist: Yes, the air inside the bag gets warm and less dense than the air around it. The cool air sinks under the warmer air. As a result, the balloon goes up!

ESK: I know that air expands when it gets heated because particles are moving really fast and really far apart!

Balloonist: You're right! Let's take a ride!

Apply It!

Make a graphic organizer like the one shown to explain why a hot-air balloon rises.

Cause		Effect
A cause is why something happens.	→	An effect is what happens.

🔊 You Are There!

The red-hot steel flows into an iron mold. Even though you are wearing a heat-fighting suit, you can sense the scorching air! You work in one of the world's most important industries. You are a steelworker. At your mill, iron ores from rocks and minerals are crushed and then heated in giant furnaces. They become liquid steel. Your job is to cast that molten steel into 2-ton blocks called ingots. The steel that you pour sets into an ingot. The ingot is placed in a huge heated pit where it reaches 1200°C (2,200°F). No wonder your job fires you up!

Lesson 1

Why does matter have energy?

Energy is the ability to cause change or do work. Heat is the total energy of moving particles in matter. The more particles something has, the more internal energy it contains.

Energy in Matter

Rub your hands together. What happens? You just used energy to make heat! Energy is the ability to change something or do work. Cool hands changed to warm ones. Whenever the place, look, or makeup of something changes, energy is used. All changes need energy!

All matter is made up of tiny particles that are always moving. In a solid, particles are closely packed. They move slightly around fixed positions. In a liquid, they are close together. They flow freely past one another. In a gas, particles are very far apart. They move in all directions. Particles in an object move because they have energy.

As an object becomes hotter, its particles move faster. As the object cools, the particles move more slowly. **Thermal energy** is energy due to moving particles that make up matter. We feel the flow of thermal energy as heat.

The colors in this thermogram or heat picture show the different amounts of heat energy.

1. ✓**Checkpoint** What is energy?
2. **Writing in Science** **Descriptive** You are sitting in a sunny place wearing a short-sleeved shirt and shorts. Write a paragraph that describes the changes to you and to the piece of chocolate on a table next to you.

351

Measuring Moving Particles

Have you ever seen a thermometer, like the one below? You measure temperature with it. Most thermometers are thin glass tubes that are joined to a bulb that holds colored alcohol. The number lines marked on the outside of the tube show degrees. One number line is scaled in degrees Celsius. The other is scaled in degrees Fahrenheit. A thermometer is based on the idea that matter expands when its particles move faster and contracts when they slow down.

If a thermometer touches matter with particles that are speeding up, particles in the liquid inside the thermometer speed up too. They move farther apart and the liquid expands. It moves up the tube. The reading on the number line shows a greater number of degrees. If the particles slow down, the liquid contracts. The shorter column in the tube marks a lesser number of degrees.

The thermometer must be on or in whatever it's measuring. If it's not touching the material, it might not measure particle motion correctly.

More particles in the larger pot mean more thermal energy.

How a Thermometer Works

This thin glass tube has a bulb filled with colored alcohol. The bulb is placed on or in the material being measured. Depending on the material's temperature, liquid travels up or down the tube. The thermometer in the photo is measuring the temperature of the air. The number lines on the outside of the tube show degrees Celsius on the right and degrees Fahrenheit on the left.

Heat and Temperature

If you wonder how hot or cold something is, you might think about its temperature. When a material has a high temperature, its particles move fast. But temperature is not a measure of how much heat the material has.

Many of us mix up the meanings of heat and temperature. The difference is in the movement of particles of matter. Temperature is the measure of the average amount of motion of particles in matter. It measures the average energy. Thermal energy measures the total energy of those moving particles. It measures both how fast the particles move and how many are moving. Heat is the transfer of thermal energy from one piece of matter to another.

For example, think of a large pot and a small pot that are each half filled with boiling water. Because the large pot holds more water, it has many more water particles than the small pot has. More particles mean more energy of motion. The large pot has more thermal energy. Since the water in each pot is boiling, the temperature of the water in both pots is the same. The average amount of motion of particles in the water is also the same. So, the size of the pot does not affect temperature!

√ Lesson Checkpoint

1. Explain why a large pot of water takes longer to begin boiling than a small pot. Both pots started with the same temperature of water, and burners for both pots are set on "high."

2. **Cause and Effect** What causes liquid in a thermometer to travel up and down the tube?

Lesson 2

How does heat move?

Heat is the transfer of thermal energy. Heat can be moved in several ways. The transfer of heat energy affects climate.

Conduction

Thermal energy flows from something warm to something cool. The transfer of thermal energy between matter with different temperatures is heat. A heat source is anything that gives off energy that particles of matter can take in. Remember when you rubbed your hands together earlier? You used mechanical energy to make heat. When solids are touching, heat energy moves by conduction. **Conduction** is the transfer of heat energy by one thing touching another.

Suppose that you place the lower part of a metal spoon in boiling water. What happens to the cool spoon? That's right, it gets hot! The spoon's particles that touch the water start to move. As they move more quickly, they crash into the particles in the spoon's handle. More and more crashes take place. Soon, heat energy from the water moves throughout the spoon. The transfer continues until both the water and the spoon are the same temperature. How do we know that the heat energy has moved? The hot spoon handle and the melting strip of wax are proof! The wooden spoon does not conduct heat energy. The handle stays cool, and the strip of wax on it doesn't melt.

Heat energy from the boiling water moves through the metal spoon. The heat causes the piece of wax to begin melting.

Conductors and Insulators

Metal Some materials let heat move through them more easily than others do. A material that readily allows heat to move is a **conductor**—like the metal spoon. Many metals, such as aluminum, copper, and iron, conduct heat well. If you place an iron pan on a burner or other heat source, it gets hot quickly.

Wood You also know that some things—like the wooden spoon—do not get too warm even when they touch something hot. They are insulators. An **insulator** is a material that limits the amount of heat that passes through it. Have you noticed that many pots and pans have wooden handles? That's because wood is a great insulator. The wooden paddle does not conduct heat to the hands of the person taking the pizza or bread from a hot oven. Heat moves around the paddle.

Marble Since ancient times, marble has been used in buildings and monuments because it is strong and beautiful. It resists fires and erosion. Marble is also an insulator. A slab of marble is helpful in the kitchen. Its cool, smooth surface is a perfect place to mix tasty treats.

Plastic Do you know why so many hot foods are served in foam containers? The plastic foam that is used to make the containers has many small air pockets. The plastic is not the only insulator. Air is a good insulator, too. So with plastic and air insulators, the foods stay warm, and your hands stay cool!

Japanese Macaque monkeys share body heat to keep warm in the snow.

1. ✓**Checkpoint** What is the difference between an insulator and a conductor?
2. **Social Studies in Science** Use reference sources such as nonfiction books, encyclopedias, and the Internet to find other materials that are used as insulators. Explain where the material is used and how it works as an insulator.

Convection

If you don't like the heat, get out of the kitchen! Have you felt how warm a kitchen gets when a stove is on? It's convection working! In convection, a fluid moves from place to place. A fluid is a substance that flows but has no definite shape. Air and water are fluids.

A pattern of flowing heat energy is a **convection current.** A convection current forms when heated fluid, such as air, expands. It becomes less dense than an equal volume of the cooler air around it. The cooler air sinks below the warmer air. The warm air is forced upward, and the pattern continues. The cool air warms and is forced upward by colder air.

Look at the two mobiles in the photo below. Can you find the heat source? It's the candles. As their energy heats the air above them, the air particles move faster. The particles move farther apart as they take in the energy. This makes the air less dense. Cooler air rushes under the less dense air. It pushes the warmer air upward. As long as the candles, the heat sources, are burning, movement of the rising warm air will make the spiral twirl and the blades turn.

One kind of much larger convection current shapes our weather. Uneven heating of the air around Earth causes currents that cover thousands of kilometers. They make Earth's major wind patterns.

1. ✓**Checkpoint** How does a convection current form?
2. **Math** in Science Choose a major city in your state. Use the Internet or other sources to find the average temperature for each month of the year. Display your data in a bar graph.

Radiators in Buildings

A radiator heats the air by convection. Water is heated in a boiler that is often located in the basement. Then the hot water or steam is pumped into pipes throughout the building. The pipes lead into radiators in each room. Radiators are made of various metals such as cast iron. As the hot water or steam moves, some of its heat energy passes through the walls of the radiator into the air. Convection currents move the air to heat the entire room. The cooler water returns to the boiler through another pipe. The heating cycle begins again.

Warm fluid is less dense.

Warm fluid is pushed upward.

Cooler fluid moves down under warmer fluid.

Cooler fluid is more dense.

Radiation

You know that the Sun is a major energy source. Every time you get warm in the Sun, you feel radiation. You feel it when you sit near a fire, too. **Radiation** is energy that is sent out in little bundles. When the radiant energy hits you, the particles in your skin move more quickly. You feel warm.

Radiation can travel through empty space or through matter. Dark-colored or dull surfaces absorb radiation. But polished, shiny surfaces reflect radiant energy or let it pass. Clear materials such as air and glass allow radiant energy inside. That is why the windows and roofs of greenhouses are made of materials such as plastic or glass. In a greenhouse, radiation provides an environment where plants grow regardless of what the climate is outdoors. People control the temperature, light, and moisture the plants receive.

Other objects that send out light also send out heat. For example, a pet lizard might need a special light to stay warm. The light sends out heat. Perhaps you've seen special lamps that restaurants use to keep food warm.

Radiation is different from conduction and convection. Conduction depends on the crashes of particles in a substance. Convection needs the spreading out of a fluid when particles crash. But radiation does not need particles. It happens all by itself. Radiation can move energy great distances, like from the Sun to the Earth.

Heat transfers through radiation in different ways. Have you warmed cold hands near a fireplace? When you do, energy moves to your hands by radiation. Like all thermal energy, radiation moves from warmer areas to cooler ones.

Radiation from the Sun passes through the windows of a greenhouse.

Conduction, Convection, and Radiation

Once the Sun's energy reaches the Earth, Earth's surface heats up. Then conduction takes place. The Earth's surface transfers heat to the air. The Earth warms the air around you. And the Earth is heated by the Sun.

But it's not just conduction that is happening! Convection currents form as the air is heated by the Earth's surface. That warm air expands and rises. As the rising air cools, the water vapor in it condenses and falls to Earth as rain or snow. Convection currents in the air cause Earth's wind and rain patterns.

Sun

Earth

Radiant Energy

The radiant energy from the Sun warms Earth's surface.

Lesson Checkpoint

1. How does energy from the Sun reach the Earth?
2. **Cause and Effect** What causes the Earth's surface to get warm?

Investigate How are thermal energy and temperature different?

Materials

measuring cup and warm water

2 large cups and 2 thermometers

ice cubes

2 plastic spoons

masking tape

What to Do

1 **Measure** carefully. Put 300 mL of warm water into cup A. Put 150 mL of warm water into cup B.

Label the cups.

A

B

300 mL

150 mL

2 Record the temperature of the water in each cup.

	Temperature of Water (°C)	
	Cup A (300 mL water)	**Cup B** (150 mL water)
Before adding ice		
After 1 ice cube melts		
After 2 ice cubes melt		
After 3 ice cubes melt		
After 4 ice cubes melt		
After 5 ice cubes melt		
Number of ice cubes completely melted when temperature reached 10°C		

Process Skills

Sometimes you can test a **prediction** by doing an experiment.

3 Put an ice cube in each cup. Stir each cup gently. Record the water temperature.

4 After an ice cube melts, record the water temperature in the cup. Add another ice cube.

5 Continue until the temperature in a cup reaches 10°C.

Make a bar graph to show your data.

Thermal Energy

To organize and display your data, construct a chart and a graph like the ones shown. They will help you examine, analyze, and evaluate the information.

Interpret your chart and graph and those of other groups. Share your results. Do not change your results just because they are different from those of other groups.

Think About It

1. Which cup has more thermal energy? How do you know?

2. Suppose you used 600 mL of your warm water. **Predict** how many ice cubes would be need to lower the temperature to 10°C. How could you test your prediction?

Go Further

Develop and conduct a scientific investigation to test the prediction you made. Design any tables, charts, graphs, or diagrams to help record, display, and interpret your data.

Using Temperature Scales

°C

120
110
100
90
80
70
60
50
40
30
20
10
0
-10
-20
-30
-40
-50

°F

250
240
230
220
210
200
190
180
170
160
150
140
130
120
110
100
90
80
70
60
50
40
30
20
10
0
-10
-20
-30
-40
-50

Boiling point of water

Normal body temperature

Hot day

Room temperature

Cool day

Freezing point of water

Cold day

Very cold day

Both the Celsius and Fahrenheit temperature scales measure temperature in degrees (°), but the degree divisions are not the same.

Notice that, on both scales, zero is a label for a point. The temperature "5°" is read "5 degrees below zero" or "negative 5 degrees."

Suppose you are asked how many 40-degree days New York has in January. Your answer depends on the scale being used. Using the Celsius scale, the answer would be "zero" because New York is never that warm in January—or in any other month! But, New York might get as warm as 40°F in January.

Take It to the NET
Temperature Scales www.sfsuccessnet.com

Decide which temperature scale is being used in each situation, the Fahrenheit scale, or the Celsius scale.

1. The outdoor thermometer reads 25 degrees, and you are water skiing.

2. The temperature is 40 degrees and you are wearing a coat at an outdoor football game.

3. The weather report uses "below freezing" and "below zero" to describe the same temperature.

4. You heat water to 100 degrees, but the water does not boil.

Lab zone Take-Home Activity

Find three different kinds of thermometers at home. They might include a weather thermometer, a fever thermometer, and a meat thermometer. Make a list of the three kinds and record the highest temperature on the Fahrenheit or Celsius scale for each one. Write a paragraph explaining why they are different for different thermometers.

Use Vocabulary

conduction (p. 354)	**insulator** (p. 355)
conductor (p. 355)	**radiation** (p. 358)
convection current (p. 356)	**thermal energy** (p. 351)

Use the vocabulary term from the list above that completes each sentence.

1. The total energy of all the particles in a body is its _____.

2. A(n) _____ limits the amount of heat that passes through it.

3. _____ is little bundles of energy that travel from the Sun through space.

4. A material that allows heat to pass through it is a(n) _____.

5. The pattern of heat energy flowing through a fluid is a(n) _____.

6. The transfer of energy by one object touching another is _____.

Explain Concepts

7. Explain how particles move differently in a solid, a liquid, and a gas.

8. Explain why the motion of particles affects a thermometer reading.

9. **Infer** why young trees and plants are sometimes kept in greenhouses before they are planted outdoors.

10. **Make a model** that shows how heat moves between objects.

11. You are sitting next to the ice rink of an outdoor hockey game. **Predict** which will keep you warmer: a dark, wool blanket or a clear, plastic sheet.

Cause and Effect

12. Fill in the missing cause and effect to show how heat is transferred.

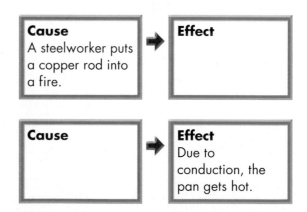

Cause		Effect
A steelworker puts a copper rod into a fire.	→	

Cause		Effect
	→	Due to conduction, the pan gets hot.

Test Prep

Choose the letter that best completes the statement or answers the question.

13. Which is the best conductor?
- Ⓐ metal
- Ⓑ wood
- Ⓒ marble
- Ⓓ plastic

14. Heat is different from temperature because
- Ⓕ heat measures the total energy of moving particles.
- Ⓖ heat measures the average energy of moving particles.
- Ⓗ temperature does not involve the movement of particles.
- Ⓘ temperature does not involve energy.

15. A large pot of boiling water has more thermal energy than a small pot of boiling water. The temperature of the water is
- Ⓐ higher in the large pot.
- Ⓑ higher in the small pot.
- Ⓒ impossible to measure.
- Ⓓ the same in both pots.

16. A thermometer measures temperature by showing
- Ⓕ particles.
- Ⓖ climate.
- Ⓗ degrees.
- Ⓘ volume.

17. When two solids touch, heat energy transfers by
- Ⓐ insulation.
- Ⓑ conduction.
- Ⓒ convection currents.
- Ⓓ liquids.

18. The Sun warms your skin by
- Ⓕ insulation.
- Ⓖ radiation.
- Ⓗ conduction.
- Ⓘ thermal energy.

19. Explain why the answer you selected for Question #13 is best. For each of the answers you did not select, give a reason why it is not the best choice.

20. Writing in Science **Informative** Use the Internet to research solar ovens. Find out what foods can be cooked in them and how cooking times compare to conventional ovens. Write an informative paragraph to share your findings.

Cooking with the Sun

Did you know that not all NASA jobs launch you into space? For example, some NASA scientists are part of the Thermal Protection Materials and Systems Branch. Their task is to develop TPS (Thermal Protection System) materials that protect spacecraft and astronauts from heat. Their research produces materials that are lightweight, yet strong and heat-resistant.

Some of the TPS material looks like a carpet. You can roll it out, cut it to shape, and even walk on it! NASA's scientists are testing it to find how well it performs.

NASA uses TPS materials in heat shields that guard spacecraft when they enter other atmospheres or come back to Earth's. One material was used on the Mars *Pathfinder*.

But the research provides information for people on Earth too. NASA's scientists use what they know about heat transfer to help others. In East Africa, poor people come to refugee camps for safety. In order to cook, they need wood. But wood is hard to find. In some parts of Africa, people spend over half the money they earn each year on cooking fuel.

NASA's Mission to Planet Earth program is helping out! It studies Earth from a global point of view. NASA's Surface Solar Energy (SSE) information lets people use their latitudes and longitudes to find the closest available solar energy. Solar Cookers International, a group that helps others learn to cook with the Sun, can zoom in on the places where solar cooking can be best used.

NASA's SSE information helps East Africans use the Sun, a natural resource and great source of heat energy, to cook. Then the people don't need to hunt for wood or spend what little money they have on fuel.

With the Sun's energy, East Africans use solar cookers to prepare meals. The Sun is a safe and clean heat source. Solar cooking does not cost much. It does not create a lot of smoke or air pollution in the environment. Solar cooking helps people harness some of the Sun's power!

Lab zone Take-Home Activity

Would you rather work as a scientist who studies TPS materials or as one who studies SSE? Tell a partner which job you'd prefer and why.

Max Planck

Max Planck was a physicist about 100 years ago. A physicist is a scientist who studies matter and energy. While studying heat and radiant energy, he noticed the ways that hot surfaces sent out light and took in radiant energy. Planck said that objects were able to send out and take in radiation in only little bunches. Planck called those bunches quanta. His ideas became known as the quantum theory.

Planck's ideas about energy quanta were different from past ideas. Scientists believed energy flowed without stopping. They knew that at times energy acted like a wave, but at other times, it acted like a collection of particles.

Then, another physicist, Albert Einstein, used Planck's theory to explain his own ideas. Einstein said that light is quantized. He meant that things that send out light do so in little bundles of energy. He thought that radiation was made up of particles, not waves.

The work of one scientist plays a part in the work of others. Planck's ideas affected Einstein's! Scientists now know that radiation has qualities of both particles and waves.

Max Planck changed physics with his theory about radiant energy.

Lab zone Take-Home Activity

The little bundles of energy that Planck described are the power source for solar cookers. Use the Internet or other resources to find other devices that use solar energy.

EC NTL 10 9 8 7 6 5 4 3 2 1

Chapter 13

Electricity and Magnetism

You Will Discover

- what causes objects to become charged.
- how electricity moves.
- why a compass needle points north-south.
- ways that electricity and magnetism are related.
- how magnetism can be transformed into electricity.

www.sfsuccessnet.com

What are some ways that energy can be changed from one type to another?

static electricity

series circuit

parallel circuit

370

Chapter 13 Vocabulary

electric current

resistance

magnetism

magnetic field

electromagnet

Explore How can static electricity affect objects?

Materials

safety goggles

balloon and string

wool cloth

What to Do

1 Tie a string to a balloon. Rub the balloon with a wool cloth for about 1 minute.

Rubbing causes your balloon to have a negative charge and your cloth to have a positive charge.

Rub all parts of your balloon.

The ballon has a negative charge.

The cloth has a positive charge.

2 Hold your balloon by the string. Hold your cloth about an arm's length away. Gradually bring them closer together. **Observe**.

3 Rub all parts of your balloon again. Hold your balloon by its string. Slowly bring it near the balloon of another group. Observe.

The effect you observe is caused by static electricity.

Both balloons have a negative charge.

Process Skills

Based on your **observations**, you made **inferences** about how charged objects affect each other.

Think About It

1. What happened as you brought together your balloon and your cloth? your balloon and the balloon of another group?

2. **Infer** How do objects with opposite charges affect each other? How do objects with the same charge affect each other?

Reading Skills

Cause and Effect

Learning to find causes and effects can help you understand what you read.

- Sometimes writers use clue words such as *because, so,* and *as a result* to signal cause and effect.

- A cause may have more than one effect. An effect may have more than one cause.

Causes and effects are marked in the advertisement below.

Magazine Advertisement

Feeling positively negative about clinging clothes?
Does static electricity rub you the wrong way?
Take charge! Try ELECTRO-NOT!

This new spray tames static electricity. Spray it on socks before putting them in the dryer. They won't stick to your shirts. Your hair will no longer stand up when you remove your winter hat. Using our patented anti-cling technology, ELECTRO-NOT neutralizes the charges that build up on your clothing. Let the sparks fly in your campfire, not on your clothes. Buy ELECTRO-NOT today. Your socks will be glad you did!

Apply It!

List some causes and effects from the advertisement. Use graphic organizers like the one shown.

Cause	➡	Effect

ZZZAPP! A jagged bolt of lightning slashes and flashes through the sky. Less than a second later, it's gone. But then more and more brilliant bolts appear, briefly connecting the clouds to the ground. Like snowflakes and grains of sand, each bolt is unique. BOOOOM!! The sound of thunder startles you. You are glad that you are indoors, watching this dazzling "spark-a-palooza" through a window. As beautiful as this super-charged sight is, you know that lightning can pack a deadly wallop. Each bolt can get as hot as 27,760° C (50,000° F).

Lesson 1

How does matter become charged?

What causes a thundercloud to make lightning? Why do socks cling in the dryer? The answer is static electricity.

Electric Charges

You dash across a carpet and touch a metal doorknob. OUCH! A jolt of static electricity and a small spark startle you.

To understand what happened, start with atoms, the tiny building blocks of everything. A sheet of paper is about one million atoms thick. Almost all atoms have three different particles. Some particles have a positive charge (+), some have a negative charge (–), and some have no charge. Matter usually has the same number of positive particles as negative particles. It is neutral.

Charged particles can move between objects that are close to each other. **Static electricity** happens when positive and negative charges no longer balance. *Static* means not moving, but eventually the static electricity does move. It may move gradually or it may move very quickly. Moving charges generate electrical energy which changes into sound, light, and heat energy.

Static Electricity

As charged particles move between atoms in storm clouds, the clouds become charged. Usually, the positive particles cluster near the top and the negative particles gather near the bottom of the clouds. In time, this static electrical energy is released as lightning. It heats up the surrounding air, making it glow. Lightning also creates a mighty sound—thunder.

1. **✓ Checkpoint** What causes static electricity on an object?
2. **Social Studies** in Science Benjamin Franklin invented the lightning rod. Use the Internet or other resources to find out what a lightning rod does.

How Charged Objects Behave

You can predict how charged objects will behave. If two objects have opposite charges—if one is positive and the other is negative—they will pull toward each other. This attraction causes an electric force. An electric force is the pull or push between objects that have a different charge.

A charged object can attract something that has no charge. If you rub a balloon on your hair, it picks up negative particles. It becomes negatively charged. Then, if you hold the balloon near lightweight neutral objects, such as scraps of paper, the neutrally charged paper moves toward it. This is why a charged balloon sticks to a wall. After awhile, the balloon loses its negative charge and falls off the wall.

Suppose you are wearing a wool cap on a chilly winter day. While you wear the cap, negative particles move from your hair to the cap. As a result, each strand of hair becomes positively charged. When you remove the cap, all the positively charged hairs stand up and move as far away as possible from the other positively charged hairs. Two objects that have the same charge push away or repel each other.

Charged amber attracts feathers.

How "Electricity" Got its Name

Millions of years ago sap oozed from a tree trunk. Gradually the sap hardened. Sometimes it trapped prehistoric insects. Amber is the fossilized tree sap. Early Greek scientists, such as Thales (625–545 BCE), noticed that amber could do amazing tricks. Amber that is rubbed on fur becomes charged. Feathers stick to the charged amber. The word *electricity* comes from "elektron," the Greek word for amber.

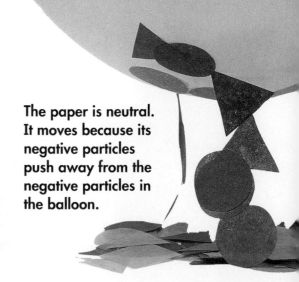

The paper is neutral. It moves because its negative particles push away from the negative particles in the balloon.

376

An Electric Field

The space around electrically charged objects is called an electric field. To represent an electric field, scientists draw lines coming out of an object. An electric field is invisible. It is strongest close to the charged object. It gets weaker farther from the object.

An electric field causes an electric force on charged objects that touch it. A positive electric field attracts negative charges. It pushes away positive charges. A negative electric field attracts positive charges and pushes away negative ones.

The balloons have the same charge. They repel each other.

The balloons have opposite charges. They attract each other.

✓ Lesson Checkpoint

1. What effect will a charged object have on an object with the opposite charge?
2. Give two examples of static electricity.
3. **Writing** in Science **Narrative** Write a story that tells a curious first grader about static electricity. Include at least two experiences you might have in a typical day.

How do electric charges flow?

How does the electric energy in a battery get to a light bulb?
To study how electricity moves, scientists build models called circuits.
Electric charges travel through different materials at different speeds.

How Electric Charges Move

Static electricity stays in one place. But most electricity is on the go. An electric charge in motion is called an **electric current.** The electric charge flows from one place to another. An electric current travels quickly and invisibly.

Learning how electricity works can be extremely dangerous. Studying a model is a much smarter way to learn how charges travel. A model of a circuit is shown on the next page. A circuit is a loop. In order for charges to flow through it, a circuit cannot have any breaks. It must be a closed circuit. In contrast, an open circuit has at least one break that interrupts the flow of electric charges. Scientists use symbols to show different parts of the circuit in diagrams. The diagram and the picture on the next page both show the same circuit.

Going with the Flow

The flow of electric charge is not the same in all materials. Some kinds of atoms become charged more easily than others. Materials made up of such atoms are conductors. The copper wire in the picture and most metals are good conductors. Silver is an excellent conductor of electric charge.

Other materials are made of atoms that do not become charged easily. Electric charge moves through them more slowly. These materials are insulators. Plastic, rubber, glass, and dry wood are good insulators. In the circuit picture, the wire is insulated. This insulation prevents the electric charges from coming in contact with other wires. Different colored insulations help show how complex circuits with many wires are connected.

A Closed Circuit

CIRCUIT SYMBOLS

Switch

Energy Source

Resistor

Energy source

The power source for this circuit is a battery. It causes the electric charge to flow.

Means of Energy Transfer

The wires provide a path through which the charge flows.

Switch

When this switch is closed, the circuit is closed. The electric charge flows without any interruptions.

Resistor

A coiled wire is inside the light bulb. This wire is made of a material with a high resistance. **Resistance** means the material does not allow electric charge to easily flow through it. Because of the resistance, the wire builds up electric energy. It gives off the built-up energy as heat and light.

Insulated Wire

The copper wire is insulated with a plastic covering.

1. ✓**Checkpoint** What is the difference between an insulator and a conductor?

2. ⟳ **Cause and Effect** What causes some materials to be good insulators of electricity?

379

Types of Circuits

In a simple circuit, known as a **series circuit**, electrical charge can only flow in one path. When the power source is turned on, the charged particles in the wire start flowing in one direction around a single loop. Any bulb along this path receives the same amount of electrical energy. If all the bulbs are identical, none will be any brighter than the others.

But, if one bulb burns out, it acts like an "off" switch and opens the circuit. The other bulbs won't receive the energy they need. They won't light either. In a series circuit, all devices wired into the circuit share the electric current equally. Today, people rarely use series circuits. Our appliances and other electric equipment need different amounts of current.

In a series circuit, one missing or burnt-out bulb opens the circuit. No bulbs will light.

Parallel Circuits

One way to prevent all the lights in a circuit from going out is to connect them in a parallel circuit. A **parallel circuit** has two or more paths for the electric charge to follow. The main loop leaves and returns to the power source. Along the loop, however, there are little loops. Each little loop is a separate path for the electric charge. How the charges flow through each little loop does not affect the flow of charges in any other path.

Circuits in your home, school, and other buildings are parallel circuits. A break in one part of the circuit does not stop the charge from flowing. Unlike a series circuit, a parallel circuit can handle electric devices that require different amounts of current.

In a parallel circuit, a missing or burnt-out bulb does not open the circuit. The other bulbs stay lit.

✓ Lesson Checkpoint

1. What is the main difference between a series circuit and a parallel circuit?
2. Why are most homes wired in a parallel circuit rather than a series circuit?
3. Art in Science Make a drawing of a parallel circuit that has light bulbs on several little loops. On one of the little loops, draw the light bulbs connected in a series circuit.

Lesson 3

What are magnetic fields?

Sometimes magnets pull together but sometimes they push apart. What causes magnets and certain other materials to behave this way?

Magnetism

A magnet is anything that attracts other things made of iron, steel, and certain other metals. **Magnetism** is the name of the force that pushes or pulls magnetic materials that are near a magnet. The word *magnet* comes from Magnesia, a part of ancient Greece that today is part of Turkey. Long ago, Magnesia was famous for having large amounts of lodestone, a naturally occurring magnetic mineral.

Magnetic Fields

How do magnets work? Each magnet has an invisible field around it. The **magnetic field** goes out in all directions. The shape of the magnetic field depends on the shape of the magnet. Look at the patterns of iron filings near the horseshoe magnet at the right and the bar magnets on the next page. The patterns are different because the magnetic fields have different shapes. But whatever the shape of the magnet, the field is strongest at the magnet's ends or poles. The pulling or pushing force is strongest at the poles.

Iron filings near a horsehoe magnet show the magnetic field is strongest near the poles.

Magnetic Poles

All magnets have two poles, a north-seeking and south-seeking pole. Opposite poles have opposite charges. Unlike charges attract each other, while like charges repel each other. So, the north-seeking pole on one magnet and the south-seeking pole on another magnet pull toward each other. But the like poles push apart.

If you break a magnet into two pieces, you'll have two magnets that each has its own north-seeking pole and its own south-seeking pole. In fact, every magnet has both a north-seeking pole and a south-seeking pole. Think of the two poles of a magnet like two sides of a coin. One cannot exist without the other.

Iron filings near a bar magnet show the magnetic field is strongest near the poles.

The north-seeking pole of one bar magnet pulls toward the south-seeking pole of another bar magnet. The iron filings show the magnetic field.

Two north-seeking poles repel each other. The iron filings show the magnetic field.

1. **✓Checkpoint** If you break a magnet into two pieces, what happens to its magnetic poles?

2. **Social Studies** in Science Use the Internet or other resources to locate places other than Magnesia where lodestone is found.

The Largest Magnet in the World

Why does a compass needle always move to the north-south direction? Many ancient sailors used compasses successfully but didn't know why they worked. Christopher Columbus used a compass when he crossed the Atlantic. Around 1600, British scientist William Gilbert suggested that the world's largest magnet is—the Earth! In other words, he proposed that Earth is a huge magnet, surrounded by an enormous magnetic field.

The Earth behaves like a large magnet. Like all magnets, its magnetic field is strongest at the poles. But, Earth's magnetic poles are not located at its geographic poles. The geographic poles are on Earth's axis, an invisible line around which our planet rotates. The magnetic north pole is located in Canada, about 1,600 kilometers (1,000 miles) from the geographic North Pole. The magnetic south pole is located near the center of Antarctica.

Why does Earth act like a magnet? Scientists aren't sure of the answer. After all, no one has actually seen the inside of our planet. But based on indirect evidence, they suggest that Earth's outer core is made of iron that is so hot that it has melted. As Earth rotates, the liquid iron flowing around and around creates a magnetic field. The inner core is probably solid iron that is also very hot. It doesn't melt because of the extremely high pressure.

If no magnet is near, the compass needle points north.

A bar magnet changes the direction the compass needle points.

How Compasses Work

A compass is a helpful, easy-to-carry tool. Wherever you are on Earth, one end of a compass needle will point to the North Pole. It follows an imaginary line that connects the magnetic poles of the Earth. Once you know which direction is north, you can easily determine south, west, and east.

For a compass to work properly, its needle must be lightweight and turn easily. The compass cannot be close to a magnet. Otherwise, the needle will respond to the pull of the magnet rather than to Earth's magnetic field.

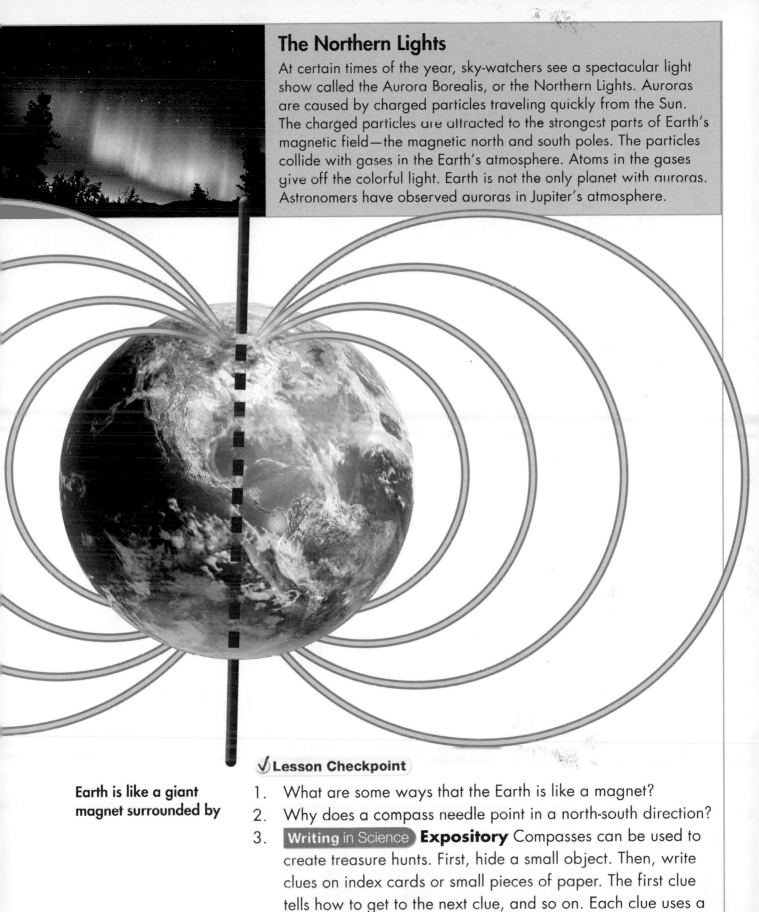

The Northern Lights

At certain times of the year, sky-watchers see a spectacular light show called the Aurora Borealis, or the Northern Lights. Auroras are caused by charged particles traveling quickly from the Sun. The charged particles are attracted to the strongest parts of Earth's magnetic field—the magnetic north and south poles. The particles collide with gases in the Earth's atmosphere. Atoms in the gases give off the colorful light. Earth is not the only planet with auroras. Astronomers have observed auroras in Jupiter's atmosphere.

Earth is like a giant magnet surrounded by

✓ Lesson Checkpoint

1. What are some ways that the Earth is like a magnet?
2. Why does a compass needle point in a north-south direction?
3. **Writing** in Science **Expository** Compasses can be used to create treasure hunts. First, hide a small object. Then, write clues on index cards or small pieces of paper. The first clue tells how to get to the next clue, and so on. Each clue uses a compass to find the right direction. Challenge a friend to use your directions to find the hidden object.

How is electricity transformed to magnetism?

Electricity and magnetism are closely related. Both are the result of charged particles moving. The combination of these forces, electromagnetism, is very useful in our daily lives.

Electromagnets

In 1820, Danish scientist Hans Christian Oersted was showing how electric current flowed through a wire. He noticed that the magnetic needle on a nearby compass moved each time he turned on the current. The electric current caused a magnetic field. The current caused the compass needle to move. Oersted saw that the forces of electricity and magnetism have a lot in common. This connection led to an important invention—the electromagnet.

The compass needles line up with the magnetic field caused by the flowing current.

When no current flows, all compasses point north.

What is an electromagnet? An **electromagnet** is a coil of wire wrapped around an iron core. When the current moves through the wire, an invisible force surrounds the electromagnet. The force is a magnetic field. When the current stops, the wire loses its magnetic power. By transforming electrical energy into magnetic energy, an electromagnet can create a very powerful magnet.

More coils make the electromagnet stronger.

More current passing through the wire makes the electromagnet stronger.

A larger core makes the electromagnet stronger.

Ways to Make the Magnet Stronger

Like a bar magnet, an electromagnet has a north and south pole. One advantage electromagnets have over natural ones is that you can change their strength. You can make an electromagnet stronger by increasing the amount of current running through the wire. Another way is by increasing the number of turns the metal coil has. A third way to boost the power of an electromagnet is by making the magnetic core larger.

1. ✓**Checkpoint** How is an electromagnet different from a magnet?
2. **Math in Science** An electromagnet with 12 coils can pick up 4 thumbtacks. You want to make the electromagnet stronger by adding coils. Predict how many coils you need to pick up 5 thumbtacks.

Uses for Electromagnets

Electromagnets are used in industry to lift heavy materials. Sometimes the materials are the resources needed for manufacturing. Sometimes they are waste materials that are being moved so that they can be used in a different way. Electromagnets are also in complex machines used by doctors and scientists.

You may not realize that electromagnets are part of many electronic gadgets that you use every day. Televisions, fans, VCRs, computers, and DVD players all work because of electromagnets. In the examples here—a doorbell, a motor, and earphones—you'll see how electromagnets help convert electric energy to magnetic energy to mechanical energy.

How a Doorbell Works

Button—Pressing the button closes the electrical circuit. Current flows to the...

Transformer—This device controls the amount of current that is sent to the...

Electromagnet—Electricity flowing in the coil of wire magnetizes the electromagnet. This pulls up the...

Contact Arm—The arm is attached to metal clapper that hits the...

Bell—This makes the sound.

Simple Electric Motor

A motor uses magnets to create motion. A simple motor has six parts.

Battery—power source

EARPHONES turn the electric current back into sound waves. A metal disc is in front of an ELECTROMAGNET in the earphone. Changes in the electric current make the magnetism weaker or stronger. The changes in magnetic strength make the disc vibrate. The vibrations are the sound waves you hear.

Armature or Rotor—a set of electromagnets, each with thin copper wire coiled around it

Permanent Magnet—works with the electromagnets in the armature. The north end of the permanent magnet pushes away the north end of the electromagnet. The south ends also push away from each other. This causes the axle to spin.

Brush—the contact point on each side of the armature that transfers power when the motor spins

Axle—holds the commutator and the armature

Commutator—switch that reverses the direction of the electric current

✅ **Lesson Checkpoint**

1. 🎯 **Cause and Effect**
   How did noticing cause and effect lead to Hans Christian Oersted's discovery?

2. Why are electromagnets used in so many electronic devices?

3. **Technology** in Science
   Use the Internet or other resources to find examples of electromagnets used in industry or medicine.

389

How is magnetism transformed to electricity?

The power of magnetism can be transformed into the power of electricity. This discovery led to the invention of the electric motor, generator, and more.

Electrical Energy

Most people take electricity for granted. They find it hard to picture daily life before electricity. They push plugs into outlets, without thinking about where the electricity comes from. They don't realize that the electrical energy that powers their televisions, refrigerators, and lamps has traveled a long way.

Today we know more ways to use magnetism to generate electricity. Sliding coiled wire back and forth over a magnet generates electricity. Spinning a coiled wire around a magnet produces electricity too.

When a magnet is moved, its magnetic field moves with it. And changing a magnetic field generates electricity. The faster the coiled wire or the magnet is moved, the stronger the electric current it produces. In contrast, the slower the movement, the weaker the current. The number of coiled loops also affects the strength of the current. More coiled loops of wire mean the magnet creates a stronger current.

Wires are wound in coils around magnets. The wires are attached to instruments that measure the electric current.

A Flashlight Without Batteries

In 1831, Michael Faraday invented a machine that used magnets to transform motion into an electric current. By turning a crank, he was able to produce electrical energy. He called this invention a dynamo. Today this technology is used in an emergency flashlight. It does not use batteries. Instead, it produces electricity when the user squeezes the handle.

Currents Currently

Most homes, schools, and businesses today get their electricity from generators. A generator is a machine that creates electric energy by turning coils of wire around powerful magnets. Modern generators are much bigger than the magnets and coils that Faraday and other scientists used in their experiments. The basic scientific principles, however, are the same. A generator uses magnets and wires to turn mechanical energy into electrical energy.

1. **✓ Checkpoint** What happens when a magnet is moved back and forth inside a coiled wire?
2. **Math** in Science How many years after Joseph Henry discovered that changing a magnetic field generates an electric current did Michael Faraday make the same discovery?

Michael Faraday

Joseph Henry

Pioneers in Electricity

In the early 1820s, British scientist Michael Faraday did many experiments with magnetism and electricity. At the same time, American scientist Joseph Henry was doing similar experiments. In 1829, Henry discovered that changing a magnetic field created an electric current in a wire. But, he didn't share his findings with other scientists for several years. In 1831, Faraday made the same discovery and shared it with other scientists. Faraday moved a magnet inside a wire coil to generate electrical energy. He used this discovery to build the first electric motor.

Discoveries in Using Electrical Energy

Thales of Miletus describes static electricity.

1600

William Gilbert suggests that Earth is a magnet.

1740s

Benjamin Franklin and Ebenezer Kinnersley describe electric charges as positive or negative.

1820

Hans Christian Oersted notices that electric currents affect a compass needle.

1829
1831

Joseph Henry (1829) and Michael Faraday (1831) produce a current by changing a magnetic field.

1870

Zenobe Gramme invents the electric generator.

1879

Thomas Edison demonstrates the incandescent light bulb.

1884

Charles Parsons develops the first successful steam turbine.

1896

Electric generator at Niagara Falls begins producing electricity for Buffalo, New York.

1980

Windfarms in the United States begin collecting the wind's energy.

How Generators Are Powered

There are many ways for a generator to create electrical energy. Some use the energy of the wind, while others rely on falling water. Still other generators are powered by steam caused by the hot temperatures deep below Earth's surface or by nuclear energy heating the water. In each kind of generator, mechanical energy spins wires around a magnet.

Wind Power
A wind turbine changes the energy of the blowing wind into electricity.

Hydroelectric Power
Generators near Niagara Falls turn the power of falling water into electricity.

Electrical Safety

Electricity lights homes, cooks food, and powers many machines. However, if you're not careful, electricity can cause a serious shock or start a fire.

The Electrical Safety Foundation urges everyone to remember the 4 R's of electrical safety:

- Respect the power of electricity.
- Read and follow the instructions that come with every electrical product.
- Replace worn or cracked electrical cords.
- Relocate, or move, appliance cords so people will not walk on or trip over them, and children or pets can't pull them.

✓ Lesson Checkpoint

1. How do magnets help generators create electricity?
2. **Math** in Science Wind turbines today generate electricity much better than they did about 25 years ago. In 1981, a wind turbine produced 25 kilowatts of electrical power. A modern turbine can create up to 750 kilowatts of electricity. How many times more powerful is a modern wind turbine?

Investigate What is an electromagnet?

Observe how an electromagnet works. Then make an operational definition. An **operational definition** of an electromagnet is a definition that tells you what you must observe to know if something *is* an electromagnet. Use this form: "An object is an electromagnet if it acts like a magnet when _____, but not when _____."

Materials

safety goggles and ruler

insulated wire and bolt

battery and battery holder

20 small paper clips

What to Do

1 Start 25 centimeters from one end of the wire. Coil the wire 30 times around the bolt near its head.

Leave a 25 centimeter piece uncoiled.

30 coils

2 Hold the bolt's head near a paper clip. Record your **observations**.

Be careful!

Wear safety goggles. Disconnect wires if any parts feel warm.

30 coils (no battery)

Process Skills

You use your experience with an object or event to help make an **operational definition** of it.

3 Make a circuit. Put a battery in the battery holder. Attach both ends of the wire to it. Find how many paper clips your electromagnet can pick up. Record. Then remove a wire from the battery holder.

30 coils

battery

battery holder

When electricity flows through the wire, the bolt works like a magnet.

4 Add 20 more coils. **Predict** how many paper clips you can pick up now. Find out.

5 Make a bar graph or select another way to show your results.

Number of Paper Clips Picked Up

10
9
8
7
6
5
4
3
2
1
0

30 coils (no battery)   30 coils   50 coils

Number of Coils

Number of Coils	Number of Paper Clips Picked Up
30 coils (no battery)	
30 coils	
50 coils	

Think About It

1. **Infer** What can make an electromagnet stronger?
2. Make an **operational definition** of an electromagnet.

Go Further

Which objects will a magnet attract? Use your electromagnet as a tool. Develop and carry out a plan to answer this or another question you may have. Write instructions others could use to repeat your investigation.

Using Numbers to Represent Electrical Charges

Positive and negative numbers are often used in science. Numbers greater than zero are positive, and numbers less than zero are negative. You have worked with positive and negative temperatures. You can also use positive and negative numbers to represent electrical charges.

When a neutral material loses particles with negative charges, it will have a positive charge. An opposite charge will make it neutral again. If the charge is +5, a charge of −5 will make it neutral again.

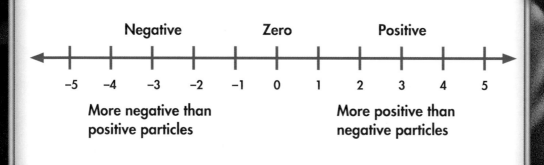

Negative	Zero	Positive

−5 −4 −3 −2 −1 0 1 2 3 4 5

More negative than positive particles

More positive than negative particles

Use the number line to answer these questions.

1. If some material has a charge of +4, what charge would make it neutral?
   A. +2
   B. −2
   C. +4
   D. −4

2. If a neutral balloon gains 3 negative charges and then loses 3 negative charges, what will its charge be?
   F. +3
   G. −3
   H. 0
   I. +6

3. If a balloon with a negative charge and a balloon with a positive charge are held up by strings next to each other, what will happen?
   A. They will move toward each other.
   B. They will move apart.
   C. Nothing will happen.
   D. They will both fall to the floor.

Lab zone Take-Home Activity

Design an experiment in which you try to stick charged balloons to a variety of objects at home, such as the refrigerator, a door, and so on. Time how long the balloon sticks to each (if it sticks at all). Make a graph that shows your results. Try this experiment in different kinds of weather.

Chapter 13 Review and Test Prep

Use Vocabulary

electric current (p. 378)	**parallel circuit** (p. 381)
electromagnet (p. 387)	**resistance** (p. 379)
magnetic field (p. 382)	**series circuit** (p. 380)
magnetism (p. 382)	**static electricity** (p. 375)

Use the vocabulary term from the list above that best completes each sentence.

1. If charged particles in an object are not balanced, the object builds up _____.

2. A charge in motion is called a(n) _____.

3. _____ is the pushing or pulling force that exists when a magnetic material is near.

4. Current flows in only one direction in a(n) _____.

5. The quality of _____ opposes the flow of electric current through a material.

6. Because of Earth's _____, a compass needle points in a north-south direction.

7. One advantage of a(n) _____ over a natural magnet is that its magnetic field can be turned off.

8. A(n) _____ can handle appliances that use different amounts of electric current.

Explain Concepts

9. Explain why copper wire is a better conductor of electricity than a rubber tube is.

10. Explain why most homes have parallel circuits rather than series circuits.

Process Skills

11. A compass needle is pointing in a north-south direction. **Predict** what would happen to the needle if a small magnet were held near the east side of the compass?

12. You rub two inflated balloons on your hair. **Infer** what happens when you hold them close to each other.

13. If you could go back in time and interview either Joseph Henry or Michael Faraday about his experiments with electricity, what two questions would you ask?

Cause and Effect

14. Complete the graphic organizer to show cause and effect for the Northern Lights.

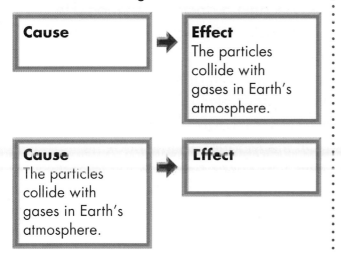

Cause		Effect
	→	The particles collide with gases in Earth's atmosphere.

Cause		Effect
The particles collide with gases in Earth's atmosphere.	→	

 ## Test Prep

15. Which of the following is NOT used to power generators?
Ⓐ Wind
Ⓑ Moving water
Ⓒ Hot rocks deep below Earth's surface
Ⓓ Static electricity

16. Lights are wired in a parallel circuit. What happens to the circuit if one bulb burns out?
Ⓕ None of the bulbs light.
Ⓖ Half of the bulbs light.
Ⓗ All bulbs but one light.
Ⓘ All bulbs light.

17. If you break a magnet into two pieces, what happens?
Ⓐ The magnetic field disappears until the pieces are put back together.
Ⓑ Each magnet piece ends up with only one magnetic pole.
Ⓒ Each new magnet has a north pole and south pole.
Ⓓ One magnet piece has two north poles and the other has two south poles.

18. Which of the following materials would be the best insulator for a metal wire?
Ⓕ Glass
Ⓖ Silver
Ⓗ Water
Ⓘ Copper

19. Explain why the answer you select for Question #18 is the best. For each of the answers you did not select, give a reason why it is not the best choice.

20. Writing in Science Expository
Suppose you are asked to give a speech to a third-grade class that explains the 4 R's of electrical safety. In your journal, write a script for your speech.

William Gilbert

William Gilbert is an important person in the history of electricity and magnetism. He studied to become a physician at St. John's College of Cambridge University in England. In 1569, he graduated and became a doctor in London. He later served as the physician for Queen Elizabeth I and King James I.

Electricity and magnetism greatly interested him. He explained that static electricity and magnetism are different forces. In 1600, he published a book called *On the Magnet.* In this book he described Earth's magnetic field. He explained that a compass needle points north-south because the Earth is a giant magnet. He also developed and conducted experiments to test his ideas about electricity and magnetism. In one of these experiments, he discovered that heating magnets changed their magnetic properties. Magnets placed in a fire lost their magnetism.

William Gilbert introduced a theory about the effect electricity and magnetism have on each other. He was also the first person to use the word *electric* to describe the force between charged objects.

His ideas influenced many scientists after him. Galileo and Johannes Kepler are two famous scientists who studied his work.

Lab zone Take-Home Activity

Benjamin Franklin and Thomas Edison are two scientists who studied electricity. Find out more about them and write what you learn in your science journal.

EC NTL 10 9 8 7 6 5 4 3 2 1

You Will Discover

- how sound travels.
- some properties of sound.
- what light is.
- how light behaves.

Chapter 14

Sound and Light

Online Student Edition

www.sfsuccessnet.com

How do sound and light travel?

reflection

transparent

translucent

absorption

opaque

frequency

wavelength

compression

Chapter 14 Vocabulary

refraction

pitch

Explore What makes sound change?

Materials

water

funnel and plastic bottle

string and marker

What to Do

1 Tie the string around the neck of a 2L bottle. Fill the bottle about $\frac{1}{3}$ full with water. Screw cap tightly onto bottle.

Use a funnel to add the water.

2 Pluck the string. Does it vibrate? **Observe** the sound.

Tie the string to the marker. Use it as a handle. Hold the marker on the desktop.

Pluck the string here.

Put on lid.

Sound is made when the string vibrates. The faster it vibrates, the higher the pitch.

$\frac{1}{3}$ full of water

almost touching the floor

3 Figure out how the sound changes when you:
   a. fill the bottle with water,
   b. pluck the string gently and hard, and
   c. shorten how far the bottle hangs down.

Think About It

1. How did adding more water affect the pitch?

2. Describe how plucking harder changes volume.

3. **Infer** How does the length of the string affect the pitch?

Process Skills

You use what you know and what you **observe** to make an **inference**.

Reading Skills

Draw Conclusions

A conclusion is a decision you reach after you think about facts and details. You can also use what you know to make a decision or form an opinion that makes sense of events.

Science Article

Fly-by-Night Creatures

Bats are flying mammals that come out at night. They use sounds to help them locate objects in the darkness. The sounds waves travel through the air and bounce off whatever they strike. This creates an echo that travels back to the bat.

The bat can tell all sorts of things from the echo. It tells the bat about an object's size, direction, distance, and speed. The bat can avoid crashing into an object like a large tree. Or if the echo is from a tiny flying insect such as a mosquito or a moth, the bat knows exactly where to catch its dinner. Even blind bats catch their food without flying into things.

Apply It!

Answer the questions by drawing conclusions from the magazine article. Use a graphic oranizer like the one at the right.

1. You see several bats swooping over a pond at dusk. Draw a conclusion as to why they are doing this.
2. What might a bat conclude from an echo it receives as it flies over the pond?

◆) You Are There!

You are standing at the shore of a lake. The water is as smooth as glass. You pick up a rock and toss it into the water. It splashes with a loud "ker-PLUNK" and vanishes—but not without a trace. A ring of ripples spreads out from the spot where your rock plunged into the lake. The outer rings grow bigger. Smaller new rings that form at the center follow them. These ripply rings are waves. Did you know that invisible waves are all around us? Lots of good things come to us in waves: sunlight, music, and even your favorite TV show!

What is sound energy?

Sound is a form of energy that travels in waves. All sounds have common characteristics that can be measured and described. Sound can travel through solids, liquids, and gases.

What Sound Is

The blare of an alarm clock, the beep of a car horn, the quack of a duck, and the rumble of thunder during a storm are all sounds. Sound is a form of energy. Sounds occur when objects vibrate. A vibration is a kind of wiggle. It is a quick back-and-forth movement.

For example, if you pluck a guitar string, the string will vibrate. The vibrating string passes energy to the air that surrounds it, so the air vibrates too. The vibrations travel through the air as sound waves. A wave is a disturbance that moves energy through matter or space. Sound waves carry sound energy. If the waves reach our ears, we hear the sound made by the guitar string.

1. ✔ **Checkpoint** What is sound?
2. **Writing in Science** **Descriptive** In your science journal, write a paragraph that describes one sound you like to hear and one sound you do not like to hear. Explain what qualities in a sound make you like it or dislike it.

407

Types of Sound Waves

As sound waves move, they set air particles into motion. The moving air particles form a pattern. Areas with groups of particles that are bunched together alternate with areas of particles that are far apart. The part of the wave where the particles are bunched together is called a **compression.**

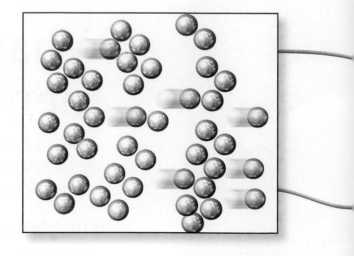

Scientists classify waves according to the way they travel through matter. There are two major types of waves.

Transverse Waves

You are probably very familiar with one type of wave. Suppose you and a friend hold opposite ends of a jump rope. You allow some slack so the middle of the rope dips toward the ground. With a quick upward flick of your wrist you send energy through the rope. The disturbance, or wave, moves through the rope to your friend's hand. However, the rope only moves, or vibrates, up and down. You created transverse waves.

In a transverse wave, the particles in the material move at a right angle to the direction that the wave travels. In other words, the wave traveled forward, toward your friend. However, the rope moved up and down. Sometimes waves in a lake or an ocean are transverse waves.

Longitudinal Waves

In a longitudinal wave, the particles in the material move parallel to the direction the wave travels. If the wave moves from right to left, then the particles also vibrate from right to left.

A spring toy can help you understand how longitudinal waves move. Suppose you lay the toy on the floor and stretch it slightly. You hold one end and your friend holds the other. Suppose you pull on the end and then push it in. You send energy through the spring. Vibrations pass along the toy. Some of the coils crowd closer together. Then, after the vibrations pass, the coils move farther apart. Sound waves are longitudinal waves. A sound wave travels as air particles are pushed together and then move apart.

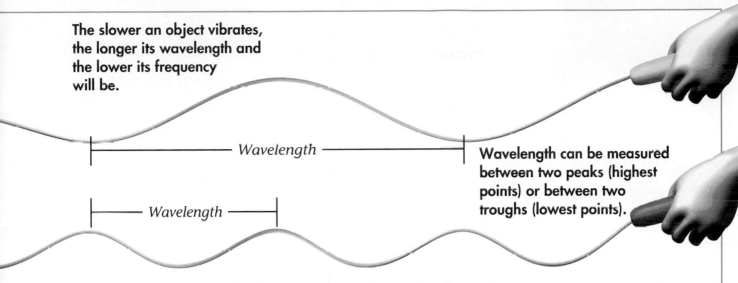

The slower an object vibrates, the longer its wavelength and the lower its frequency will be.

Wavelength

Wavelength

Wavelength can be measured between two peaks (highest points) or between two troughs (lowest points).

The faster an object vibrates, the shorter its wavelength and the higher its frequency will be.

Frequency and Wavelength

Waves travel in different ways. They can carry different amounts of energy. But, all waves have certain properties. Frequency and wavelength are two of those properties.

The **frequency** of a wave is the number of waves that pass a point in a certain amount of time. The faster an object vibrates, the higher its frequency will be. Frequency is often described as the number of complete cycles a wave makes in one second. A cycle is a vibration.

Most sounds consist of sound waves of several frequencies. **Wavelength** is the distance between a point on one wave and a similar point on the next wave.

Compression

Wavelength is the distance from a compression to the next compression.

1. **✓Checkpoint** What are two types of waves?
2. **Health in Science** The unit used to measure sound frequency is the hertz. One cycle per second equals one hertz. A person with normal hearing can hear sounds in the frequency range of 20 to 20,000 hertz. People older than 70, however, cannot always hear sounds above 6,000 hertz. Do they have trouble hearing high-frequency or low-frequency sounds?

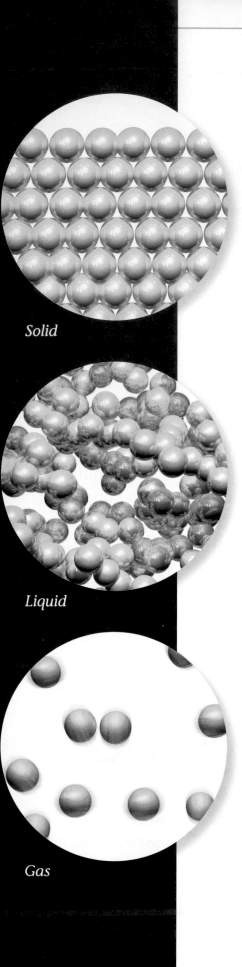

Solid

Liquid

Gas

How Sound Travels

Sound waves need a medium in which to travel. A medium is any kind of matter. Gases, liquids, and solids are mediums through which sound waves can travel.

A sound wave travels at different speeds through different mediums. As it travels, the sound wave compresses the particles in the medium. How fast the sound moves through the medium depends on how tightly the particles are packed.

Particles in a solid are crowded close together. When a sound wave causes a particle in a solid to vibrate, the vibration quickly passes to nearby particles. So, a sound wave passes quickly through the solid.

In a liquid, the particles are a little farther apart. Vibrations take a little longer to pass from one particle to another. So, sound waves travel slower in a liquid medium than they do in a solid.

In a gas, such as air, particles are the farthest apart. When a sound wave causes a gas particle to vibrate, the vibrating particle must travel a distance before it bumps into another particle. It passes energy to that particle, causing it to vibrate. Sound waves travel slowest in a gas.

If you were floating around in outer space, you would be traveling in complete silence. This is because space is a vacuum—an empty place that contains no matter. Since there are no particles of matter in a vacuum, sound waves would not be able to travel to your ears.

Approximate Speed of Sound

Speed (meters per second) vs. Type of Medium

Type of Medium	Speed
Air at 0°C	~300
Fresh Water at 25°C	~1,500
Brick	~4,200
Steel	~5,200

Scientists use echoes to map the ocean floor.

Echoes

As a sound wave travels, it often bumps into objects. If it hits a hard, smooth surface, the wave reflects. That means that the sound bounces back. For example, if you shout your name into a cave, you will hear your name softly repeated. The sound waves bounced off the cave wall and traveled back to you. A reflected sound is called an echo.

Scientists use sound waves to learn about the bottom of the ocean. The sound waves travel down, hit the ocean floor, and return to the surface as echoes. By measuring the time that passes between sending the sound wave and receiving the echo, scientists can figure out how deep the ocean is at that point.

✓ Lesson Checkpoint

1. Why does sound travel fastest in solids and slowest in gases?
2. How does an echo form?
3. 🎯 **Draw Conclusions** A bird perched in a tree hears the chirping of another bird. A whale hears the song-like sound made by another whale swimming near it. Which sound travels faster, the bird's chirping or the whale's singing? Explain how you decided.

411

How is sound made?

Vibrating objects produce all types of sound. The way an object is made and the way it vibrates affect the type of sound we hear. The frequency and the amount of energy in the sound wave also affect the sound we hear.

Loudness

When you describe a sound, one of the first things you think about is loudness. You whisper around a sleeping baby, but you might give an ear-splitting shout when your favorite baseball player hits a home run. Your shout is a lot louder than the whisper, but what exactly is loudness? Loudness is a measure of how strong a sound seems to us. Loudness is related to the amount of energy in a sound wave.

If you are far from the source of a sound, it will not sound as loud as if you were standing nearer to it. Suppose you are sitting next to a friend who is playing the drums. The sound waves do not have far to travel to your ears, so they will sound loud. But if you were across the street, the sound of the drums would be softer. The sound waves do not lose some of their energy as they travel through the air. The energy just spreads out to cover a larger area, like waves on a pond.

Pitch

Another characteristic of sound is pitch. **Pitch** is what makes a sound seem high or low. Pitch depends on a sound's frequency. Objects that vibrate quickly, those with high frequencies, have a high pitch. Objects that vibrate slowly have a low frequency and a low pitch. The material of the object making the sound and its size and shape affect the sound you hear.

A gong is a percussion instrument. When a person hits a gong, the metal vibrates. Its sound is a blend of pitches.

When a tuning fork is struck, it vibrates at a single frequency. It gives off a pure tone of a certain pitch.

The flute is a wind instrument. When the flute player blows across a hole in the flute, the column of air inside the instrument vibrates.

The violinist rubs the bow across the strings causing them to vibrate. The strings that play the highest notes are thin metal wires.

1. ✓Checkpoint What type of pitch does a high-frequency sound have?

2. Social Studies in Science The sounds from machinery, traffic, construction, and airplanes make noise pollution. Many towns have rules that limit noise levels. Suppose you were part of your local government. Write one rule you would make to keep noise from becoming a problem.

How Instruments Make Sound

Guitars, violins, harps, and other string instruments make sound when a musician plucks, rubs, or hits the strings. This sends vibrations through the instrument.

Strings on a guitar are stretched between the top and bottom of the instrument. A guitarist plays notes by plucking the strings. The note depends on the length and thickness of the string and how tightly it is stretched. A guitarist tunes the guitar by tightening the strings to make the pitch higher or loosening them to make it lower.

Sound waves travel slowest through the thicker, heavier strings. These strings vibrate slowest and play the lowest pitches. Waves travel more quickly through the thinner strings. They vibrate faster and have higher pitches.

To shorten a string and raise its pitch, a musician presses down on the metal frets or bars along the neck of the guitar.

The longer recorder has a lower pitch than the shorter instrument.

Percussion Instruments

Drums, xylophones, and maracas are examples of percussion instruments. Percussion instruments make sounds when something like a hand or a stick strikes them. For example, when you hit a bongo drum with your hand, the skin across the top of the drum vibrates and produces sound.

Wind Instruments

In a wind instrument such as a recorder, the musician blows air across a hole. This causes particles in a column of air inside the instrument to vibrate. The vibrations produce the sound you hear. The shorter the instrument, the shorter the column of air and the higher its pitch will be.

The Piano

A piano has more than 200 strings. Each key on a piano matches a group of strings. When you press a key, a padded hammer strikes the group of strings. The strings vibrate and produce a tone. Pressing a key extra hard will not change either frequency or pitch. But it will make the sound louder.

A tuning key is used to tighten or loosen each string.

Hitting a drum closer to the center lowers the pitch.

The piano has features of both percussion and string instruments.

How We Hear

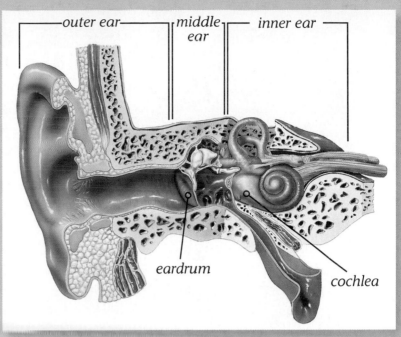

outer ear — middle ear — inner ear

eardrum

cochlea

The outer part of the human ear funnels sounds into the ear canal. Inside the ear canal, the sound waves hit the eardrum. The sound waves make the eardrum vibrate. The vibrating eardrum causes three tiny connected bones in the middle ear to vibrate. Because of their shapes, the bones are named the hammer, the stirrup, and the anvil. Next, the vibrations move into the cochlea in the inner ear. The cochlea is a snail-shaped organ that is filled with a liquid. When the liquid in the cochlea starts to vibrate, tiny hairs in the cochlea move. They convert the vibrations into signals that travel along the auditory nerve to the brain. The brain interprets the signals as sound.

✓ Lesson Checkpoint

1. How does a wind instrument produce sound?
2. How does the pitch of a thick guitar string compare to that of a thinner string?
3. **☉ Draw Conclusions** By shortening or tightening a guitar string, you raise the pitch. What do you conclude will happen to the pitch if you tighten the skin stretched across the top of a drum?

415

Lesson 3

What is light energy?

Light has much in common with sound. Both are forms of energy. Both travel as waves. Only a tiny fraction of light energy can be seen by the human eye.

Sources of Light

Like sound, light is a form of energy. The Sun, a bonfire, a street lamp, and a firefly are just a few sources of light energy. No light source is more important to us than the Sun. Without a constant supply of energy from the Sun, Earth would be a dead planet. It would be too cold and dark for any kind of life. Plants, for example, convert sunlight into chemical energy, which they use to make food. Plants are part of the food chain. Without plants, animals and people could not survive.

Some animals give off light called bioluminescence. The light is a result of chemical reactions inside the animal's body. Some sea animals that live near the bottom of the ocean—where it is pitch black—are bioluminescent.

Long, long ago, humans discovered that they could make their own light. The discovery of fire opened up a whole new world. No longer did almost all activities have to stop as soon as the Sun went down. People could light a campfire and stay warm, cook food, or work even after dark.

The firefly is a bioluminescent insect.

416

Thomas Edison demonstrated this type of lamp in the United States in October 1879.

The Light Bulb

In the 1870s, American inventor Thomas Edison and British inventor Joseph Swan discovered that electric current would heat up a filament, or thread, until it gave off both heat energy and light energy. They put the filament inside a hollow glass ball. They passed an electric current through the filament. It got very hot. It glowed, but it did not catch fire! This invention was the light bulb.

Shadows

Light travels in straight lines called rays that fan outward from the source of the light. You can easily see how light travels by looking at a shadow.

Stick puppets cast their shadows on a screen. The shadows can be made larger by moving the puppets closer to the light source.

If you hold your hand in front of a wall and then shine a flashlight on it, a hand-shaped shadow will show up on the wall. Your hand blocks the path of the light rays. A shadow, or dark area, appears where the light rays cannot reach the wall. The size of the shadow can change. If you hold your hand very close to the wall and shine the flashlight on it, the shadow will be about the same size as your hand. If you move your hand away from the wall and closer to the flashlight, the shadow will be larger than your hand.

The angle that the light strikes the object also affects the size of the shadow. Think of your own shadow on a sunny day. Around noon, when the Sun is highest in the sky, your shadow is short. Early in the morning or late in the day, the Sun is lower in the sky. Your shadow is longer.

✓ Checkpoint

1. What do the Sun, a bonfire, and a street lamp have in common?
2. Art in Science You can put on a shadow puppet play with only a source of light and a darkened room. Use your fingers and hands to create "characters" such as birds, rabbits, and other animals. Write a short script and put on a play for some friends or classmates.

Light Waves We See

The light we can see makes up only a thin slice of the universe's light energy. Scientists refer to all forms of light energy as electromagnetic radiation. Visible light, the light we see, is the most familiar form of electromagnetic waves.

Light energy travels as a wave. Like all waves, light waves have wavelengths and frequencies. The human eye can see only the wavelengths and frequencies of the colors in the visible spectrum. White light, such as light from a lamp or the Sun, is actually a blend of the colors in a rainbow. Sunlight that passes through the raindrops is split into individual colors. The colors are red, orange, yellow, green, blue, and violet.

These colors always appear in the same order because of their wavelength and frequency. As you move from left to right on the spectrum, wavelength decreases and frequency increases. So, red light has the longest wavelength and the lowest frequency. Violet light has the shortest wavelength and the highest frequency.

Electromagnetic Waves We Cannot See

Most of the waves in the electromagnetic spectrum are not visible. Radio waves, microwaves, and infrared waves are invisible because their wavelengths are too long for the human eye to see. Ultraviolet waves, X-rays, and gamma rays are high-energy waves. They are invisible because their wavelengths are too short.

Scientists use special equipment to study the invisible waves in the electromagnetic spectrum. These invisible waves behave the same as the visible light waves. All electromagnetic waves travel at the same speed through empty space. They all carry energy. This energy can be absorbed by an object and then changed to another form of energy such as heat.

Large amounts of high-energy waves can harm living cells. For example, ultraviolet waves from the Sun can damage the eyes or cause sunburn or cancer. But in smaller amounts, these waves can be helpful. Ultraviolet waves are used to kill bacteria. Microwaves are radio waves that cook or warm food. X-rays show doctors such things as a broken bone inside a patient's body.

Red light is at the left end of the spectrum of visible light. It has the longest wavelength and the lowest frequency.

Microwaves passing through the food cause particles in it to vibrate quickly. The vibrations produce heat.

Black holes and other mysterious objects in outer space give off gamma rays. Earth's atmosphere blocks gamma rays. Special telescopes in spacecraft are used to detect gamma rays.

Ultraviolet waves, X-rays, and gamma rays have short wavelengths and low frequencies.

Violet light is at the right end of the spectrum of visible light. It has the shortest wavelength and the highest frequency.

X-rays pass through soft body parts such as skin but are absorbed by hard substances such as bone.

Radio and television stations send out signals on different radio wave frequencies. When you change the channel, you are changing the frequency of the radio wave that your radio or TV receives.

✓ **Lesson Checkpoint**

1. What colors of light make up the visible spectrum?
2. Why can't humans see X-rays?
3. 🔄 **Draw Conclusions** Laser light waves all have the same wavelength. What can you conclude about the color of laser light?

How do light and matter interact?

Light may behave in different ways when it strikes matter. What happens depends on the type of matter the light waves strike.

Light and Matter

Light rays travel in straight lines—as long as nothing is in their way! But light can change when it strikes an object. The light rays may pass through the object. They may reflect off the object. Or, they may be absorbed by the object.

Light waves reflect at least a little off most objects. **Reflection** occurs when light rays bounce, or reflect, from a surface back to our eyes. Some objects reflect more light rays than others. When you brush your teeth in front of a mirror, the smooth, shiny surface of the mirror reflects almost all the light rays that hit it. The rays reflect back to your eyes at the same angle. You see a clear image, or reflection, of your toothpaste-filled mouth.

Light waves can also be absorbed. **Absorption** occurs when an object takes in the light wave. After a light wave is absorbed, it becomes a form of heat energy.

Reflection

Absorption

Color and Light

We see colors because objects absorb some frequencies of light and reflect others. The shirt at the right looks red because it reflects light rays of the red frequency. It absorbs light rays of other visible color frequencies.

Black and white objects are special cases. When light hits a white T-shirt, for example, all color frequencies in the visible spectrum are reflected. When the colors all blend, they look white. An object looks black because it absorbs all colors of the visible spectrum. On a sunny day, black objects feel warm because the light energy they absorb changes into heat energy.

Letting Light Through

Materials can be grouped by how they react to light. Materials that transmit nearly all of the light rays that hit them are **transparent.** This means that materials let the light rays pass through them. You can clearly see what is on the other side of transparent material. Air, clean water, and tinted windows are transparent. Transparent objects that are colored reflect and transmit only that color. They absorb the other colors. For example, sunglasses that are tinted blue reflect and transmit only blue frequencies. They absorb all others.

Materials that let some light rays pass through but scatter other rays are **translucent.** You can see that light passes through a translucent material, but what is on the other side of it looks blurry. Waxed paper, lampshades, frosted glass, and beeswax are translucent.

Materials that do not let any light pass through are **opaque.** You cannot see through an opaque object. An opaque material either reflects or absorbs the light rays that strike it. Aluminum foil is an example of an opaque material that reflects light. The light bounces off the foil, making the surface look bright and shiny. Wood is an opaque material that absorbs light.

✓ Checkpoint

1. How does light behave when it strikes a transparent object?
2. **Math** in Science Sunglasses help protect the eyes by causing some light rays to be absorbed, scattered, or reflected away from the eyes. A typical pair of sunglasses might transmit $\frac{3}{10}$ of visible light rays. What fraction of visible light do the glasses reflect, scatter, or absorb?

How Light Changes Direction

The light rays refract, or bend, as they travel from air to water. That's why the pencil looks broken.

Light can be transmitted, reflected, and absorbed, but that's not all. Light can also be bent!

Unlike sound, light does not need a medium to travel through. In fact, light travels fastest through the empty space of a vacuum such as outer space. Light slows a little when it travels through various mediums. Light travels slower in a gas such as air than in a vacuum. Suppose a light wave travels from a vacuum to gas. As the wave hits the gas, it slows down.

Particles in a liquid are closer together than the particles in a gas. So, light travels through a liquid slower than through a gas. Light moves slowest through the tightly packed particles in solids.

When light moves at an angle from one medium to another, some of the light is reflected, some is absorbed, and some passes through and changes directions. It bends! This bending is called **refraction.** As a light ray moves at an angle from one transparent medium to another, it changes speed. The change in speed causes the light to refract, or bend. In white light that is separated into individual colors, each color bends differently. The longer the color's wavelength, the less it bends. The picture of the pencil shows what happens when light that is moving through air strikes a transparent solid that contains a transparent liquid.

Rays of light bend and separate into individual colors when they strike a piece of glass known as a prism. Red light bends the least. Violet light bends the most

The Human Eye

The human eye is a fluid-filled ball with a bony area around it. A transparent covering protects the front of the eye. The covering also refracts light that enters the eye. A donut-shaped muscle called the iris is behind the covering. The iris is the colored part of the eye. The

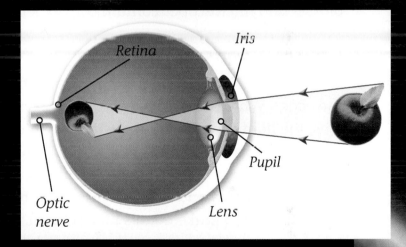

dark opening in the center of the iris is called the pupil.

The iris controls how much light enters the eye. In bright light, the iris closes and the pupil gets smaller. In dim light, it opens and the pupil gets larger. The light that enters then passes through the lens of the eye. The lens refracts the light rays even more. The rays form an upside-down image on the retina at the back of the eye. Cells in the retina change the light into signals that travel along the optic nerve to the brain. You see a right-side up image.

1. **✓ Checkpoint** In which medium does light travel faster, a gas or a liquid?
2. **Math in Science** Suppose you are using a magnifying glass that makes objects seem 3 times their real-life size. How long would an insect that measures 1 centimeter look through the magnifying glass?

Lenses

Lenses are curved pieces of clear glass or plastic that refract light that passes through them. Lenses can be used to help people see things that are very small or very far away. There are two main types of lenses: convex and concave.

Convex Lenses

A convex lens is thicker in the middle than at the edges, somewhat like a football. When light passes through a convex lens, the light rays bend in toward the middle of the lens. The bent light rays come together and meet at a point on the other side of the lens. A convex lens can magnify things, or make them look larger. Magnifying glasses and microscopes contain convex lenses.

Concave Lenses

A concave lens is thinner in the middle than at the edges. When light passes through a concave lens, the light rays bend out toward the thicker edges of the lens. The light rays spread apart. So, the object appears smaller than it really is.

Concave lenses and convex lenses are often used together to make details look sharper. Many telescopes that are used to view distant objects have both concave and convex lenses.

Convex lenses make things look larger.

Concave lenses make things look smaller.

1st century A.D.: Roman thinker Seneca notices that a glass ball filled with water magnifies letters.

1275: On a visit to China, Italian traveler Marco Polo sees people wearing eyeglasses.

1609: Italian scientist Galileo uses a telescope to look at objects in the sky.

1668: English scientist Isaac Newton invents a new type of telescope with a reflecting mirror.

424

Ways Light Is Used

Lasers

A laser is a narrow but powerful beam of light. Laser light can be visible or invisible. It can travel long distances and still focus on a small area. You use laser light when you play or store information on a CD. Laser light is used to read bar codes in stores and libraries. It is used in printers and scanners.

Laser light has a great deal of heat energy. In industry, it is used to cut, drill, and bond materials together. In medicine, doctors use lasers to treat certain problems with internal organs, the eye, and the skin.

Optical Fibers

Optical fibers are very thin glass or plastic fibers that are bundled together in a coated, flexible tube. A light source, often a laser, is at one end of the tube. A human eye, a camera, or some other detector is at the other end. The tube can be twisted or bent without affecting the image that is sent.

Optical fibers are made from transparent materials that transmit visible, ultraviolet, and infrared light. The information they carry quickly travels long distances. Optical fibers are used in communication, medicine, and industry.

✓ **Lesson Checkpoint**

1. What happens to light energy when it is absorbed by an object?
2. What does a convex lens look like?
3. **Draw Conclusions** What happens when light rays strike a mirror?

1670s: Dutch scientist Anton van Leeuwenhoek becomes the first person to look at tiny life forms with a microscope.

1784: American Benjamin Franklin invents bifocal glasses that help people see both near and far objects.

1800s: German scientist Joseph von Fraunhofer uses two different types of lenses to make a compound lens.

1888: Contact lenses are placed directly on the eye to correct eyesight.

Guided Inquiry

Investigate How does light travel?

Light travels in straight lines, but you can make it bend.

Materials

scissors

shoe box with hole

metric ruler and
black paper

black paper square
with slits

flashlight and mirror

cup and water

Process Skills

You can make **inferences** based on your **observations**.

What to Do

1 Tape the black paper square over the hole in the box. Measure the bottom of the box. Cut black paper to fit.

2 Hold the flashlight about 60 cm back from the box. Shine the light through the slits. See how the black paper absorbs most of the light, but some light goes through the slits. **Observe** the light's path inside the box.

60 cm

3 Tilt a mirror in the box to reflect the light. Observe the light's path.

Do you see 2 straight lines?

60 cm

Find objects in your classroom that reflect light like a mirror.

4 Put an empty plastic cup in the box. Shine light through the slits and the cup. Observe how light passes through air in the cup. Add water. Observe how it refracts the light.

Which objects are opaque?

60 cm

What things are transparent?

5 Draw a sketch or diagram to show the path of the light from the flashlight, through the slits, through the water, and beyond.

Think About It

1. Compare how light is affected by the air, the cup, the water, the box, the black paper, and the mirror. Use the terms *reflect, absorb, opaque,* and *transparent.*

2. Describe the light's path through the box and the cup with water. **Infer** what happens when light travels from air to water.

Go Further

How is light affected by translucent materials, such as wax paper? Develop and carry out a written plan to answer this question or one of your own. When finished, give an oral report to your class or make a written report in your science journal.

Math in Science

Comparing Speeds

Sound travels through air at about 1,190 kilometers per hour. That means a sound can travel the length of a football field in about one third of a second. Many machines travel just as fast as sound. Some machines travel even faster than sound. The display below compares the speed of some of the world's fastest machines to the speed of sound.

Machines vs. Sound

World's fastest train

Supersonic passenger jet

Sound wave in air

Jet airplane

Jet-powered car

World's fastest spy plane

In the display, the bar for the supersonic passenger plane is about twice as long as the bar for the speed of sound in air. This shows that the plane flies about twice as fast as sound travels in air.

Use the data in the display to answer the questions. Explain how you could find each answer just by comparing the bars.

1 Which machine travels at about the same speed as sound?

2 Which machine travels about three times as fast as sound?

3 Which machine travels about one third as fast as sound?

Lab zone **Take-Home Activity**

In one minute, a sound wave can travel about 12 miles, or 63,360 feet. Find out how fast you walk compared to the speed of sound. Walk down a sidewalk for one minute while an adult times you. Then use a tape measure to find the distance you covered. How much faster is the sound wave, in feet per minute?

Chapter 14 Review and Test Prep

Use Vocabulary

absorption (p. 420)	**reflection** (p. 420)
compression (p. 408)	**refraction** (p. 422)
frequency (p. 409)	**translucent** (p. 421)
opaque (p. 421)	**transparent** (p. 421)
pitch (p. 412)	**wavelength** (p. 409)

Use the term from the list above that best completes each sentence.

1. Clear glass is an example of a _____ material.

2. Light rays cannot pass through a material that is _____.

3. A sound wave with a high frequency will also have a high _____.

4. The distance from one point on a wave to the next similar point on a wave is known as _____.

5. _____ is bending that results from a light wave changing speed as it moves at an angle from one medium to another.

6. When a light wave is taken in by an object, _____ occurs.

7. Materials that let some light rays pass through but scatter some of the other rays are _____.

8. A wave bouncing back off an object or surface is known as _____.

9. A _____ is the part of a sound wave where particles are close together.

10. The number of times a wave makes a complete cycle in a second is its _____.

Explain Concepts

11. Explain why a wave with a short wavelength has a high frequency.

12. Why does a light wave travel slower through a gas than through a vacuum?

Process Skills

13. **Predict** what a note played on a tuba would sound like if you were standing in front of the tuba player. Then **predict** what the note would sound like if the tuba player were at one end of a basketball court and you were standing at the other end.

14. The Sun gives off light energy in the visible and invisible parts of the electromagnetic spectrum. The pie circle graph shows the different kinds of light the Sun gives off. **Interpret the data** and explain whether most of the light energy given off is in the visible or the invisible part of the spectrum.

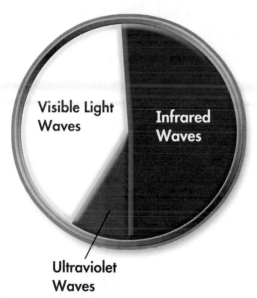

Visible Light Waves

Infrared Waves

Ultraviolet Waves

Draw Conclusions

15. Make a graphic organizer like the one shown below. Fill in facts that you might lead you to the conclusion.

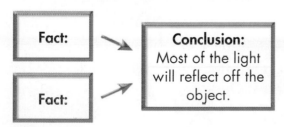

Fact:

Fact:

Conclusion: Most of the light will reflect off the object.

Choose the letter that best completes the statement.

16. A sound wave cannot travel through a _____.
- Ⓐ gas
- Ⓑ liquid
- Ⓒ solid
- Ⓓ vacuum

17. To hear a higher-pitched note on a guitar string you should
- Ⓕ loosen the string.
- Ⓖ shorten the string.
- Ⓗ pluck the string harder.
- Ⓘ make the string vibrate slower.

18. Radio waves, ultraviolet rays, and gamma rays are all
- Ⓐ part of the visible spectrum.
- Ⓑ part of the electromagnetic spectrum.
- Ⓒ longitudinal waves.
- Ⓓ used to broadcast television and radio programs.

19. Explain why the answer you selected for Question #18 is best. For each of the answers you did not select, give a reason why it is not the best choice.

20. Writing in Science **Expository** Write a paragraph explaining what happens to a ray of sunlight as it passes from the air through a clear glass filled with water.

Optometrist

The eye is a sensitive organ and requires special care. Optometrists help us take care of our eyes. Sometimes people do not see everything clearly. They may see things that are close, but things that are far away may be blurry. They are near sighted. Other people can see things far away but have a hard time seeing things up close. They are far sighted. An optometrist can prescribe lenses to correct these problems.

The kind of lens an optometrist prescribes depends on the kind of vision problem that needs to be corrected. The shape of the lens changes how light enters the eye.

Optometrists can help with other eye problems. They can diagnose and treat some eye diseases. They can check to see how well you see colors. They may recommend exercises to help your eyes work together better. Optometrists also can test your depth perception, the ability to judge how far away something is.

If you want to help people see better, you might like to become an optometrist. You must earn a college degree. The next step is to earn a Doctor of Optometry degree. You also must pass a test given by the state where you want to be an optometrist.

Lab zone > Take-Home Activity

The way a camera works is similar to the way an eye works. Use your library or the Internet to find out how a camera works.

EC NTL 10 9 8 7 6 5 4 3 2 1

You Will Discover

- how types of motion are described.
- how forces affect motion.
- how forces, motion, and energy are related.

Chapter 15
Objects in Motion

Online
Student Edition

www.sfsuccessnet.com

What causes motion and how does it affect us?

relative motion

friction

velocity

434

force

work

Chapter 15 Vocabulary

frame of reference

speed

gravity

kinetic energy

potential energy

Explore What can change a marble's speed?

Materials

marble and ruler
with groove

books

meterstick and
masking tape

timer and calculator or
computer (optional)

Process Skills

You **interpret data** when you use data to help answer questions.

What to Do

1 Roll a marble down a ramp. Time how long it takes to move 180 cm. Find the speed.

$$speed = distance \div time$$

Place marble at end of ruler.

about 10 cm

book

ruler with a groove

Starting Line — Begin timing here.

180 cm

Ending Line — Stop timing here.

2 **Predict** how lowering the ramp would change the speed. Test your prediction by removing 1 book.

Think About It

1. **Interpret** Make a bar graph to show your results.
2. **Infer** How did lowering the ramp change the speed of the marble?

Reading Skills

TARGET SKILL Sequence

Sequence refers to the order in which events happen. Sometimes writers use clue words such as *first*, *next*, *then*, *after*, and *finally* to signal sequence.

Science Journal

Rolling Along

First, my friend gave me a ruler with a groove in the center. I put one end of the ruler on the floor and propped the other end on a book to form a ramp. Next, I put a marble in the groove at the high end of the ruler and let it go. After the marble stopped rolling, my friend used a piece of tape to mark how far it had traveled. Finally, I measured the distance the marble rolled on the floor.

Apply It!

Use clue words to help you complete a graphic organizer that shows the order in which things happened in the journal entry.

Add as many boxes as you need to show the entire sequence of events.

First

⬇

Next

⬇

Then

⬇

🔊 You Are There!

You thought the stairs would never end, but finally you're at the top. You lower yourself into the steep, looping tube as water swirls around your feet. Then you let go. Suddenly, you're sliding, twisting, turning, faster and faster. At each curve, you fear that you'll fly right out of the tube, but your body slams against the wall and bounces back into the cushion of rushing water. After one last loop, you shoot out the end of the tube. Whoosh! You splash into the pool. You can't wait to go again, but you just don't know if you have the energy to climb all those stairs. If only you could slide up the stairs too! Why can't you?

What is motion?

All kinds of things around you move in different ways. Cars, trucks, and buses transport people and goods from place to place. You can describe and measure their motion in different ways.

Types of Motion

Different things move in different ways. One way objects can move is in a straight line. A baseball player racing for home plate is likely to run in a straight line. Trains on a track often travel in straight lines.

Objects can also move in a curved path. A car turning a corner moves in a curved path. Curved motion takes place around a center point. A bicycle wheel follows a curved path around its axle. Earth moves in a curved path around the Sun.

Another way things can move is back and forth. When a player plucks a guitar string, the string moves back and forth. This back and forth motion is known as vibration.

But as you ride your bicycle or walk down your street, you pass plants, buildings, and other things that do not move. They are fixed in place. When you pass a fixed object, you know you are moving. When you stand still, you can tell that a car you see moves because it changes position. Your understanding of motion is related to the things around you. Every day, you compare objects that change position with objects that don't. The change in one object's position compared to another object's fixed position is **relative motion.**

Toy cars change speed as they race around the track.

Sometimes the cars move in a straight path.

Sometimes the cars move in a curved path.

1.   ✓**Checkpoint** What are three different types of motion?
2.   ⦿ **Sequence** Describe the sequence of events of the yellow race car as it travels around the track above.

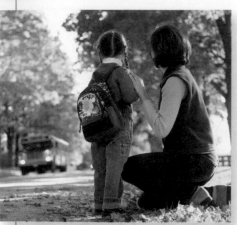

From your frame of reference on the sidewalk, the bus and the people on it are moving.

From your frame of reference on the bus, everything on the bus seems to be standing still.

From your frame of reference on the bus, everything outside the bus seems to move.

How You Know You Are Moving

How do you know if a person on a water slide moves? How do you know if the water moves? You look at the changing positions of the person and the water. You compare their changing positions to the fixed position of the slide. You use the relative motion of the objects around you to decide what is moving and what is not moving.

The objects you use to detect motion are your **frame of reference.** How an object seems to move depends on your frame of reference. Your frame of reference is like your point of view.

Suppose you are on a float in a parade. Your friend is on the same float. Your float begins moving down the parade route. You wave at the people sitting and watching the parade as your float moves past them. From your frame of reference on the float, the people seem to be moving. But, your friend hasn't moved a bit. From your friend's frame of reference, you haven't moved either. As the parade moves down the street, people on the sidewalk see you and your friend pass by. From their frame of reference, you and your friend are both moving.

Suppose you use your classroom as your frame of reference. If you were sitting at your desk, you would say that you are not moving. But suppose you choose the Sun as your frame of reference. Now you would say that you are moving, because Earth carries you along with it as it travels around the Sun.

Measuring Motion

Speed is the rate at which an object changes position. It measures how fast an object moves. The unit for speed is a unit of distance divided by a unit of time, such as kilometers per hour. A car moving at a high speed changes position faster than a car moving at a slow speed. To find an object's average speed, divide the distance the object moves by the total time spent moving.

Velocity combines both the speed and the direction an object is moving. Some words that describe direction are *north*, *south*, *east*, and *west*. Others are *left*, *right*, *up*, and *down*.

Any change in the speed or direction of an object's motion is an acceleration. Starting, speeding up, and slowing down are accelerations. The roller coaster accelerates as it speeds up. It is changing speed. A roller coaster on a curved path accelerates even if its speed does not change. That is because it changes direction as it moves around the curve.

✓ **Lesson Checkpoint**

1. What is a frame of reference?
2. What are two ways that a roller coaster can accelerate?
3. **Writing in Science** **Descriptive** Write a paragraph that describes the difference between speed and velocity.

The roller coaster slows as it moves up to the top of the loop. It goes faster heading downhill. The velocity changes as the coaster changes direction from up to down.

As the roller coaster moves uphill again, its velocity changes. Its speed decreases.

This roller coaster reaches its greatest speed at the bottom of the loop.

Lesson 2

How does force affect moving objects?

Objects do not just move on their own. Something must make a ball start to roll. Something must also make a rolling ball stop.

Force

A **force** is any push or pull. Force can make an object that is standing still start to move. It can also make a moving object move faster, slow down, stop, or change direction. The object moves in the same direction as the force.

Some forces act only on contact. These forces must touch an object to affect it. A marble on a level surface will not move until you hit it with your finger or another object. Contact force starts the ball rolling.

Other forces can act at a distance. These forces can affect objects without touching them. For example, without any contact, a magnet can pull a piece of iron toward it. The magnet has a force that acts on the iron from a distance.

Pushing or pulling can change both the position and motion of an object. The size of the change depends on the strength of the push or pull. For example, the harder you push a swing, the higher and faster it will move. Also, a strong magnet will pull a piece of iron toward it from farther away than a weak magnet will.

A moving marble hits one that is standing still. The contact force of the moving marble starts the other marble moving.

A marble that is standing still moves when it is bumped by another marble.

Magnets can make things move without touching them.

Magnetism is a force that can act at a distance. Magnetic force has an effect on metals like iron and steel.

442

Combining Forces

All forces have both size and direction. Notice the dogs pulling on the rubber toy. They are combining forces, but they are working against each other. They are pulling in opposite directions, but with the same force. As long as they both pull with the same force, the forces are balanced. The toy will not move. But if one dog pulls with more force, the forces will be unbalanced. The toy will move toward the dog with the greater force.

Many objects are acted upon by more than one force. Suppose you push on a door to open it. Your friend on the other side of the door also pushes on it with the same size force. But your friend is pushing the door in the opposite direction. The forces are balanced and the door does not move. But suppose you continue to push the door while your friend pulls it. Now both forces are acting on the door in the same direction. The door moves—quickly—in your friend's direction. The total force on the door can be found by adding the forces together.

Two train engines pull together in the same direction. They are combining forces and working together. The total force of the engines is equal to the sum of the two forces.

1. ✓**Checkpoint** What causes objects to move or moving objects to stop moving?
2. ↻ **Sequence** Describe the sequence of events if the dog on the right suddenly stops pulling on the toy.

Force and Motion

Recall that if two dogs tug on a toy with balanced force, the toy will not move. If two or more forces acting on an object in opposite directions are balanced, the forces cancel each other. The object's motion does not change. A still object will not start moving unless the forces acting on it change. The resistance an object has to any change to its motion is called inertia.

In the same way, a moving object changes its motion only when a force acts on it. If balanced forces are applied to a moving object, it will keep moving at the same speed and in the same direction. The moving object will not slow or turn until the forces acting on it change.

The amount of force acting on an object affects how that object changes speed and direction. When you ride a bike, you first start pushing on the pedals. Next you push harder. The bicycle goes faster. Then you squeeze the brakes. The bicycle slows. You turn the handlebars. The bicycle changes direction.

More force is needed to change the motion of an object with more mass. That's why football players find big players are harder to tackle than smaller players. That's why you can easily move an empty wagon. When your friends climb in, you must pull with more force to move the wagon and its passengers.

Force is needed to move the plow. Even more force would be needed to move larger equipment.

Friction

You learned that a moving object will not slow until the forces acting on it change. You also know that unless an object is coasting downhill, moving objects do slow down. You know that if you don't pull a wagon, it will eventually slow and stop. Actually, the wagon slows because there is a force acting on it

Friction is a force that acts when two surfaces rub together. Friction can slow or stop moving objects. It can also keep objects from starting to move. The amount of friction between two surfaces depends on each object's surface and its mass.

The surface of every object has high and low spots. On a rough surface, you can see and feel these uneven places. When objects with rough surfaces rub, the high spots catch on each other. This causes a lot of friction. On a smooth surface, the uneven places are too tiny to see or feel. When objects with smooth surfaces rub, there is less friction. The objects move more easily.

The amount of friction also depends on the weight of the objects that are pressing together. If you push a box of feathers along the floor, it moves easily. What would happen if you fill the same box with books? The weight of the box presses against the floor with more force. This causes more friction, and the box is harder to push.

If you can't change the surfaces or the weight of the objects you are trying to move, you can reduce friction in other ways. You can use oil or wax to make the surfaces smoother. Less friction means you need less force to move the objects.

The surface of the Super Slide is very smooth.

Ball bearings reduce friction because they roll rather than drag across each other. Oil makes their surfaces smoother.

✓ **Lesson Checkpoint**

1. What is friction?
2. **Writing in Science** **Descriptive** Write a short story describing what would happen if suddenly there was no friction.

445

Lesson 3

How are force, mass, and energy related?

The force of gravity acts between all objects. How gravity and other forces act depends on the mass, distance, and motion of the objects.

The heavier the weight is, the more it stretches the spring.

Mass and Weight

Mass and weight are not the same. Mass is the amount of material in an object. Weight is a measure of the force of gravity acting on that object's mass. The Moon's mass is much less than Earth's mass. So the Moon pulls things toward it with only one-sixth as much force. This means that people on the Moon weigh only one-sixth as much as they do on Earth. But their mass does not change.

The Force of Gravity

When you drop a ball, it doesn't hang in the air. Instead, it falls to the ground. A force acts on the ball to make it fall. That force is **gravity**, which makes objects pull toward each other. The force of gravity between two objects depends on their masses and the distance between them.

The force of gravity is stronger if objects are close together. As the objects move farther apart, the force of gravity between them becomes weaker.

The force of gravity between massive objects is strong. As the mass of the objects is reduced, so is the force of gravity between them. Doubling the mass of one object doubles the force of gravity between it and another object.

The ball you drop falls because Earth's large mass pulls on it. The ball also pulls on Earth, but the ball's mass is too small to move the massive Earth.

The astronaut weighs about 900 newtons on Earth but only about 150 newtons on the Moon.

Sir Isaac Newton made many discoveries that relate force and motion.

Measuring Force

The amount and direction of many forces can be measured. A spring scale is one tool used to measure force. A spring scale has a hook on the bottom. When you hang an object from the hook, the spring stretches. How much the spring stretches depends on the object's weight. Weight is a measure of the force of gravity acting on an object's mass. The heavier an object is, the stronger the force. And the stronger the force, the more the spring will stretch. Look at the springs in the picture at the top of page 446. The heaviest weight stretched the spring the most.

The marker shows the size of the force that has stretched the spring. As the spring stretches, the marker moves along a row of numbers on the scale. These numbers are the unit of force that scientists call the newton. One newton (1 N) is about the force you would need to lift a small apple. The newton was named after Sir Isaac Newton, who explained how force and motion are linked.

1. ✓**Checkpoint** What two factors affect the force of gravity between two objects?
2. **Math in Science** If a dog weighed about 240 newtons on Earth, how much would it weigh on the Moon?

447

Energy and Motion

Scientists define energy as the ability to do work. **Work** is the ability to move something. When work is done, a change happens. Energy is the source of that change. Any change in motion requires energy.

You should know about two kinds of energy. The energy of motion is **kinetic energy.** All moving things have kinetic energy. The amount of kinetic energy depends on an object's speed and mass. The faster the giant swing moves, the more kinetic energy it has. The swing also has more kinetic energy if the cage is full of riders. That is because the added mass of the riders has increased the total mass of the cage.

The wrecking ball has a great deal of kinetic energy before it crashes into the building.

Stored Energy

When the swing reaches the top of its path, it stops for a moment. The swing is not moving, so it has no kinetic energy. But now it has another kind of energy. **Potential energy** is stored energy. The swing has potential energy because of its position at the top of its path. The swing has the most potential energy when it is as high as it can possibly be. As soon as the cage starts to swing down toward the ground, it starts to use its potential energy. Now that the cage is moving, the stored energy is changing to energy of motion.

Objects that are stretched or squeezed also have potential energy. A stretched rubber band has potential energy. So does the tightened spring in a wind-up toy.

Like a roller coaster, the energy of this giant swing constantly changes back and forth between potential energy and kinetic energy.

Changing Kinds of Energy

Potential energy can change into kinetic energy and back again. Picture a child winding the spring of the toy bird. Each turn winds the spring tighter, which adds more stored energy. Then the child releases the toy. The spring unwinds, and the bird hops forward. The energy stored in the spring is changing into the energy of motion.

At the top of its path, the giant swing has potential energy. As it swoops toward the ground, stored energy changes to kinetic energy. Then it swings back up. Now the energy of motion is changing back into the energy of position. At the top of the path, the swing has regained its high position. The energy of motion has become the stored energy of position. When the giant swing starts back down the path, the process starts again.

In the giant swing, you saw that energy can change from one type to another. By nudging a rock so that it starts rolling down a hill, you change its potential energy into kinetic energy. The potential energy that fuel gives a rocket on the launch pad changes to kinetic energy when the rocket blasts off. Energy cannot be made or destroyed. The total amount of energy never changes.

The wound spring inside this toy has potential energy.

Changing Types of Energy		
Type of Stored Energy	**How the Energy Is Used**	
Fossil fuels store potential energy from the Sun.	Fossil fuels burn to give vehicles kinetic energy.	
Plants store potential energy from the Sun.	The energy is released to support the animals that eat the plants.	
The water behind a dam has potential energy.	A hydroelectric power plant produces electric energy.	

✓ **Lesson Checkpoint**

1. What kind of energy does a stretched rubber band have?
2. How is energy changed in the toy bird?
3. **Technology in Science** Use the Internet or other sources to find out how Niagara Falls became a source of electrical energy.

Investigate How does friction affect motion?

Materials

Ramp Angle Protractor

cardboard

sandpaper and waxed paper

tape

toy car and eraser

calculator or computer (optional)

Process Skills

You can use a table or a chart to **collect** and record **data**.

What to Do

1 Tape the sandpaper to the cardboard.

2 Put the car and the eraser on the ramp. Have someone in your group hold the Ramp Angle Protractor.

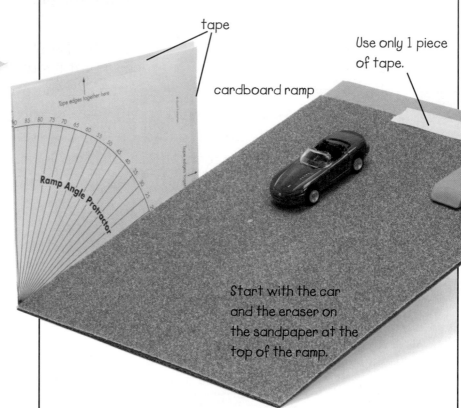

tape

cardboard ramp

Use only 1 piece of tape.

Ramp Angle Protractor

Start with the car and the eraser on the sandpaper at the top of the ramp.

3 Slowly raise the ramp. **Observe** the angle of the ramp. When each object reaches the bottom of the ramp, record the angle. Repeat 2 more times. **Collect** and record your **data**.

Take It to the NET
More Activities www.sfsuccessnet.com

4 Based on your observations, **predict** what would happen if you replaced the sandpaper with waxed paper. Test your prediction 3 times. Record your data.

5 Make a bar graph of your results.

	Angle at Which Object Reached Bottom of Ramp (degrees)			
	Sandpaper Surface		Waxed Paper Surface	
	Car	Eraser	Car	Eraser
Trial 1				
Trial 2				
Trial 3				
Average				

Find the averages. Your teacher might ask you to use a calculator or a computer to find the averages.

Sandpaper is rougher than waxed paper. The force of friction is greater.

Average Angle at Which Object Reached Bottom of Ramp

Angle (degrees)

70
60
50
40
30
20
10
0

Car	Eraser	Car	Eraser
Sandpaper Surface		Waxed Paper Surface	

Think About It

1. **Interpreting Data** How did using waxed paper instead of sandpaper affect the angle at which the objects moved?

2. What force pulled the eraser down the ramp? What force kept the eraser from moving until the ramp was steep enough?

Go Further

How could you increase or decrease the force of friction between the objects and the ramp? Design and conduct a scientific investigation to find out. Provide evidence for your conclusion.

Relating Distance, Speed, and Time

The distance a moving object travels is the product of its average speed and the time it travels. You can use the formula below to find distance.

Distance = average speed × time

Take It to the NET
Distance, Speed, Time www.sfsuccessnet.com

In the 1850s, wagons on the Oregon Trail traveled at an average speed of 3 km per hour. At this pace, they could travel only 3 × 8 km, or 24 km, in 8 hours. Today, at highway speeds, you can travel 24 kilometers in 15 minutes or less.

Use the distance formula to answer each question.

1 Today, a car traveling on a highway might have an average speed of 92 kilometers per hour. How far would the car travel in 8 hours?

2 A jet passenger plane might have an average speed of 775 kilometers per hour. If an international flight takes 8 hours, how far has the plane traveled?

3 A roller coaster travels an 852-meter track in 3 minutes. What is the average speed of the roller coaster in meters per minute?

Lab zone Take-Home Activity

Plan a trip with the following conditions. You have 4 hours to travel each way. You may go by car, train, or airplane. Choose a destination you could reach from home by your choice of transportation in 4 hours.

Use Vocabulary

force (p. 442)	**potential energy** (p. 448)
frame of reference (p. 440)	**relative motion** (p. 439)
friction (p. 445)	**speed** (p. 440)
gravity (p. 446)	**velocity** (p. 441)
kinetic energy (p. 448)	**work** (p. 448)

Use the vocabulary term from the list above that best completes each sentence.

1. A child at the top of a slide has _____.

2. When you push or pull on a wagon, you make a _____ act on the wagon.

3. _____ tells both the speed and direction that something is moving.

4. _____ is done when you move an object.

5. A change in the position of one object compared to the position of a fixed object is called _____.

6. The force that makes a ball fall toward the ground is _____.

7. The objects you use to detect motion are called your _____.

8. The energy that a bicycle has when it moves down a hill is called _____.

Explain Concepts

9. Why do you need to use force to move a ball up a ramp when it moves downward by itself?

10. Use vocabulary terms to explain why a soccer ball that is quickly rolling across a grass field slows and finally stops rolling.

Process Skills

11. Infer why it is easier to push an empty grocery cart than one that is filled with canned foods.

12. Predict what would happen if you tried to walk on a sidewalk where there was no friction between your shoes and the sidewalk.

13. Copy the chart below. Then **classify** each motion as straight line, curved, or vibration.

Motion	Kind of Motion
Swinging back and forth on a swing	
Riding on a merry-go-round	
Crossing the street at a crosswalk	

 Sequence

14. Complete a graphic organizer to show the order in which things happen on a roller coaster ride.

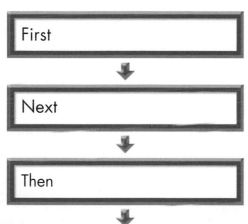

First

⬇

Next

⬇

Then

⬇

 Test Prep

Choose the letter that best completes the statement or answers the question.

15. Gravity is a force that makes objects
 Ⓐ push apart.
 Ⓑ pull toward each other.
 Ⓒ stop moving.
 Ⓓ move uphill.

16. Which object has kinetic energy?
 Ⓕ a ball lying on the floor
 Ⓖ a stopped merry-go-round
 Ⓗ a dog running through a yard
 Ⓘ a car parked in a garage

17. What happens to the force of gravity between two objects when the mass of one of the objects is increased?
 Ⓐ It increases.
 Ⓑ It decreases.
 Ⓒ It stays the same.
 Ⓓ It pushes the objects apart.

18. Speed is expressed in units of
 Ⓕ time per distance.
 Ⓖ direction per time.
 Ⓗ distance per time.
 Ⓘ force per time.

19. Explain why the answer you selected for Question #16 is best. For each answer you did not select, give a reason why it is not the best choice.

20. Writing in Science **Descriptive**
Write a paragraph describing what types of motion take place during a tug-of-war.

Space Engineer

Would you like to be part of the space program when you grow up? Even if the thought of flying in space is not something you would like to do, you can still work for NASA.

Most space engineers do not go into space. Their work is here on Earth. An engineer at NASA might work on many different projects. Engineers design the space shuttle, the computers, and everything that the space vehicle needs to safely reach its destination, complete its tasks, and return home. Engineers design such things as the place where the astronauts will live or how to land the space shuttle.

Engineers also design simulations on Earth. A simulation is a model of an actual event that helps us learn about the real thing. Simulations of gravity in space or of flying in a space shuttle help engineers design the space shuttles. Simulations also help astronauts learn what to do in different situations when they are in space. The simulations prepare astronauts for how life in space will be different from life on Earth.

Math skills are used often in engineering. If engineering interests you, you will want to start now. Study all the math and science you can.

Estela Hernandez is a flight simulation engineer for NASA.

Lab zone Take-Home Activity

Think of something you would like to improve. Maybe you want skates with better brakes or a clock that tells what the weather is like. Write about your idea.

You Will Discover

- how simple machines help us do work.
- how simple machines work together as parts of complex machines.

Chapter 16

Simple Machines

www.sfsuccessnet.com

64mm

How do simple machines make work easier?

fulcrum

effort

lever

pulley

inclined plane

load

458

Chapter 16
Vocabulary

wheel and axle

wedge

screw

Explore How can a machine ring a bell?

Materials

2 markers

2 metric rulers

eraser

marble

bell

What to Do

1 Set up a machine that can ring a bell. Your machine could look like the one in the picture.

 Push down.

2 Test the machine.

Process Skills

You can **communicate** information about the machine you made by drawing a diagram.

Think About It

1. Draw a diagram that **communicates** how to make the machine. Draw another diagram that communicates how the machine works.

2. How else could you use the machine? What else could you make with the parts?

Reading Skills

Summarize

A summary is a short retelling of something you have read.

- When you write a summary, include only the most important ideas.

- Leave out most details, and do not add any new ideas.

- Use your own words when you summarize.

- A graphic organizer can help you organize the main ideas for your summary.

Science Article

Musical Levers

Many musical instruments use levers to play different notes. A piano key is connected to levers inside the piano. The levers move a hammer that hits a group of strings that make the sounds. Flutes and clarinets have levers that open and close small holes. Opening and closing different holes make different sounds. Drummers use levers attached to hammers that strike the drums.

Apply It!

Read the magazine article. Use a graphic organizer like this one to choose ideas for your summary. Then write a one- or two-sentence summary about "Musical Levers."

Detail →

Detail → Summary

Detail →

You Are There!

On the way home from school, you walk by an empty lot. You see a huge machine digging a hole. A shovel on the end of a long arm scoops up dirt. It dumps the dirt into a dump truck. You watch carefully for a while, thinking about how the parts of the machine work together. Some parts look familiar. This big machine isn't so hard to figure out. It is made up of many smaller, simpler machines.

Lesson 1

What is a machine?

The lever is a simple machine. It helps people do work. Other simple machines include the wheel and axle, pulley, inclined plane, wedge, and screw.

Machines and Work

A machine can be just one piece or it can have many moving parts. But all machines help us do work. Do you think that work means doing homework or chores around the house? In science, work has a special meaning. Work means using force—pushing or pulling —in order to move an object or make a change.

You could use a lot of force but not do any work. Can you think of a way? Suppose you push as hard as you can on a brick wall. You may be pushing very hard, but you won't move the wall one tiny bit. Because nothing moves or changes, you aren't doing any work.

Machines make work easier. Some simple machines allow you to to use less force to do work. The heavier the object, the more force you must use to move it. Without simple machines, we couldn't budge heavy things.

Other simple machines change the direction of the force you use. You can push or pull in one direction and get work done in a different direction.

You will learn about simple machines that have just one or two parts. Yet each of these machines makes work easier. Some basic types of simple machines are the lever, the pulley, the inclined plane, the wheel and axle, the wedge, and the screw.

1. **✓Checkpoint** How do you use force to do work?
2. **Math in Science** Distance is a quantity, or amount, of space between two things. Amounts can be measured. What tools would you use to measure the distance someone pushes a wheelbarrow? In what units would you measure the distance?

Levers

One useful machine is the lever. A **lever** is a long bar with a support. The weight of both the bar and what it carries rests on the support. We call this support the **fulcrum.** The object you want to lift or move is the **load.** When you use a lever, you have to apply some effort or force. The **effort** is a push or a pull on the bar that makes the load move in some way.

A lever doesn't make you stronger, but it does make doing hard work easier. It adds to your force. It can also change the direction of the force. When you use a lever, you can make some choices about the best way to get the work done. The pictures show how moving the fulcrum changes the amount of force you need to use.

Levers help us lift things that are very heavy.

Effort	Fulcrum	Load
4 rings		4 rings

4   4

The effort and the load are equal. They are both 4 units from the fulcrum. The lever is balanced.

The first picture shows a lever with the fulcrum exactly halfway between the load and the effort. When you use this kind of lever, the effort you use matches the downward force, or weight, of the load. The lever changes the direction of the force.

Effort	Fulcrum	Load
4 rings		8 rings

4   2

On this lever, the load is closer to the fulcrum. So, the same effort balances a larger load.

In the second picture, the fulcrum is much closer to the load than to the effort. Notice that the load, on the right, is a stack of eight metal rings. The effort, on the left, is a stack of four rings. When the fulcrum of a lever is closer to the load, the force is applied over a greater distance. You use the same effort to lift a heavier object.

For any lever, the effort multiplied by its distance from the fulcrum is equal to the load multiplied by its distance from the fulcrum. The equation below matches the second picture.

Effort	×	Distance	=	Load	×	Distance
4	×	4	=	8	×	2
		16	=			16

464

Types of Levers

Levers can be classified into three different groups. In the first group of levers, the fulcrum is between the effort and the load. Levers with the load between the effort and the fulcrum are in the second group. When the effort is between the load and the fulcrum, the lever is in the third group.

Groups of Levers

Some levers have two bars that work together. Levers with two bars can also be divided into groups.

Group 1

The fulcrum on the pliers is between the effort and the load. The effort is the part of the pliers you squeeze, and the load is the object you want to hold or turn.

Group 2

The fulcrum on the nutcracker is at the closed end. The effort is at the open end, where you squeeze. The load is the nut you want to crack open. It is between the fulcrum and the effort.

Group 3

The fulcrum on the tongs is at the closed end. The load is at the open end, which picks up the ice cube. The effort is in the middle, where you squeeze. It is between the fulcrum and the load.

1. ✓**Checkpoint** Define fulcrum, load, and effort.
2. **Math** in Science A load of 3 rings is 4 units from the fulcrum of a lever. When 2 rings are placed on the other side of the fulcrum, the lever balances. How far are the 2 rings from the fulcrum?

Wheel and Axle

The **wheel and axle** is a special kind of lever that moves or turns objects. The axle is a rod that goes through the center of the wheel. The steering wheel on a car is a wheel and axle. When the driver turns the steering wheel, the axle that connects with the car's front wheels also turns. The force the driver uses to turn the steering wheel is increased to turn the car's wheels.

A screwdriver is another example of a wheel and axle. The handle is the wheel and the metal blade is the axle. The end of the blade fits into a slot on the screw. The force you use to turn the handle increases. The blade turns and tightens the screw.

In this type of wheel and axle, you put force into turning the doorknob, which is the wheel. This force changes into a larger force that turns the axle. The axle is the turning shaft inside the doorknob. That makes it easy to turn.

Look at the picture of the garden hose reel. You turn the crank and the long hose winds onto the reel. The crank you turn is the wheel. It is joined to the axle, which goes through the center of the reel. You use effort to turn the crank and with each turn, more hose is wound up!

Pulley

A **pulley** is a wheel with a rope, wire, or chain around it. This pulley is actually two pulleys. At the top is a fixed pulley, which is fastened to one place. At the bottom is a movable pulley. It moves up or down along with the load that is hanging from the hook.

One thing a pulley does is change the direction of force. Look at the picture again. The force scale on the right shows how much force is being used to raise the weight. The direction that this strong pull is coming from is down and to the right. The pulley has changed the direction of the force.

Block and Tackle

When you use two or more pulleys together, you are using a system of compound pulleys. When one of the pulleys is fixed, the compound pulley is known as a block and tackle. Each pulley you add to a compound system reduces the amount of effort needed to lift a load. A system with many pulleys allows you to lift a heavy load using only a fraction of the effort you'd need without the pulleys.

Look at the pictures of the compound pulleys. Which system do you think would be best for lifting a piano?

A pulley can also reduce the amount of force needed to lift a load. This is true, however, only when at least two pulleys are used together—as in this picture. You may have noticed that there is only one length of rope between the top pulley and the pulling arm to the right. But there are two lengths of rope between the two pulleys. Because those two lengths both carry weight, the person or machine operating the pulley can use less force to lift the load.

✔ Lesson Checkpoint

1. How does an axle fit into a wheel?
2. How does a fixed pulley help you lift a load?
3. **⊙ Summarize** How many ways can you use pulleys? Briefly describe at least three ways.

Lesson 2

How can machines work together?

The inclined plane is a simple machine. The wedge and the screw are special kinds of inclined planes. Simple machines can be connected to do all kinds of work.

Inclined Plane

Suppose you want to put a box of books on your desk. You could lift the box from the floor straight to your desk—ouch! Can you think of an easier way?

Did you think of making a ramp? If you could find a long, strong board, you could place one end on the floor and one end on the edge of the desk. Then you could push the heavy box up the flat, smooth surface of the ramp (the board). That would be a lot easier than lifting the box straight up!

In science, a ramp is simple machine called an **inclined plane.** You use the same total amount of force when you lift an object straight up as when you slide it up to the same level on an inclined plane. On an inclined plane, less force is applied over a greater distance. You don't need to work as hard to move the object up to its new location.

Factors that Affect force

Inclined planes can help move objects up or down. Several factors affect the amount of force needed to move an object. If two ramps are the same height, a greater force is needed to move an object up the shorter, steeper ramp.

Friction can slow things as they move along an inclined plane. Friction is a force that develops between two surfaces that touch and rub. Friction makes it harder to push, drag, or slide things.

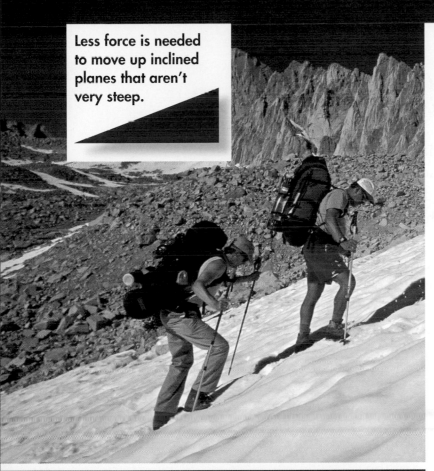

Less force is needed to move up inclined planes that aren't very steep.

More force is needed to move up a steep inclined plane.

A box near the top of an inclined plane often stays where it is because the force of friction balances the downward-pulling force of gravity.

However, if you attach wheels to the bottom of the box, it will probably roll down the inclined plane. The wheels take away most of the friction. The forces are unbalanced. Now the gravity has more force than friction

Suppose two boxes are at the bottom of an inclined plane. One box is very heavy. The other is light. Which box would you have to push harder to get to the top? That's right, the heavy box. You use more force to move heavier things.

Now, suppose you and a friend time how long each of you takes to push the heavy box to the top of the inclined plane. Who do you think used more force? Whoever took less time used more force. The stronger a force is, the faster it will move an object.

1. ✅**Checkpoint** You move a heavy box up an inclined plane, farther than if you lifted it straight up to the same height. Is using the inclined plane a good idea? Explain your answer.

2. **Social Studies** in Science
   Many roads in mountainous areas are built as zigzag inclined planes called switchbacks. What effect do the switchbacks have on the effort travelers use and the distance they travel?

469

Wedges

The **wedge** is a special kind of inclined plane. Think of a wedge as two inclined planes put together. To do its work, the wedge must be moving. A force aimed against the end of the wedge drives the inclined planes forward. The force can drive the thin edge of the wedge deep into an object.

Wedges can be used to split things apart or to move things. They can also be used to hold things in place.

In the picture below, you can see a wedge being driven into part of an old tree trunk. The force of the hammer pounding on the flat end of the wedge drives the pointed end of the wedge deeper and deeper into the wood. The wedge changes the downward force of the hammer into a sideways force that will split the wood into smaller pieces.

A nail is a kind of wedge. You drive a nail into wood by striking the flat end of the nail with a hammer. The nail fastens the wood to something else.

A wedge used as a wheel block stops much larger objects from moving

470

Screws that Drill Holes

An auger is a type of screw. It is used to drill holes. The auger twists downward. At the same time, pieces of the material being drilled move upward.

The people in the photo are drilling a hole in the ice sheet in Antarctica. They will study the ice that the auger brings from deep in the hole to the surface.

Screws

Another simple machine is the **screw.** Perhaps you have seen someone using a screwdriver to tighten a screw. Did you look closely at the screw? It is like a small stick with slanting ridges wrapped all around it. We call these ridges *threads* of the screw.

Actually, the screw is a type of inclined plane. If you could unwrap a screw's threads, you would clearly see the inclined plane. The pictures at the right will help you see how this might look.

Screws are used in many ways. They can fasten things. They can also lift things. A screw holds pieces of wood together better than a nail does because the threads make it hard to pull out the screw. To tighten a screw, you must make many turns with a screwdriver. But you would probably use less total effort with the screwdriver than you would using a hammer to drive a nail.

1. **✓ Checkpoint** What part does an inclined plane play in a wedge? in a screw?

2. **Writing in Science** **Persuasive** Suppose you have made an auger for a special purpose. Write an advertisement to persuade people to buy it. Be sure to explain the special type of work the auger is designed to do.

471

Complex Machines

Simple machines are often put together to do bigger jobs. complex machines have parts that are simple machines working together. *Complex* means "having many parts."

At home, you probably have a can opener in your kitchen. Does it look like the one below?

Which simple machines are parts of the can opener? You can see circle shapes, so there are probably wheels and axles. Some of the wheels have spikes or points. They are *gears*. The spikes are called *teeth*. A gear is a kind of wheel. Gears are often used in pairs to change speed or direction of motion.

Look carefully at the garden shears. Levers combined with wedges on the cutting blades make this a complex machine.

The sharp edge that you use to cut into the top of the can is a wedge.

What kind of simple machine do you think the long handles are? You open and close, or "squeeze" them. They are levers.

When you turn the winding handle, an axle turns the gears. The gears change the motion into a cutting action that opens the can.

You can easily see one wheel and axle in the lawnmower. What other simple machines can you find?

The picture above shows another complex machine. This machine has a different source of power than the can opener. Instead of your muscle power, this machine uses solar energy, or energy from sunlight. The box on the left is filled with solar cells. They change the energy of the Sun's rays into electricity that the machine can use.

Now look carefully at the other parts of the machine. You will see some simple machines.

There is more than one wheel and axle. Can you find them? You will also see some gears. Can you tell how two gears are changing the direction of motion?

The machine is lifting a load. Does the lifting part remind you of a simple machine? What is it?

This machine has wheels and axles and a pulley. It may have some other simple machines that you aren't able to see.

You can easily see one wheel and axle in the eggbeater. Do you see more than one? What other simple machines do you see?

✓ Lesson Checkpoint

1. Name three kinds of work that a screw can do. Give an example of each.
2. What is a complex machine?
3. **⊙ Summarize** Write two or three questions that would help you summarize what you know about a can opener.

Investigate What tasks can a machine do?

Materials

safety goggles

common objects

What to Do

1 Plan a device to do a task. Your device could make a toy car move, push a marble, make noise, or lift something. Or make a device do something else.

2 Think about how your task could be done. Design and build a device made of 2 or more simple machines to do your task. Describe your device. **Predict** whether your device will do its task.

What materials and tools did you use?

3 Test your prediction. **Investigate** how well your device does the task. Investigate what might have caused problems.

Process Skills

A **prediction** tells what result is expected. You test your prediction by trying out your device.

4 Change your device so it works even better.

5 Make a chart. Record your task you chose, the materials and tools you used, your prediction, your test and the results of your test, and how you changed your device.

Task	
Design (Describe and draw your device.)	
Materials and Tools Used	
Prediction	
Test and test results	
Change	

When you take off the clothes pin this device will knock down the dominoes.

Think About It

1. What task did you decide to do?
2. How did you test your **prediction**?
3. **Communicate** Explain how your change made your device work better.

Go Further

How would removing one part of your device affect how well it works? Demonstrate that in an object consisting of many parts, the parts usually influence or interact with one another.

Using Half the Force

Pulleys can be very helpful for moving heavy loads. Using a moveable pulley, the force needed to move an object is only half of what it would be without a pulley. Another way to say it is that the force needed without a pulley is twice the force needed with a moveable pulley. Remember, to find half of a number, you can divide by 2. Finding twice a number is the same as multiplying it by 2.

Copy and complete the chart below.

Job Number	Force Needed without a Pulley	Force Needed with a Moveable Pulley
1.	500 Newtons	
2.	290 Newtons	
3.		1,000 Newtons
4.		380 Newtons

Lab zone Take-Home Activity

Use a ruler and a stack of books to make an inclined plane. Tape a rubber band to the side of a small plastic container. Measure how far you have to pull the rubber band to start moving the empty container up the inclined plane. Then do the same with the container half-full of pennies and then full of pennies. Record the measurements on a chart and compare them.

Use Vocabulary

effort (p. 464)	**pulley** (p. 466)
fulcrum (p. 464)	**screw** (p. 471)
inclined plane (p. 468)	**wedge** (p. 470)
	wheel and axle (p. 466)
lever (p. 464)	
load (p. 464)	

Use the vocabulary word from the list above that best completes each sentence.

1. The support on which a lever rests is the _____.

2. The _____ is a simple machine with slanted threads along its sides.

3. The pointed end of a moving _____ can split things apart.

4. A _____ can be made from a rope and wheel or a chain and wheel.

5. The _____ is a push or squeeze that makes a lever move .

6. A windup key on a toy is an example of a _____.

7. A wheelchair ramp is a type of _____.

8. A scissors is a kind of _____.

9. In a simple machine, a weight to be lifted or moved is the _____.

Explain Concepts

10. Explain how moving the fulcrum on a lever changes the amount of force needed to move an object.

11. Explain how a simple machine differs from a complex machine.

12. How are inclined planes, wedges, and screws alike?

Process Skills

13. **Infer** You meet two carpenters. One uses nails, but the other prefers screws. Write one possible reason for each carpenter's choice.

14. **Classify** each picture as a simple machine or a complex machine.

Summarize

15. Make a graphic organizer like the one shown below. Write three facts about levers. Use the facts to summarize what you know about levers.

Detail

Detail → Summary

Detail

 Test Prep

Choose the letter that best completes the statement or answers the question.

16. In science, *work* means
  Ⓐ using force to move or change something.
  Ⓑ how far something moves.
  Ⓒ doing a job.
  Ⓓ how hard you push on something.

17. Which object is NOT a lever?
  Ⓕ a pair of scissors
  Ⓖ a nutcracker
  Ⓗ a gear
  Ⓘ a crowbar

18. A gently slanting driveway on a hill is
  Ⓐ a wedge.
  Ⓑ a pulley.
  Ⓒ a lever.
  Ⓓ an inclined plane.

19. Explain why the answer you chose for Question 16 is the best. For each of the answers you did not choose, give a reason why it is not the best choice.

20. Writing in Science **Expository**
Suppose someone you know has never seen a pair of scissors. You want to explain how to use the scissors and what is happening when they cut. Using what you know about simple machines, write a paragraph that tells this person how scissors work.

Archimedes

Archimedes was perhaps the greatest scientist of the ancient world. He was born about 287 B.C.E. in Syracuse, a Greek colony in Sicily. Archimedes and King Hielo II of Syracuse were friends. They may have been related. Archimedes probably studied in Alexandria, Egypt. Historians think that while he lived in Egypt, he invented a device that could raise water from the Nile River to irrigate nearby farmland. The device, which was a type of auger, became known as Archimedes' Screw. It is a simple machine that has been used in the Nile Valley for thousands of years.

Archimedes discovered laws for the use of simple machines such as levers and screws. He also developed many complex machines. Some were weapons used in battle. Others were devices that could move heavy loads. One device was a system of pulleys that could raise and move a whole ship, even a ship with passengers on it! In explaining how the lever can be used, he is said to have told King Hielo, "Give me a place to stand on, and I will move the entire Earth."

Lab zone Take-Home Activity

Make a list of objects in your home that have pulleys, wheels, screws, levers, wedges or inclined planes.

Unit C Test Talk

Use Information from Text and Graphics

Sometimes information that you need is given in a graphic organizer, a table, a graph, or some other display. Once you understand exactly what the display shows, you can decide how to use it. Then, by adding new facts to the facts you already know, you can answer the questions.

In a graph or a table, look for a pattern to see how the data compare. A pattern can also help you estimate the answer. If the data are in a table or chart, changing the order of the items may make it easier to use the new information.

Read the passage. Then use the data in the table to answer the questions.

One substance may sink under or float on top of another substance. To decide what happens, you compare the density of the two substances. Density is mass divided by volume. The substance with the greater density sinks under the other substance.

Substance	Density at 20°C
Corn Oil	0.93
Corn Syrup	1.38
Gold	19.32
Honey	1.4
Lead	11.35
Mayonnaise	0.91
Milk	1.03
Piece of apple	0.6
Salt	2.16
Water	1.00

Use What You Know

Suppose a sample of each substance were put into the same container. Use the information in the table to answer the questions about what would happen.

1. Which would float at the top?
   - Ⓐ Corn Oil
   - Ⓑ Mayonnaise
   - Ⓒ Piece of apple
   - Ⓓ Water

2. Which is the best explanation why the two substances might be hard to tell apart in the container?
   - Ⓐ Corn syrup and corn oil are both made from corn.
   - Ⓑ Gold and a piece of apple are both solids.
   - Ⓒ Honey and corn oil are both golden colored.
   - Ⓓ Milk and water have about the same density.

3. How would you arrange the items to make the information easier to use?
   - Ⓐ Keep the items in alphabetical order.
   - Ⓑ List all of the liquids first.
   - Ⓒ List all of the solids first.
   - Ⓓ List items in order of their densities.

4. Suppose you make a bar graph from the data. Which substances would you have bars that were almost the same length?
   - Ⓐ Corn oil and mayonnaise
   - Ⓑ Gold and iron
   - Ⓒ Milk and honey
   - Ⓓ Piece of apple and salt

Unit C Wrap Up

Chapter 11

How can matter be compared, measured, and combined?
- We use tools to measure the mass and volume of matter.
- Observations and measurements help us to compare matter.
- Physical and chemical changes can happen when matter is combined.

Chapter 12

What are some ways that heat energy can move from one object to another?
- Heat energy can move from one object to another by conduction.
- Heat moves through liquids and gases in a pattern called convection.
- Energy from the Sun comes to the Earth by radiation.

Chapter 13

What are some ways that energy can be changed from one type to another?
- Electric charges can move through wire as electric current.
- Electric current can produce magnetic fields.

Chapter 14

How do sound and light travel?
- Sound travels in waves through solids, liquids, and gases.
- Light travels as electromagnetic waves.

Chapter 15

What forces cause motion and how do they affect us?
- Forces start objects moving, speed them up, slow them down, or stop them.
- Changes in motion require energy.

Chapter 16

How do simple machines make work easier?
- Simple machines change the direction a force is applied.
- Simple machines can also change the amount of force you need to apply.

Performance Assessment

Height and Potential Energy

Find out if the height of an object affects its potential energy. Use modeling clay to make three balls of the same size. Place a ball in a plastic bag and put it on the floor. Hold a thick book flat above the ball. Release the book so that it lands on the clay. Remove the flattened ball from the bag and trace its outline on a sheet of paper. Repeat the procedure using the other balls of clay. Drop the book from different heights. Record your procedures. Write your observations. Based on your observations, draw a conclusion about height and potential energy.

Read More About Physical Science

Look for books like these in the library.

A force is needed to move the snow.

Experiment How is motion affected by mass?

A force can cause an object to move. In this **experiment** you will find out how the mass of an object affects the distance the object will move.

Materials

½ of a cup and marble

2 metric rulers

2 books

4 pennies and tape

balance and gram cubes

calculator or computer (optional)

Process Skills

You **experiment** when you carry out a fair test of your **hypothesis**.

Ask a question.

How does the mass of a cup affect the distance a rolling marble will move the cup?

State a hypothesis.

If the mass of a cup is increased, then will the distance the cup is moved by a rolling marble increase, decrease, or remain the same? Write your **hypothesis**.

Identify and control variables.

You will increase the mass of the cup by taping pennies to the cup. You will **measure** the distance the cup moves. Everything else must remain the same.

Take It to the NET
More Activities www.sfsuccessnet.com

Test your hypothesis.

1 Roll a marble down a ramp into a cup. **Observe** and record the results.

ramp

about 5cm

Measure the distance the cup moves.

Place the open end of cup at the end of the ruler.

2 Use a balance and gram cubes to find the mass of the cup. Record the mass in grams.

3 Tape a penny on top of the cup. Move the cup back to the end of the ramp.

4 Roll the marble down the ramp into the cup. Record the results. Then find the mass of the cup with the penny taped on it. Record the mass.

5 Repeat using 2, 3, and 4 pennies.

penny taped on cup

Collect and record your data.

Number of Pennies	Distance Cup Moved (cm)	Mass of Cup with Pennies (g)
0		
1		
2		
3		
4		

Make a table to record your data.

Interpret your data.

Use your data to make a line graph. Look at your graph closely. Describe how the distance the cup moved was affected by the mass of the cup with pennies.

Your teacher may wish you to use a computer (with the right software) or a graphing calculator to help collect, organize, analyze, and present your data. These tools can help you make tables, charts, and graphs.

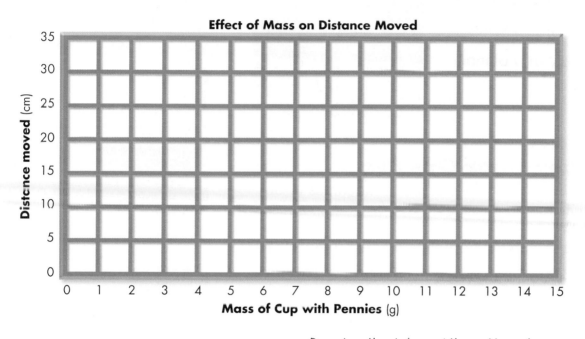

Effect of Mass on Distance Moved

You may wish to use graph paper.

Based on the data and the pattern shown by your line graph, predict the distance the cup would move with 5 pennies.

State your conclusion.

Explain how mass affects the distance that the cup moves. Compare your hypothesis with your results. **Communicate** your conclusion.

Go Further

How would changing the height of the ramp affect how the cup moves? Design and carry out a plan to investigate this or other questions you may have. Make sure to write a procedure others can understand and use to repeat your experiment.

A Pinhole Camera

A camera uses light to form images on photographic paper.

Idea: Make a pinhole camera.

Build a Better Door Opener

People invent and then improve machines to do different jobs.

Idea: Use common objects to make a machine that will do a simple task such as close a door, water plants, crack an egg, or open a window. Name the machine and design a box or container to package it. Make a diagram with labels to show all the simple machines included in the new machine.

Battery Power

Like other power sources, batteries have different life spans.

Idea: Use several different brands of batteries. You will need a flashlight for each brand. Make sure all batteries are the same size. Turn on all of the flashlights and time how long each battery brand keeps the flashlight lit.

EC NTL 10 9 8 7 6 5 4 3 2 1

Unit D

Space and Technology in Indiana

Did you know that you can observe the motions of the planets and stars? There are many stargazing clubs in Indiana where people gather to make observations and exchange information.

Space and Technology in Indiana

What do weather and climate, time zones, questions about the universe, and satellite technology have in common? They all provide opportunities to learn about space and technology in Indiana. You will learn more about the science behind these topics in Unit D.

Indiana Forecast Office

Changes in the earth's orbit and tilt cause differences in the solar energy received by Earth. Scientists at the Indiana Forecast Office in Indianapolis carefully predict weather and changes in Indiana's climate. You will learn more about weather and climate in Chapter 17.

Time Zones

You can easily get confused when you ask, "What time is it?" in parts of Indiana. The chart shows summer and winter times in parts of Indiana. You will learn more about comparing hours of daylight in Chapter 17.

Indiana Times		
Summer Times		
77 counties	10 counties	5 counties
Eastern Standard Time	Central Daylight Time	Eastern Daylight Time
10:00 A.M.	10:00 A.M.	11:00 A.M.
Winter Times		
77 counties	10 counties	5 counties
Eastern Standard Time	Central Standard Time	Eastern Standard Time
10:00 A.M.	9:00 A.M.	10:00 A.M.

Indiana Space Grant Consortium

Scientists at the Indiana Space Grant Consortium work with NASA to answer questions about the universe. You will learn more about the universe in Chapter 18.

Communications Satellites

Communications satellites are spacecraft that orbit the earth. Using the Global Positioning System, or GPS, people can determine their location using radio signals transmitted from satellites. Indiana's emergency services use GPS to locate the closest response vehicle. You will learn more about satellite technology in Chapter 19.

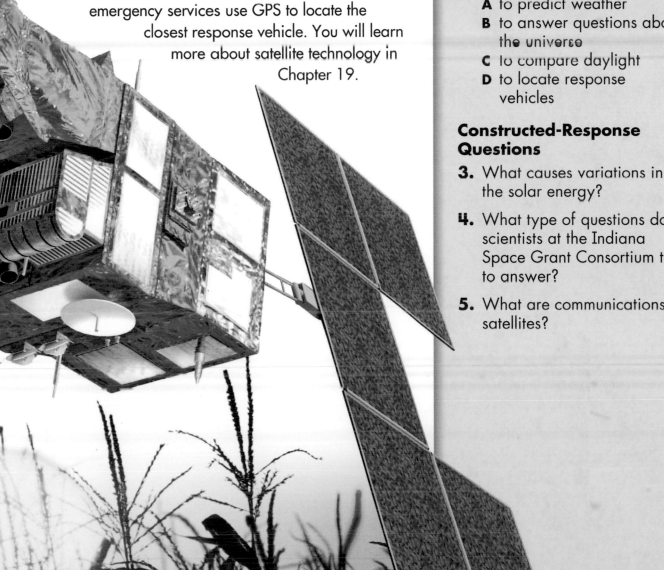

Answer the questions below. Write your answers on a separate sheet of paper.

Multiple-Choice Questions

1. During the summer, when it is 2:00 P.M. in Marian County (EST), what time is it in Warrick County (CDT)?

A 12:00 P.M.

B 1:00 P.M.

C 2:00 P.M.

D 3:00 P.M.

2. How do Indiana's emergency services use the Global Positioning System (GPS)?

A to predict weather

B to answer questions about the universe

C to compare daylight

D to locate response vehicles

Constructed-Response Questions

3. What causes variations in the solar energy?

4. What type of questions do scientists at the Indiana Space Grant Consortium try to answer?

5. What are communications satellites?

3

Field Trip

Prairie Grass Observatory at Camp George Cullom

Prairie Grass Observatory in Frankfort is an excellent spot for viewing the motions of the planets. It is well away from city lights. Some light from nearby towns can be seen, but otherwise the sky is very dark. Indiana stargazers gather to share telescopes and observe planets, stars, and meteor showers.

Astronomers like to know ahead of time if viewing conditions will be favorable. The "Clear Sky Clock" at Prairie Grass Observatory forecasts the following information.

Condition	Forecast
Cloud cover	Forecasts percentage of cloud cover
Transparency	Forecasts how clear the air will be
Darkness	Forecasts how dark the sky will be

Find out more:

Research to find out more about astronomy clubs in Indiana.

- Write about the various activities in which members of astronomy clubs participate.
- Present your findings to the class.

EC IN 10 9 8 7 6 5 4 3 2 1

Chapter 17

Earth's Cycles

You Will Discover

- o different ways the Earth moves.
- o what causes the seasons.
- o why the shape of the Moon appears to change throughout the month.
- o that groups of stars can be seen in the sky.

Online Student Edition

www.sfsuccessnet.com

What can daily and seasonal cycles tell us about the Earth, Moon, and Sun?

revolution

axis

rotation

eclipse

lunar eclipse

orbit

ellipse

solar eclipse

constellation

Explore What is the shape of a planet's path?

Materials

paper

heavy cardboard

tape

2 pins

metric ruler

piece of string

What to Do

1 Tape the paper onto the cardboard. Stick a pin in the center. Tie a knot to make a loop of string. Put the loop over the pin. Use a pencil and the string to draw a circle. Hold the pencil upright against the stretched string as you draw your circle.

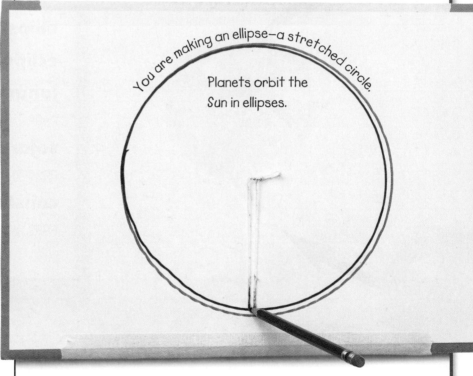

You are making an ellipse—a stretched circle.

Planets orbit the Sun in ellipses.

2 Put a second pin about 5 mm away from the first pin. Put the loop of string over both pins. Try to draw another circle. **Observe** the shape carefully. Is the length from the center to the edge the same in all directions?

Think About It

Predict the effect of moving the second pin farther from the center. How would the new ellipse be different?

How to Read Science

 Cause and Effect

Linking causes and effects can help understand what you read. Writers sometimes signal cause and effect with words such as *because, since, so,* and *as a result.* A cause may have more than one effect. An effect may have more than one cause.

Science Magazine

The Earth spins like a top. At the same time, it travels around the Sun. However, the Earth's axis—the imaginary line it spins around—is tilted compared to Earth's path around the Sun.

Each half of the Earth tilts toward the Sun for about half of the year. Sunlight reaching that hemisphere heats the Earth more. Also, because the Sun is higher in the sky, there are more hours of daylight. So, the temperatures are higher. During the rest of the year, this half of the Earth tilts away from the Sun. There are fewer hours of daylight, and temperatures are lower.

As the Earth revolves around the Sun, these differences in temperature and the hours of daylight cause the seasons.

Apply It!

Use causes and effects in the article to answer the questions.

• If one half of the Earth is tilted toward the Sun, how does that affect the amount that sunlight heats that half of the Earth?

• How does the position of the Sun in the sky affect the number of daylight hours?

• When the Earth has moved in its orbit to the other side of the orbit, which hemisphere is then tilted toward the Sun?

🔊 You Are There!

Do you remember riding on a train when you were very young? You could hear the sound of the train moving along the tracks. You looked out the window and saw trees, buildings, signs, and telephone poles zipping by. Did you think they were moving, while you stayed in the same place? For thousands of years, people have wondered why the stars seem to move in the sky. For a long time, people thought the stars moved around Earth. That was what they seemed to see when they looked at the sky. But do stars really move? Or is it Earth that moves?

Lesson 1

How does Earth move?

The Earth spins like a top as it circles around and around the Sun. The Earth is tipped to one side as it moves. This tilt causes the changing seasons.

Earth Seems to Stand Still

Everyone agrees that the Earth doesn't seem to move. You can't sense its movement because you are moving right along with it! Everything on the Earth moves at the same speed as the part of the Earth just below it. Another reason you don't sense Earth's motion is that it moves steadily and smoothly.

Even though you can't feel Earth's motion, you can find some clues to it. One clue is that to people on Earth, the Sun and the stars seem to move across the sky. This happens because the Earth is turning. Another clue is that the seasons change during the year. In some areas of the world, the difference in seasons is more dramatic than in other regions. The seasonal changes are partly caused by the way Earth moves through space.

Today, scientists use telescopes, cameras, and computers to study how the stars and other objects in the sky seem to move. We have learned a lot about the stars since people looked at the sky thousands of years ago.

1. ✅**Checkpoint** Why does the Earth seem to be standing still?
2. **Social Studies** in Science Use the Internet or other sources to find out about early people whose ideas about the Sun, the stars, and the Moon had an effect on their rituals or customs. Write a report explaining what you learned.

Earth's Rotation

If you have ridden on a merry-go-round, you know that it turns around a pole that runs through its center. Earth turns around its **axis,** an imaginary pole that goes through its center. Earth's axis passes through the North Pole, the center of the Earth, and the South Pole.

The spinning of the Earth around its axis is called its **rotation.** Each time Earth makes a full turn around its axis, it has made one rotation. Earth takes 23 hours and 56 minutes to make one rotation. When Earth rotates, it turns from west to east. Because of Earth's rotation, objects such as the Sun and the other stars appear to move from east to west in the sky.

The Earth rotates from west to east as it spins around its axis.

Why Shadows Change

Another result of Earth's rotation is that shadows change their positions and sizes during the day. When light shines on an object and does not pass through it, the object casts a shadow. As the Earth rotates, sunlight shines on an object from different angles. The length and position of the object's shadow changes. Earth's rotation also causes day to change into night and night into day. When a place on Earth is turned toward the Sun, it has daytime. It has nighttime when it is turned away from the Sun.

An object's shadow is longest in the morning and in the evening when the Sun is low in the sky. It is shortest at the middle of the day, when the Sun is overhead.

Like the Sun, the other stars appear to move in the sky from east to west. You cannot see these stars in the daytime because the light from the Sun is too bright. If you watch for several nights, if the sky is clear, and if you are in a place that does not have many bright lights, you can see that stars appear to change their positions in the sky.

Daylight Hours

The number of hours of daylight at every place on Earth changes during the year. The graph shows the number of hours of sunlight in one day for a city in the Northern Hemisphere.

Hours of Daylight Throughout the Year

Month	March	June	September	December
Number of Hours	12.0	13.9	12.3	10.4

Viewed from the same location on Earth, the Sun's position changes depending on the time of day and the time of year.

Evening ← → Morning

Summer

Winter

1. Why do the Sun and the stars appear to move from east to west in the sky?

2. **Writing in Science** **Expository** Write an article for a newspaper's weather page to explain how and why shadows change their positions during the day. Include some examples from things around you.

Earth's Revolution

As Earth rotates, it travels around the Sun. The movement of one object around another is a **revolution.** A complete trip around the Sun by the Earth is one revolution. The path Earth follows as it revolves around the Sun is its **orbit.**

The Earth takes about 365 days, or 1 year, to complete one revolution. During that year, Earth and everything on it travels about 940,000,000 kilometers at an average speed of about 1,700 kilometers per hour.

Earth's orbit is an **ellipse.** An ellipse is like a circle stretched out in opposite directions. As the Earth moves in its orbit, its distance from the Sun changes. Earth is farther from the Sun in some parts of its orbit. It is closer to the Sun in other parts.

Gravity is a force that pulls two objects toward one another. It can act at a distance. The gravity between the Earth and the Sun keeps the Earth revolving around the Sun. Without gravity, the Earth would fly off into space. If the Earth stopped moving, the attraction between Earth and Sun would make them crash into each other.

When the North Pole tilts away from the Sun, the rays strike the Northern Hemisphere at a lower angle, and the Southern Hemisphere gets more direct sunlight.

The midnight Sun moves across the sky just above the horizon.

Earth's Tilted Axis

Earth's axis is always tilted. As Earth revolves around the Sun, its axis is always tilted in the same direction. The end of the axis at the North Pole always points toward the North Star. This tilt affects how places on Earth receive sunlight. In different parts of Earth's orbit, different places directly face the Sun.

In late June, the Northern Hemisphere, or northern half of the Earth, tilts toward the Sun. It is summer and daylight is longer than night. But it is winter in the Southern Hemisphere. Nights are longer than daylight. In late December, the Southern Hemisphere tilts toward the Sun. Now, it is winter in the Northern Hemisphere and summer in the Southern Hemisphere. Earth's axis is not tilted toward the Sun in spring and fall. The lengths of daylight and night are more nearly equal in spring and fall.

The Northern Hemisphere gets more direct sunlight when it tilts toward the sun. Direct sunlight heats this hemisphere more and daylight lasts longer. As a result, temperatures are higher. It is summer. At the same time, the Southern Hemisphere tilts away from the Sun. The days are shorter and temperatures are lower. It is winter. In spring and fall, temperatures are more moderate in both hemispheres.

When the North Pole tilts toward the Sun, the Northern Hemisphere gets more direct sunlight.

✓ Lesson Checkpoint

1. Why is it summer in the Northern Hemisphere when it is winter in the Southern Hemisphere?
2. **Cause and Effect** Explain what causes Earth's seasons.

The Midnight Sun

For several weeks of a hemisphere's summer, the area near the pole gets some sunlight all day and all night. The "midnight Sun" takes an almost circular path close to the horizon. The Sun does not rise high overhead and it does not set. During summer in the Northern Hemisphere, the midnight Sun is seen north of the Arctic Circle. During summer in the Southern Hemisphere, the midnight Sun is seen south of the Antarctic Circle.

Lesson 2

What patterns can you see in the sky?

As the Moon orbits the Earth, the same side of the Moon always faces the Earth.

You see stars in different parts of the night sky as the Earth rotates on its axis and revolves around the Sun. The Moon revolves around the Earth. It also rotates on its own axis. All these movements cause changes in the patterns that you see in the sky.

Sun, Moon, and Earth

Sometimes you can see the Moon at night. Sometimes you can even see it during the day. The Moon looks as if it is shining with its own light, just as the Sun does. But the Moon does not really produce its own light. You can see the Moon because sunlight reflects off the Moon's surface.

Like Earth's orbit around the Sun, the Moon's orbit around Earth is shaped like an ellipse. The gravity between the Moon and Earth keeps the Moon in its orbit. Because it moves, the Moon stays in its orbit and doesn't crash into the Earth. The Moon makes a complete revolution around the Earth in about 29 days.

Like the Earth, the Moon rotates around its axis. Each time it rotates once around its axis it revolves once around the Earth. As a result, the same side of the Moon is always facing the Earth. That is the only side you can see from Earth.

New Moon: Since the Moon's dark, unlighted side faces Earth, you can't see a new moon. The new Moon begins a new set of phases.

Crescent: A sliver of lighted Moon appears.

First quarter: One half of the lighted half of the Moon, or one quarter of the Moon is visible.

The Phases of the Moon

If you look at the Moon at different times of the month, its shape appears to change. Half of the Moon faces the Sun and sunlight is reflected from the surface of that half. When the lighted half of the Moon directly faces the Earth, the Moon appears as a full circle of light. It is called a full Moon.

We see a full Moon only briefly each time the Moon revolves around the Earth. The rest of the time, only part of the lighted half of the Moon faces Earth. Then, you can see only part of the full circle of light. For a short time, you cannot see any of the lighted part of the Moon. So, you do not see the Moon at all. Between the times you see the full Moon and the time you can't see any Moon at all, the Moon appears to have different shapes. All the Moon's shapes are called the phases of the Moon.

Full Moon: The entire half of the Moon that faces Earth is lighted. You see the Moon as a full circle. A full Moon appears about a week after the first quarter.

Last quarter: Gradually, you see less and less of the Moon. About a week after the full Moon, the Moon appears as half of a circle. You see half of the lighted half, or one quarter of the entire Moon.

1. **✓ Checkpoint** What causes the apparent repeated changes of the Moon's shape?
2. **Math in Science** About how many times does the Moon revolve around Earth in one year?

Eclipses

An **eclipse** occurs when one object in space gets between the Sun and another object, and casts its shadow on the other object. This occurs when the Moon passes through the Earth's shadow and when the Moon's shadow falls on part of the Earth.

Most of the time, reflected sunlight lights up the Moon. However, during some full moons, the Moon and the Sun are on exactly opposite sides of the Earth. Often, the Moon passes above or below Earth's shadow. But sometimes it passes through the Earth's shadow. Then a **lunar eclipse** occurs.

If only part of the Moon is in Earth's shadow during the eclipse, the Moon might look as if something took a bite out of it. This is a partial eclipse. If the whole Moon is in the Earth's shadow, the eclipse is a total lunar eclipse. A lunar eclipse can last as long as 100 minutes. It can happen several times in the same year. Each eclipse is visible only in certain places. Where on Earth the eclipse can be viewed depends on the Moon's position in Earth's shadow.

During a total lunar eclipse, the Moon does not disappear completely. Earth's atmosphere bends and scatters some sunlight, so some of the Sun's rays reach the Moon. The Moon appears to be copper colored.

During a lunar eclipse, the Moon moves into and out of Earth's shadow.

During a total solar eclipse, the Sun may not be visible at all. Sometimes in a solar eclipse a thin, bright ring of sunlight appears to circle the Moon.

Solar Eclipses

A **solar eclipse** occurs when the Moon passes between the Sun and the Earth and casts its shadow on the Earth. Notice in the picture that the Moon's shadow covers only a small part of Earth. A solar eclipse can be seen only at the places on Earth where the Moon casts its shadow.

During a total solar eclipse, the day can become as dark as night. Total solar eclipses last up to 7.5 minutes. Solar eclipses occur two to five times each year.

Viewing a Solar Eclipse Safely

NEVER look directly at the Sun, even during an eclipse. Looking through binoculars, sunglasses, smoked glass, exposed film, or a telescope does not protect your eyes. Using them to watch the Sun, even for a very short time, could cause permanent damage to your eyes, including blindness.

To view a solar eclipse safely, view its image cast on a screen. Sit or stand with your back to the Sun. Punch or cut a small hole, up to 2 mm across, in a sheet of paper or thin cardboard. Hold it up in front of you. Place a second piece of paper or cardboard behind the first sheet. As sunlight passes over your shoulder and through the hole in the first sheet, you can see an image of the eclipse on the second sheet. Try it out before the eclipse starts so you know how to place the paper. The eclipse will not last long.

1. ✓ **Checkpoint** How is a total lunar eclipse different from other lunar eclipses?
2. **Health** in Science Why should you never look directly at the Sun?

Stars

Scientists estimate that there may be 1,000,000,000,000,000,000,000 stars in the known universe. That's 1 billion trillion, or 1 followed by 21 zeroes! The Sun is the star that is nearest the Earth and is most important for us. It provides energy and light to living things on Earth.

Like all stars, the Sun is a hot ball of gas. It is a very ordinary star. Many stars are much bigger, brighter, or hotter than the Sun. Others are smaller, dimmer, and cooler.

During the day, you cannot see stars because the Sun is so bright. Even at night, if you are in a city that has many lights, or if the sky is not clear, you may be able to see only a few of the brightest stars. The light from stars that are very far away appears faint when it reaches the Earth. The stars look like tiny dots of light. Many stars in the sky are so faint or far away that you cannot see them at all with your own eyes. But you could see some of them through a telescope.

During late fall and winter in the Northern Hemisphere, Cassiopeia is almost directly overhead. It looks somewhat like the letter W.

Polaris

Star Patterns

For thousands of years, people have noticed that the stars appear in shapes and patterns in the sky. These star patterns are called **constellations.** Astronomers divide the sky into 88 constellations. People often identify the stars by the constellations they are part of. The constellations are very far away from us. The stars in each constellation appear to be close to each other. Actually, they may be very far apart in space.

As the Earth rotates around its axis, stars appear to move across the sky. At the equator, the stars seem to move in straight lines. They rise in the east and set in the west every 24 hours. If you are near one of the poles, the stars appear to rotate in a circle in the sky. People in the Southern Hemisphere don't see the same constellations as people in the Northern Hemisphere.

In the Northern Hemisphere, the North Star, or Polaris, appears in the sky above the North Pole. The Earth rotates around its axis, and the North Pole is at the northern end of the axis. Polaris does not seem to move in the sky. The stars near it do not rise or set. They seem to rotate around Polaris. These stars are in the constellations Ursa Major (the Great Bear), Ursa Minor (the Little Bear), Cepheus (the King), Cassiopeia (the Queen), and Draco (the Dragon).

Seven stars in the constellation Ursa Major make up the Big Dipper. The two stars that form the end of the dipper's bowl can help you find Polaris. Look at the pictures to see how the positions of the constellations change during the year.

Orion

During the winter in the Northern Hemisphere, that bright constellation you see in the southern sky is Orion, the Hunter. Orion has 7 bright stars, more than any other constellation. Three stars in a line form his belt. To find Orion in the sky, look for these 3 stars. Then trace up to his left shoulder. The bright star there is named Betelgeuse. It is about 400 times larger than the Sun and much brighter too. But it is also much farther from Earth. Rigel, the bright star in Orion's right foot is also much larger, brighter, and farther from Earth than the Sun is. In March, the stars in Orion drop too low in the sky for you to see.

Polaris

During the summer, Cassiopeia appears much lower in the sky. Now it looks like the letter M.

✓ Lesson Checkpoint

1. Why does the Moon remain partly visible during a lunar eclipse?
2. Why do distant stars that are actually very far from each other appear to be close together in the sky?
3. 🌀 Cause and Effect What kinds of motion cause solar and lunar eclipses? Explain.

Guided Inquiry

Investigate How can you make a star finder?

Materials

Star Finder Pattern

Star Wheel

folder

scissors and glue

stapler

Process Skills

You **observe** when you gather information using your eyes.

What to Do

1 Glue the Star Finder Pattern on a folder.

Place the edge of the Star Finder along the folded edge of the file folder as shown.

After gluing, cut out the oval.

2 Close the folder. Cut out the star finder.

Cut along the edge of the Star Finder.

Do not cut the folded edge.

Staple the front of folder to the back.

3 Cut out the Star Wheel. Slide it into the Star Finder.

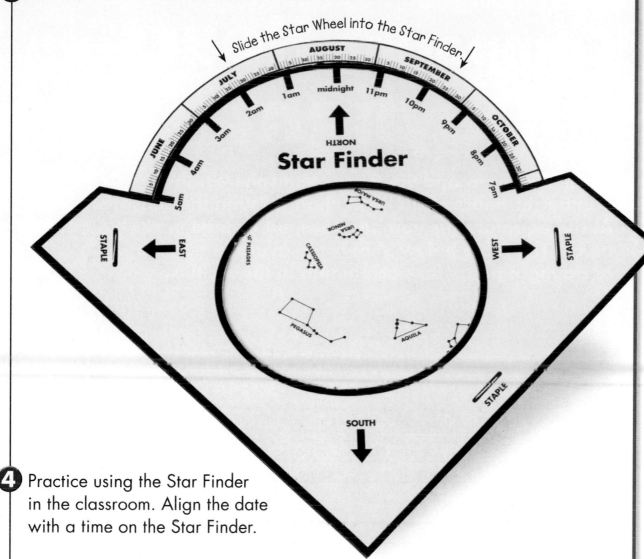

Slide the Star Wheel into the Star Finder.

Star Finder

4 Practice using the Star Finder in the classroom. Align the date with a time on the Star Finder.

5 Suppose you were going to **observe** the sky on April 1 at 9 P.M. Set the dial for 9 P.M. on April 1. Record the constellations you could see. Now set the dial for midnight. Record the constellations you could see.

Think About It

Which constellations you could **observe** at 9:00 P.M. that are not visible at midnight? Explain why.

Go Further

Do all stars have the same brightness, size, and color? How do stars move daily and seasonally? If possible in your area, use your star finder to help find out. Also, look for star patterns, such as the Big Dipper.

Math in Science

Comparing Hours of Daylight

In the Northern and Southern Hemispheres, the number of hours of daylight changes with the seasons. At the equator, this number does not change very much. The table below shows the average number of daylight hours for each month in three cities.

Average Number of Daylight Hours			
Month	Chicago, IL	Quito, Ecuador	Rio de Janeiro, Brazil
January	9.5	12.1	13.4
February	10.6	12.1	12.9
March	12.0	12.1	12.2
April	13.4	12.1	11.6
May	14.6	12.1	11.0
June	15.2	12.1	10.8
July	14.9	12.1	10.9
August	13.8	12.1	11.4
September	12.5	12.1	12.0
October	11.0	12.1	12.6
November	9.8	12.1	13.2
December	9.2	12.1	13.5

Use the data in the table to answer the questions.

1 Find the average number (mean) hours of daylight in Chicago for October, November, and December.

2 In June, how many more hours of daylight are there in Chicago than in Rio de Janeiro?

3 Notice the pattern in the data for each of the three cities. How are the patterns different?

4 In which month is the data for the three cities the most alike?

Lab zone Take-Home Activity

Find data about the average number of daylight hours for each month in your area. Compare this data with the data for Chicago, IL. Write a paragraph about why the data is similar or different.

Chapter 17 Review and Test Prep

Use Vocabulary

axis (p. 496)	**orbit** (p. 498)
constellation (p. 505)	**revolution** (p. 498)
eclipse (p. 502)	**rotation** (p. 496)
ellipse (p. 498)	**solar eclipse** (p. 504)
lunar eclipse (p. 502)	

Use the term from the list above that best completes the sentence.

1. The Earth spins around its _____.

2. Earth completes one _____ each day.

3. A(n) _____ is part of the sky used to identify stars.

4. The Earth's _____ around the Sun takes a year.

5. During a(n) _____, the Moon casts its shadow on the Earth.

6. During a(n) _____, the Moon passes through the Earth's shadow.

7. The Earth takes a year to complete one _____ around the Sun.

8. A(n) _____ occurs when an object in space gets between the Sun and another object.

9. Earth's path around the Sun is shaped like a(n) _____.

Explain Concepts

10. Explain how and why shadows change during the day.

11. Explain why you always see the same side of the Moon.

Process Skills

12. The graph shows daylight hours in Miami, Florida (red bars) and Boston, Massachusetts (blue bars). Where do the daylight hours vary more? **Infer** why this is so.

Hours of Daylight During the Year

13. Many stars are actually much bigger and brighter than the Sun. **Form a hypothesis** about why the light that we see from these stars may be very faint.

14. Suppose you have located where Earth is today on a map showing the Sun and all of the planets. **Predict** where the Earth will be in six months.

◎ Cause and Effect

15. Explain what changes with the seasons and what causes those changes by using the following ideas to make a graphic organizer such as the one below.

- Earth revolves around the Sun.
- Earth's axis is tilted.
- Earth's path in the sky changes.
- Sunlight is more direct or less direct.
- Hours of sunlight vary.
- Temperatures vary.

 Test Prep

Choose the letter that best completes the statement.

16. The Sun rises in the east and sets in the west because
   Ⓐ it depends on which hemisphere you are in.
   Ⓑ the Sun moves in the same direction as the Moon.
   Ⓒ Earth rotates from east to west.
   Ⓓ Earth rotates from west to east.

17. One reason seasons change on Earth is that
   Ⓕ the Sun's gravity is very strong.
   Ⓖ the Earth's axis is tilted.
   Ⓗ Earth revolves around the Sun in an ellipse-shaped orbit.
   Ⓘ Earth rotates around its own axis.

18. The constellations in the Northern Hemisphere that never appear to rise or set are
   Ⓐ near Polaris.
   Ⓑ in Ursa Major.
   Ⓒ near the edge of the visible sky.
   Ⓓ the largest ones.

19. Explain why the answer you selected for Question #18 is best. For each of the answers you did not select, give a reason why it is not the best choice.

20. Writing in Science **Expository**
Earth spins on its axis and orbits the Sun. Yet, to us, Earth doesn't seem to move. Write a paragraph that explains this to a younger child.

RBE

Robert B. Lee III is a NASA research scientist. His projects include CERES and ERBE.

Robert B. Lee III grew up in Norfolk, Virginia. Like three of his seven brothers and sisters, young Robert had a job. When he was 11 years old, he began a 10-mile paper route. As he collected payment from his customers, he learned to make change quickly with the money he had. This combined two things he enjoyed, problem solving and mathematics.

He made toy airplanes from reeds and other materials that grew in swampy areas near his home. Airplanes fascinated him. He liked the challenge of making his airplanes fly better. Robert was in junior high school when the United States launched its first rocket. His project for metal-working class was a model rocket.

Robert participated in various sports and in math and science competitions in high school. As part of a training program at Norfolk State College, he began working at NASA's Langley Research Center in Hampton, VA. After he graduated from college, he became a staff scientist at Langley.

Much of Mr. Lee's research focuses on remote sensing. This means using instruments on Earth or in satellites to take measurements of the Sun, Earth's upper atmosphere, and atmospheres of other planets. Mr. Lee and his team compare data to find unusual results. They have collected data on the Sun's radiation. The data show changes in the brightness of the Sun, the causes of the changes, and how the changes may affect Earth's climate.

Robert B. Lee III travels to other countries to share the results of his research. But he still does most of his problem solving close to his boyhood home.

Lab zone Take-Home Activity

As part his research, Mr. Lee is tracking sunspots. Use the Internet or other sources to find information about sunspots. Write a paragraph in your science journal to summarize what you learn.

512

EC NTL 10 9 8 7 6 5 4 3 2 1

You Will Discover

- what makes up our solar system.
- the characteristics of the planets.
- what keeps planets and moons in motion.

Chapter 18

Inner and Outer Planets

Discovery CHANNEL SCHOOL DVD Library

www.sfsuccessnet.com

How is Earth different from other planets in our solar system?

galaxy

universe

astronomy

craters

514

Chapter 18
Vocabulary

solar system

space probe

satellite

Explore How can you compare the sizes of planets?

Materials

Planets 1 and Planets 2

scissors

metric ruler

What to Do

① **Measure** the diameter of each paper "planet." Then use your measurements and chart to find each planet's name. Label each planet. Cut out each planet.

② Use the cutouts as **models** of the planets. Put them in order by size. Compare the sizes of the planets.

Name of Planet	Diameter of Planet (km)	Diameter of Model (mm)	Distance from Sun (km)
Mercury (Label it M)	4,900 km	5 mm	57,900,000 km
Venus	12,100 km	12 mm	108,200,000 km
Earth	12,800 km	13 mm	149,600,000 km
Mars	6,800 km	7 mm	227,900,000 km
Jupiter	143,000 km	143 mm	778,600,000 km
Saturn	120,500 km	121 mm	1,435,500,000 km
Uranus	51,000 km	51 mm	1,780,000,000 km
Neptune	49,500 km	50 mm	4,495,100,000 km
Pluto	2,300 km	2 mm	5,870,000,000 km

③ Put the planets in order by distance from the Sun.

Process Skills

You identified the paper "planets" by **measuring** them. The paper **models** are about 1 billionth of the diameter of the real planets. The paper planets are scale models.

Think About It

1. Explain how **measuring** helped you identify each paper **model**.

2. Compare the sizes of Earth, Venus and Jupiter?

3. How many planets are smaller than Earth? larger than Earth?

How to Read Science

Predicting

- A prediction is a statement about what you think will happen in the future. To make a prediction, you think of what you have learned in the past. You make observations and measurements. Then you look for patterns to tell you what to expect in the future.

- The information you read in the newspaper article gives you clues to future events.

Newpaper Article

Comet to Return!

March 5, 1986 Edmund Halley noticed that a comet visible in 1682 followed the same long, narrow path as comets in 1607 and 1531. He studied the laws of motion and data from past comets. He said that all three were really the same comet. In 1705, he predicted that the comet would return in 1759. Seventeen years after his death, his prediction came true. The comet was named in his honor. Halley's Comet appeared again in 1835, 1910, and now, 1986 it will come close to us again.

Apply It!

Use what you know and the information from the paragraph to predict when Halley's Comet will appear next.

You Are There!

On a clear night you gaze up at the sky. You see thousands and thousands of stars. Some are brighter than others. You notice a cloudy band that stretches across the sky. You are seeing part of the Milky Way, our home galaxy. The Milky Way has so many stars that you could not count them in a lifetime. We cannot see our galaxy as a whole, but scientists can see other galaxies that they think are similar to ours. Cameras sent into space years ago have only recently left the very small part of our galaxy that we call home, the solar system.

Lesson 1

What makes up the universe?

Our solar system travels around the Sun. Earth is a small part of the solar system. The solar system is only a small part of a vast universe.

The Universe and the Milky Way

You know your home address, but do you know your address in the **universe**? The universe is all of space and everything in it. Most of the universe is empty space.

The universe has millions of galaxies. A **galaxy** is a system of billions of stars, gases, and dust clustered together. We live in the Milky Way galaxy. The Milky Way is shaped like a flat spiral. Other galaxies have different shapes. Our Sun is located near the edge of our galaxy. It is just one of billions of stars in the Milky Way.

People have always watched objects move across the sky. The study of the Sun, Moon, stars, and the other objects in space is **astronomy**. Experts think that when the Great Pyramids in ancient Egypt were built, they lined up with the stars.

The Egyptians were not the only ones who used principles of astronomy. Greeks, Arabs, Indians, and other early civilizations all used astronomy to decide when they should plant or harvest crops. Sailors on the open sea did not have landmarks to tell them where they were. They used the Sun and the stars.

1. **✓Checkpoint** Describe what makes up the universe.
2. **Social Studies** in Science Use the Internet or other sources to find how early civilizations used the positions of certain stars for such buildings as Mayan pyramids or Greek temples. Draw a picture that shows what you learned.

Our Solar System

The **solar system** includes the Sun, the planets, their moons, and other objects. Everything in the solar system revolves around the Sun. That is, each object moves in a path, or orbit, around the Sun. A planet is a very large, ball-shaped object that moves around a star, such as the Sun. Planets are cooler and smaller than stars. They don't give off their own light, either. They may seem to shine because they reflect the light from the star they orbit.

Our solar system has inner and outer planets. The inner planets are Mercury, Venus, Earth, and Mars. The outer planets are Jupiter, Saturn, Uranus, Neptune, and Pluto. An area called the asteroid belt is between the inner planets and outer planets. Asteroids are rocky objects that also orbit the Sun but are too small to be called planets. As you probably inferred, the asteroid belt is a part of the solar system that has many asteroids.

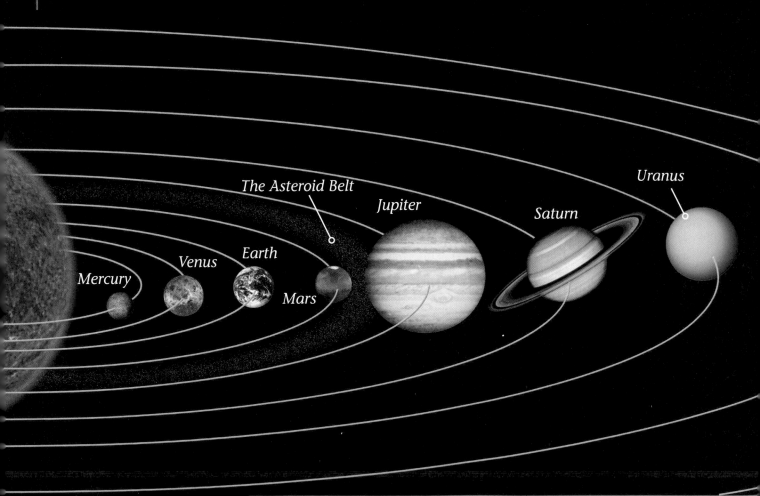

Mercury
Venus
Earth
Mars
The Asteroid Belt
Jupiter
Saturn
Uranus

When they observe the Sun, scientists use special telescopes with special cameras. They use special filters to photograph and record radiation from the Sun. Looking at the Sun can damage your eyes. You should never look directly at the Sun or use an ordinary telelscope to observe the Sun.

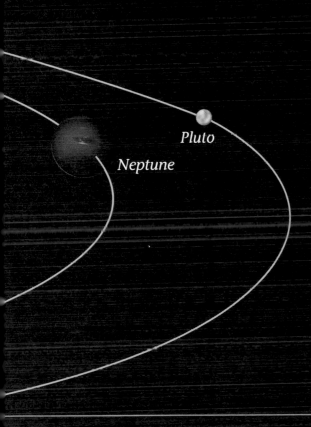

Pluto

Neptune

Gravity is the force that keeps the Earth and other objects in their orbits. Planets tend to move in a straight line. But the force of gravity affects the motion of the planets. Because the Sun is so huge, its gravity pulls the planets toward it. As a result, the planets move in curved paths around the Sun. The force of gravity between each planet and the Sun keeps even the outer planets in their orbits. The orbits are elliptical. That is, they are slightly flattened circles. The orbits of planets closest to the Sun are almost circular. The orbits of the outer planets are longer and narrower.

Astronomers have discovered other planets in orbit around other stars. So, it is possible that there are other solar systems besides ours.

The Sun

Our Sun is a medium sized star. It is the largest body in the solar system. Like all stars, the Sun is a huge ball of hot, glowing gases. Energy from the Sun provides light and heat for Earth. The outer parts of the Sun are much cooler than the inner parts. Scientists estimate that the outer part of the Sun is about 5,500° C (10,000°F). They think that the inner core is as hot as 15,000,000°C!

Like Earth, the Sun has magnetism. The Sun's magnetic field can become very strong in some places. Large loops of gas can extend from the Sun's surface in these areas. Dark spots called sunspots also appear at places where the magnetic field is very strong.

✓ Lesson Checkpoint

1. Why do planets orbit around the Sun?
2. Name three different types of objects in our solar system.
3. **Writing in Science** **Descriptive** Descriptive Describe the characteristics of the Sun.

Lesson 2

What are the inner planets?

The four planets closest to the Sun are known as the inner planets. Mercury, Venus, Earth, and Mars are all small rocky planets.

Mercury

Mercury is the planet closest to the Sun. It is a small planet, a little bigger than Earth's moon. Mercury is covered with thousands of dents. The dents are shaped like bowls and are called **craters**. Craters were made when meteorites crashed into Mercury's surface long ago. A meteorite is a rock from space that has struck the surface of a planet or a moon.

In 1974 scientists sent the Mariner 10 space probe to visit Mercury. A **space probe** is a vehicle that carries cameras and other tools for studying different objects in space.

This picture of Mercury was made by joining many smaller photos that were taken by Mariner 10. No photos were taken of the area that looks smooth.

Mercury Facts

Distance from Sun
57,909,175 km (35,983,100 mi)

Diameter
4,879 km (3,032 mi)

Length of day as measured in Earth time
59 days

Length of year as measured in Earth time
88 days

Average surface temperature
117° C (332° F)

Moons
none

Weight of a person who is 100 lb on Earth
38 lb

Too Hot and Too Cold

Mercury has almost no atmosphere. Because it is so close to the Sun, Mercury is scorching hot during the day. Daytime temperatures are four or five times greater than the hottest place on Earth. But with no atmosphere to hold in the heat, Mercury is very cold at night.

Venus

Venus is the second planet from the Sun. It is about the same size as Earth. Like Mercury, Venus is very hot and dry. Unlike Mercury, Venus has an atmosphere made of thick, swirling clouds. The clouds of Venus are burning hot and poisonous! There are strong winds and lightning. The clouds also are good at reflecting the Sun's light. This makes Venus one of the brightest objects in the night sky.

Venus Facts

Distance from Sun
108,200,000 km (67,200,000 mi)

Diameter
12,104 km (7,521 mi)

Length of day as measured in Earth time
243 days

Length of year as measured in Earth time
255 days

Average surface temperature
464° C (867° F)

Moons
none

Weight of a person who is 100 lb on Earth
91 lb

1. ✓**Checkpoint** What are some reasons why people cannot live on Mercury or Venus?
2. **Math** in Science How much farther from the Sun is Venus than is Mercury?

Earth

Earth, our home, is the third planet from the Sun. It is also the solar system's largest rocky planet. Earth is the only planet that has liquid water on its surface. In fact, most of Earth's surface is covered with water.

Earth is wrapped in a layer of gas that is about 150 kilometers (93 mi) thick. This layer of gas, or atmosphere, makes life possible on Earth. It filters out some of the Sun's harmful rays. It also contains nitrogen, oxygen, carbon dioxide, and water vapor. Plants and animals on Earth use these gases. Earth is the only planet in the solar system known to support life.

Earth Facts

Distance from Sun
149,600,000 km (93,000,000 mi)

Diameter
12,756 km (7,926 mi)

Length of day as measured in Earth time
24 hours

Length of year as measured in Earth time
365 days

Average surface temperature
15°C (59°F)

Moons
1

Weight of a person who is 100 lb on Earth
100 lb

The Moon

Moons are **satellites** of planets. A satellite is an object that orbits another object in space. Just as planets revolve around the Sun because of gravity, moons revolve around planets. The force of gravity between a planet and its moon keeps the moons in their orbits.

Earth has one large moon. The Moon is about one-fourth the size of Earth. The Moon has no atmosphere. It has many craters that formed when meteorites crashed onto its surface.

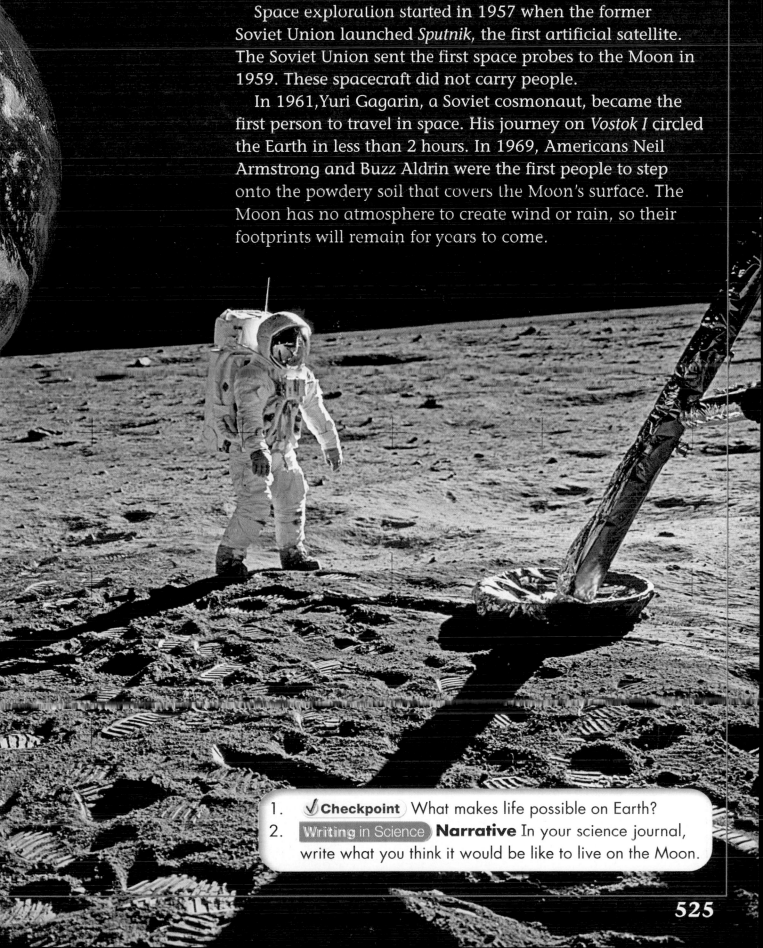

Space exploration started in 1957 when the former Soviet Union launched *Sputnik*, the first artificial satellite. The Soviet Union sent the first space probes to the Moon in 1959. These spacecraft did not carry people.

In 1961, Yuri Gagarin, a Soviet cosmonaut, became the first person to travel in space. His journey on *Vostok I* circled the Earth in less than 2 hours. In 1969, Americans Neil Armstrong and Buzz Aldrin were the first people to step onto the powdery soil that covers the Moon's surface. The Moon has no atmosphere to create wind or rain, so their footprints will remain for years to come.

1. ✔**Checkpoint** What makes life possible on Earth?
2. **Writing in Science** **Narrative** In your science journal, write what you think it would be like to live on the Moon.

Mars

The fourth planet from the Sun is Mars. The rocks and soil that cover much of Mars contain the mineral iron oxide. This mineral is reddish-brown in color. It is the same material that makes up rust. This has given Mars its nickname, the "Red Planet." Mars has two deeply cratered moons. Phobos, one of the moons, is very close to Mars. It is closer to Mars than any other moon is to any other planet.

Mars Facts

Distance from Sun
227,900,000 km (141,600,000 mi)

Diameter
6,794 km (4,222 mi)

Length of day as measured in Earth time
25 hours

Length of year as measured in Earth time
686 days

Average surface temperature
−63°C (−85°F)

Moons
2

Weight of a person who is 100 lb on Earth
38 lb

The atmosphere on Mars does not have enough oxygen to support life forms that need oxygen. Winds on Mars cause dust storms. The dust storms are sometimes so large that they cover the entire planet.

Mars has polar caps that grow in the Martian winter and shrink in the summer. Mars has many volcanoes. It also has a canyon that's bigger than Earth's Grand Canyon. This canyon, the Valles Marineris, is more than 3000 kilometers (1,864 mi) long. Earth's Grand Canyon in Arizona is 800 kilometers (497 mi) long.

About $\frac{4}{5}$ of the surface of Mars is dry and is covered by dust and rocks.

Several probes have successfully landed on Mars. The first one, *Viking I*, touched down on Mars in 1976. In January 2004, the twin robot Mars Exploration Rovers *Spirit* and *Opportunity*, landed. *Spirit* and *Opportunity* gathered and sent data back to Earth. Scientists hope the data will provide much information about materials that make up Mars. They hope some of the data will provide evidence that Mars has or once had water.

✔ **Lesson Checkpoint**

1. Why is the soil on Mars red?
2. What characteristics do Earth and Mars have in common?
3. ◉ **Predict** What might scientists predict if the Rovers find water on Mars?

527

What do we know about Jupiter, Saturn, and Uranus?

Jupiter, Saturn, and Uranus are the first of the outer planets. Their orbits are beyond the asteroid belt. These three planets are gas giants. They all have many moons.

Jupiter

Jupiter, the fifth planet from the Sun, is a gas giant. A gas giant is a very large planet made mostly of gases. Jupiter's atmosphere is mainly hydrogen and helium. Jupiter is the largest planet in our solar system. In fact, it is so big that all of the other planets could fit inside it!

Jupiter Facts

Distance from Sun
778,600,000 km (484,000,000 mi)

Diameter
142,984 km (88,846 mi)

Length of day as measured in Earth time
10 hours

Length of year as measured in Earth time
12 years

Average surface temperature
–148°C (–234°F)

Moons
at least 63

Rings
yes

Weight of a person who is 100 lb on Earth
214 lb

Jupiter's atmosphere has a weather system called the Great Red Spot that has been raging for centuries. It is a disturbance that is more than three times the size of Earth.

Jupiter's Moons

Jupiter has many moons. Galileo was the first person to see the four largest moons through his telescope in 1610. They are about the size of Earth's moon. Jupiter also has rings, but they are too dark to be seen from Earth.

Io has more active volcanoes than any other body in the solar system. The volcanoes give off sulfur. The sulfur shows up as yellows, oranges, and greenish yellows. Io is the solar system's most colorful moon.

Europa is the smoothest object in the solar system. Its crust is frozen, but a liquid ocean might lie beneath the crust. Some scientists believe there may be living organisms on Europa.

Ganymede is the largest moon in the solar system. It is bigger than Mercury and Pluto. Ice covers one third of its surface. It may even have a saltwater ocean!

Callisto is the more heavily cratered than any other object in the solar system. The impacts of meteorites have left large cracks in its surface. Scientists think there is a frozen ocean beneath its crust.

1. ✓ **Checkpoint** What is a gas giant?
2. **Art** in Science Draw a picture of what you think it would look like on the surface of one of Jupiter's moons.

Saturn

The sixth planet from the Sun, Saturn is also a gas giant. Like Jupiter, Saturn's atmosphere is mostly hydrogen and helium. Saturn is very large, but it has only a small amount of matter.

The *Voyager* space probe explored Saturn's rings. It showed that the particles that make up the rings range in size from tiny grains to boulders. They are probably made of water, ice, dust, and chunks of rock.

Galileo's Handles

When Galileo saw Saturn through his telescope, he was surprised. He saw what looked like a planet with handles! The "handles" were actually the brilliant ring system that orbits the planet.

Galileo lived from 1564 to 1642. He was a mathematician and astronomer. He agreed with Copernicus that all planets revolve around the Sun. Galileo invented an astronomical telescope and used it to oserve the Moon and planets.

Saturn Facts
Distance from Sun   1,426,725,000 km (886,000,000 mi)
Diameter   120,536 km (74,897 mi)
Length of day as measured in Earth time   11 hours
Length of year as measured in Earth time   30 years
Average surface temperature   −134°C (−220°F)
Moons   at least 31
Rings   yes
Weight of a person who is 100 lb on Earth   74 lb

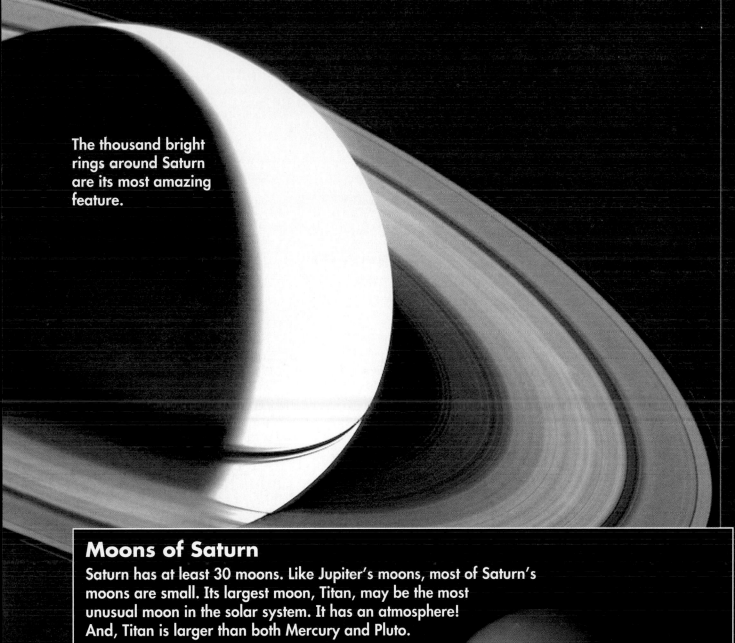

The thousand bright rings around Saturn are its most amazing feature.

Moons of Saturn

Saturn has at least 30 moons. Like Jupiter's moons, most of Saturn's moons are small. Its largest moon, Titan, may be the most unusual moon in the solar system. It has an atmosphere! And, Titan is larger than both Mercury and Pluto.

Pan Atlas Prometheus Janus Enceladus Mimas Tethys Dione Rhea Titan Hyperion Iapetus Phoebe Pandora Epimetheus

1. ✔ **Checkpoint** What are Saturn's rings made of?
2. **Writing** in Science **Expository** Research the life of Galileo. Write what you learn in your science journal.

Uranus

In 1781, William Herschel discovered a seventh planet orbiting the Sun. The gas giant Uranus is the farthest planet you can see without a telescope. Its atmosphere is hydrogen, helium, and methane. Uranus is so cold that the methane is a liquid. Tiny drops of liquid methane form a thin cloud that covers the planet. This gives Uranus its fuzzy blue-green look. Like the other gas giants, Uranus also has a ring system and many moons. But, unlike Saturn's bright ring system, the rings of Uranus are dark and hard to see with Earth-based telescopes. A space probe discovered the rings in 1977.

Rolling Through Space

Uranus rotates on its side. No one knows for sure why Uranus has this odd tilt. Scientists think that a very large object may have collided with the planet when the solar system was still forming. This bump may have knocked Uranus onto its side.

Uranus Facts

Distance from Sun
2,872,000,000 km (1,784,000,000 mi)

Diameter
51,118 km (31,763 mi)

Length of day as measured in Earth time
17 hours; spins backward

Length of year as measured in Earth time
84 years

Average surface temperature
−216°C (−357°F)

Moons
at least 27

Rings
yes

Weight of a person who is 100 lb on Earth
86 lb

Uranus is a gas giant with a large liquid core.

The Moons of Uranus

Today we know the planet has at least 27 moons, and more may yet be discovered. The moons farthest from Uranus are hard to see using telescopes on Earth. The moons closer to the planet were first seen with telescopes during the 1700s. They are larger moons with deep valleys, craters, and steep ridges.

Ariel

Oberon

Titania

Miranda

Umbriel

✔ Lesson Checkpoint

1. How is the atmosphere of Uranus different from that of Saturn?
2. How is Uranus different from other gas giants?
3. **Math in Science** How many years passed between the discoveries of Uranus and its ring system?

What do we know about Neptune, Pluto, and beyond?

Neptune's atmosphere is similar to that of Uranus. Like Uranus, the gas methane gives Neptune a blue color. Neptune has bands of clouds and storms similar to those on Jupiter.

Neptune is a gas giant. Pluto, however, is not a giant. In fact, it is the smallest planet in our solar system. Scientists are discovering more objects beyond Pluto.

Neptune

Neptune is the eighth planet from the Sun. It is the smallest of the gas giants. Even so, if Neptune were hollow, it could hold about 60 Earths. It is so far away that it can't be seen without a telescope. In 1846 astronomers discovered Neptune. A few days later they spotted, Triton, Neptune's largest moon.

Because Neptune is so far from the Sun, its orbit is very long. It takes more than one hundred Earth years for Neptune to orbit the Sun. It is a very windy planet. Its winds blow the Great Dark Spot across the planet.

The Voyager 2 space probe took a picture of Neptune. The picture showed a huge storm. It is called the Great Dark Spot.

Neptune Facts

Neptune Facts	
Distance from Sun 4,495,100,000 km (2,800,000,000 mi)	
Diameter 49,528 km (30,775 mi)	
Length of day as measured in Earth time 16 hours	
Length of year as measured in Earth time 165 years	
Average surface temperature −214°C (−353°F)	
Moons at least 13	
Rings yes	
Weight of a person who is 100 lb on Earth 110 lb	

How Neptune Was Discovered

British astronomer John Couch Adams studied planets and other objects in space. He noticed that Uranus was not orbiting the way that he calculated it should. He concluded that the force of gravity between Uranus and another planet was affecting the orbit.

A mathematician named Urbain Leverrier made calculations of his own. He used these data to predict the position and size of the proposed planet. He shared his findings with astronomers. On September 23, 1846, Johann Galle aimed his telescope where the predictions suggested he should look. He saw Neptune!

The Moons of Neptune

Neptune has at least 13 moons. The largest, Triton, may be the coldest body in our solar system. Its surface temperature is about –235°C.

Astronomers think that Triton didn't form with Neptune. Instead, they think it formed farther from the Sun and was captured by Neptune's gravity.

1. **✓ Checkpoint** How does Neptune compare in size with other planets?
2. **Math in Science** How much colder is the average temperature on Triton than on Neptune?

Triton

Neptune's ring

Neptune

535

Pluto

In 1930, Clyde Tombaugh discovered a ninth planet, Pluto. It is the only outer planet that is not a gas giant. It has an icy, solid surface. Pluto is the smallest planet in the solar system. It is even smaller than Earth's moon!

Pluto's only moon, Charon (cair' un), is slightly smaller than Pluto. Charon is very close to Pluto. Many astronomers consider Pluto and Charon a double planet system since they are so close together and similar in size. Also, astronomers think the two share the same atmosphere when they are closest to the Sun.

Pluto

Charon

Pluto Facts

Distance from Sun
5,906,000,000 km (3,670,000,000 mi)

Diameter
2,302 km (1,430 mi)

Length of day as measured in Earth time
6 days (spins backward)

Length of year as measured in Earth time
248 years

Average surface temperature
−223°C (−375°F)

Moons
1

Weight of a person who is 100 lb on Earth
8 lb

NASA's Hubble Space Telescope looked more than 3 billion miles into space and captured this image of the small, icy Pluto.

Charon

Pluto

An Odd Orbit

Pluto has an odd orbit. The other planets travel around the Sun at the same angle, while Pluto's orbit is tilted. During parts of its orbit it is closer to the Sun than Neptune. This occurred from 1979 to 1999. The next time this will occur is in 2237.

Sedna

Sedna

Pluto

Is Sedna the tenth planet? Astronomers discovered Sedna in November, 2003. It is smaller than Earth's moon, but it is the largest body discovered in the solar system since 1930 when Pluto was first seen. Sedna is as far as 84 billion miles from the Sun. Its temperature is a chilly –240°C. Like Mars, it is a red object.

Astronomers have observed other objects beyond Pluto. These objects also seem to be too small to be planets.

✓ Lesson Checkpoint

1. List the planets in order from smallest to largest.
2. **Math** in Science At the closest point of its orbit, Pluto is 4,436,820,000 km from the Sun. At the farthest point, Pluto is 7,375,930,000 km from the Sun. How much farther is this?
3. ⟳ Predict Will astronomers find evidence of life on Sedna?

Investigate How does spinning affect a planet's shape?

Materials

large construction paper

metric ruler

scissors

stapler

hole punch

dull pencil

Process Skills

Models are different from the real thing they represent, but can be used to learn about the real thing. By constructing, operating, and analyzing your model, you learned how spinning might affect a planet's shape.

What to Do

1 Cut 2 strips of construction paper. Cross the strips at their centers. Staple as shown.

Each strip should measure about 2.5 cm × 46 cm.

2 Bring the 4 ends together and overlap them. Staple them as shown to form a sphere.

3 Use the punch to make a hole through the center of the overlapped ends.

4 Push about 5 centimeters of the pencil through the hole.

5 Hold the pencil between your palms and move your hands back and forth to make your **model** spin. Record your observations in a chart like the one below.

You have made a model of a spinning planet.

Shape When Not Spinning	Shape While Spinning
⬭	

Think About It

1. Did the sphere change shape when you spun it? Make an **inference** about what happened.

2. How is your **model** similar to a spinning planet? How is it different?

Go Further

Be your own model of a spinning planet. Stand in an open area far from other students with your arms hanging loosely at your sides. Spin around twice. Feel your arms move out. Be careful not to get dizzy!

Using Data About Planets

Each planet in the solar system has the shape of a sphere. The diameter of a sphere is the distance from one point on the surface of the sphere to a point on the opposite side, passing through the center. Think of digging a tunnel that passes through the center of Earth, to the opposite side. The length of that tunnel would be the diameter.

The table below gives the diameter in kilometers of each planet in the solar system.

Planet	Diameter
Mercury	4,879 km
Venus	12,104 km
Earth	12,756 km
Mars	6,794 km
Jupiter	142,984 km
Saturn	120,536 km
Uranus	51,118 km
Neptune	49,528 km
Pluto	2,390 km

Copy the table on page 540. Add a third column, with the heading "Rounded Diameter".

1. Round each diameter to the nearest thousand kilometers. Write the rounded number in the table.

2. List the 9 planets with their rounded diameters in order from least to greatest. What is the median rounded diameter? Which planet has that diameter?

3. Which planet has a diameter about 10 times that of Venus?

4. Which planet has a diameter less than half that of Mercury?

Lab zone Take-Home Activity

Choose your favorite planet and do some research about it. Write a news article or a science fiction story about your planet.

Use Vocabulary

astronomy (p. 519)	**solar system** (p. 520)
craters (p. 522)	**space probe** (p. 522)
galaxy (p. 519)	
satellite (p. 524)	**universe** (p. 519)

Use the vocabulary term from the list above that completes each sentence.

1. A _____ is a vehicle that carries cameras and other tools into space.

2. The study of the universe, including the Sun, Moon, stars, and planets is called _____.

3. A _____ is an object that orbits another object in space.

4. Billions of stars clustered together form a _____.

5. _____ are bowl shaped holes made by meteorites.

6. The _____ is all of space and everything in it.

7. The Sun, the planets, their moons, asteroids, and other objects that revolve around the Sun make up the _____.

Explain Concepts

8. Describe the orbits of all the planets.

9. Explain what makes Earth unique in our solar system.

10. Explain why some scientists consider Pluto to be a double planet.

11. Describe the features of the Sun that show in this photograph and explain what causes them.

Process Skills

12. **Sequence** Order the planets from closest to the Sun to farthest from the Sun.

13. **Infer** All of the gas giants have many moons. With two moons, Mars holds the record for the most moons for the smaller rocky planets. Infer why gas giants have more moons than rocky planets.

Predicting

14. All planets in our solar system orbit the Sun. Scientists have identified more than 100 planets orbiting other stars. Suppose they discover one of these planets is similar to gas giants in the solar system. **Predict** other characteristics of this planet.

Test Prep

Choose the letter that best completes the statement or answers the question.

15. The smallest of the gas giants is
Ⓐ Pluto.
Ⓑ Uranus.
Ⓒ Saturn.
Ⓓ Neptune.

16. The object in our solar system with the strongest gravitational pull is
Ⓕ Jupiter.
Ⓖ the Sun.
Ⓗ the Earth.
Ⓘ the Moon.

17. Who discovered the planet Pluto?
Ⓐ John Couch Adams
Ⓑ Urbain Leverrier
Ⓒ Clyde Tombaugh
Ⓓ Johann Galle

18. What kind of storm sometimes cover the entire planet of Mars?
Ⓕ thunderstorms
Ⓖ tropical storms
Ⓗ dust storms
Ⓘ ice storms

19. Explain why the answer you chose for Question #18 is best. For each of the answers you did not choose, give a reason why it is not the best choice.

20. Writing in Science **Persuasive** Astronomers have observed many moons orbiting planets. Which planet do you think is likely to have moons that astronomers have not yet discovered? Give reasons to convince others why your choice is reasonable.

Nicolaus Copernicus

Nicolaus Copernicus was born in Thorn, Poland on February 19, 1473. He attended the University of Krakow where he studied many subjects including astronomy.

In his astronomy classes, Nicolaus learned about Ptolemy's model of the universe. Ptolemy was an astronomer in Alexandria, Egypt around 150 AD. Ptolemy used his observations to develop a model of the universe. According to this model, the Earth was at the center of the universe. Everything else revolved around the Earth. Copernicus studied the works of Ptolemy and other astronomers. Copernicus developed a different theory of how to model the universe. He said objects in space moved in different ways than those Ptolemy had described. He thought the Earth moved around the Sun.

Throughout his lifetime, Copernicus carefully recorded what he observed. He also considered what others observed. In 1543, he published *On the Revolutions of Heavenly Spheres.* This book said that Earth rotates on an axis and revolves around the Sun. Copernicus was open to new ideas even though they were diffferent from the beliefs of his time. He paved the way for modern astronomers.

Lab zone Take-Home Activity

Be a sky-watcher like Copernicus. each night for 2 weeks, look at the sky directly overhead at sunset. Write about what you see in your **science journal.**

Chapter 19
Effects of Technology

You Will Discover

- how technology meets the challenges of our lives.
- how we use technology in communication and transportation.

Online
Student Edition

www.sfsuccessnet.com

How do the devices and products of technology affect the way we live?

technology

optical fibers

communication

546

Chapter 19 Vocabulary

telecommunications

vehicle

547

Explore How do communications satellites work?

Communications satellites orbiting Earth help move signals from place to place.

Materials

large coffee can

black and white construction paper

scissors and tape

metric ruler and clay

mirror and flashlight

What to Do

1 **Make a model** of a communications satellite as shown, moving a signal halfway around the Earth.

2 Place the mirror so the light from the flashlight hits the white paper.

flashlight = transmitter

can = Earth

paper = receiver

mirror = communications satellite

Think About It

Infer How do you think a communications satellite helps to send signals from place to place?

Process Skills

After you observe how light is reflected in your **model**, you can **infer** how a communications satellite works.

Take It to the NET
More Activities www.sfsuccessnet.com

Reading Skills

Main Idea and Details

The main idea is the most important idea in a reading selection or a picture.

- Identify the main idea of each paragraph. It is usually found in the topic sentence, which is often the first sentence of a paragraph.

- Read the selection carefully. Take note of details that make the main idea clearer. Some details may explain the main idea. Other details may give examples to support the main idea.

- Some of the main ideas and details might be familiar to you. As you read, think about what you already know.

Now read the following part of a newspaper article about magnetic resonance imaging (MRI). The main idea, and details are highlighted.

Newspaper Article

Since it was first used on people in 1977, magnetic resonance imaging (MRI) has become a major problem-solving tool for doctors. This medical technology uses electromagnetic waves. The waves make 3-D images of the body. Doctors can find problems inside the body without cutting into it. They are able to see right through bones and tissue. They are able to diagnose injuries and diseases.

Apply It!

Why is magnetic resonance imaging an effective problem-solving tool for doctors? Use the graphic organizer to help answer.

Detail	Detail	Detail

Main Idea

◆))You Are There!

You are late for work! You hop into your sleek Skymobile. Sensors in one of the onboard computers react. "Where to?" appears on the screen in front of you. You have barely finished saying "Work" as you zoom away at 350 mph. The skyway is crowded, but not as jam-packed as the highway below! Your Skymobile uses the latest technology to get you where you need to go. With just one or two touches of your finger, your Skymobile does the rest. You sit back and relax. In just a few more minutes, you will coast into the parking port on top of the skyscraper in which you work. Thanks to technology, your commute was quick. Maybe you won't be late after all.

How does technology affect our lives?

People use technology to make their lives more comfortable and productive. But using technology to solve one problem can cause a different problem.

Creating New Challenges

You may not be zooming through the skies in your Skymobile just yet. But you are using technology, in many ways, in your own life right now. **Technology** is the knowledge, processes, and products that we use to solve problems and make our work easier. It helps us meet our needs and make our lives more comfortable, healthy, and useful.

Technology has a huge effect on people and other living things. Some developments have unintended effects. Some products of technology can hurt people, animals, and plants. Motor vehicle emissions, industrial waste, and insecticides have some bad side effects. Many countries, like the United States, face problems with air, water, soil, and water pollution.

Most people agree that technology has helped us greatly. New technologies are always changing the ways people do their jobs. In many cases, machines now do things that people once did. And that can mean that people lose their jobs. But at the same time technology makes unexpected problems, it can solve them, too. New technologies may lead to machines that do dangerous work that was once done by people. And, new technologies create new jobs—many in the electronics industry.

1. **✓Checkpoint** What trouble has some technology caused in the United States and other countries?
2. **Writing** in Science **Informative** Write an informative paragraph about the forms of technology you have used in the last 24 hours. Explain whether each form of technology has helped make your life more comfortable, more productive, or more healthy.

From Hitchhiker to Invention

Prickly with tiny hooks, the burr has been known to hitch rides on animals! This little bit of nature led to an important product that people make. An engineer was pulling burrs off his clothing and from his dog's fur. He got the idea for Velcro™, a sticky fastener made of tiny hooks and loops. Velcro™ is made of nylon or polyester. It is used in clothing, medical equipment, and sports gear. Maybe your shoes are fastened with it!

Technology and Materials

This extreme rollerblader is too busy concentrating on the next move to notice all the products of technology. Materials that are not found in nature have come our way because of technology. In-line skates and gear are made from different materials such as plastic, metal, rubber, and nylon. Some of these materials are made mainly from natural resources. But others are made from materials that people have made from natural resources.

Iron ore, a natural resource, is heated to make the steel for the bearings, screws, and axles. To make these parts, liquid metal is poured into different molds. Plastic is made from chemicals. Then it is shaped into shoe parts, buckles, and protective gear. The covering on knee and elbow pads and wrist guards may be made from nylon, a type of plastic. The cloth that lines the inside of the rollerblades may be polyester. Clothing can be made from polyester too. Certain threads, like polyester, are made by people from chemicals or recycled plastic materials. Each day technology leads to new inventions and improves old ones.

Technology Keeps Us Healthy

You know that technology helps keep us safe and healthy. It's watching out for the rollerblader! The materials used in protective gear help lower the number of serious injuries that come with in-line skating. What happens if the rollerblader takes a fall? The helmet will help protect the rollerblader's head. Plastic cushions in the knee and elbow pads and in the wrist guards will also absorb some of the crash.

Technology is used to design and produce equipment that protects us.

Always wear a helmet when rollerblading! The outer shell is often made from a hard material. Helmets are light, and they protect your head from impacts.

Knee and elbow pads are made of a kind of foam covered by a layer of plastic. Pads can be slipped on or held with Velcro™ straps.

Most wrist guards have a thin, tough nylon spine. This supports the wrist and protects the palm.

Wheels on in-line skates are made of polyurethane. It is made with chemical technology.

Controlling Waste

Many companies make waste and pollution as they manufacture items for our use. Many companies are working to make products out of things that will decompose, or break down. These things will become part of the Earth again. But some materials do not break down easily. They are not part of nature because they have been made by people. In fact, they have been made through technology. We should recycle plastic, glass, aluminum, and other materials that are results of technology.

1. **✓Checkpoint** How did an item found in nature play a role in the invention of Velcro™?

2. **◎ Main Idea and Details** Which details support the main idea that in-line skating gear is made from many different materials?

553

Technology and Medicine

Medical technology has greatly changed the tools that are used to treat illness and injuries. The changes have improved medical care. Now, instead of using small, sharp knives in operations, doctors sometimes use lasers. A laser beam can remove tissue. It can unclog blocked arteries and fix broken blood vessels.

Today, doctors often use tools with **optical fibers.** These very thin tubes allow light to pass through them. Doctors use cameras with optical fibers to see inside the body without making a large cut. They can decide what the problem is and the best way to treat it. Sometimes they decide very little surgery is needed inside the body.

Keyhole surgery is one way that technology has improved the care doctors are able to give. The patient may have less pain and heal faster because the doctor makes only a small cut, about the size of a keyhole.

Technology and Food

You know proper nutrition is part of good health. Nature gives us food. Technology gives us some control over nature. People in many areas use tractors, chemical fertilizers, and pesticides. They are able to grow many kinds of plants. The crops they harvest provide different foods needed for a healthy diet.

But with these good things come drawbacks, too. The same fertilizers and pesticides that help crops grow can harm the environment.

The combine harvester in the photo allows the grain from huge fields to be gathered—quickly!

X-rays and More

Machines that help doctors determine what is wrong are a great move forward in medicine. Perhaps you know someone who has had an X-ray of a broken bone. After the doctor sees where the bone is broken and what the break looks like, fixing the bone is easier.

People make machines to do things they would not be able to do in other ways. In 1895 Wilhelm Roentgen (1845–1923) discovered X-rays. He did not understand his discovery right away. In science, X is a symbol for the unknown. Roentgen called his finding X-rays. For the first time, doctors saw inside the body—without touching it!

Have you had your teeth X-rayed at your dentist's office? An X-ray picture marks the spot where a cavity is found. Doctors take X-rays to find broken bones or tumors. X-rays are also used to treat cancer. But the same technology that is so helpful can be harmful, too. Too much contact with X-rays can cause burns and cancer.

Today, Nuclear Magnetic Resonance or NMR technology allows doctors to identify the chemical make up of matter. They can use magnetic resonance imaging (MRI) technology to learn about things that don't show up on X-rays. They can get a detailed look at what is happening inside blood vessels, for example.

✓ Lesson Checkpoint

1. How do doctors use new medical technology in surgeries?
2. Compare and contrast the benefits of X-rays with the harmful qualities.
3. **Descriptive** You are a doctor living in 1895. You have just seen Wilhelm Roentgen demonstrate a new X-ray machine. Write a journal entry to describe what you saw. Include your thoughts about this new technology.

How X-Rays Work

X-rays pass through skin and other organs. Bones, metal and other objects block the rays and cast clear shadows on film. We call the shadow picture an X-ray.

Lesson 2

How has technology changed communication and transportation?

We depend on communication and transportation. Without technology, communications would be limited. Transportation would not run.

Communication

Have you called someone, written a letter, sent an email or an Instant Message lately? Then you have communicated! **Communication** is the process of sending any type of message from one place to another. You communicate to have your needs met and to stay safe and well. You also communicate to interact with other people. You may use speech or writing. But there are many other ways to get your message across.

Good communication takes three things. You must send a message. The message must be received. And it must be understood. Sending an email through the World Wide Web is one example of the process. But without technology, speech only goes a short way. As time passes, we may not remember all the details of the original spoken message.

Can you think of other ways to send messages? Through writing, you can send them with ink and paper. With speech, you can use a phone. With photography, you can use a camera. Without technology, communication is limited. After the invention of writing about 8,000 years ago, messages could be sent long distances, and the ideas in them could be stored for a long time. But the messages had to be written by hand.

A quill—the hollow shaft of a feather—was first used as a pen around 600 AD.

Dried and cleaned goose, swan, or turkey feathers were most popular. Their thick shafts held the ink. The tip was shaved to a point with a knife.

By 1455, a German goldsmith, Johannes Gutenberg, had invented a way of making type with single letters. Hard metal punches were carved with letters.

In Guttenberg's workshop, workers set movable letter blocks by hand. After they printed as many copies as they needed, the letters could be reused. Printing brought the benefits of writing to a wider group.

A .—	J .———	S ...	2 ..———
B —...	K —.—	T —	3 ...——
C —.—.	L .—..	U ..—	4 ....—
D —..	M ——	V ...—	5 .....
E .	N —.	W .——	6 —....
F ..—.	O ———	X —..—	7 ——...
G ——.	P .——.	Y —.——	8 ———..
H	Q ——.—	Z ——..	9 ————.
I ..	R .—.	1 .————	0 —————

The earliest form of telecommunication was the electric telegraph. An electric current shot along a wire in short bursts called Morse code.

Early motion picture cameras used film that moved from one reel to another reel. After the film was developed, another machine was needed to view it.

Telecommunications

Communication paired with electricity completely changed the way of life in the 19th century. The time that passed between a message being sent and received shrunk. Messages that used to take several days or even weeks arrived in seconds. In time, people could talk from one continent to another. The world became smaller, the pace of life faster. Today, many forms of communication take only a split second to reach hundreds of people.

Telecommunications are communications that are done electronically. A transmitter sends out a signal with information. The signal travels to a receiver. The receiver turns that signal back into a clear message. Communication satellites send telephone, radio, TV, and other signals from one part of the Earth to another. They are also used for navigation by cars, trucks, aircraft, and ships.

Early video cameras took moving pictures and could also play them back!

1. **✓Checkpoint** In what ways did life change when electricity was used with communication?

2. **Social Studies** in Science Use sources such as nonfiction books, encyclopedias, and the Internet, to discover more about methods of communication. Create a poster, a diagram, or a model, to share your findings.

Transportation Systems

Transportation systems move people and goods from place to place. Most transportation systems use a vehicle. A **vehicle** carries the people and goods. Cars, trucks, trains, ships, planes, and rockets are vehicles. Vehicles move on roadways, railways, waterways, and through airways. Long trips that once took days or weeks may now take only hours. Which vehicles have you traveled in or on?

To make vehicles safe, engineers test and improve new designs. Seat belts, air bags, and new bumpers make safer cars. But, the extra costs of making safety items means that the car costs more to buy.

1807: Robert Fulton builds the *Clermont*. It is the first steamboat that carries passengers—and stays in business.

1890s: Electric trolley streetcars begin to replace horse-drawn trolleys for public transportation in cities.

1914: Henry Ford's factory mass produces automobiles. More people can afford to own a car.

1869: The transcontinental railroad across the United States links the east and the west. The railroad is completed at Promontory, Utah. The last spike is made of gold.

1903: Bicycle makers Orville and Wilbur Wright build a powered airplane. Orville flies 120 feet in 12 seconds.

Have you seen a conveyor belt? Have you ever taken an escalator or elevator? These systems are also designed, built, run, and used by people.

Today's transportation systems often use computer technology. Computers keep systems on time and running properly. Space transportation systems use computer technology, too. Scientists use computers and computer models to solve problems of great distances, weightlessness, and airlessness.

The Technology of Time Measurement

Time can be measured in the seconds it takes to move parts from one place to another on an assembly line. It can be the days a truck takes to cross the continent or the weeks a huge cargo ship takes to cross the ocean. Keeping track of time has always been important to us. In ancient Egypt, astronomers used the Sun's movement to tell time. Later, people used machines. Mechanical motions repeated over and over again. Today, we use clocks and watches that can measure time in fractions of seconds.

1959: Transcontinental jet service connects New York City and Los Angeles.

Early 1980s: Articulated buses carry passengers in large cities.

1937: British inventor Sir Frank Whittle builds the first successful jet engine.

1964: High-speed electric "bullet trains" begin operating in Japan.

2004: In Shanghai, China, the world's first commercial maglev rail system begins operating.

1. ✓ **Checkpoint** How does the way we measure time today differ from the way the ancient Egyptians measured it?

2. **Main Idea and Details** What are some details that support the main idea that most modern transportation systems use vehicles?

559

Lab zone — Guided Inquiry

Investigate Why are satellite antennas curved?

Materials

index card

scissors

metric ruler

foil

round bowl

black construction paper

clay and flashlight

Process Skills

You can use what you **observe** and what you already know to make an **inference**.

What to Do

1 Cut out 4 slits in an index card.

Use clay to hold the index card straight up.

5 mm

4 cm

Use clay to tip the flashlight slightly downward.

about 45 cm

2 Fold the square of foil twice in half to make a strip as shown.

Do not wrinkle the foil!

3 Bend the foil around the bowl to make a smooth curve.

bend

560

Take It to the NET
More Activities www.sfsuccessnet.com

4 In a dark room turn on the flashlight. **Observe** how the light reflects off the foil. Find where the light comes together at one spot. If necessary, slightly curve the foil closer together or farther apart.

5 Copy and complete the drawing. Use dotted lines to show how the light reflects off the foil.

Path of Light

The curved foil reflector gathers the light in one spot. A satellite antenna has a curved reflector to gather an invisible signal in one spot. At that one spot, a receiver detects the signal and passes it on.

Think About It

1. **Infer** If a very weak signal were coming from space, would you need a large or small satellite antenna to detect it?

2. Compare and contrast your model of a satellite antenna with the real thing.

Go Further

What would be the effect of a more powerful signal or a larger antenna? Change your model to help answer this or other questions you may have.

Scale Models and Scale Drawings

Inventors often make a scale model or a scale drawing. This helps them when they design new products. A scale model or scale drawing is exactly like the new product it represents, but either much larger or much smaller. A scale is a special type of ratio. A ratio compares two quantities. If there are 12 boys and 15 girls in your class, the ratio of boys to girls would be 12 to 15. Ratios can be written several ways: 12 to 15, 12:15, or $\frac{12}{15}$. A scale compares size on a model to size on the actual object.

This model of a Solar Powered Car has a scale of 1 cm:25 cm. That means that a length of 1 cm on the model represents a length of 25 cm on the actual car. If the model is 10 cm long, how long is the actual car?

$$\frac{1 \text{ cm}}{25 \text{ cm}} = \frac{10 \text{ cm}}{?}$$ Write the ratios in fraction form.

$$\frac{1 \times 10}{25 \times 10} = \frac{10}{250}$$ Work with equivalent ratios the same way as equivalent fractions.

The actual car is 250 cm long.

A map is a scale drawing. Any distance on the map is much less than the actual distance it represents.

A map has a scale of 1 cm:4 km and two cities are shown 5 cm apart on the map. What is the actual distance between the two cities?

$$\frac{1 \text{ cm}}{25 \text{ cm}} = \frac{5 \text{ cm}}{?}$$

$$\frac{1 \text{ cm} \times 5}{4 \text{ km} \times 5} = \frac{5 \text{ cm}}{20 \text{ km}}$$

The actual distance between the cities is 20 kilometers.

Use the model car on page 562 and the map described above to answer each question.

1. If the model car is 5 cm wide, how wide is the actual car?

2. If the model car is 3 cm tall, how tall is the actual car?

3. Two rivers are 6 cm apart on the map. What is the actual distance between the rivers?

4. The mapmaker wanted to draw a line showing a straight road that is actually 36 km long. How long should the line be on the map?

Lab zone Take-Home Activity

Make a scale model or scale drawing of a room in your house. You will need to find the actual measurements of the room and everything in it. Decide on a scale to use. Then find the measurements for the model or drawing.

Chapter 19 Review and Test Prep

Use Vocabulary

communication (p. 556)	**technology** (p. 551)
optical fibers (p. 554)	**telecommunications** (p. 557)
	vehicle (p. 558)

Use the term from the list above that best completes each sentence.

1. _____ are messages that are sent by electronic means.

2. A _____ carries people and objects from one place to another.

3. Very thin tubes that let light pass through them are _____.

4. _____ is the knowledge, processes, and products that we use to make our lives better.

5. Writing a letter to a pen pal is an example of _____.

Explain Concepts

6. Explain how a machine or tool has helped people do something they could not do without it.

7. Explain how one scientific advance might have been influenced by or related to an earlier one.

8. Explain how technology in medicine has helped both doctors and patients.

Process Skills

9. Employees of a small company take orders over the phone. They enter the order in a computer program that sends it to be filled. The company buys a new computer system. Now customers enter their own orders. **Infer** why the company and its employees might have very different reactions to the new system.

10. **Make a model** that shows how creating technology to solve one problem might cause other unexpected problems.

11. **Predict** how transportation technology might develop even more advanced ways of moving people and objects. Explain how you arrived at your ideas.

12. Velcro™ was invented after a scientist pulled burrs off his clothes and his dog. **Form a hypothesis** about how Post-it® notes were invented.

Main Idea and Details

13. Make a graphic organizer like the one shown below. Fill in the missing details that support the main idea.

| Detail | Detail | Detail |

The way people communicate has changed a great deal over time

🦉 Test Prep

Choose the letter that best completes the statement or answers the question.

14. Through technology, we have materials that do not appear in
- Ⓐ science.
- Ⓑ medicine.
- Ⓒ nature.
- Ⓓ telecommunications.

15. In the 19th century the way of life changed when _____ was used with communication.
- Ⓕ electricity
- Ⓖ television
- Ⓗ time
- Ⓘ transportation

16. Throughout history, people have used various ways to keep track of
- Ⓐ optical fibers.
- Ⓑ telecommunications.
- Ⓒ lasers.
- Ⓓ time.

17. Sometimes technology can cause
- Ⓕ the world to seem bigger.
- Ⓖ unexpected problems.
- Ⓗ us to stop making machines.
- Ⓘ the pace of life to slow down.

18. Which has brought people closer together?
- Ⓐ optical fibers.
- Ⓑ clocks and watches.
- Ⓒ standard time zones.
- Ⓓ modern transportation.

19. Explain why the answer you selected for Question #17 is best. For each answer you did not select, give a reason why it is not the best choice.

20. **Writing** in Science **Persuasive** What is the best or worst effect of technology? Use words to persuade others to share your opinion.

Telemedicine

When you are sick, your mother or father might take you to the doctor. The doctor has learned how to help make you feel better and has the special tools he or she needs to find out what is wrong. What if you lived in a place that was far from a doctor? Your parent could call a doctor who would tell her or him what to do. The problem is that your parent doesn't have the same special tools a doctor has to examine you.

This same problem applies to astronauts in space. They are many miles from the nearest doctor. NASA is developing technologies to solve this problem. Computers, satellites, and digital imaging technology help astronauts talk to, write, and send pictures to doctors on Earth. The information the doctors receive helps them decide how to care for the astronauts in space.

Astronaut Guion Bluford monitors his blood pressure. This information is recorded to track his health while in space.

In the same way that astronauts in space can "visit" doctors on Earth, people in areas far from cities can "visit" a doctor. Some places on Earth have very few doctors. Other places do not have doctors who have special training to treat specific illnesses. NASA is working with businesses, hospitals, and doctors to solve this problem. They are using a process called telemedicine. It means giving medical help to people who are far away.

One place that uses telemedicine is Harlingen, Texas. Some people in Harlingen need help from doctors in San Antonio. Traveling 250 miles to San Antonio is expensive, difficult, and takes a lot of time. NASA and several businesses have worked together to provide telemedicine facilities for this area. Doctors from South Texas Hospital in Harlingen can send patient information such as heart rate, blood pressure, or x-ray images to doctors in San Antonio. After the doctors in San Antonio study the information they can tell the doctors in Harlingen how to treat their patients to make them better.

The technology that NASA is developing is helping people all over the world receive better medical care.

Lab zone Take-Home Activity

With your family, look for objects that have "tele-" as part of their name. What do these objects have in common?

Otis Boykin

Inventor Otis Boykin

You have learned about the great steps made in medical technology. The pacemaker is one of them. It is an electronic device. It runs on batteries. Strange though it may sound, it sends electric shocks to the heart! It keeps the heart beating at the proper rhythm. The pacemakers of people who have heart disease do not work properly. The heart slows down or beats too fast. For them, the pacemaker is a lifesaver. It keeps their hearts beating just right. And they have Otis Boykin to thank.

Otis Boykin (1920–1982) attended college in Dallas, Texas and Chicago, Illinois. After that, Boykin worked in a lab. It was not long, though, before he began inventing! He invented the electrical devices used in all guided missiles and in IBM™ computers. He also developed a burglarproof cash register and a chemical air filter. All together, he made 26 electrical devices. One was part of the pacemaker.

Have you heard the word *ironic* before? Something that is ironic is strange. It is the opposite of what you would expect. Sadly, it is quite ironic that Otis Boykin, the inventor of a major part of the pacemaker, died of a heart attack.

Otis Boykin invented part of the pacemaker. Placed near the heart, the pacemaker helps the heart beat in rhythm.

Boykin's computer device

Test-Taking Strategies

Find Important Words

Choose the Right Answer

Use Information from Text and Graphics

 Write Your Answer

Write Your Answer

To answer the following test questions, you need to write your answer. Read the passage and then answer the questions.

For centuries people have watched the stars move across the sky. Ancient Greek, Babylonian, Arab, and Egyptian sky-watchers noticed patterns in how certain groups of stars moved. Perhaps star groups formed pictures to them. Modern astronomers have divided the sky into 88 constellations. A constellation is a group of stars in a certain region of the sky. Many of the constellations are named by a pattern of stars in that region. Many stars are identified by the constellation they are part of. The stars in each constellation may look close together, but they are really far apart.

Stars can tell you the time whether you are on land, on sea, or in the air. You can watch constellations rise and set at the time and place you expect. The paths of the constellations moving across the sky are the same year after year.

Astronomers classify stars according to size, brightness, or temperature. To us, the Sun is the most important star in the sky. But based on one classification system, the Sun is an average star. Many other stars are hotter, bigger, or brighter.

Stars appear to be different colors because of the temperature of their atmosphere. The hottest stars are blue. The temperature of blue stars is at least 11,000°C. The star Rigel in the Orion constellation is blue. Next hottest stars are white, followed by yellowish white and then yellow. The Sun is a yellow star. Its temperature ranges from 5100°C to 6,000°C. The temperature of orange stars is between 3600°C and 5100°C. Red stars, such as Betelgeuse in Orion, are the coolest of all. Their temperature is between 2000°C and 3600°C.

Use What You Know

To write your answer to each question, you need to read the passage and the test question carefully. Write your answers in complete sentences. Then read your answer to make sure it is complete, correct, and focused.

1. In what ways is the Sun an average star?

2. Sirius is a white star. It is the brightest star in the sky. How do you know it is not the hottest?

3. What is a constellation?

4. Suppose last night you helped your friend locate Orion in the sky. How will your friend know where to find Orion a year from now?

Unit D Wrap Up

Chapter 16

How are cycles on Earth affected by the Sun and the Moon?
- Earth's movement around the Sun causes the seasons.
- The shape of the Moon appears to change as it revolves around the Earth.
- Eclipses occur as a result of the Moon revolving around the Earth.
- Earth's rotation is the reason groups of stars seem to move across the sky.

Chapter 17

How is Earth different from the other parts of the solar system?
- The part of the universe known as the solar system is made up of the Sun, planets, moons, other objects, and mostly empty space.
- Each planet in the solar system rotates on its axis and revolves around the Sun.
- Some planets have similar characteristics.

Chapter 18

How has technology changed the way of life?
- Advances in technology make our work easier and give us products that keep us safe and comfortable.
- Faster systems of transportation and communication are results of technology.

Performance Assessment

How Technology Helps Scientists

Give examples of kinds of technology that help scientists learn about Earth and space. Make drawings or models that show the technology and write a brief description of what scientists have learned by using the technology.

Read More About Space and Technology

Look for books like these in the library.

Experiment How does payload affect the distance a model rocket can travel?

Rockets launched from Earth have carried satellites, telescopes, and astronauts into space. The mass a rocket can carry is called its payload. In this **experiment** you will make a model rocket and find out how the payload affects the distance a model rocket travels.

Materials

safety goggles

Rocket Pattern and scissors

tape and 2 L plastic bottle

straw and clay

4 large paper clips

meterstick

Process Skills

You **control variables** when you change only one thing in an **experiment**.

Ask a question.

How does the payload affect the distance a model rocket can travel?

State a hypothesis.

If you increase the payload, then will the distance a model rocket travels remain the same, increase, or decrease? Write your **hypothesis**.

Identify and control variables.

You will change the payload your model rocket carries by changing the number of paper clips taped to the rocket. You will measure the distance the rocket travels. Everything else must remain the same. Always (a) use the same rocket, (b) launch the rocket from the same height and at the same angle, and (c) squeeze the bottle with the same force.

What is the independent variable?
What is the dependent variable?
What are some controlled variables?

Take It to the NET
More Activities www.sfsuccessnet.com

Test your hypothesis.

Make a model of a rocket.

1 Cut out the Rocket Pattern.

2 Roll the rocket into a cone and fasten with tape.

3 Make a launcher. Put a straw about 4 cm into a 2 L bottle. Seal the opening around straw with clay.

Wear safety goggles!
Why do you think you must wear safety goggles?

4 Put the rocket on the launcher.

⑤ Squish!

Hold your rocket launcher in the same position for each launch. Squeeze the bottle with the same force each time.

Be careful!

Make sure no one is in the way when you launch your rocket!

⑥ Launch your rocket 3 times. **Measure** the distances the rocket travels. Record the farthest distance.

⑦ Repeat your test with 2 large paper clips taped to your rocket. Tape the paper clips on the side of the rocket, at the top.

⑧ Repeat your test with 4 large paper clips taped to your rocket.

Hold the bottle at about this angle every time.

Collect and record your data.

Payload (number of paper clips)	Farthest Distance Rocket Traveled (cm)
0	
2	
4	

Take It to the NET
More Activities www.sfsuccessnet.com

Interpret your data.

Use your data to make a bar graph. Look at your graph closely. Analyze how the number of paper clips carried by your rocket affected the distance it traveled.

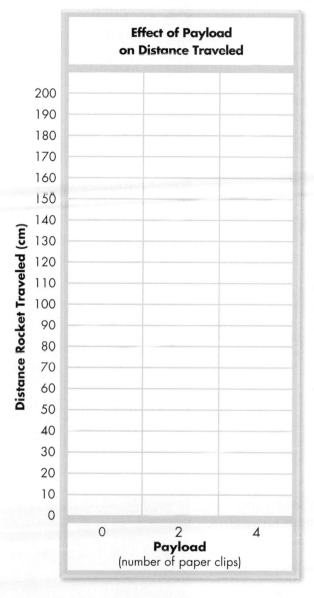

Effect of Payload on Distance Traveled

Distance Rocket Traveled (cm): 200, 190, 180, 170, 160, 150, 140, 130, 120, 110, 100, 90, 80, 70, 60, 50, 40, 30, 20, 10, 0

Payload
(number of paper clips): 0, 2, 4

What pattern do you find in your data? What is a reasonable explanation for the results of your experiment?

State your conclusion.

Explain how the payload affects the distance your model rocket travels. Compare your hypothesis with your results. **Communicate** your conclusion.

Go Further

How would adding fins affect how far the rocket travels? Write and carry out a plan to investigate. Develop a hypothesis. Include a safety procedure. Keep a record in a science journal. Select a way to show your results. Write a report or share your results orally with your class.

Science Fair Project

Discovery Channel School

How Heavy Is Heavy?

Idea: Weigh an object such as a heavy shoe to determine its Earth weight. Determine how much the object would weigh on each of the other planets in the solar system. Use the information to make an exhibit that shows the weight of the object on Earth and its weight on each of the other planets.

Objects in Space

Idea: Make models of the planets and other space objects. Be sure to tell if you model shows the relative sizes or the relative distances of the objects. Make a poster that has one interesting fact about each object.

Phases of the Moon

Idea: Make a flipbook to show how the phases of the Moon change during the month. Make a drawing that shows how the Moon looks each day of the month. Then put them in order to make the booklet. Make sure the pages of your booklet are firmly attached before you flip them.

What Time Is It?

Idea: Find what the latitude is for your home. Use the information to make a sundial to show how shadows the sundial creates can be used to tell time.

Metric and Customary Measures

The metric system is the measurement system most commonly used in science. Metric units are sometimes called SI units. SI stands for International System because these units are used around the world.

These prefixes are used in the metric system:

kilo- means *thousand*
1 kilometer equals 1,000 meters

milli means *thousandths*
1,000 millimeters equals 1 meter

centi means *hundred*
100 centimeters equals 1 meter

Length and Distance

1 meter

1 yard

Area
One meter is longer than 1 yard.

Mass
One kilogram is greater than 2 pounds.

1 pound

1 kilogram

Volume
One liter is greater than 4 cups.

1 liter

1 cup

Temperature
Water freezes at 0°C or 32°F. Water boils at 100°C or 212°F.

Glossary

absorption (page 420) the taking in of light energy by an object

anemometer (page 195) a tool that measures wind speed

astronomy (page 519) the study of planets, stars, and other objects in space

axis (page 496) an imaginary line that goes through an object; Earth has its own axis, which goes through the North and South Poles

barometer (page 194) a tool that measures air pressure

carnivores (page 84) consumers that eat only animals

cause (page 109) why something happens

cell (page 7) the building block of life

chemical change (page 336) a change that results in a new substance

chlorophyll (page 49) green material in plants that captures energy from sunlight for photosynthesis

chloroplast (page 8) a special part of a plant that traps the energy in sunlight for making food

communication (page 556) the process of sending any type of message from one place to another

community (page 82) different populations that interact with each other in the same area

compare (page 5) to say how things are alike

competition (page 114) when two or more species in an ecosystem must use the same limited resources

compression (page 408) the part of the wave where the particles are closest together

conclusion (page 45) a decision reached after thinking about facts and details

condensation (page 187) the process of water vapor, a gas, changing to a liquid

conduction (page 354) the transfer or passing of energy

conductor (page 354) a material that allows heat to pass through it

conservation (page 296) using only what you need as efficiently as possible

constellation (page 504) any one of 88 areas in the sky that are used to identify and name the stars

contrast (page 5) to say how things are different

convection current (page 356) the pattern in which heat energy flows; formed when heated liquid or gas expands and is less dense than a cooler liquid or gas around it

crater (pages 270, 522) a large hole shaped like a bowl in the surface of a planet, moon, or other object in space

cytoplasm (page 8) a gel-like liquid inside the cell membrane that contains the things that the cell needs to carry out life processes

decomposers (page 87) organisms that eat the waste and remains of dead plants and animals

density (page 326) the property of matter that compares the mass of an object to its volume

deposition (page 267) the laying down of pieces of Earth's surface by water, ice, and wind

details (page 213) individual pieces of information that support a main idea

dormant (pages 62, 271) in a state of rest

earthquake (page 272) a shaking of Earth's crust caused by sudden, shifting movements in the crust

eclipse (page 502) a temporary situation in which an object in space casts its shadow on another object

ecosystem (page 79) all the living and nonliving things in an environment and the many ways they interact

effect (page 109) what happens as a result of a cause

effort (page 464) the force used on a simple machine

electric current (page 378) the flow of an electric charge through a material

electromagnet (page 387) a coil of wire that creates a magnetic field when current moves through the wire. If the coil is wrapped around an iron core, the core concentrates the field.

ellipse (page 498) an oval-shaped curve that is like a circle stretched out in two opposite directions

endangered (page 120) a species whose population has been reduced to such small numbers that it is in danger of becoming extinct

epicenter (page 272) the point on Earth's surface directly above the focus of an earthquake

erosion (page 266) the moving of weathered pieces and particles of rock by water, ice, and wind

evaporation (page 186) the change from liquid water to water vapor

extinct (pages 120, 271) no longer living, as an entire species, or active, as a volcano

fault (page 272) a break or crack in rock where Earth's plates move

fertilization (page 56) the process by which an egg cell and a sperm cell combine

force (page 442) any push or pull

fossil fuels (page 294) fuels including coal, petroleum, and natural gas that are made from fossils, or the remains of living things that died millions of years ago and were trapped in rocks

frame of reference (page 440) the objects you use to detect motion

frequency (page 409) the number of times a wave makes a complete cycle in a second

friction (page 445) force that acts when two surfaces rub together

front (page 190) the boundary or line where the two different air masses meet

fulcrum (page 464) the support on which a lever plus the load it is carrying rests

galaxy (page 519) a group of stars

genus (page 12) a grouping that contains similar, closely related animals

gravity (page 446) force that makes objects pull toward each other

hazardous waste (page 126) substances that are very harmful to humans and other organisms

herbivores (page 84) consumers that get energy by eating only plants

host (page 117) an organism that is harmed by a parasite

humidity (page 190) the amount of water vapor in the air

humus (page 289) a dark brown part of soil that is made up of decomposed plants and animals

hurricane (page 215) a dangerous storm made up of swirling bands of thunderstorms with wind speeds of at least 119 kilometers per hour

igneous rock (page 246) rock that forms from molten (melted) rock

immune system (page 161) the organs in your body that defend against disease

inclined plane (page 12) a simple machine like a ramp

infectious disease (page 158) a disease that can pass from one organism to another

insulator (page 355) a material or substance that limits the amount of heat that passes through it

invertebrates (page 22) animals without backbones

involuntary muscles (page 146) muscles that you cannot choose to control

kinetic energy (page 448) energy of motion

landform (page 263) a natural feature on Earth's surface; landforms include mountains, hills, valleys, plains, plateaus, and coastal features

landslide (page 268) a rapid downhill movement of large amounts of rock and soil

lever (page 464) a simple machine made of a bar resting on a support

load (page 464) the weight that is to be lifted or moved

lunar eclipse (page 502) the passage of the Moon through the Earth's shadow

luster (page 240) the way a mineral's surface reflects light

magnetic field (page 382) the invisible force around a magnet when a magnetic object moves into the field. The force is strongest at the magnet's poles, or ends.

magnetism (page 382) the pulling or pushing force that exists around a magnet due to the arrangement of electrons

main ideas (page 213) the most important information in a reading passage or display

metamorphic rock (page 248) rock that has changed as a result of heat and pressure

meteorologist (page 194) a scientist who studies and measures weather conditions

mineral (page 239) natural, nonliving solid crystal that makes up rocks

mixture (page 328) a combination of two or more substances that keep their individual properties

neuron (page 154) basic working unit of the nervous system or the nerve cell

niche (page 82) the specific role an organism has in its habitat

nucleus (page 8) the control center of the cell

EM4

omnivores (page 84) consumers that eat both plants and animals

opaque (page 421) describes materials that do not let any light pass through them

optical fibers (page 554) very thin tubes that allow light to pass through them; often used by doctors in medical procedures

orbit (page 498) the path followed by one object as it revolves around another object, such as Earth's orbit around the Sun

ore (page 294) a mineral-rich rock deposit that can be removed from the Earth and used to make products

ovary (page 56) the thick bottom part of the pistil where the egg cells are stored

parallel circuits (page 381) two or more paths in which an electric charge can flow

parasite (page 117) an organism that lives on or in another organism, helping itself but hurting the other organism

pathogens (page 158) organisms that cause disease

petroleum (page 294) a crude oil that is found in rocks; a nonrenewable energy source

photosynthesis (page 48) the process in which plants make their own food

physical change (page 332) a change in the size, shape, or state of matter

pistil (page 55) a female structure in plants that produces egg cells

pitch (page 412) a measure of whether a sound seems high or low, determined by the sound's frequency

population (page 82) all the members of one species that live within an area of an ecosystem

potential energy (page 448) stored energy

precipitation (page 187) any form of water falling from the air to Earth's surface

predict (page 517) make a statement about what might happen next

pulley (page 467) a simple machine made of a wheel with a rope around it

radiation (page 358) energy that is sent out in the form of infrared rays or waves

recycling (page 297) saving, collecting, or using materials again instead of turning them into waste

reflection (page 420) the bouncing back of a wave off an object or surface

refraction (page 422) bending of light caused by the change of speed that occurs when light rays pass from one transparent medium to another

relative motion (page 439) change in position of one object compared to the position of some fixed object

resistance (page 379) a quality of an object which means that electric current cannot flow easily through it

revolution (page 498) the repeated motion of one object around another, much more massive object; for instance, the motion of the Earth around the Sun

rotation (page 496) the spinning of a planet, moon, or star around its axis

satellite (page 524) something that orbits a planet

screw (page 471) a simple machine made of a stick with ridges called threads wrapped around it

sediment (page 242) weathered bits of rock, soil, shells, and dead plant and animal matter that settles at the bottoms of lakes, rivers, and oceans

sedimentary rock (page 242) rock that forms when sediments are cemented together and harden

sepal (page 55) one of several leaf-like parts that cover and protect the flower bud

sequence (page 77) the order in which things happen

series circuit (page 380) a simple circular path in which an electric current flows only one way through each part of that circuit

solar cells (page 293) electric cells that convert the Sun's energy into electricity

solar eclipse (page 503) the passage of the Moon between the Sun and the Earth; the Moon casts its shadow on the Earth

solar energy (page 287) the energy given off by the Sun

solar system (page 520) a system of planets and other objects that move around the Sun

solubility (page 331) ability of one substance to dissolve in another

solute (page 330) the substance that is dissolved in a solution

solution (page 330) a combination of two or more substances where one is dissolved by the other

solvent (page 330) the substance that dissolves another substance in a solution

space probe (page 522) a vehicle that carries cameras and other tools for studying distant objects in space

species (page 12) a group of similar organisms that can mate and produce offspring

speed (page 440) the rate at which an object's position changes

stamen (page 55) male structure in plants that makes pollen

static electricity (page 375) the imbalance of positive or negative charges between objects

storm surge (page 219) a swell of water at the eye of a hurricane over the ocean

succession (page 118) gradual change from one community of organisms to another

summarize (page 337) give only the main points

summary (page 237) a short retelling of something read

technology (page 551) the knowledge, processes, and products that we use to solve problems and make our lives easier

telecommunications (page 557) communications sent by telephone, fax, television, satellite, and radio

thermal energy (page 351) total energy of motion

tornado (page 222) a rapidly spinning column of air that comes down out of a cloud and touches the ground

translucent (page 421) describes materials that let some light rays pass through but scatter some of the other rays

transparent (page 421) describes materials that let nearly all the light rays that hit them pass through

tropical depression (page 216) a low pressure air mass that forms over warm water with swirling winds can be as strong as 61 kilometers per hour

tropical storm (page 216) a low pressure air mass that forms over warm water with swirling winds that are more than 61 kph but less than 119 kph

universe all of the objects that exist in space

vaccine (page 161) an injection of dead or weakened pathogens that causes you to be immune to a disease

vehicle (page 558) something that carries people and objects from one place to another; includes automobiles, trucks, trains, ships, airplanes, and rockets

velocity (page 441) the speed and the direction an object is moving

vertebrates (page 18) animals with backbones

volcano (page 270) a cone-shaped landform with an opening at the top; hot rocks, gases, and ashes are shot out of its top at times

voluntary muscles (page 146) muscles that you can choose to control

vortex (page 223) a spinning, funnel-shaped area in a fluid

wavelength (page 109) distance between one point on a wave to the next similar point on a wave

weathering (page 264) a gradual wearing away or changing of rock and soil caused by water, ice, temperature changes, wind, chemicals, or living things

wedge (page 470) a simple machine that is made of two inclined planes put together and that can be driven into another material

wheel and axle (page 466) a simple machine made of a wheel and a rod joined to the center of the wheel

wind vane (page 195) a tool that shows the direction from which the wind is blowing

work (page 448) using force in order to move an object a certain distance

Index

This index lists the pages on which topics appear in this book. Page numbers after a *p* refer to a photograph or drawing. Page numbers after a *c* refer to a chart, graph, or diagram.

Credits

Illustrations

8-32 Marce Laverdet; 9, 43, 49, 57 Robert Ulrich; 80-94, 184-198, 352-359 Bob Kayganich; 106-128, 189, 380-383, 408-410, 419, 442, 500 Peter Bollinger; 216-224, 288, 294 Tony Randazzo; 242-244, 264-272 Alan Male

Photographs

Every effort has been made to secure permission and provide appropriate credit for photographic material. The publisher deeply regrets any omission and pledges to correct errors called to its attention in subsequent editions.

Unless otherwise acknowledged, all photographs are the property of Scott Foresman, a division of Pearson Education.

Photo locators denoted as follows: Top (T), Center (C), Bottom (B), Left (L), Right (R), Background (Bkgd).

1 (Bkgd) ©Zig Leszczynski/Animals Animals/Earth Scenes, (CR) ©Richard LaVal/Animals Animals/Earth Scenes; 2 (BL) ©Ken Cole/Animals Animals/Earth Scenes, (T) ©Martha J. Powell/Visuals Unlimited, (B) ©Dorling Kindersley; 3 ©Ralph A. Clevenger/Corbis, (BR) ©Ralph A. Clevenger/Corbis; 5 ©Gusto Productions/SPL/Photo Researchers, Inc., (Bkgd) ©Martha J. Powell/Visuals Unlimited; 6 (T) ©Martha J. Powell/Visuals Unlimited; 8 (BR) ©Eye of Science/Photo Researchers, Inc., (TL) ©Carolina Biological/Visuals Unlimited, (CL) ©SIU/Visuals Unlimited, (BL) ©Alfred Pasieka/Photo Researchers, Inc.; 10 (B) ©Stephen Dalton/NHPA Limited; 11 (BL) ©Ken Cole/Animals Animals/Earth Scenes, (CL) Getty Images, (BR) ©Craig Tuttle/Corbis; 12 (CL) ©Ken Cole/Animals Animals/Earth Scenes, (CL) Getty Images, (BL) ©Dorling Kindersley; 13 (TC) ©Dorling Kindersley, (TCL) ©Dorling Kindersley, (TL) ©Dorling Kindersley, (TC) ©Ken Cole/Animals Animals/Earth Scenes, (TC) ©John Conrad/Corbis, (TCR) ©Ray Richardson/Animals Animals/Earth Scenes, (TCR) © Dorling Kindersley, (TCR) ©Dorling Kindersley, (TR) ©Dorling Kindersley; 14 (L) ©John Durham/Photo Researchers, Inc., (L) Sue Atkinson/©Dorling Kindersley; 15 (BL) ©Dorling Kindersley, (TL) Karl Shone/©Dorling Kindersley, (BL) Dave King/©Dorling Kindersley; 16 (T) ©Wolfgang Kaehler/Corbis, (TR) Getty Images, (CL) ©Dorling Kindersley; 17 (BC) ©Larry Lee/Corbis, (T) ©Richard Hamilton Smith/Corbis, (CC) ©Steve Terrill/Corbis; 18 (TR) ©Dorling Kindersley, (B) ©Dorling Kindersley, (BL) ©Dorling Kindersley, (BL) ©Dorling Kindersley, (BL) ©Ray Richardson/Animals Animals/Earth Scenes; 20 (TR) ©Jim Tuten/Animals Animals/Earth Scenes, (BL) ©Dorling Kindersley, (BR) ©Dorling Kindersley; 21 (B) ©Dorling Kindersley, (TR) ©Dorling Kindersley, (BR) ©Dorling Kindersley; 22 ©Philip James Corwin/Corbis, (TR) ©Dorling Kindersley; 23 (BC) Jerry Young/©Dorling Kindersley, (CL) ©Andrew Syred/Photo Researchers, Inc., (BR) ©F. J. Jackson/Robert Harding Picture Library Ltd., (TR) Dave King/©Dorling Kindersley; 24 ©Dwight R. Kuhn, ©Dwight R. Kuhn; 25 (TL) ©Dwight R. Kuhn, ©Dwight R. Kuhn, ©Kevin Summers/Getty Images; 26 ©Dorling Kindersley; 27 ©John Conrad/Corbis, (TL) ©Peter Johnson/Corbis; 28 (TL) ©Ray Richardson/Animals Animals/Earth Scenes, (CL) ©Ray Richardson/Animals Animals/Earth Scenes, (BL) ©Dorling Kindersley, (BL) ©E. R. Degginger/Color Pic, Inc.; 29 (BR) Digital Stock, © Dorling Kindersley; 30 ©Ray Richardson/Animals Animals/Earth Scenes; 31 (TL) ©Ken Cole/Animals Animals/Earth Scenes, (BL) ©Steve Kaufman/Corbis, (CL) ©Ralph A. Clevenger/Corbis; 32 (TR) ©Eric Baccega/Nature Picture Library, (B) ©Anup Shah/Nature Picture Library; 33 ©Manoj Shah/Getty Images; 34 ©Martin B. Withers; Frank Lane Picture Agency/Corbis, (TL) ©Dorling Kindersley, (CL) ImageState, (BL) ©Dorling Kindersley, (TR) ©Lonny Kalfus/Getty Images; 35 (TL) ©Martin B. Withers; Frank Lane Picture Agency/Corbis, (TL) ©Dorling Kindersley, (CL) ImageState, (BL) ©Dorling Kindersley, (R) ©Dorling Kindersley; 36 (BL) ©Dorling Kindersley; 37 (CL) ©Dorling Kindersley, (TR) Getty Images, (BL) ©Dorling Kindersley, (CCB) ©John Gerlach/Animals Animals/Earth Scenes, (CR) ©Allan Davey/Masterfile Corporation, (BL) ©Dorling Kindersley, (BC) ©Dorling Kindersley, (BR) Jerry Young/©Dorling Kindersley; 39 (TR) ©Dorling Kindersley; 40 (B) ©M. P. Kahl/Photo Researchers, Inc.; (TL) NASA 41 (TCL) Getty Images, (Bkgd) PhotoLibrary.com; 42 (B) © Royalty-Free/Corbis, (TL) ©George D. Lepp/Corbis; 43 (BR) ©Carolina Biological Supply Company/Phototake; 46 (TL) ©George D. Lepp/Corbis; 48 (TL) ©Dorling Kindersley; 49 (BC) ©Dr. Jeremy Burgess/Photo Researchers, Inc.; 50 (TL) ©Dorling Kindersley; 51 (TR) ©Dorling Kindersley, (R) Getty Images, (BR) ©Dorling Kindersley; 52 (TL) © Dorling Kindersley, (TL) ©Gary Moss/Getty Images, (BL) Brand X Pictures, (BR) ©Dorling Kindersley; 53 (TR) ©Carolina Biological /Visuals Unlimited, (CR) ©Dorling Kindersley; 54 (BC) © Royalty-Free/Corbis, (TL) © Dorling Kindersley; 55 (TL) ©David Sieren/Visuals Unlimited, (TL) ©Owaki-Kulla/Corbis; 56 (TR) ©W. Treat Davidson/Photo Researchers, Inc., (B) ©Dorling Kindersley, (B) ©Merlin Tuttle/BCI/Photo Researchers, Inc.; 58 (TL) ©Dorling Kindersley, (BR) ©Dorling Kindersley, (BL) ©Dorling Kindersley, (BL) ©Dorling Kindersley, (BC) ©Dorling Kindersley; 59 (BC) ©Dorling Kindersley; 60 (CL) Stephen Oliver/©Dorling Kindersley, (TL) ©Dorling Kindersley, (BL) ©Dorling Kindersley; 61 (Bkgd) ©Merlin Tuttle/BCI/Photo Researchers, Inc.; 62 (TL) ©Ed Reschke/Peter Arnold, Inc., (B) ©Carolina Biological Supply Company/Phototake, (BL) ©John Shaw/Tom Stack & Associates, Inc., (TL) © Dorling Kindersley; 63 (Bkgd) ©Dwight R. Kuhn, (TR) Neil Fletcher and Matthew Ward/©Dorling Kindersley; 64 (TL) ©Dorling Kindersley, (BCL) ©Dorling Kindersley, (L) ©Dorling Kindersley; 65 (L) ©Dorling Kindersley; 66 (TR) ©Joseph Devenney/Getty Images; 68 (BL) ©Dorling Kindersley; 71 (TR) © Royalty-Free/

Corbis; 72 (Bkgd) ©Neale Clark/Robert Harding Picture Library Ltd., (TL) NASA; 74 (T) ©Andrew Brown; Ecoscene/Corbis, (BR) ©George H. H. Huey/Corbis, (BL) ©Kennan Ward/Corbis; 75 (TR) ©Raymond Gehman/NGS Image Collection, ©Jim Brandenburg/Minden Pictures; 77 (Bkgd) ©Andrew Brown; Ecoscene/Corbis; 78 ©Andrew Brown; Ecoscene/Corbis; 80 (CL) ©David Keaton/Corbis, (BL) ©Steve Terrill/Corbis; 81 ©Andrew Brown; Ecoscene/Corbis, (TR) ©Michael Townsend/Getty Images, (BR) ©David Muench/Corbis; 82 (TL) ©Steve Kaufman/Corbis, (B) ©Konrad Wothe/Minden Pictures; 83 (C) ©Raymond Gehman/NGS Image Collection, (TL) ©Steve Kaufman/Corbis, (TC) ©Tim Fitzharris/Minden Pictures, (T) ©George H. H. Huey/Corbis, (TL) ©Gerry Ellis/Minden Pictures, (CR) ©Jim Brandenburg/Minden Pictures, (BC) Getty Images, ©Buddy Mays/Corbis; 84 (TL) ©Biophoto associates/Photo Researchers, Inc.; 85 (TR) ©Frank Lane Picture agency/Corbis, (CR) ©Joe McDonald/Corbis, (TL) ©John Gerlach/Animals Animals/Earth Scenes, (CL) ©D. Robert & Lorri Franz/Corbis, (TL) ©Dorling Kindersley, (BR) ©George H. H. Huey/Corbis; 86 (BL) ©Buddy Mays/Corbis, (BR) ©Jeff Foott/Nature Picture Library, (BC) ©John Cancalosi/Nature Picture Library; 87 (TL) ©Sally A. Morgan/Corbis, (CR) ©Brian Milne/Animals Animals/Earth Scenes; 88 (TR) ©Stephen J. Krasemann/DRK Photo, (BR) ©Kennan Ward/Corbis, (CL) ©Kennan Ward/Corbis, (L) ©Michael Llewellyn/Getty Images; 89 (TR) ©Tom Brakefield/Corbis, (BL) ©Kevin Schafer/Corbis, (TC) Getty Images, ©Steve Kaufman/Corbis, (BR) ©Michael & Patricia Fogden/Corbis; 90 (TL) ©Randy Wells/Getty Images, (BL) ©Roland Birke/Peter Arnold, Inc., (CL) ©Dorling Kindersley; 91 (BR) ©Ralph White/Corbis, (TR) Getty Images, (BL) ©Georgette Douwma/Getty Images; 92 (BR) British Antarctic Survey/SPL/Photo Researchers, Inc., (L) © Royalty-Free/Corbis, (BR) ©Roland Birke/Peter Arnold, Inc., ©Dorling Kindersley; 93 (BR) ©W. Perry Conway/Corbis, (TL) © Royalty-Free/Corbis, (CL) ©George D. Lepp/Corbis; 95 ©David Samuel Robbins/Corbis, (BC) ©Vaughn Fleming/SPL/Photo Researchers, Inc., (TR) ©Eric and David Hosking/Corbis; 96 (TR) ©John & eliza Forder/Getty Images; 98 (TR) ©Neil McIntyre/Getty Images, (BL) ©D. Robert & Lorri Franz/Corbis; 101 (TR) ©Dorling Kindersley; 102 ©Roger Ressmeyer/Corbis; 104 (BR) ©Alan G. Nelson/Animals Animals/Earth Scenes, (L) ©Tom Edwards/Animals Animals/Earth Scenes, (TL) ©George Rinhart/Corbis Bottmann; 105 ©E. R. Degginger/Color Pic, Inc., (TR) ©Michael Fogden/Animals Animals/Earth Scenes 106 ©Orion Press/Corbis; 106 (BR) Getty Images; 107 (TR) ©Frank Blackburn; Ecoscene/Corbis, ©Sullivan & Rogers/Bruce Coleman Inc., ©Barbara Von Hoffmann/Animals Animals/Earth Scenes; 109 (Bkgd) ©Orion Press/Corbis; 110 (C) ©Orion Press/Corbis; 112 (CC) ©David Muench/Corbis, (C) ©Lynda Richardson/Corbis, (T) ©Art Wolfe/Getty Images, (TC) ©Dorling Kindersley, (BC) ©Gary W. Carter/Corbis, (TL) Getty Images, (C) Getty Images, (BR) Hans Neleman/Getty Images; 115 ©Dorling Kindersley, (B) ©Ron Austing; Frank Lane Picture Agency/Corbis; 116 (B) © Royalty-Free/Corbis; 117 (BR) AP/Wide World Photos; 118 (BL) ©David Muench/Corbis, (R) ©Jon Sparks/Corbis; 119 (TR) ©Frank Blackburn; Ecoscene/Corbis; 120 ©Gary W. Carter/Corbis; 121 (BR) ©Peter Scoones/SPL/Photo Researchers, Inc.; 122 (BR) ©Martin B. Withers; Frank Lane Picture Agency/Corbis, (C) ©1999 Tom Bean/DRK Photo, (CR) ©Marty Cordano/DRK Photo; 123 (CR) DRK Photo; 124 ©Bettmann/Corbis, (R) Getty Images; 125 (R) ©Bettmann/Corbis; 126 (BL) ©Adrian Lyon/Getty Images, (R) ©Vince Streano/Corbis; 127 (TR) ©Bruce Hands/Getty Images; 128 (BL) ©Sullivan & Rogers/Bruce Coleman Inc., (R) ©Barbara Von Hoffmann/Animals Animals/Earth Scenes, (L) Getty Images, (BL) ©Doug Sokell/Visuals Unlimited; 129 (BR) ©Dorling Kindersley, ©Dorling Kindersley, (TR) ©Ed Reschke/Peter Arnold, Inc., (TR) ©Myrleen Ferguson Cate/PhotoEdit; 130 (TR) ©Georg Gerster/Photo Researchers, Inc.; 132 (Bkgd) ©Steve Allen/Getty Images , (Inset) ©Alain Choisnet/Getty Images, (BL) Getty Images, (BC) Getty Images, (BR) Getty Images; 136 (BR) NASA, ©Jerry Driendl/Getty Images; 137 ©Dr. Dennis Kunkel/Visuals Unlimited; 138 (BR) ©Dr. Kari Lounatmaa/Photo Researchers, Inc.; 139 (BL) ©Dr. Donald Fawcett & E. Shelton/Visuals Unlimited; 141 (BR) Getty Images; 142 (L) ©Dr. Donald Fawcett/Visuals Unlimited, (C) ©Dr. Richard Kessel & Dr. Randy Kardon/Tissues and Organs/Visuals Unlimited; 144 (BL) ©CNRI/Photo Researchers, Inc., (TL) ©Science Photo Library/Photo Researchers, Inc.; 147 (TR) ©SPL/Photo Researchers, Inc., (TR) ©Innerspace Imaging/Photo Researchers, (TR) ©Dr. Donald Fawcett/Visuals Unlimited; 152 (BC) ©Reuters/Corbis; 155 (TR) ©Alfred Pasieka/Photo Researchers, Inc.; 157 (BR) ©Prof. P. Motta/Dept. of Anatomy/University "La Sapienza", Rome/Photo Researchers, Inc., (TR) ©Susumu Nishinaga/Photo Researchers, Inc., ©Dr. Fred Hossler/Visuals Unlimited; 158 (CR) ©Dr. Kari Lounatmaa/Photo Researchers, Inc.; 159 (CR) ©Science Source/Photo Researchers, Inc.; 160 (L) ©Bettmann/Corbis, (R) ©Bettmann/Corbis, (B) ©Bettmann/Corbis, (R) ©Bettmann/Corbis, 161 (TL) ©Dr. Donald Fawcett & E. Shelton/Visuals Unlimited, (TL) ©Dr. Donald Fawcett & E. Shelton/Visuals Unlimited; 162 (TR) Getty Images; 164 ©Scott Camazine/Photo Researchers, Inc., ©Scott Camazine/Photo Researchers, Inc., ©Dr. Wolf Fahrenbach/Visuals Unlimited, ©Tim Flach/Getty Images; 165 Getty Images; 168 ©Dr. Donald Fawcett & E. Shelton/Visuals Unlimited, (B) ©Bettmann/Corbis, (TR) Corbis, (BR) Corbis 169 (TR) ©Daniel Zupanc/NHPA Limited 176 Jerry Young/©Dorling Kindersley; 177 (Bkgd) ©Steve Wilkings/Corbis; 178 (BR) Getty Images, (BR) ©Dorling Kindersley; 179 (CR) ©David Lees/Corbis, (BL) ©Dorling Kindersley, (TR) Stephen Oliver/©Dorling Kindersley; 182 (Bkgd) ©Earth Satellite Corporation/Photo Researchers, Inc.; 184 (B) ©Tom Van Sant/Corbis; 186 (B) ©Charles O'Rear/Corbis; 189 (CR) ©Dorling Kindersley, (Bkgd) ©Darwin Wiggett/Corbis; 190 (L) ©David Lees/Corbis; 191 (TR) ©Leonard Lessin/Peter Arnold, Inc., (C) ©Dorling Kindersley; 194 (BL) ©Dorling Kindersley, (BR) Getty Images; 195 (TR) Stephen Oliver/©Dorling Kindersley; 195 (BR) ©Dorling Kindersley; 198 (BR) ©Dorling Kindersley; 199 (T) ©British Antarctic Survey/Photo Researchers, Inc.; 200 (T) ©Mark Lewis/Getty Images; 204 ©Jim Craigmyle/Corbis, (Bkgd) ©Layne Kennedy/Corbis; 208 (BL) ©Jim Brandenburg/Minden Pictures; 209 (Bkgd) Getty Images, (CL) Getty Images; 210 (T) ©Sygma/Corbis, (B) ©Dorling Kindersley; 212 (N) ©NASA/Corbis; 214 (Bkgd) ©Sygma/Corbis; 217 (TR) ©Adastra/Getty Images; 218 (B) ©Dorling Kindersley; 219 (TL) ©Morton Beebe/Corbis 223 (CR) ©H. Hofinger/FLPA-Images of Nature;